Commodity Activism

Commodity Activism

Cultural Resistance in Neoliberal Times

EDITED BY

Roopali Mukherjee
and Sarah Banet-Weiser

NEW YORK UNIVERSITY PRESS
New York and London

NEW YORK UNIVERSITY PRESS
New York and London
www.nyupress.org

References to Internet websites (URLs) were accurate at the time of writing.
Neither the author nor New York University Press is responsible for URLs
that may have expired or changed since the manuscript was prepared.

Library of Congress Cataloging-in-Publication Data

Commodity activism : cultural resistance in neoliberal times /
edited by Roopali Mukherjee and Sarah Banet-Weiser.
p. cm. — (Critical cultural communication)
Includes bibliographical references and index.
ISBN 978-0-8147-6400-8 (cl : alk. paper)
ISBN 978-0-8147-6401-5 (pb : alk. paper)
ISBN 978-0-8147-6402-2 (ebook)
ISBN 978-0-8147-6301-8 (ebook)
1. Consumption (Economics)—Social aspects. 2. Consumption (Economics)—
Political aspects. 3. Consumers—Political activity. 4. Consumer behavior.
5. Social action—Economic aspects. 6. Social responsibility of business.
I. Mukherjee, Roopali. II. Banet-Weiser, Sarah, 1966–
HC79.C6C6353   2012
306.3—dc23   2011046956

New York University Press books are printed on acid-free paper,
and their binding materials are chosen for strength and durability.
We strive to use environmentally responsible suppliers and materials
to the greatest extent possible in publishing our books.

Manufactured in the United States of America
c 10 9 8 7 6 5 4 3 2 1
p 10 9 8 7 6 5 4 3 2 1

Contents

Acknowledgments

This project would have had little chance of getting off the ground had it not been for an entirely exhilarating late-night conversation with Radhika Parameswaran in which the central paradoxes of "commodity activism" first emerged in the form of a tentative but ambitious anthology. The book, likewise, would have had little chance of completion had it not been for a conference roundtable on the topic a year later, where Sarah Banet-Weiser and I made the remarkably fortuitous decision to collaborate as editors on the project. Beyond our rigorous interlocutions over the course of the project, *Commodity Activism* is a reminder of how academic collaborations can shape the deepest friendships, formative of the ways in which the political is always personal. Thank you, Sarah, for your unquestioned support and tireless energy on this project. As the project took shape, Ralina Joseph, Joy Fuqua, and Laurie Ouellette helped us bring a remarkable group of contributors together for the collection. Tom Schumacher, Madhu Dubey, Priya Jaikumar, David Kazanjian, Rick Maxwell, Nizan Shaked, Jeff Maskovky, Jonathan Buchsbaum, Jonah Engle, and John Pittman listened to these ideas with patience and attention. Josefina Saldana, Rudolf Gaudio, and my brother, Sandeep Mukherjee, provided kind and good counsel. I am grateful to each of them for making *Commodity Activism* a complex and compelling endeavor for me.

Roopali Mukherjee

Coediting an anthology about a topic in which one is deeply invested is invigorating, provocative, and indeed complex. Simply put, this volume would not exist were it not for the intellectual efforts, passionate commitment, and collaborative spirit of Roopali Mukherjee, and I consider the friendship I have with her the book's deepest reward. My warmest thanks are to her and her vision. We extend our immeasurable gratitude to the authors who contributed to this volume, for their patience throughout this process, and for their remarkable and varied insights on the current state of commodity activism. Kent Ono offered crucial insight and suggestions from the beginning of this project, and we are deeply grateful to him for his faith in us and for his part in shaping this volume. At New York University Press, Eric Zinner and Ciara McLaughlin had confidence in this project from the beginning, and we are tremendously grateful for their patience and guidance throughout the process. The anonymous readers who critically engaged the manuscript pushed us to think about critical issues and inspired lively and inspiring conversations that transcend these pages. This volume could not have been completed without the invaluable research assistantship of Jess Butler, Kevin Driscoll, and Lori Lopez. Josh Kun, Marita Sturken, Cara Wallis, Laura Portwood-Stacer, D. Travers Scott, Larry Gross, Taj Frazier, Melissa Brough, Cynthia Chris, and Inna Arzumanova all offered guidance, insight, and reassurance during the development of this anthology, and I owe them my deepest thanks. Finally, thank you to my family, for their patiently giving me up for so many hours, their steadfast confidence in me, and their continual love and support.

Sarah Banet-Weiser

Foreword

———— MARITA STURKEN ————

The sense of a crucial historical shift is a key structure of feeling of our times. Upheaval, restructuring, shift, and dramatic social and economic change are not only the prevailing contemporary discourses but also likely to be how our moment in time will be characterized historically in the future. While modernity's upheaval created a sense of instability and unrootedness, in the contemporary intersection of neoliberalism and digital media, the boundaries between culture and the economic have been redrawn in dramatically new and consequential ways. So many aspects of our society, including formerly unquestioned solid social institutions such as finance, politics, education, newspapers, magazines, art criticism, the music and other culture industries, are in such upheaval that the feeling of rapid social change, both traumatic and liberating, is rampant. Boundary crossing is a common theme of contemporary understandings of these upheavals—the traversing of national boundaries through information technologies, the mixing of genres, the traffic between art and consumerism, the erosion of distinctions of popular and high culture. Key among these is the boundary crossing of commodity culture/consumerism and activism/social resistance. The uniquely pervasive quality of contemporary consumerism and the transformation of the category of cultural/social resistance are crucial shifts that have transformed social life, cultural consumption and production, politics, and people's daily lives to an unprecedented degree. Yet, as always, understandings of these social shifts have tended to lag behind the daily experience of them, and our language for describing them seems ever out-of-date.

This volume, *Commodity Activism: Cultural Resistance in Neoliberal Times*, intervenes into this unstable terrain in ways that enable us to see the stakes involved in understanding these social shifts. What happens when the boundaries between brand culture, commodity culture, activism, and humanitarianism are blurred? What is resistance today, and what are the stakes in our capacity to define resistance? What do new modes of consumerism tell us about the different kinds of subjectivities emerging in the context of neoliberal societies? What do social activism and social change become in such contexts? The authors of this volume move beyond the simple binaries of the mainstream and the margins, acquiescence and resistance, and consumerism and activism to delve into the new forms of consumerism and activism that have rendered such opposing structures meaningless.

Clearly, activism is not what it used to be. Resistance was never what it was understood to be. And, capitalism is always reinventing itself. The power of capitalism as a global force has always been in its capacity as a system to adapt, incorporate, and expand. Yet the prevailing sense that capitalism is undergoing a new phase in relationship to activism and resistance is palpable. It is in this shifting, murky, hard-to-define terrain that critical consumer studies has emerged as an important new field of study. *Commodity Activism* is indicative of how vital this emergent field of study can be. It provides insights into how practices of consumerism have changed over time and are integral to social imaginaries, and it helps provide the means for understanding how economic relations and the workings of capitalism have transformed public life, concepts of citizenship, social movements, and the nature of political action itself.

The work of *Commodity Activism* extends critical consumer studies into the terrain of political activism, thus engaging with the crucial and ever-difficult question of what gets to count as activism, and what constitutes social and cultural resistance. The stakes are high here, precisely because the goals are myriad and complex. What does cultural resistance aim to do—empower, expose ideological frameworks, change the culture industries, make us feel better? Can resistance be pragmatic, instrumentalist, and embedded in consumer practices? To rethink resistance in relationship to commodity culture is, of course, a radical act in itself.

Contradictions are inevitable here. Activism as consumerism. Celebrity humanitarianism. Commodity-driven social resistance. Neoliberal activism. Yet, perhaps the most important insight that we can take away from a book such as this is that seeing it all as contradiction does not help us anymore, that a sense of contradiction is derived from remaining in an outdated mode of thinking. We cannot dismiss these modes as simply hypocrisy, incorporation, or corporate appropriation. They demand a more complex, less cynical, less dismissive approach. Indeed, these very practices of consumer activism demand a recognition of the key relationship of consumerism and affect, the emotional content of consumer transactions. They thus demand new models for taking the emotional effects of consumer transactions seriously rather than seeing them as uncritical and acquiescent. This book is a powerful step toward forging these new paradigms and modes for thinking about the role of commodities in the context of social activism and political change.

Introduction

Commodity Activism in Neoliberal Times

———— SARAH BANET-WEISER AND ROOPALI MUKHERJEE ————

Buying Product RED items—ranging from Gap T-shirts to Apple iPods to Dell computers—means one supports the Global Fund to help eliminate AIDS in Africa. Consuming a "Caring Cup" of coffee at the Coffee Bean and Tea Leaf indicates a commitment to free trade and humane labor practices. Driving a Toyota Prius, likewise, points to the consumer's vow to help resolve the global oil crisis as well as fight global warming. Purchasing Dove beauty products enables one to participate in the Dove Real Beauty campaign, which encourages consumers to "coproduce" nationwide workshops to help girls and young women tackle problems of low self-esteem, many of which are created by the beauty industry itself, within which Dove has been a significant player. Using their star capital and the force of their celebrity, public figures such as Angelina Jolie, Brad Pitt, and Kanye West launch social activist programs ranging from UN-sponsored humanitarian actions to protesting the global trade in blood diamonds to rebuilding low-income neighborhoods in hurricane-ravaged New Orleans. All of which is to say that within contemporary culture it is utterly unsurprising to participate in social activism by buying something.

This book explores the range of that participation and the contradictions inherent in grafting philanthropy and social action onto merchandising practices, market incentives, and corporate profits. Drawing upon a series of examples, the essays in this volume are dedicated to thinking through the proliferation of these modes of activism within contemporary culture in the US, and the emergence of what we term "commodity activism" in the neoliberal moment, a moment in which realms of culture and society once considered "outside" the official economy are harnessed, reshaped, and made legible in economic terms. Through these explorations, we attempt to understand current struggles over what social activism means, who takes shape as activists in contemporary society, and whom such activism is imagined to serve.

These shifts indicate, among other things, a powerful turn in the modes
and meanings of social activism so that within the contemporary cultural
economy in the US, social action, we suggest, may itself be shifting shape
into a marketable commodity. As is characteristic of the commodity form—
produced through labor for purposes of trade and profit within markets and
fetishized in culture—commodity activism, as we encounter it today, offers
critical insights into both the promise and the perils of consumer-based
modes of resistance as they take shape within the dynamics of neoliberal
power. What, we ask, does it mean to "do activism" in a sociocultural context increasingly defined by neoliberal ideas about self-reliance, entrepreneurial individualism, and economic responsibility? In what ways do these
discourses shape contemporary conceptions of citizenship and community,
of marginality and resistance? What sociohistorical and institutional forces
can we trace to historicize the emergence of commodity activism? And what
account can we make of the political consequences of civic engagement and
action being increasingly defined by the logics of the marketplace?

It seems appropriate that a book on shifting forms of social activism
should appear at this historical moment, in the midst of renewed laments
over the marauding triumph of capital, the decline of heroic social movements, indeed, as some argue, the ethical futility of popular resistance itself.
Marked by a new generation of "posts"—postfeminism, postrace, postpoli-
tics—neoliberalism, we are warned, has hastened the "death of civil rights,"
the "end of feminism," the "collapse of the Left."[1] Certainly, social movements
and their modes of organizing have witnessed dramatic shifts over the past
half century. Thus, we find, for example, radical leaders of the past, iconic
figures like Che Guevara and Malcolm X, deployed within mainstream culture as little more than fashion statements. Likewise, we find the resistance
strategies of historic social movements co-opted into tactics of "brand aid"
and "shopping for change" campaigns led, with little hint of irony, by corporations, corporate philanthropies, and media celebrities.[2] As the tactics of
social and political critique then, appear to survive as little more than diverting spectacles, neither mainstream nor leftist approaches to activism seem to
escape the paradigmatic force of neoliberal capital. The proliferation of commodity activism, in other words, serves as a trenchant reminder that there
is no "outside" to the logics of contemporary capitalism, that resistance, to
indulge the popular cultural refrain, has, perhaps, become futile.

We may, on the one hand, characterize these forms of commodity activism as corporate appropriations, elaborate exercises in hypocrisy and arti-
fice intended to fool the consumer, sophisticated strategies aimed at securing

ever-larger profits. On the other hand, commodity activism may illuminate the nettled promise of innovative creative forms, cultural interventions that bear critically, if in surprising ways, on modes of dominance and resistance within changing social and political landscapes. Eschewing both uncritical exuberance and blanket condemnation, the essays in this collection move away from an either/or logic of profit versus politics, from clear distinctions between cultural co-optation and popular resistance that have characterized these debates within cultural studies.[3] Instead, we situate commodity activism within its larger historical contexts, its emergence over time revealing the vexed and contradictory means by which individuals and communities have marshaled the ideological and cultural frameworks of consumption to challenge, support, and reimagine the political and social dynamics of power.

The essays in this collection plumb the paradoxes of celebrity patronage and corporate philanthropy—both as showy spectacles that build brand loyalty, star iconicity, and profits, and as openings for critical thought and action—to argue that contemporary modes of commodity activism resist easy generalization, each deserving careful study and exploration. Thus, working from the vantage point of a single illustrative case, each essay in this volume unpacks the symbolic, rhetorical, and discursive means by which historical traditions of social activism are being hollowed out and rearticulated in commodity form. At the same time, the authors critically challenge the idea that hard-and-fast certainties separate capitalist power and popular resistance. The range of questions marking the ethical practices of commodity activism, we suggest, deny clear distinctions between modes of social action that appear to have collapsed into co-optation and others that seem to operate "outside" the logics of neoliberal capitalism.

Centrally engaging the conundrum of "resistance" within the current moment in the history of capital, then, each of our contributors critically assesses the cultural resonance and tactical significance of marketized modes of "fighting back"—who fights, how they fight, and whether such interventions have any "real" power to make social change. The essays in this volume indulge neither the fatalism of the "postpolitical," the idea that resistance is so profoundly co-opted by capital that it has been rendered meaningless, nor a romantic nostalgia for an imagined "outsider politics." Indeed, acknowledging that one can no longer—if one ever could—stand outside the system to critique it, this collection is instead geared toward careful examination of the contradictions that commodity activism necessarily ushers into the dynamics of contemporary capitalist power as well as the form and force of modes of resistance organized in the context of those dynamics. If commodity activism tethers mythologies of resistance to institutions and practices of capitalism, each case study we include grapples with the historical implications of such marketized modes of resistance in the neoliberal moment—what the function and value of such "resistance" might be, how its interventions enable and repress our collective imaginations, how it influences the history of struggle and solidarity—discursively, mythically, and tactically at the current moment in history.

Against press accounts in the US that breathlessly proclaimed "the death of capitalism" in the wake of the global financial crisis of 2008,[4] the essays in this volume unpack the consequences of commodity activism with a pointed recognition of the lasting ravages of capitalist power on individual and collective subjectivities. Ongoing shifts in the legitimacies of the liberal welfare state and the coincident turn in attitudes toward social and redistributive programs hitherto managed and administered by the state raise troubling questions about the merits and meaning of social action in the "postfeminist," "post–civil rights," "postcapitalist" eras. The essays we present here share a conviction that free market ideologies that dominate the discursive formations of contemporary neoliberalism offer us key openings to reevaluate Marxist theories of social power and resistance as well as to critically assess the promissory scope and limits of commodity activism. In opposition to circulating laments over the limitations of Marxist approaches to cultural critique, the essays in this volume are dedicated to thinking through the consolidation of commodity activism precisely as it redefines material histories of capitalist power, identity construction, and resistance.

Recognizing the analytical power of Marxist cultural critique, the contributors to this volume resist easy answers to these dilemmas, instead critically reassessing the form, function, and futility of resistance in the contemporary moment. On the one hand, promoting the consumption of goods, services, and celebrities as an act of charity and/or resistance, notions of social activism and philanthropy are increasingly defined by and within the rituals of media consumption. Popular media retain significant power as crucial sites for the domestication and containment of cultural imaginaries of political protest. As social action is increasingly styled by and manifest through commercialized popular culture, the case studies in this collection bring into relief the troubling ironies of anticapitalist resistance that is increasingly orchestrated and managed by capitalist media institutions.

On the other hand, this volume also illuminates vulnerabilities within totalizing categories like "domination" and "resistance," enabling fresh insights into the lurking promise of political resistance *within* the bounds of commodified popular culture and mainstream media. Our contributors take seriously the potential, for example, of the conditions of possibility of activism, which, despite commodification and bowdlerization in the neoliberal era, also reveals itself as a productive force for politics and the constitution of critical subjectivities and solidarities. In this sense, the collection serves centrally to illuminate how abiding axes of oppression and inequity—race, gender, class, and so on—interact with consumer cultures to reinvent grassroots identifications as well as tactical strategies for resistance and reimagination. These shifts in the relationships between citizenship and civic action, we suggest, are neither linear nor predetermined.

Activist, Citizen, Consumer: Historical Relations

As many historians of consumer culture have pointed out, dominant ideologies in the US have long sustained the mythic belief that the consumer is qualitatively different from the citizen. While surely citizens are also consumers and vice versa, there have historically been important ideological stakes in keeping these subject positions distinct. As economic historians John Kenneth Galbraith, Lizabeth Cohen, Lawrence Glickman, and others have noted, there remains a residual ethos (in the popular, political, and academic spheres) that Americans acted first as virtuous citizens before *transforming* or, from a more critical vantage point, *deteriorating*, into consumers.[5]

These transformations are seen to originate at different historical moments, but there is a general consensus that a heightened form of the "citizen-consumer" emerged in force during the late 20th and early 21st centuries in the US. Postwar affluence and conspicuous consumption spurred state discourses encouraging consumption practices as "patriotic" and the transformation of social institutions within the "Consumers' Republic." An increasingly superficial cultural sphere emerged over this period dominated by celebrities, advertising, and profit-oriented media institutions. Populist mythologies of a voracious and meddling state bureaucracy paved the path to widespread Reaganite deregulation; rampant, and often, rogue, corporatism; and market bubbles collapsing cyclically into fiscal scandal and crisis. The confluence of these economic and cultural forces advanced a nation of consumer-citizens, perhaps most visibly represented in the ever-growing divides between rich and poor, moral panics scapegoating "welfare queens" and other state dependents, and cultural mythologies celebrating individually minded folks bent on "enterprising themselves" rather than collective action and social justice.

While it is certainly true that these economic transitions facilitated the discursive transformation of a nation of citizens into a nation of consumers, and consonant cultural shifts from collective civic sensibilities to a bootstraps ethos of individualist entrepreneurship, ideological categories of "the consumer" and "the citizen" have neither clearly nor consistently been diametrically opposed.[6] That is, the history of citizenship as it has taken shape within consumer culture in the US is not a linear one with noticeable, disruptive—and regressive— breaks between citizens and consumers. While this book situates its examples within the historical moment of neoliberalism, we note that commodity activism did not emerge anew from the discursive formations of neoliberal capital. Rather, within the evolutionary history of capitalism, consumers have consistently—and often contradictorily—embraced consumption as a platform from which to launch progressive political and cultural projects.

For example, shifts from bourgeois consumption to mass consumption that began in the late 18th century were brought into bold relief within the industrial and political revolutions of the 19th and 20th centuries. Immigrant cultures consolidated new consumer communities in the US, making consumption practices a key platform for struggles over class, race, and gender formations in the late 19th and 20th centuries. Each of these historical junctures represents a crucial transition in the relations between individuals, their consumption habits, and their political subjectivities.[7] That is, citizenship in the US has historically been understood and fashioned *through* consumption practices, providing us with a wealth of examples from early protests against taxation to boycotts for labor and civil rights to the "shopping for change" campaigns of today.

In particular, histories of consumer movements in the US demonstrate a tradition of consumer-citizens acting in ways that are intimately connected with community or collective politics. For instance, as Victoria de Grazia, Kathy Peiss, Jennifer Scanlon, and Lynn Spigel, among others, have documented, many middle- and working-class women crafted new experiences of personal autonomy outside the home in 19th-century Europe and the US via pleasurable rituals of shopping and material acquisition.[8] Importantly, gendered habits of shopping for clothing, buying and wearing cosmetics, and acquiring newfangled gadgets and appliances for the bourgeois home were not merely about the identification of consumption with femininity; nor were they only about patriarchal domesticity in which women were charged with provisioning for the home. Indeed, while it may be the case that consumption practices stand in as metonyms for sexual and social oppressions, mass consumption also arguably "liberated" women from a stifling domesticity, encouraging new independent gendered subjectivities and, in some situations, subverting traditional gendered relations in both public and private spheres. As de Grazia explains,

> It is the capacity of commodities to move between the customarily female spaces of the market and the household, between the world of production and the world of reproduction, wreaking havoc with the very polarities—of public and private, calculation and desire, commercial sphere and domestic space, male and female—that have forged modern definitions of womanhood in Western society, as well as the terms for interpreting women's subordination.[9]

It is important, in other words, to recognize the variety of ways that consumption practices reshaped and reimagined gendered subjectivities and relations, and that the consumer-citizen did indeed facilitate broader activist impulses that were geared to political goals and aspirations larger than those limited to individual desires and subjectivities.

Likewise, practicing consumer citizenship was crucial for immigrants, African Americans, and other racialized constituencies in the 19th- and 20th-century US as a means to mitigate and challenge racist practices and cultural exclusions. Projecting political aspirations onto commodities and consumption practices, disenfranchised racialized communities organized boycotts of segregated public spaces, collectively invested in independent businesses, and engaged in strategic consumption practices that called into question hegemonic relations of racial power and inequity. As Robert Weems Jr., Lizabeth Cohen, Jason Chambers, and others have documented, for instance, the civil rights movement that transformed racial formations in the mid-20th century US was notably organized around issues of consumption and access—in retail stores, at lunch counters, and on city buses—as a means to enfranchise African Americans.[10] Each of these struggles, it must be noted, was founded on the promise of the *market* to deliver social acceptance and democratic rights, and on the force of mobilizations of *consumers* to effect social and political change.[11] In each instance, tactics of social action engaged with rituals and institutions of commerce and capitalist exchange to demand political freedom and equality.

Likewise, the founding of consumer protection agencies in the US, the mass organizing efforts of consumer activist Ralph Nader starting in the 1950s, and the passage of federal laws regulating deceptive advertising practices, consumer fraud, and products endangering public health and safety were aimed at making corporations and markets more accountable to consumer needs and concerns.[12] These programs instilled corporate ethics of "customer service," securing the profitability of corporations that reoriented their business practices to be more responsive to consumers while they emboldened consumers to collectively demand higher standards in goods and services in exchange for brand loyalties. Taking a different tack, anticonsumerist mobilizations organized by countercultural groups like the hippies during the 1960s and 1970s in the US sought to debunk cultural associations between material acquisition and personal happiness and were geared to "simple living" and ecologically sustainable lifestyles. Calling for the outright rejection of material needs and desires, assumed to be fabricated by greedy corporations and foisted on hapless consumers, these struggles revealed their own political paradoxes over time as campaigns like "Buy Black," the *Whole Earth Catalog*, and publications like *AdBusters* proffered anticonsumerist critiques that, ironically, urged consumerism itself.[13]

Throughout the 19th-century and early to mid-20th-century US, then, consumer movements emphasized collective action and the formation of consumer communities geared to political goals, each marked by its own paradoxes and contradictions. The "Consumers' Republic" that Lizabeth Cohen so carefully delineates throughout the mid-20th century in the US had an emphasis on civic virtues of consumerism, that is, consumer citizenship was largely understood as enabling broader goals of equal access, social justice, and community building. Emphasizing collective mobilization, these movements marshaled political goals beyond those that addressed individualized consumptive desire and identity. They mobilized around issues of access—for the poor, the working classes, immigrants, and disenfranchised racialized groups—and toward leveraging the market so it would function more efficiently and responsively for all kinds of consumers. Such consumer politics, it must be noted, were neither antimarket nor anticapitalist. Rather, they focused on the liberatory promise of the market itself, buoyed by the conviction that capitalist exchange was key to transforming the political condition of consumer-citizens.[14]

Cultural Resistance in Neoliberal Times

The *longue durée* of consumer activism in the US, then, encapsulates a two-centuries-long trajectory that is scored with tensions over the ethics and expediency of consumer activism. In the contemporary moment commodity activism is marked by both the legacies of and transitions from these historical antecedents. As the neoliberal moment is witness to ever-sharper delineations of the marketplace as constitutive of our political imaginaries, our identities, rights, and ideologies are evermore precisely formulated within the logics of consumption and commodification rather than in opposition to them. Here, cultural notions of liberal democratic subjectivity transform into capitalist citizenship, and rituals of consumption increasingly stand in for other modes of democratic engagement with profound consequences for what counts as "civic resistance."[15] And, as participation within public spheres is increasingly shaped and secured by one's capacities to consume, these transitions exact their heaviest price from marginalized constituencies—women, nonwhites, and the poor.[16] Thus, commodity activism reveals new challenges that become legible within the historical and institutional particularities of neoliberalism.

While there are competing definitions of the idea of neoliberalism and significant theoretical debate over its implications, we draw from David Harvey here for whom neoliberalism is

> in the first instance a theory of political economic practices that proposes that human well-being can best be advanced by liberating individual entrepreneurial freedoms and skills within an institutional framework characterized by strong private property rights, free markets, and free trade. The role of the state is to create and preserve an institutional framework appropriate to such practices.[17]

Thus, neoliberal society has reimagined not just economic transactions and resources but also social and individual relations, the dynamics of affect and emotion, modes of social and political resistance, and the terrain of culture itself. It is not simply that neoliberalism has seized realms of life hitherto sheltered from the relations of production but that neoliberalism reorganizes society and culture such that "the role of culture has expanded in an unprecedented way into the political and economic at the same time that conventional notions of culture have largely been emptied out."[18] In this milieu, individual rights and freedoms are guaranteed not by the state but rather by the freedom of the market and of trade.[19]

The constitutive force of neoliberalism as it shapes the ethical and material contours of commodity activism is notably revealed in the surge, in recent years, in practices of "ethical consumption" or "corporate social responsibility" (CSR). The emergence of neoliberalism, as Milton Friedman famously heralded it in the *New York Times Magazine* in 1970, reopened enduring questions about the prudence and folly of corporate commitments to social and political causes. Railing against those who argued that "business is not concerned 'merely' with profit but also with promoting desirable 'social' ends; that business has a 'social conscience' and takes seriously its responsibilities for providing employment, eliminating discrimination, avoiding pollution," Friedman asserted, to the contrary, that the "sole social responsibility of business was to increase its profits."[20]

Friedman's contention notwithstanding, corporate relationships with social and political causes—sweat-free labor, the environment, funding for AIDS and cancer research—proliferated rather than dwindled under the aegis of neoliberal capital and, as the cases of commodity activism we present in this volume reveal, social causes reoriented themselves to assimilate rather than oppose the logics of profit and capitalist gain. Indeed, in recent decades, the role of corporations in building a better planet, achieving world peace, curing Alzheimer's disease, and so on, is so commonplace, it is often hard to take seriously. To wit, the fast-food chain McDonald's maintains a website entitled "Values in Practice" that features posts on sustainable supply chains, environmental responsibility, nutrition, and well-being. Coffee mega-retailer Starbucks has a program entitled Starbucks Shared Planet™, that uses the tagline "You and Starbucks. It's bigger than coffee" with little recognition of the irony that the term "shared planet" is now a trademarked commodity. Similarly, the clothing company Geoffrey Beene places a card in the folds of its garments that details the various causes the company is committed to, with the words "Enjoy your new Geoffrey Beene garment . . .because nothing feels better than giving back."

Within the discursive formations of neoliberalism, then, CSR aligns corporate support of social issues with building corporate brands and consolidating brand revenues while social justice transforms into yet another strategic venture to secure the corporate bottom line. CSR, in other words, is "good for business," and within the neoliberal context, this means exploiting what David Vogel terms "the market for virtue." Vogel highlights this historical shift in the logic and practices of CSR with a compelling example about consumer activists who, in the 1960s and 1970s, protested pharmaceutical giant Dow Chemical's production of napalm for use in the war in Vietnam:

> The antiwar activists who, during the 1960s, pressured Dow Chemical to stop producing napalm, framed their argument exclusively in moral terms: they neither knew nor cared whether producing napalm would affect Dow's earnings. In contrast, the contemporary environmental activists who are working with Dow to reduce its carbon emissions argue that doing so will make Dow more profitable by lowering its costs.[21]

Vogel's case reveals key differences in activist paradigms across time, but here we are also offered a critical opportunity to unpack shifts in the moral frameworks undergirding commodity activism. Moral virtue, in this context, is reframed as *consonant with* the interests of contemporary capitalism and, as Vogel points out, commands an increase in cultural and economic capital. Part of the discourse of contemporary neoliberal capital, then, is the notion that profit is achieved not by ruthless, inhumane practices or by unrestrained avarice but, rather, by both the corporation and the consumer acting "virtuously." Thus, even as the labor practices of multinational corporations and trade agreements across the globe remain sharply skewed in the interests of economic elites, corporations align themselves with social causes to bolster their reputations as good citizens. As Laurie Ouellette points out in this volume, as a public relations venture directed at consumers in the US, social responsibility is embraced as a pro-business strategy.

Activist Consumption and the "Enterprising" Self

Within the political economy of neoliberalism, however, it is not simply that social realms have become recoded as economic but that individuals, and in the specific case of this collection, consumer-citizens, have themselves become reconstituted as economically productive. These "enterprising" selves, as Michel Foucault has argued,[22] become key actors within neoliberalism, expressed not only through a retreat from collectivity and public spheres but also, as Alison Hearn in this volume suggests, through a normalizing of individual entrepreneurialism and the branding of the neoliberal self. The current transition, then, shifts from a 20th-century focus on consumer movements to a neoliberal emphasis on the individual consumer—a shift from a collective reimagining of the market to a retooling of capitalist practices and strategies to better accommodate the self-interests of citizen-consumers. What distinguishes commodity activism from earlier consumer movements is its mode of mobilization, the emphasis having shifted from larger political goals to consumers themselves "as the chief beneficiaries of political activism."[23] Likewise, as the essays in this anthology reveal, movement tactics and paradigms of collective organizing themselves reveal a kind of "commodity creep" so that even radical imaginaries of social critique seem to falter under the seductive force of neoliberalism. Thus, as political imaginaries and subjectivities are reshaped to fit the individualized ethos of neoliberal capitalism, mooring them evermore securely to the logics of consumption and marketization, commodity activism emerges as both symptomatic of and tailored to this historical transition.

Consumer-citizens, in this moment, increasingly practice moral and civic virtue principally through their pocketbooks. Within the logics of commodity activism, "doing good" and being a good consumer collapse into one and the same thing. Thus, as Samantha King, Josée Johnston and Kate Cairns, Jo Littler, and others in this collection suggest, the practices of "ethical consumption" need to be interrogated not only as a means to historicize shifts in relative autonomy enabled by neoliberal ideologies but, as important, to understand what is lost in them. For example, ethical consumption practices are designed for the wealthy, evidenced not only by the higher prices of, say, food produced for organic markets or "green nappies" for middle-class mothers but also by the fact that most consumer activists in the US tend to be more affluent and educated. Our attention to these activist practices, then, offers clues to the means by which working-class Americans may be gradually edged out of political activism by the class dynamics of commodity activism.

Likewise, our explorations in this collection take seriously the paradoxes of commodity activism as it reimagines "value" within neoliberal culture. From a variety of perspectives, the scholars in this collection locate the proliferation of commodity activism within shifts in what constitutes labor, and consequently, how value is generated within late capitalist markets. For example, the contemporary moment is characterized by ongoing shifts in definitions of "interactivity" and "agency," changes that have been hastened by the development of rapid, inexpensive media technologies, and viral circulation of content enabled by such mobile, miniature innovations. Given the democratizing potential of such "do-it-yourself" (DIY) activity and user-generated content, for instance, this collection enables fresh perspectives on the extent of control that media gatekeepers continue to enjoy over the production of popular culture and vernacular practices. Although traditional expert knowledges are indeed tempered by innovations in viral media technologies and their vernacular practices, as Mark Andrejevic reminds us,[24] consumer-generated content does not simply empower the consumer. It also creates opportunities for corporations to offload labor onto consumers in the name of democratic openness. Thus, while commodity activism demands reevaluations of traditional binaries between popular and commercial culture, vernacular and mainstream production, and media producers and consumers, as a number of our contributors in this collection reveal, activists engaged in "shopping for change" campaigns contribute to the profitability of corporate brands, the commodification of cultural identity, the marketization of political dissent, and so on. Each marks the collapse of boundaries between producers and consumers, and each reveals an instance of labor that is unrecompensed and, indeed, unrecognized by corporations that neverthe-less derive substantial market value from it.

Within these relations of production, commodity activism generates value as it is created by the fetishization of social action as a marketized commod-ity, that is, value created by the "sign value" of consumption and consumer practices.[25] Mindful of Marx's insistence that capitalism renders invisible the social relations of production, we suggest that commodity activism hints at new dilemmas raised by the emergence of "affective" or "immaterial" labor,[26] ideas that Sarah Banet-Weiser, Alison Hearn, and others in this collection pursue further. In other words, as commodity activism produces market value in affective relations with brands, celebrities, and political virtue, our work in this collection reveals how new forms of labor are made available by the marketization of dissent. Moreover, the value generated by such labor yields new modes of objectification and exploitation. If commodity fetishism results in objects becoming humanized and human relations being objec-tified, the commodification of social activism engages profound questions about the reach of contemporary capitalism into the circumstances of our choices as producers, consumers, and moral citizens.

Buying Good, Doing Good: The Contradictions of Commodity Activism

As it has taken shape, this anthology engages with scholarly dialogues about how neoliberal capitalism both enables and confounds modes of social activ-ism at the present moment. We situate commodity activism as a specific kind of product emerging from labor in the neoliberal capitalist economy. We theorize how the phenomena of commodity activism open up new pos-sibilities for the construction of identities and solidarities. We focus on the role of consumers in the formation of new cultural expressions and cultural production within emerging economic landscapes. Finally, we offer careful substantiation for new theoretical frameworks that refuse the traditional and nostalgic binaries that position politics in opposition to consumerism.

This book illuminates some of the central contradictions that are made visible through commodity activism. However, our goal is neither simply to "expose" commodity activism as a clever hoax intended to bring in greater profits for corporations nor to celebrate commodity activism as an ideal form of social action for 21st-century consumers. Rather, it is our hope that this col-lection offers a variety of ways to understand and situate commodity activism within the contemporary era by avoiding the pitfalls of binary thinking that separate consumption practices from political struggles. The creation of value continues to drive capitalism, yet the meaning of "value" shifts and is reimagined within the context of neoliberal capitalism. The commodity in question is not only a tangible product (though tangible products are still clearly important within the current political economy) but also intangible attributes that include cultural responsibility, moral virtue, political ethics, and social action itself.

These are the questions that we maintain must be asked at this particular juncture in the history of capitalism—questions that revolve not simply around whether commodity activism empowers or disempowers the consumer but rather about how practices of consumption, structures of political economy, and the creation of political and cultural subjectivities are entangled within contemporary values of neoliberalism. This book wrestles with these questions, despite the fact that due to changing media and technological platforms, instabilities and crises confronting Western capitalism, and shifting imaginaries about the state's role in culture and society, our answers to such questions may be, at best, partial, perishable, and provisional. More than anything, through the essays in this collection, we offer a range of points of entry into a larger cultural and political conversation about who and what consumers are and should be, about shifts that notions of citizenship and the state are currently enduring, and, as well, about larger social goals that contemporary commodity activism may be uniquely poised to meet.

From global health campaigns sponsored by pharmaceutical corporations to social movements capitulating to mantras of individualism and entrepreneurial responsibility, this anthology engages the ways in which the radical potential of social activism is being transformed in a variety of ways. Each of the cases we include serves to explore the vicissitudes of what it means to pursue politically activist work in this historical moment.

To these ends, this anthology is organized as a multidisciplinary, methodologically diverse project; our contributors work from a variety of scholarly and disciplinary homes, including communication, cultural and media studies, ethnography, sociology, and critical policy studies. We situate this book within the nascent field of "critical consumer studies," a field that takes consumer culture and consumption habits seriously as sites of scholarly inquiry, and which is dedicated to careful investigations of the contradictions and ruptures within capitalist consumerism in order to discern both the promise and the limits of political action. Drawing from film, television, and other media texts, consumer activist campaigns, and cultures of celebrity and corporate patronage, each empirical case serves to highlight a robust range of theoretical problematics including, for example, the spectacularization of catastrophe to profitable ends within the logics of disaster capitalism, the glamorization of suffering within public relations portfolios of media celebrities, the corporate production of cultural identities, and the capitalization of difference in ways that yoke politics to profits.

NOTES

1. Stanley Aronowitz, *How Class Works: Power and Social Movement* (New Haven: Yale University Press, 2003); Pierre Bourdieu, *Acts of Resistance: Against the Tyranny of the Market*, trans. Richard Nice (New York: New Press, 1999); Todd Boyd, *The New H.N.I.C. (Head Niggas In Charge): The Death of Civil Rights and the Reign of Hip Hop* (New York: NYU Press, 2003); Wendy Brown, "Women's Studies Unbound: Revolution, Mourning, Politics," *Parallax* 9, no. 2 (2003): 3–16; Nick Couldry, *Listening beyond the Echoes: Media, Ethics and Agency in an Uncertain World* (London: Paradigm, 2006).

2. Dwight F. Burlingame and Dennis R. Young, eds., *Corporate Philanthropy at the Crossroads* (Bloomington: Indiana University Press, 1996); Joseph Heath and Andrew Potter, *Nation of Rebels: Why Counterculture Became Consumer Culture* (New York: Collins Business, 2004); Jo Littler, *Radical Consumption: Shopping for Change in Contemporary Culture* (Buckingham: Open University Press, 2008); Hamish Pringle and Marjorie Thompson, *Brand Spirit: How Cause Related Marketing Builds Brands* (New York: Wiley, 1999); Anita Roddick, *Take It Personally: How Globalisation Affects You and Powerful Ways to Challenge It: An Action Guide for Conscious Consumers* (London: Element Press, 2003); Myra Stark, "Brand Aid: Cause Effective," *Brandweek* 40 (1999): 20–22; Sara A. Tinic, "United Colors and Untied Meanings: Benetton and the Commodification of Social Issues," *Journal of Communication* 47 (1997): 3–25; David Vogel, *The Market for Virtue: The Potential and Limits of Corporate Social Responsibility* (Washington, DC: Brookings Institution Press, 2006).

3. Danae Clark, "Commodity Feminism," *Camera Obscura* 9, nos. 1–2 (1991): 181; John Fiske, *Reading the Popular* (London: Routledge, 1989); Jim Mcguigan, "What Price the Public Sphere?" in *Electronic Empires: Global Media and Local Resistance*, ed. Daya Kishan Thussu (London: Arnold, 1998); Meaghan Morris, "Metamorphoses at Sydney Tower," *New Formations* 11 (Summer 1990): 5–18.

4. Peter Foster, "No End to Capitalism," *Financial Post*, September 18, 2009, http://Network.Nationalpost.Com/Np/Blogs/Fpcomment/Archive/2009/09/18/Peter-Foster-No-End-To-Capitalism.Aspx#Ixzz17vwi36fq (accessed September 2, 2010).

5. John Kenneth Galbraith, *The Affluent Society* (New York: Mariner, 1987); Lizabeth Cohen, *A Consumers' Republic: The Politics of Mass Consumption in Postwar America* (New York: Knopf, 2003); Lawrence B. Glickman, ed., *Consumer Society in American History: A Reader* (Ithaca: Cornell University Press, 1999).

6. Sarah Banet-Weiser, *Kids Rule! Nickelodeon and Consumer Citizenship* (Durham, NC: Duke University Press, 2007); Anne M. Cronin, *Advertising and Consumer Citizenship: Gender, Images and Rights* (New York: Routledge, 2001); Scott C. Martin, ed., *Cultural Change and the Market Revolution in America, 1789–1860* (Lanham, MD: Rowman and Littlefield, 2005); George Yúdice, "The Vicissitudes of Civil Society," *Social Text* 14, no. 4 (1995): 1–25; Susan Murray and Laurie Oullette, eds., *Reality TV: Remaking Television Culture*, 2nd ed. (New York: NYU Press, 2003).

7. Cohen, 2003; Gary Cross, *An All-Consuming Century: Why Commercialism Won in Modern America* (New York: Columbia University Press, 2000); Victoria de Grazia (with Ellen Furlough), ed., *The Sex of Things: Gender and Consumption in Historical Perspective* (Berkeley: University of California Press, 1996).

8. de Grazia, 1996; Kathy Peiss, *Hope in a Jar: The Making of America's Beauty Culture* (New York: Macmillan, 1999); Jennifer Scanlon, ed., *The Gender and Consumer Culture Reader* (New York: NYU Press, 2000); Lynn Spigel, *Make Room for TV: Television and the Family Ideal in Postwar America* (Chicago: University of Chicago Press, 1992).

9. de Grazia, 1996, 7–8.

10. Robert Weems, *Desegregating the Dollar: African American Consumerism in the Twentieth Century* (New York: NYU Press, 1998); Cohen, 2003; Jason Chambers, *Madison Avenue and the Color Line: African Americans in the Advertising Industry* (Philadelphia: University of Pennsylvania Press, 2009.

11. Elizabeth Chin, *Purchasing Power: Black Kids and American Consumer Culture* (Minneapolis: University of Minnesota Press, 2001); Arlene M. Dávila, *Latinos, Inc.: The Marketing and Making of a People* (Berkeley: University of California Press, 2001); Andrew R. Heinze, *Adapting to Abundance: Jewish Immigrants, Mass Consumption, and the Search for American Identity* (New York: Columbia University Press, 1990); Paul R. Mullins, *Race and Affluence: An Archaeology of African America and Consumer Culture* (New York: Kluwer Academic/Plenum, 1999); Katherine Sender, *Business, Not Politics: The Making of the Gay Market* (New York: Columbia University Press, 2004).

12. Lawrence B. Glickman, *Buying Power: A History of Consumer Activism in America* (Chicago: University of Chicago Press, 2009).

13. Glickman, 2009; Max Haiven, "Privatized Resistance: *Adbusters* and the Culture of Neoliberalism," *Review of Education, Pedagogy, and Cultural Studies* 29 (2007): 85–110; Paul Kingsnorth, *One No, Many Yeses: A Journey to the Heart of the Global Resistance Movement* (London: Free Press, 2003); George Ritzer, *Enchanting a Disenchanted World: Revolutionizing the Means of Consumption* (New York: Pine Forge Press, 2005); Bill Talen, *What Should I Do If Reverend Billy Is in My Store?* (New York: New Press, 2003); Fred S. Turner, *From Counterculture to Cyberculture: Stewart Brand, the Whole Earth Network, and the Rise of Digital Utopianism* (Chicago: University of Chicago Press, 2008).

14. Matthew Hilton, *Prosperity for All: Consumer Activism in an Era of Globalization* (Ithaca: Cornell University Press, 2009).

15. Joy James, "Academia, Activism, and Imprisoned Intellectuals," *Social Justice* 30, no. 2 (2003): 3–7; Peter Miller and Nikolas Rose, "Mobilizing the Consumer: Assembling the Subject of Consumption," *Theory, Culture and Society* 14 (1997): 1–36; Nikolas Rose, *Powers of Freedom: Reframing Political Thought* (Cambridge: Cambridge University Press, 1999).

16. Lauren Berlant, *The Queen of America Goes to Washington City: Essays on Sex and Citizenship* (Durham, NC: Duke University Press, 1997); Inderpal Grewal, *Transnational America: Feminisms, Diasporas, Neoliberalisms* (Durham, NC: Duke University Press, 2005); Chandra Mohanty, *Feminism without Borders: Decolonizing Theory, Practicing Solidarity* (Durham, NC: Duke University Press, 2003); Aihwa Ong, *Neoliberalism as Exception: Mutations in Citizenship and Sovereignty* (Durham, NC: Duke University Press, 2006).

17. David Harvey, *A Brief History of Neoliberalism* (Oxford: Oxford University Press, 2005), 2.

18. George Yúdice, *The Expediency of Culture: Uses of Culture in the Global Era* (Durham, NC: Duke University Press, 2003), 9.

19. Harvey, 2005, 7.

20. Milton Friedman, "The Social Responsibility of Business Is to Increase Its Profits," *New York Times Magazine*, September 13, 1970, 32–33, 122–26.

21. Vogel, 2006, 24.

22. Michel Foucault, "Governmentality," in *The Foucault Effect: Studies in Governmentality*, ed. Graham Burchell, Colin Gordon, and Peter Miller (Chicago: University of Chicago Press, 1991), 87–104.

23. Glickman, 2009.

24. Marc Andrejevic, "Watching Television without Pity: The Productivity of Online Fans," *Television and New Media*, 9, no. 1 (2008): 24–46.

25. Jean Baudrillard, *The Consumer Society: Myths and Structures* (London: Sage, 1998).

26. Michael Hardt, "Affective Labor," *Boundary 2*, 26, no. 2 (Summer 1999): 89–100; Maurizio Lazaratto, "Immaterial Labor," in *Radical Thought in Italy: A Potential Politics*, ed. Paul Virno and Michael Hardt (Minneapolis: University of Minnesota Press, 1996), 133–47.

PART ONE

Brand, Culture, Action

The titles are revealing: *Love Marks*; *Emotional Branding*; *Citizen Brand*. All are books written in the past several years meant to guide marketers and advertisers on how to navigate the increasingly blurred relationships between advertising, branding, emotion, and politics. In the late 20th and early 21st centuries, it became clear that advertising and brand managers were developing new strategies to capture the attention of ever-more-savvy consumers by appealing to affect, emotion, and social responsibility. Indeed, the definition of the contemporary "consumer" does not simply point to what kinds of purchases one might make; more than that, the "consumer" is a political category. And, consumption itself is part of what one *is*, part of the complex framework that constitutes identity. In the contemporary terrain of global, national, and narrow-scale marketing, brands have begun to assume increasingly complex sets of political and activist functions. Within the multidimensional contexts of branding, marketers are increasingly turning to campaigns that encourage consumers toward highly cathected and deeply emotional relationships to brands, so that products bear what is called, in market-speak, "love marks."

The chapters in this part explore, from different vantage points, the contradictions that characterize the contemporary relationship of consumer culture, the commodity activist, and branding. Neoliberalism and the technological and cultural apparatuses that support and validate this political economy have hastened critical transformations in the interrelations between the consuming subject and political culture. As such, in order to theorize who, and what, the "consumer" is in the current era of neoliberalism and branding, we need different conceptualizations for key terms like "participation," "activism," "mainstream," "authenticity," "consumer," and "producer." Moreover, as our definitions of what constitutes the "political" shift under the impact of "new" media convergence and mobilized forms of cultural production and circulation, we need new analytics for understanding the contemporary activist subject and the ways in which this subject both creates and experiences "social activism."

The authors in this part thus ask questions such as: What does it mean to "be" a consumer activist? How do we craft identities within the context of branding and marketing? What are some of the tensions between consumption behavior and political action within these contexts? The chapters do not arrive at the same set of answers for these questions, and indeed engage in provocative debate about what, and who, a "commodity activist" is: Is she a girl who participates in a Dove Soap–sponsored workshop on "self-esteem"? Should our conception of "commodity activist" include media conglomerates like ABC and its efforts to "build community"? How do we situate "green branding" within the context of commodity activism? Indeed, is the "commodity activist" a brand in and of itself?

The chapters in this part explore these questions by analyzing a series of examples of contemporary commodity activism. To begin, Alison Hearn theorizes the subject position of the "branded self" in contemporary consumer culture to make the argument that within neoliberal modes of governmentality and the symbolic and discursive logics of flexible accumulation and post-Fordism, self-branding emphasizes the instrumental crafting of a notable self-image. Such branded versions of subjectivity, collapsing and fusing with capitalist processes of production and consumption, Hearn argues, produce a "self" that is always already interpellated as highly individuated, competitive, self-interested, and image-oriented. This is a "self," in other words, that effectively undermines any claims to community activism and solidarity. Exploring tensions between these modes of hyperpromotionalism and collective affiliation as they emerge on and through the youth websites "Ecorazzi: the latest in green gossip" and "Ecostilleto," as well as the Disney-owned, green initiative "Friends for Change," Hearn's essay probes the consequences of the emergence of the neoliberal branded self for youth culture and community activism, specifically environmentalism.

Next, Sarah Banet-Weiser looks at the ways in which contemporary neoliberal capitalism offers a new, market-inspired definition of "self-esteem" for young girls and women through the lens of the Dove Real Beauty campaign. Critics of this campaign frame their concerns within the discourse of hypocrisy; it seems, on the face of it, phony or duplicitous to launch a social activism campaign that targets the beauty industry by using—and thus promoting—Dove beauty products, a key player in the global beauty industry. However, Banet-Weiser argues that within neoliberal capitalism, this kind of strategy makes perfect sense: in a context in which distinctions between "authentic" and "commercial" politics are blurred through the retraction of public and social services, claims of "hypocrisy" make sense only if there is a clear distinction between culture and commerce. Commodity activist campaigns such as the Dove Real Beauty campaign are made legible within a broader context of brand culture, in which the "social activist" herself is shaped into a kind of brand.

Laurie Ouellette examines a cultural product—television, and specifically, the media network ABC—that has historically operated as a private, for-profit industry, tracing the development and transformation of TV in its role as a responsible "citizen" in a neoliberal context. Examining the ABC Better Community initiative as a case of the growing role of television as an agent of civic responsibility, Ouellette unpacks the campaign not as a "corporate ruse" interested only in promotion and profit but rather as a "template" for a kind of "good government" that is both created and sustained by neoliberal governmentality. The transformation of the public sector within the context of neoliberalism reveals how "do good TV" adds to the "value" of a media conglomerate such as ABC as it shifts from an overt compulsion to profit to a more "virtuous" commitment to social responsibility—a responsibility that is ultimately realized and sustained through profit.

We close this part with an essay by Jo Littler, who examines a broader expression of brand culture, "green branding," arguing that the discursive ironies of green branding work as a form of commodity activism that encourages individuals to address environmental, social, and political concerns through consumption. Littler reminds us that green products navigate a range of contradictions—they may operate as a fetish serving the needs of a small group of people, they may mark the emergence of a liberating form of grassroots democracy-from-below, and they may also epitomize a gross instance of corporate "greenwash." Tracing the conceptual relations between "green governmentality" and "productive democracy" through her analysis of a single green product, the nappy, Littler reminds us that green commodity activism as it takes form within neoliberal brand culture remains double-edged. While neoliberal culture insistently contains possibilities for their full emergence, contemporary modes of green activism and branding can paradoxically be forceful in spurring social action toward broader progressive objectives—regulating corporate behavior, changing popular expectations, and, crucially, pushing beyond green capitalism into green cooperativism.

1

Brand Me "Activist"

ALISON HEARN

In 2006, *Time* magazine named "YOU" person of the year. Arguing that the Internet and social network sites had facilitated the emergence of "community and collaboration on a scale never seen before," the magazine went on to celebrate Web 2.0's revolutionary political possibilities, suggesting that the new Web demonstrated "the many wresting power from the few," which might then lead to "a new kind of international understanding."[1] But, what kind of power does creating a Facebook profile, posting personal videos on YouTube, designing a cool avatar on Second Life, or "tweeting" your thoughts hourly constitute? What form of revolution is fomented when individuals follow their favorite celebrities' "green dos and don'ts" or vote on which green project Disney should support with 1 million of its billions of dollars? Who *is* this "ME" imagined by *Time*'s interpellation "YOU" anyway?

This chapter will examine the versions of selfhood assumed and partially produced by contemporary forms of "commodity activism," with reference to three popular "green" websites emanating from, and totally dependent on, the economy of Hollywood celebrity: ecorazzi.com, ecostiletto.com, and Disney's friendsforchange.com. I argue that *Time* magazine's imperative "YOU" and its concomitant response "ME" mark the conflation of selfhood with neoliberal modes of governmentality, the economic logics of post-Fordism, hyperconsumerism, and promotionalism, and marries this conflation to social activism. As the boundaries between work and life erode, broad-based structural, systemic, and collective problems are routinely reduced to issues of "personal responsibility" and "the reflexive project of the self,"[2] or the constitution of "ME," becomes a distinct form of labor in the guise of self-branding. This chapter interrogates the naturalized elision seen in many contemporary forms of commodity activism between radical individual empowerment, necessary for the market, and collective and communal affiliation, necessary for long-lasting political change. While acknowledging that new media technologies and social networks *can* enable increased social and ethical accountability on the part of corporations and government, this accountability is never simply given. This chapter insists that, in order for significant social change to take place, dominant templates for meaningful selfhood must also be remade; ultimately, a conceptualization of selfhood tightly bound to the logic of neoliberalism and the post-Fordist market is one of the core components, and central limitations, of "commodity activism."

The Empty Self in Consumer Society

American psychotherapist Philip Cushman argues that the "self" is a cultural construct, which expresses "the shared understanding within a community about what it is to be human."[3] Cultural historian Warren Sussman asserts that procedures of self-production and self-presentation have always reflected the dominant economic and cultural interests of the time. Invariably, "changes in culture do mean changes in modal types of character."[4] In other words, our forms of self-production and self-understanding are deeply conditioned by our economic and social context; dominant modalities of "self" are both summoned into being and illustrated in our cultural discourses and institutions. The ways we come to internalize or embody these versions of "selfhood" are always contested and in flux, constituting examples of biopower in action. As Michel Foucault has famously written, "Nothing in man—not even his body—is sufficiently stable to serve as a basis for self-recognition or for understanding other men."[5]

During the 20th century, Anthony Giddens argues, we have been "disembedded" from more traditional forms of sociality and community, such as the church or family. As we develop ever more abstract systems, institutions, and technological forms, which pull us out of our cultural, spatial, and temporal situatedness, established modes of identity and selfhood are dislodged and thrown into crisis.[6] Cushman describes the terrain of modernity as marked by social absences and a lack of coherence and tradition. We experience this "interiorly as a lack of personal conviction and worth," and we embody it "as a chronic and undifferentiated emotional hunger" that "yearns to acquire and consume as an unconscious way of compensating for what has been lost."[7] Cushman describes the modality of selfhood in the growing post–World War II consumer landscape, then, as an "empty self"; this self must perpetually consume in order to be filled, organized, and effectively identified, but it can never truly be satiated. As Zygmunt Baumann writes, midcentury consumer society "proclaims the impossibility of gratification and measures its progress by ever-rising demand";[8] desire is its principle engine.

Under the conditions of post–World War II consumer society, the self must personally maintain its coherence over time and does this through the reflexive creation of its own story, or biography: "A person's identity is not to be found in behavior, nor—important though this is—in the reactions of others, but in the capacity to keep a particular narrative going."[9] For Giddens, as for Cushman and Baumann, this reflexive project of the self is intimately linked to the processes of consumption. And, while these sociologists differ in their views about the potential pitfalls and benefits associated with self-production as consumption, they all agree that self-production inevitably involves the production of a coherent *narrative of self* built up through "the possession of desired goods and the pursuit of artificially framed styles of life,"[10] in which "self-actualisation [is] packaged and distributed according to market criteria."[11] In the absence of larger frames of meaning, perpetual attention to the construction of "self" through processes of consumption provides the only remaining continuity, or through-line, in our lives. Baumann concurs: "It is me, my living body or that living body which is me, which seems to be the sole constant ingredient of the admittedly unstable, always until further notice composition of the world around me."[12]

The Post-Fordist, Neoliberal "Self"

The late modern (or postmodern) logics of capitalism and neoliberalism constitute the contemporary parameters within which we come to construct our personal biographies. How, then, can we come to understand the modalities of selfhood held out for us to occupy under these contemporary conditions?

David Harvey and others describe the current "post-Fordist" mode of production as marked by processes of "flexible accumulation," which include strategies of permanent innovation, mobility and change, subcontracting, and just-in-time, decentralized production.[13] Flexible accumulation is heavily dependent on communication networks and on lateral flows of information and production, as opposed to hierarchical ones, and tends to emphasize the production and consumption of knowledge and symbolic products, including packaging, image design, branding, and marketing, over concrete material production.[14] As post-Fordism focuses on the creation and deployment of ephemeral images, images come to play a larger and larger role in capital accumulation: "Investment in image-building . . .becomes as important as investment in new plants and machinery."[15]

Neoliberalism is the mode of governmentality that accompanies these economic developments. Simply put, neoliberalism "proposes that human well-being can best be advanced by liberating individual entrepreneur-ial freedoms and skills within an institutional framework characterized by strong property rights, free markets and free trade."[16] The role of the state is to advance and protect these freedoms through deregulation, privatiza-tion, and reduced social welfare benefits. Individual responsibility is stressed, while communitarian or state-run social or cultural initiatives are discour-aged. Perhaps most important, under neoliberalism, market exchange is seen as "an ethic in itself, capable of acting as a guide to all human action, and substituting for all previously held ethical beliefs."[17]

The working self under hypernetworked conditions of flexible accumula-tion and the market-driven ethos of neoliberalism is increasingly precarious and unstable. French sociologists Luc Boltanski and Eve Chiapello describe contemporary work conditions marked by flexibility, casualization, segmen-tation, intensity, and increased competition.[18] Autonomous Marxist crit-ics, such as Antonio Negri, Michael Hardt, Maurizio Lazzarato, and Paolo Virno, argue that the increased production of immaterial commodities, such as design, symbols, knowledge, and communication, necessitates new forms of labor, which involve creativity, innovation, and the manipulation of per-sonal emotion and affect. This "immaterial labour" is defined by Lazzarato as "the labour that produces the informational and cultural content of the commodity . . . the kinds of activities involved in defining and fixing cultural and artistic standards, fashions, tastes, consumer norms."[19] Immaterial labor demands that the worker put his or her own life experience, communica-tive competency, and sense of self into the job; here we see "the very stuff of human subjectivity" put to work for capital.[20] Paul du Gay notes the rise of an "enterprise culture" in the workplace, where workers are expected to be "entrepreneurs of the self,"[21] engaged in the "continuous business of living to make adequate provision for the preservation, reproduction, and reconstruc-tion of [their] own human capital."[22] As the boundaries between working and nonworking life erode, we see the rise of the "social factory," in which human creative capacity is subsumed to the logic of capital and modes of capitalist accumulation extend into all activities of human life.[23]

The modality of selfhood that arises from these conditions has been termed the "flexible personality":[24] perpetually active, willing to innovate and change personal affiliations on a dime. But this perpetual flexibility and instability come with a price. As Virno argues, in the precarious dog-eat-dog world of the flexible entrepreneurial workplace, we no longer trust in any overarching system of values. In order to hedge against our "stable instabil-ity,"[25] we look to exploit every opportunity and grow increasingly cynical as we recognize that work is a game and that its rules do not require respect, but only adaptation. Along with this comes "disenchantment," as we realize that there are "no secure processes of collective interpretation"[26] in which to invest, and no longer any stable identity systems worth believing in.

And so, under the conditions of neoliberalism and flexible accumulation, the processes of commodified and narrativized self-production described by Giddens intensify, accompanied by increasing cynicism and opportunism. As broad-based structural and systemic problems are "dumped at the feet of the individual," we, in turn, "seek biographical solutions to systemic contradictions";[27] under these conditions our "self" becomes, both, the source and the solution for large-scale social problems. But, more than this, "the self" and its modes of presentation—affect, creativity, communicative capacities, and the ability to forge social relationships—becomes directly productive for capital. We see a shift from a working self to the self *as* work in the form of the self-brand.

The Branded Self in Promotional Culture

Under post-Fordist capitalism, the processes of symbolic production, including marketing and branding, have become central activities. These activities, however, are entirely dependent on the processes of meaning making, relationships, and sociality of consumers as they not only buy but also "live through" the brand, contributing directly to processes of social production. As Adam Arvidsson writes, branding practices work to contain or colonize our meaning-making activities as they "unfold naturally" through our lived experiences.[28] So, branding practices produce sets of images and immaterial symbolic values in and through which individuals negotiate the world *at the same time* as they work to contain and direct the expressive, meaning-making capacities of social actors in definite self-advantaging ways, shaping markets and controlling competition. Within current branding practices, consumers' behavior, relationships, bodies, and *selves* become "both the object and the medium of brand activity."[29] As Foucault writes:

> The body is . . . directly involved in a political field; power relations have an immediate hold upon it; they invest it, mark it, train it, torture it, force it to carry out tasks, to perform ceremonies, *to emit signs*. This investment of the body is bound up, in accordance with complex reciprocal relations, with its economic use. It is largely as a force of production that the body is invested with relations of power and domination.[30]

Andrew Wernick outlines a specific example of the body forced to be economically useful and to emit signs of its utility in his book *Promotional Culture*. Writing in 1991 and anticipating the economic and cultural developments associated with the rise of flexible accumulation and its focus on image, marketing, and branding, Wernick argues that the commodity form cannot be separated from its promotional form and that consumption activity is bound to the production of promotional meanings and brands. For Wernick, promotion is a mode of communication, a "species of rhetoric," more notable for what it does than what it says. Promotional discourse is thoroughly instrumental; its function is to bring about some form of "self-advantaging exchange."[31] The intensification and generalization of the processes of promotion and marketing produce a "promotional culture" and era of "spin," where what matters most is not "meaning" per se, or "truth" or "reason," but "winning"—attention, emotional allegiance, and market share.

Promotionalism is the dominant symbolic language and mode of expression of advanced corporate commodity capitalism, and branding practices and consumer campaigns are the places where the dominant mode of production, transnational corporate capitalism, literally and figuratively *becomes* culture.[32] As promotionalism names the ubiquity of market values and discourses in all areas of life, good, services, corporations, and, most centrally, people are all implicated in its logic. Wernick describes the fate of the "self" in a promotional culture; "the subject that promotes itself, constructs itself for others in line with the competitive imaging needs of the market. Just like any other artificially imaged commodity, then, the resultant construct is a persona produced for public consumption."[33]

This "persona produced for public consumption" might also be understood as a "branded self." Elsewhere I have defined the "branded self" as an entity that works and, at the same time, points to itself working, striving to embody the values of its working environment. The self as commodity for sale on the labor market must also generate its own rhetorically persuasive packaging, its own promotional skin, within the confines of the dominant corporate imaginary. Self-branding is a form of affective, immaterial labor that is purposefully undertaken by individuals in order to garner attention and, potentially, profit.[34]

Practices of self-branding first emerge in management literature in the late 1990s. Against the backdrop of neoliberalism, flexible accumulation, and the rise of a culture of promotionalism with the brand as life-defining resource, self-branding is positioned as a way to establish some form of security in the extremely precarious work world of 21st-century capitalism.[35] In this literature, success is dependent not upon specific skills or motivation but on the glossy packaging of the "self" and the unrelenting pursuit of attention. Those in quest of a personal brand are encouraged to expose their best attributes, or "braggables," in every venue available to them by launching a "personal visibility campaign."[36] Carefully crafted appearance and maximum image exposure, such as writing in newsletters, giving talks, or appearing on TV, are crucial.

The idea that self-construction and self-promotion are forms of profit-producing work is now very common. We can see the labor of self-branding every day on reality television programs and experience it ourselves in many workplaces, such as retail stores and call centers, where workers are asked to both physically and emotionally "represent" their employer's brand image. And, we most likely engage in a form of it ourselves as we craft our profiles on social network sites, such as Facebook. There can be no doubt that self-branding is a function of an image economy, where attention is monetized and notoriety, or fame, is capital. As Jonathan Beller writes, "Not only do the denizens of capital labor to maintain ourselves as image, we labor in the image. The image . . . is the mise-en-scene of the new work."[37]

But who determines the parameters of this visibility? Where do the templates for constructing an effective self-brand come from, and whose interests do they serve and reflect? Writing about laboring bodies in 14th-century England, labor historian Kellie Robertson recalls Foucault's claims about the body as overwritten by relations of power; while Robertson speaks to a quite different inflection of the brand—that of hot iron burned into human flesh—her characterization of the brand's uses bears an eerie resemblance to the branded bodies and selves of the 21st century. Writing about branding as a way of both disciplining renegade workers and rendering visible the power of their masters, Robertson states:

> The symbolic nature of the brand asserted not only that a laborer was the equivalent of his or her badly performed work, but also that it was permissible for the state to legislate a person's identity publicly in terms of his or her work through this penal semiotics. The body's surface was to become the page upon which a coercive, textualized identity was enacted.[38]

While it might seem ludicrous to suggest that contemporary forms of self-branding are the product of coercion, there can be no doubt that highly instrumentalized, self-interested persuasion is at the very heart of our promotional culture, and that the templates for achieving a notable image or persona are derived, for the most part, from the epicenter of that culture—the mainstream commercial media industries and their celebrity brands. Can the branded, neoliberal styles of selfhood manufactured by the mainstream culture industries and propagated in the form of the celebrity also serve as effective templates for social activism?

The Celebrity-Brand Activist and the Cause Célèbre

We can now begin to consider the implications and inflections of the branded self for, and in, contemporary activism, specifically green activism. I would like to argue that the logic of self-branding is both foundational to and perpetually reinforced by the types of activism enacted on the three websites chosen for examination here: Ecorazzi.com, Ecostiletto.com, and Disney's Friendsforchange.com. This logic pervades the sites' aesthetic and political parameters and their core assumptions about their interlocutors', or users', "self"-defined political agency. On all these sites we see a veritable cyclone of promotional convergence between products, services, and celebrity brands, which serve as models for environmental activism. The sites use a highly individualized mode of address, which assumes the desire of individuals to self-brand as "activist" through the processes of active consumption and celebrity emulation. But, while all these sites seem to work the same thematic and aesthetic terrain, they are not equal in terms of their industry origins and modes of production.

The role of the celebrity is central to much commodity activism, just as it is central to the post-Fordist industrial model of immaterial labor, which is defined by Maurizio Lazzarato as "the labor that produces the informational and cultural content of the commodity . . . the kinds of activities involved in defining and fixing cultural and artistic standards, fashions, tastes, consumer norms."[39] Paolo Virno argues that individual virtuosity—a capacity for improvised performance, linguistic, and communicative innovation, which inevitably requires the presence of others—is a core component of immaterial labor. Since the culture industries are where "the virtuoso begins to punch a time card,"[40] the practices of the culture industries have become "generalized and elevated to the rank of *canon*,"[41] providing models of virtuosic profitability in the form of the celebrity brand. Insofar as "productive labour, in its totality, appropriates the special characteristics of the performing artist,"[42] Lazzarato and Virno both argue that "subjectivity ceases to be only an instrument of social control . . . and becomes directly productive" for capital.[43]

The Hollywood celebrity is *the* paradigmatic model for self-branding and, perhaps more profoundly, for meaningful contemporary selfhood defined as it is by ever-increasing levels of public visibility, flexibility, cross-promotional capacity, and profit potential. Celebrity as image-currency is the apotheosis of social capital and provides a quick and effective way to garner attention for other issues. But, more often than not, the issue, or cause, and the celebrity use each other in a mutually reinforcing synergy of promotion, leaving open the question of whether the cause or the celebrity benefits most from the bargain.

The website "Ecorazzi: The Latest in Green Gossip" uses the medium of the celebrity to foreground its "green" message but also "exists to help celebrities further their good messages—and to offer the general public a way to follow their favorite celebs and perhaps learn something at the same time."[44] In fact, the site explicitly addresses green issues only insofar as they are enacted by, or relate to, celebrities, admonishing readers not to "overlook . . . how some people are using their fame as a vehicle to highlight and educate on issues important to them."[45] In a tacit acknowledgment of its role as celebrity flack, the site admits that, "in the spirit of fair play," it will point out who's "slacking and who's deserving of recognition."[46] Ecorazzi claims to have successfully fulfilled people's "two passions—the environment and celebrity gossip," without "being too serious."[47]

The site itself looks like many other celebrity gossip sites, such as perezhilton or ohnotheydidnt, with featured items in distinct text boxes and advertising for other websites and products down the right side of the page. For the most part, the site simply aggregates stories from other media outlets, such as actress Alicia Silverstone's interview about being a vegan in *Health* magazine or MTV's interview with the cast of *Twilight* about their desire to "give back." The site also includes a plethora of items that appear to be copied directly from press releases sent by corporate social responsibility (CSR) offices, such as clothing retailer Gap's news that it now serves cage-free eggs in its corporate cafeteria. It also replicates press releases from media producers and celebrity managers, such as the news that actress Hillary Duff is visiting Colombia delivering "blessings in a backpack," or that the film *Wolverine* is working on increased production sustainability. Occasionally the site features items critical of celebrities or their production companies; a recent piece taken from the BBC overtly criticizes U2's carbon footprint.[48]

Founded by a web content developer and green blogger, David d'Estries, and former corporate marketer and green activist Rebecca Carter, Ecorazzi has been in operation since 2006. Field reporters include a former red-carpet correspondent and an "eco-chic" event planner from Los Angeles. Ecorazzi claims to attract college-educated urban women between the ages of twenty-five and forty-five with household incomes above $50,000. These targeted "influencers" are Internet-savvy and are willing to pay more for eco-friendly items.[49] Testimonials about the site repeatedly note that, because of its eco-friendly focus, the site allows readers to indulge "guilt-free" in celebrity gossip.

While Ecorazzi focuses on reporting how it feels to *be* a green celebrity, prioritizing the value of celebrity self-branding and product promotion above any more substantive engagement with environmental issues,[50] a similar website, Ecostilleto.com, emphasizes how to *buy* green like celebrities. Claiming to provide the secrets to "smart and sexy green living," the site promises to explain what constitutes "eco-friendly choices" in "real girl terms" to its "over-20, primarily affluent female market."[51] Citing television celebrity Kelly Rutherford, the site insists: "EcoStilleto is for the woman who wants to do the right thing and still look great doing it."[52]

Ecostilleto mimics other women's magazines by providing special interest sections such as "Beauty and Health," "Fashion," "Design," and, of course, "Ecocelebrity." The tone is not overly proselytizing. Indeed, similar to Ecorazzi's promise of "guilt-free" celebrity gossip, Ecostilleto maintains the centrality of consumer pleasure above any kind of self-sacrifice; it provides green shopping alternatives to its readers, "because everyone wants to make a difference, but no one wants to give up the little things that we love." The site confesses that it is "not about guilt" but "about information" and makes a distinction between "sustainability" and being a "sustainabully."[53]

Like Ecorazzi, Ecostilleto is full of celebrity "news" (read: promotion). *Grey's Anatomy* star Jessica Capshaw produces a "celebrity baby blog" where she confesses she has gotten greener with the birth of her son. The site covers actress Mariel Hemingway's "healthy-living" book signing and the launch of LIV GRN—a "unique lifestyle brand dedicated to perpetuating the health of our planet"—owned by Larry Frazin, former manager of the indie rock band No Doubt. The site often features descriptions of celebrity parties; Ecostilleto itself seems to throw many parties in and around the Los Angeles area. This party coverage inevitably includes the promotion of clothing designers, retailers, caterers, and, of course, other celebrity brands. In addition, the site aggregates eco-friendly home, fashion, and lifestyle information for readers, much of which tends to feature celebrity endorsements.[54]

Both Ecorazzi and Ecostilleto speak to and actively produce a "self" who is a highly individualized, neoliberal, image-savvy consumer and potential self-brander, deeply connected to the paradigmatic symbol of the neoliberal, post-Fordist order: the celebrity. While both sites tout the importance of each individual's contribution to social change, beyond Hollywood parties and corporate-sponsored media events, there is no discussion of how individuals might work collectively around their common environmental concerns. Both sites simply assume that their online communities of readers and subscribers *are* the collectivities and communities that will make environmental change happen. This assumption—that the mere fact of the Internet's interactivity and social networking capacities will generate political and economic change—is very common nowadays. New media forms are seen to facilitate increased social production in the form of human relationships and connections, the free exchange of ideas, and the aggregation of collective intelligence, which occur outside the cash nexus and will eventually produce a new form of value distinct from the capitalist accumulation of profit.[55] And yet, on the websites examined here, there appears to be no environmental cause that cannot be addressed *through* consumption. While the phrases "simplify" and "responsible consumption" appear occasionally, these sites offer no deeper analysis of broad-based, global structural environmental issues or any assessment of the limitations of consumerism itself.[56] On the contrary, they go out of their way to reaffirm and solidify a way of life and a version of selfhood that support the hyperconsuming status quo by actively excusing individuals from taking a more self-sacrificing, collectively oriented approach to the issues. As well intentioned as they might be, on these sites the neoliberal logic of self-branding and celebrity culture trumps all, and environmentalism becomes a chic, branded cause célèbre.[57]

Ecorazzi and Ecostilleto were both started by young green-conscious entrepreneurs, interested in marrying environmental responsibility with market viability. Initially self-financed, both sites have since grown their advertising base and taken on other investors due to their online success.[58] One way of understanding the productive cultural work of these sites, then, is as a form of "outsourced" corporate branding service, which focuses specifically on social responsibility for various products and celebrities. Certainly, major corporations have intensified their focus on social issues in recent years, largely as a result of the antibrand, antiglobalization protests of the 1990s and the growing recognition on the part of corporations that their brand identity has to mesh with consumers' changing value systems.[59] Corporate branding increasingly foregrounds corporations' own work, through CSR offices, to integrate broader social, economic, and environmental concerns into their own internal practices, insisting that the corporate brand is "supported by an ethical corporation" behind the scenes.[60] Ecorazzi and ecostilleto claim to provide a glimpse into the ethical behavior "behind" various celebrity brands and consumer products and to hold others accountable for their dishonesty or lack of environmental ethics. But, in this neoliberal era of perpetual promotion and self-branding, where visibility is currency and the boundary between work and life has collapsed, how can we even begin to distinguish between public and private, authentic or inauthentic, self-interested or ethical, other-directed behavior?

One of the most cynical and opportunistic examples of environmentalism as cause célèbre emanates directly from the corporate responsibility offices of one of the world's largest media industries, Disney, in the form of its youth initiative Friends for Change: Project Green. On the site, Disney child stars, such as the Jonas Brothers, Miley Cyrus, and Demi Lovado solicit kids to register and to take a pledge to "make a difference." Pledges include turning the lights off when leaving a room or turning the water off when brushing your teeth. In exchange for registering and for alerting other kids to the site, users get a chance to "vote" for one of five green projects that Disney will support with $1 million of its money. The site also includes a new song and video, made by the Disney child stars, entitled "Send It On," which exhorts us "to send a bright idea to a friend and encourage them to make a change"; this is accompanied by a "Behind-the-scenes" video of the music video production. Listed as an initiative of Disney's CSR office, the site includes pop-ups of very general environmental information and links to Disney movies, merchandise, parks, music, and television products.[61]

Asking kids to vote on allocating Disney's million dollars summons them to align their interests with those of a transnational corporate behemoth. It also naturalizes a view that corporate philanthropy is the real power behind social change, even as it promotes individual responsibility as paramount. Disney's "initiative" is not about providing promotional services in order to stimulate green consumption, arguably a benign activity, nor does it support young entrepreneurs attempting to find a way to marry profit to environmental responsibility. Rather, it is an opportunistic ploy to aggregate more email addresses for the Disney marketing department and increase promotion for Disney in general through the distribution of the song and behind-the-scenes video and its celebrity brands—all this under the aegis of corporate social responsibility.[62]

The "making of" music video is most telling in terms of the form of commodity activism at work here and the version of the "self" produced and summoned by it. In it, we see the stable of current Disney child stars horsing around with each other and expressing earnest desires to promote "the big movement that [they're] trying to make happen." Singer Selena Gomez innocently names the truth behind what she no doubt truly believes is occurring: "It's not just about us wearing cute clothes and performing on stage, it's about getting this message out"; what, exactly, "this message" is and why it is important to "get it out" remain completely unaddressed. As the coup de grâce, at the end of the video, singer Miley Cyrus points her finger toward to the camera and states emphatically "no-one else is needed but YOU!"[63]

Brand Us Activists

Can the "branded," neoliberal "self" be an effective agent of social change? To what degree can the environmental good intentions expressed on sites like Ecorazzi and Ecostilleto and, to a more limited extent, Disney's Friends for Change be said to be making a significant cultural difference?

Some critics contend that the broader technological environment of hypersocial connection within which these questions are posed will eventually generate such intense social scrutiny that everyone, including corporations, will be forced to behave ethically.[64] While it is (thankfully) true that the productive impulses of people set in motion by new media technologies can never fully be contained by corporate interests, I am less optimistic about the potential for liberation from capitalism presumably congealed in these new technological forms. Rather, I would argue that we should focus our attention on the content circulated via these technologies and on the versions of selfhood this content holds open for us to adopt or occupy. On the sites examined here the celebrity, branded self is championed and tied directly to the practices of extravagant consumerism, and both are inextricably bound to the logic of late post-Fordist capital. This has profound implications for environmental activism; if the "self" is seen to be a biography constructed out of market purchases, and the branded self is perceived as a form of value-generating property, how can we even begin to "make over" the planet in ways that require collective political organizing, the reduction of consumption, and individual self-sacrifice? Activist efforts, green and otherwise, face an uphill battle; they must work to reconceptualize the "YOU" interpellated by *Time* magazine, Disney, and countless other corporate interests. Contemporary progressive activists must work to reimagine an "US" populated by "yous" who are yearning for, and committed to, the formation of durable, caring, noninstrumental social connections beyond the self-interested, divisive, and acquisitive relations of the promotional post-Fordist market.

NOTES

1. Lev Grossman, "Time's Person of the Year: You," *Time*, December 13, 2006.

2. Anthony Giddens, *Modernity and Self-Identity: Self and Society in the Late Modern Age* (Stanford, CA: Stanford University Press, 1991), 9.

3. Philip Cushman, "Why the Self Is Empty: Toward a Historically Situated Psychology," *American Psychologist* 5, no. 45 (1990): 599.

4. Warren Sussman, *Culture as History: The Transformation of American Society in the 20th Century* (New York: Pantheon, 1984), 285.

5. Michel Foucault, *Language, Counter-Memory, Practice*, ed. Donald Bouchard. (Ithaca: Cornell University Press, 1990), 153.

6. Giddens, 1991.

7. Cushman, 1990, 600.

8. Zygmunt Baumann, "Consuming Life," *Journal of Consumer Culture* 1, no. 1 (2001): 13.

9. Giddens, 1991, 53.

10. Giddens, 1991, 196.

11. Giddens, 1991, 198.

12. Baumann, 2001, 22.

13. David Harvey, *The Condition of Post-Modernity* (Oxford: Blackwell, 1990).

14. Robert Goldman and Stephen Papson, "Capital's Brandscapes," *Journal of Consumer Culture* 6, no. 3 (2006): 327–53; Harvey, 1990.

15. Harvey, 1990, 280.

16. Harvey, 1990, 2.

17. Harvey, 1990, 3.

18. Luc Boltanski and Eve Chiapello, *The New Spirit of Capitalism* (London: Verso, 2005).

19. Maurizio Lazzarato, "Immaterial Labor," in *Radical Thought in Italy: A Potential Politics*, ed. Paolo Virno and Michael Hardt (Minneapolis: University of Minnesota Press, 1996), 133.

20. Brett Neilsen and Ned Rossiter, "From Precarity to Precariousness and Back Again: Labour, Life and Unstable Networks," *FibreCulture Journal*, no. 5 (2005), http://journal.fibreculture.org/issue5/neilson_rossiter.html (accessed August 8, 2009).

21. Paul du Gay, *Consumption and Identity at Work* (London: Sage, 1996), 70.

22. Colin Gordon, "Governmental Rationality: An Introduction," in *The Foucault Effect: Studies in Governmentality*, ed. Graham Burchell, Colin Gordon, and Peter Miller (Chicago: University of Chicago Press, 1991), 44.

23. Michael Hardt and Antonio Negri, *Empire* (Cambridge: Harvard University Press, 2000); Lazzarato, 1996.

24. Brian Holmes, "The Flexible Personality: For a New Cultural Critique," *Transversal* (2002), http://transform.eipcp.net/transversal/1106/holmes/en (accessed August 8, 2009).

25. Paolo Virno, "The Ambivalence of Disenchantment," in *Radical Thought in Italy: A Potential Politics*, ed. Paolo Virno and Michael Hardt (Minneapolis: University of Minnesota Press, 1996), 17.

26. Holmes, 2002, 10.

27. Baumann, 2001, 15–16.

28. Adam Arvidsson, "Brands: A Critical Perspective," *Journal of Consumer Culture* 5, no. 2 (2005): 249.

29. Elizabeth Moor, "Branded Spaces: The Scope of the New Marketing," *Journal of Consumer Culture* 3, no. 1 (2003): 42.

30. Michel Foucault, *Discipline and Punish: The Birth of the Prison*, trans. Alan Sheridan (New York: Vintage, 1977), 25, emphasis added.

31. Andrew Wernick, *Promotional Culture: Advertising, Ideology and Symbolic Expression* (London: Sage, 1991), 181.

32. For more on these processes, see Sarah Banet-Weiser's essay in this volume.

33. Wernick, 1991, 192.

34. Alison Hearn, "Meat, Mask, Burden: Probing the Contours of the Branded 'Self,'" *Journal of Consumer Culture* 8, no. 2 (2008): 197–217.

35. Hearn, 2008, 200.

36. Tom Peters, "The Brand Called You," *Fast Company* 10 (1997): 83.

37. Jonathan Beller, *The Cinematic Mode of Production: Attention Economy and Society of the Spectacle* (Hanover, NH: Dartmouth College Press, 2006), 1.

38. Kellie Robertson, *The Laborer's Two Bodies: Labor and the "Work" of the Text in Medieval Britain, 1350–1500* (New York: Palgrave Macmillan, 2006), 17.

39. Lazzarato, 1996, 133.

40. Paolo Virno, *A Grammar of the Multitude* (New York: Semiotexte, 2004), 56.

41. Virno, 2004, 58.

42. Virno, 2004, 54–55.

43. Lazzarato, 1996, 142.

44. About Ecorazzi.com, http://www.ecorazzi.com/about-2/ (accessed August 19, 2009).

45. About Ecorazzi.com.

46. About Ecorazzi.com.

47. Ecorazzi Media Kit, http://www.ecorazzi.com/advertise-with-ecorazzi/ (accessed August 19, 2009).

48. All examples were found on Ecorazzi's home page, http://www.ecorazzi.com/, on August 19, 2009.

49. Ecorazzi Media Kit.

50. By "substantive engagement" I mean, both, collective, grassroots forms of broad-based, or local, political action around specific environmental issues and in-depth and detailed coverage of, and information about, these same issues.

51. Ecostilleto Media Kit, available online at http://www.ecostiletto.com/index.php?/Beauty/about/ (accessed August 19, 2009).

52. Ecostilleto home page, http://www.ecostiletto.com (accessed August 19, 2009).

53. About Ecostilleto, http://www.ecostiletto.com/index.php?/Beauty/about/ (accessed August 19, 2009).

54. All examples were taken from Ecostilleto's home page, "Ecocelebrity" and "Press and Parties" sections (accessed August 19, 2009).

55. Adam Arvidsson and Nicolai Peitersen, *The Ethical Economy*, http://www.ethicaleconomy.com/info/book (accessed August 19, 2009); Daniel Solove, *The Future of Reputation: Gossip, Rumor and Privacy on the Internet* (New Haven: Yale University Press, 2007); Tara Hunt, *The Whuffie Factor: Using the Power of Social Networks to Build Your Business* (New York: Crown, 2009).

56. Some of these structural global issues include global warming, renewable forms of energy, water and wildlife conservation and protection, and food security. Environ-

mental groups that stress collective, grassroots, nonconsumerist-based forms of activism and who provide in-depth information on their issues include global efforts with local chapters around the globe, such as the slow food movement (slowfood.com) and Friends of the Earth (foei.org), and local initiatives, such as wildlife and wilderness preservation effort earthroots.org and alternative power facilitators ourpower.ca, both located in my hometown of Toronto.

57. For more on the emergence and propagation of celebrity activism, see essays in part 2 of this volume.

58. Rachel Lincoln Sarnoff, email correspondence with author, August 15 and 17, 2009.

59. Guido Palazzo and Kunal Basu, "The Ethical Backlash of Corporate Branding," *Journal of Business Ethics* 73, no. 4 (2007): 333–46.

60. Palazzo and Basu, 2007, 340.

61. Disney Friends for Change: Project Green homepage, http://disney.go.com/disney-groups/friendsforchange/#/disneygroups/friendsforchange/ (accessed August 19, 2009).

62. Laurie Ouellette's essay in this volume also explores the ways in which Disney is working to attach its brand to forms of social activism.

63. "Send It on Official Behind the Scenes Video," http://www.youtube.com/watch?v=_LKiCktltVw (accessed August 19, 2009).

64. Indeed, there are signs, exacerbated by the global economic collapse, that even multinational corporations sense that the definitions of value are changing and that capitalism may be on its way out. See Arvidsson and Peiterson, 2009; Anthony Faiola, "The End of American Capitalism?" *Washington Post*, October 10, 2008; Phillip Blond, "Outside View: The End of Capitalism as We Know It?" *The Independent,* March 23, 2008.

2

"Free Self-Esteem Tools?"

Brand Culture, Gender, and the
Dove Real Beauty Campaign

SARAH BANET-WEISER

> For any way of thought to become dominant, a conceptual apparatus has to be advanced that appeals to our intuitions and instincts, to our values and desires, as well as to the possibilities inherent in the social world we inhabit.
>
> David Harvey, *A Brief History of Neoliberalism*

In October 2006, promotion company Ogilvy and Mather created "Evolution," a viral video for Dove Soap, the first in a series of videos stressing the importance of girls' healthy self-esteem and encouraging critique of beauty industries. "Evolution" depicts an "ordinary" woman going through elaborate technological processes to become a "beautiful" model: through time-lapse photography, the woman is seen having makeup applied and hair curled and dried. The video then cuts to a computer screen, where the woman's face undergoes airbrushing to make her cheeks and brow smooth, as well as photo-shopping and computer manipulation to elongate her neck, widen her eyes, narrow her nose. The video does not make a subtle critique; rather, it intends to point out the artificiality and unreality of the women produced by and within the beauty industry. Indeed, the concluding tagline reads, "No wonder our perception of beauty is distorted. Take part in the Dove Real Beauty Workshops for Girls."

According to its website, the Dove Campaign for Real Beauty is "a global effort that is intended to serve as a starting point for societal change and act as a catalyst for widening the definition and discussion of beauty."[1] Harnessing the politicized rhetoric of commodity feminism, the "Evolution" video is clearly a product of a postfeminist environment, making a plea to consumers to act politically but through consumer behavior—in this case, by establishing brand loyalty to Dove products. Dove posted the video on YouTube, and it quickly became a viral hit, with millions of viewers sharing it through email and other media-sharing websites.[2] Well received outside of advertising, the video also won the Viral and Film categories Grand Prix awards at Cannes Lions 2007.

With its "self-esteem" workshops and bold claim that the campaign can be a "starting point for societal change," the Dove Real Beauty campaign is a contemporary example of commodity activism, one of the new ways that advertisers and marketers have used brands as a platform for social activism. As we discuss throughout this volume, commodity activism is a practice that merges consumption behavior—buying and consuming products—with political or social goals, such as challenging the highly unattainable beauty norms produced by media and other industries. More specifically, however, contemporary forms of commodity activism are often animated by and experienced through brand platforms. Individual consumers act politically by purchasing particular brands over others in a competitive marketplace; specific brands are attached to political aims and goals, such as Starbucks coffee and fair trade, or a Product RED Gap T-shirt and fighting AIDS in Africa. Brands and, more generally, brand culture are the context in which contemporary commodity activism positions political action within a competitive, capitalist brand landscape, so that such activism is reframed as possible only when supporting particular brands. Thus, the vocabulary of brand culture is mapped on to political activism, so that the same forces that propel and legitimate competition among and between brands do the same kind of cultural work for activism. The brand is the legitimating factor, no matter what the specific political ideology or practice an individual might support.

Brand Culture and Commodity Activism

This chapter takes a closer look at this connection between brand culture and commodity activism by focusing on a specific case, the Dove Real Beauty campaign. In particular, this chapter looks at some of the elements of contemporary brand culture—consumer-generated content, digital technologies, immaterial labor, and, more generally, political subjectivities—as a way to demonstrate how the connections between brand culture and commodity activism are made normative in contemporary US culture. How do specific political goals—raising the self-esteem of young girls, for example—become understandable within the language of brands and the market? Related to this, how do brands become the most logical mechanism through which one can be active politically? How does brand culture utilize digital technologies

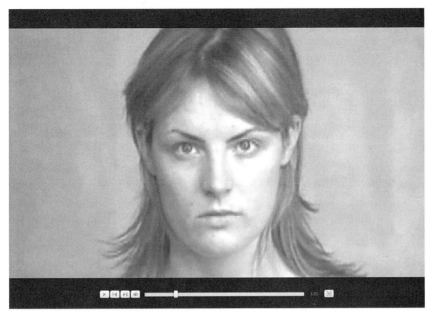

2.1. The "Before" picture in Dove's "Evolution" video.

2.2. "Transforming" through photo-shopping, Dove "Evolution" video.

and consumer labor, especially through the practice of consumer-generated content, as a way to help construct an activist citizen-consumer?

As we state in the introduction to this volume, certainly commodity activism did not appear as a direct result of neoliberal capitalism. Consumer boycotts, as in US civil rights movements for equal rights for African American consumers, Ralph Nader's consumer advocacy of the 1960s and 1970s, and the emergence of "ethical consumption" in the 1980s could accurately be called commodity activism.[3] However, I am interested in the relationship between neoliberal capitalism and brand culture—a relationship that seems to provide a particularly rich context for contemporary modes of commodity activism. The context of neoliberalism—roughly from the 1990s until the contemporary moment—provides a characteristic cultural economy, technological apparatuses, and emergent brand culture for a commodity activism shaped differently than in previous eras. Neoliberalism privileges a kind of "brand strategy" in its production of goods, services, and resources that manages, contains, and actually designs identities, difference, and diversity as particular kinds of brands.

The Dove campaign is but one part of the conceptual apparatus of neoliberal capitalism, as David Harvey suggests in the epigraph to this essay. Importantly, it is a compelling example of commodity activism, one that illustrates the contradictions, contingencies, and paradoxes shaping consumer capital, as well as the contemporary logics connecting merchandising, political ideologies, and consumer citizenship. The Dove campaign helps illuminate what Josée Johnston and Judith Taylor note as a transition particular to contemporary commodity activism: "While formal opportunities for citizenship seemed to retract under neoliberalism, opportunities for a lifestyle politics of consumption rose correspondingly."[4] Dove offers a productive lens into this rise, one that asks consumers to act and empower themselves as individuals. Such personal empowerment is ostensibly realized through occupying a particular subject-position, that of the "consumer-citizen" who can satisfy "competing ideologies of consumerism (an idea rooted in individual self-interest) and citizenship (an ideal rooted in collective responsibility to a social and ecological commons)."[5]

In order to reconceptualize economic strategies, such as branding, as cultural practices—as "culture" itself and as a context for commodity activism—we need to think in terms of how one "values" culture. How do specific elements of culture adopt different understandings of capital? As Hearn points out in this volume, the appending of "brand" to "culture" indicates tracing the contemporary revaluing of culture, mapping out the dimensions of the moment when brand culture *becomes* culture. Culture is a dynamic process within which a constellation of forces cohere: aesthetic values, technological practices, affective connections. Raymond Williams, in his classic essay "Culture Is Ordinary," considered culture a conjunction of understandings, seen "to mean a whole way of life—the common meanings; [and] to mean the arts and learning—the special processes of discovery and creative effort."[6] Culture is "ordinary," Williams insisted, a process and production of everyday life, of individual and collective experience. It is also, as Vicki Mayer reminds us, "a sense of place, its physicality and material environment [and] each place has a history, shaped by struggles over resources and authority."[7] Culture is something, some place, that is made and remade, and therefore depends on individuals in relation to a system of production. Thus, when examining brands and branding practices as a kind of culture, it makes sense to look not only at their role as a function of capitalist exchange but also as a vehicle through and within which individuals create particular kinds of political and cultural identities.

It is this role of brand culture, as a mechanism through which individuals construct political and cultural identities, that I am most concerned with here. As an industry, branding, like advertising, is key for the persistence of the global capitalist economy: the competitive landscape of brands; the subindustries sustained by brands such as corporate social responsibility, the practice of self-branding, city planning, and so on; and increasing transnational flows of global brands, among other things, are crucial for global capitalism to continue to function smoothly.[8] Brands also have, of course, a ubiquitous material presence: signs, advertisements, logos, musical jingles, symbols, viral and digital media. This design element of brands is essential for the normalization of branding in the everyday life of individuals.[9] The oft-cited statistics on how many advertisements people in the US see per day (last count over 3,000) remain important, but in the early 21st century it is perhaps more pertinent to ask when people do *not* visually confront a brand name, logo, or symbol, not when they *do*. It is no longer possible to analyze brands and branding as separate from culture; rather, they are an integral element of contemporary neoliberal culture in the US. As such, brand culture forms what Celia Lury notes as "a set of relations between products and services."[10] This set of relations functions as what Lury calls the "logos" of the contemporary economy, which is taken to mean not only the visual and textual significations of brands (such as signs or slogans) but also "the kind of thought or rationality that organizes the economy."[11] The individual-as-commodity has a presence within brand culture, which emerges from the expansion of neoliberal capitalism and its adoption of cultural characteristics that feel distinctly noncapitalist. My interest in the Dove brand culture lies in this kind of brand "logos," and, through the case of the Dove Real Beauty campaign, in the structuring ideologies and rationalities that organize the contemporary postfeminist cultural economy.

Additionally, part of the contemporary logic of branding involves a reconfigured consumer subject who moves effortlessly from traditional advertising (print or television, for example) to nontraditional media such as the Internet. The meteoric rise in consumer-generated content (Web 2.0), together with its service to corporations as well as in the crafting of "empowered" citizens, must be taken into account when examining contemporary neoliberal brand culture and the role of commodity activism within this context. Contemporary brand culture, supported by interactive, networked media technologies, and a heightened presence of consumer participation, represents a kind of compromise between the previous historical moment of mass consumption and that of niche marketing. It is one in which culture itself is built from affective producer-consumer relationships.[12] The contemporary era, however, needs to be theorized as not simply a more innovative expansion of earlier capitalist logics that structured mass consumption or niche culture. Thinking about brand culture as functioning as a kind of lifestyle politics for consumers—something one is or does or makes, rather than pointing to a particular consumer good one purchases—is a means to conceptualize the ways in which consumer citizenship is situated in the contemporary neoliberal economy. The current cultural economy, in other words, is not necessarily a logical advance, the subsequent point on a continuum of consumer culture. Rather, a focus on the ways in which brands, such as Dove, enable and animate particular forms of commodity activism and forms of citizenship/ political subjectivity offers a way to better understand what sociohistorical and institutional forces enabled and supported the current commodification of social activism.

The contemporary digital economy, with its flexible labor force and blurred consumer/producer identities, is part of this transition, enabling and supporting late 20th-century and early 21st-century individuated marketing and neoliberal brand culture. The individual cultural entrepreneur is celebrated as one who populates a radically "free" market, one that is no longer supported or even regulated by the state. Boundaries between consumerism and politics are ever more destabilized, a process enabled by a retraction of the notion of the public, a shift of resources from social services to individual entrepreneurs, and a general increase in social-change rhetoric as part of promotional culture. Thus, the "commodity activist" makes a particular kind of sense as a subject position within brand culture. Brands and branding do not simply materialize within neoliberal capitalism as individualized acts of self-promotion or specific modes of community-constitution; rather, identities, acts, and communities that are constructed through brands and branding describe larger historical shifts within contemporary culture.

Free Self-Esteem Tools: The Dove Real Beauty Campaign

Dove has an extensive history as part of an industry long known (by feminists) for the insidious ways in which it capitalizes on feminine insecurities about the gendered body, using a market-inspired rhetoric of "self-esteem" and "real beauty" as a primary promotional vehicle, which is characteristic of the contradictions of a postfeminist ethos. Those spaces historically understood (if perhaps not experienced) as noncapitalist or antagonistic to consumer capital (in this case, the empowerment of girls) have been reimagined as new markets within the expansion of capitalism. In part because of these contradictory dynamics, critics have charged Dove with duplicity, claiming that the way it produces many beauty products (including Axe, a young men's soap/cologne line advertised with highly stylized and stereotypical representations of heteronormative hypermasculinity) is at odds with the company's positioning of itself and its consumers as commodity activists. Dove, however, understands this activism as a deliberate use of commodity culture's products, advertising, and promotional media to publicize the problem of girls, self-esteem, and damaging disciplinary practices of femininity—realized and operationalized, of course, through the brand platform of Dove itself.

Indeed, the "empowerment" of girls to develop "healthy self-esteem" has been traditionally understood as the development of political and cultural identity outside of consumer culture (especially since low self-esteem for girls is widely recognized as a specific result of unattainable gender norms represented in media and consumer culture). However, self-esteem for girls has emerged in the past decade as an important element of the *market* for consumer and media products for girls. Indeed, self-esteem itself is a kind of postfeminist product one can acquire through consumption of the proper commodities, thus working as part of new ground for the expansion of neoliberal capitalist practices.

The Dove Real Beauty campaign is particularly illustrative of ongoing debates over the relationship between gender and consumer culture, one that "pivots around the question of whether women have been empowered by access to the goods, sites, spectacles, and services associated with mass consumption."[13] As Victoria de Grazia, Susan Bordo, Lynn Spigel,[14] and many others have pointed out, there are a variety of points of entry into this debate, ranging from historical analyses of consumer culture's empowering expansion of middle-class women's social and institutional boundaries to examinations of consumer-culture representations of women and the female audience.[15] My examination of the Dove Real Beauty campaign approaches this form of commodity activism as one of many contemporary examples of a neoliberal strategy that recontextualizes corporate and managerial practices (such as those of Dove's parent company, Unilever) into political (in this case, feminist) and social contexts. One result of this neoliberal recontextualization is a restructuring and management of identities (such as gender) and social relations (such as consumer/producer) that occurs in the service of capital.

Commodity feminism, as elaborated by Robert Goldman, Deborah Heath, and Sharon L. Smith, is an advertising strategy emerging in the later decades of the 20th century that seeks to appeal to an exhausted, cynical, and media-savvy (primarily female) audience through the appropriation of feminist icons and ideals for commercial purposes.[16] In this appropriation, and as an extension of Marx's commodity fetishism, feminist ideologies and practices are emptied of their political valence and meaning and offered to consumers as commodities. However, contemporary commodity activism, I argue, is more than a kind of corporate appropriation in the vein of commodity feminism. Rather, as this analysis demonstrates, the Dove Real Beauty campaign illuminates the dynamics between and within neoliberal brand culture, audience participation, and social and commodity activism.

Historically, soap and beauty products have been a rich vehicle for the rhetoric of consumption as a kind of civic duty. Even in the 19th century, as Anne McClintock has shown, soap (and other commodities) stood in for values that traversed the cleanliness of the physical body into the "cleanliness" of the social body.[17] In particular, in the colonial building of empire of the 19th century, "soap flourished not only because it created and filled a spectacular gap in the domestic market but also because, as a cheap and portable domestic commodity, it could persuasively mediate the Victorian poetics of racial hygiene and imperial progress."[18] In the mid-20th century, feminine beauty products continued to be associated with national identity and rhetorics of American progress.[19] Because of the changing position of the middle-class woman in postwar American culture (brought on by various social forces, including suburban migration, emergent ideologies of the idealized nuclear family, and marketing to the housewife), feminine beauty products are particularly illuminative of dynamics of the mass-consumption/mass-production era. Historian Kathy Peiss, for example, argues that women's consumption of cosmetics needs to be understood within a broader context of struggles between consumer conformity and female empowerment.[20] Cosmetics marketing in the early to mid-20th century not only was about capitalizing on individual insecurities for profit but also created and perpetuated a changing definition of womanhood. That is, the cosmetics industry helped to create a market exclusively for women, and thus invited women to participate in the market, shifting and challenging previously held notions of public and private spheres. While surely the marketing of cosmetics contributed to the commodification of gendered and racialized identity (where particular "types" of women are branded as products), as Peiss argues, such practices also destabilize traditional gendered hierarchies based on notions of public and private and helped establish a kind of cultural legitimacy for women.[21] Such historicizing of the marketing strategies that sold beauty products to women as ways to establish cultural legitimacy allows for examining contemporary practices, such as the Dove Real Beauty campaign, as part of a larger cultural transition.

Consider, then, the current manifestation of a Dove soap ad. Dove in 2004 (through the work of Ogilvy and Mather) created the "Dove Campaign for Real Beauty" website. Part advertising, part pedagogy, part social activism—*all* made legible by brand culture—the campaign capitalized and built upon the consumer/producer subject position as the privileged identity of a neoliberal cultural economy. As a part of the website and a concurrent billboard campaign, Dove featured images of "real, everyday" women. Taglines asked consumers to make choices such as "Fat/Fabulous?" and "Withered/Wonderful?" Consumers were invited to text in their "vote" for the best choice, with results displayed in real time, encouraging consumer participation in the development of the campaign. Ostensibly empowered by "choice," consumers are asked to vote for the not-so-subtle correct answer—wonderful, fabulous—even in a brand context that has historically not only supported but created an entire industry around "fat" and "withered" as problems women need to address.[22] By participating through casting a vote, female consumers become a kind of citizen in the Dove nation; through their consumer-generated content, they help build the brand.

Indeed, participatory culture in the context of digital media is especially rich for demonstrating the connection between brand culture and commodity activism. Furthering this participatory aim, soon after the campaign began, a subsidiary initiative, the Dove Self-Esteem Fund, was launched to address eating disorders for young women and girls. The pedagogical function of the campaign—educating women and girls on how to have "healthy self-esteem"—has a particular shape in the current cultural economy. Tapping into the discourse of the consumer/producer, the Dove workshops imply that consumers not only are helping to produce ads but also are charged with producing a healthier gender culture.[23]

On the Dove website, for example, one can choose from a number of options as ways to participate in the campaign. Consumers can participate in Dove online workshops and download "free self-esteem tools." (Once a participant has completed three tools, she can "receive [her] very own self-esteem certificate," which thus acquires symbolic use-value for Dove consumer-citizens.) The "self-esteem tools" include "TrueYou!" workbooks that offer "simple self-esteem exercises for moms and girls to do together" and are described as guides to "help your daughter feel more beautiful." There is also "You're the Editor!," which offers tips for girls to create their own magazines, and the "Self-Esteem Bubble," where girls can "surround [themselves] with a self-esteem bubble and allow [one's] confidence to grow." One can sign up for the national workshop tour (through which apparently 3,308,796 "lives have been touched to date"). The company commissioned a report, *Real Girls, Real Pressure: A National Report on the State of Self-Esteem*, inviting consumers to "play a role in supporting and promoting a wider definition of beauty." The emphasis of the rhetoric on the individual consumer—"You're the Editor!" "Play a Role," "TrueYou"—clearly distracts attention from the role that capitalist industry has not only in creating low gendered self-esteem but also in the simultaneous creation of a market to help combat this issue. Indeed, on the very same web page that offers "free self-esteem tools" are advertisements for Dove products, such as Dove Body Wash, which apparently gives its users a "nourishing boost," as well as an appeal to consumers to "try NEW Dove Daily Treatment Conditioners FREE!" Another, for Dove Beauty Bar, has the tagline "Just because the economy is drying up, it doesn't mean your skin should. With Dove Beauty Bar, beautiful skin is still affordable." In a direct way, this Dove ad informs consumers that larger social and economic problems—indeed, crises—need not be of concern as long as one attempts individual beauty. It is difficult, in obvious ways, to reconcile the cultural work performed by Dove beauty products, which are created for women and girls to more closely approximate a feminine ideal, with the Dove Real Beauty workshops, the invitations for consumer coproductions, and the critique of the beauty industry's role in low self-esteem. But this kind of reconciliation is precisely the kind of cultural work that postfeminism does, and moreover, reveals why the Dove campaign has a particular political logic within brand culture.

Media Technologies and Brand Culture: Immaterial Labor and "Participation"

Enabling media technologies and their surrounding rhetoric of empowerment provides support for the productive consumer who builds emotive relationships within brand culture. The blurring of boundaries between consumer/producer so celebrated in Web 2.0 technoscapes is often signaled as the tipping point in contemporary society in terms of formation of individual subjectivity. The celebration of this boundary collapse, especially in the rhetoric of advertising and marketing, hinges upon the notion of the disappearance of the former middleman or gatekeeper between consumers and producers. Consumers are afforded greater latitude and freedom than ever before to produce individually meaningful material. Fixed distinctions between "production and consumption, labor and culture" are questioned and denaturalized, and the resulting space opened up becomes the space of individual empowerment.[24] It is within this context of celebratory rhetoric about this new consumer/producer, coming from profit-seeking advertisers and marketers, that it makes sense for a brand, such as Dove, to entreat its consumers to "download your free self-esteem tools."

The work that Dove is asking its consumers to perform, in both the Real Beauty campaign and the purchasing of Dove products, is part of a larger dynamic that characterizes labor within a neoliberal era. By inviting consumers to be involved in coproduction of the Dove brand, Dove provides the context for the lived experience of brand culture, where consumers participate in a critique of the norms of beauty culture, even while supporting and expanding the brand boundaries of a company firmly entrenched within this culture. The Dove campaign is not simply about the acquisition of beauty knowledge and skills (such as how to put on makeup or how to lose weight) that can be explained relatively easily as corporate appropriation of feminist pedagogical tropes but rather about creating and supporting a *shifted* manifestation of the citizen-consumer, one who is critical of marketing and unrealistic norms and is therefore *invited* to develop this narrative in conjunction with corporate culture.

Dove's workshops and its invitation to this kind of consumer coproduction also signal a labor practice, characteristic of the neoliberal era, that, on

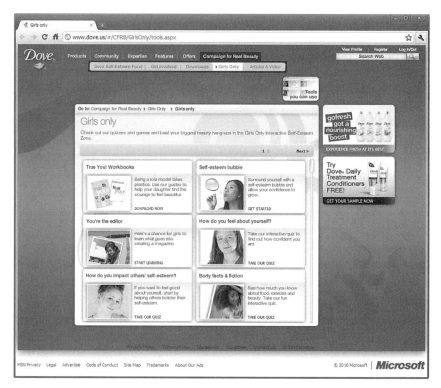

2.3. The Dove Campaign for Real Beauty website, offering tips for self-esteem.

the one hand, implements specific forms of production (e.g., voting, creating videos for the campaign, workshopping) but, on the other, implies a form of labor not generally recognized as such (e.g., participating in media production, DIY practices, consumer-generated content). This "immaterial labor" produces affect, cultural desire, and emotional sensibilities (manifest in "healthy self-esteem," gender identity, shifted practices of femininity and desire).[25] It emerges as part of the expansion of neoliberal cultural economies and is "part of a process of economic experimentation with the creation of monetary value out of knowledge/culture/affect."[26]

Unlike the more familiar corporate appropriation of identity and culture, such as that critiqued by feminist theorists under the rubric of commodity feminism, immaterial labor within neoliberalism needs to be understood as what Tiziana Terranova calls a "channeling" of "collective labor (even as cultural labor) into monetary flows and its structuration within capitalist business practices."[27] The Dove campaign, in other words, is not simply an insidious, manipulative attempt by advertisers to disrupt and co-opt an "authentic" formation of gender identity. Indeed, as others in this volume argue, the Dove campaign is but one example from the contemporary marketing landscape that demonstrates the futility of a binarized understanding of culture: authentic versus commercial.

Within neoliberalism, the logic that motivates the Dove Real Beauty campaign is precisely *not* illogical—rather, it makes a kind of perfect sense. The perceived hypocrisy apparently embodied by Dove's parent company, Unilever, may not be hypocritical at all, given a context in which codes of capitalism are used and stretched in ways previously seen as impossible, in which culture is a commodity and a resource, and in which identities take on meaning at the precise moment they are recognized as market categories. Mark Andrejevic, in his work on "participatory culture" in Web 2.0 technologies,[28] argues that the consumer/user empowerment promised by new technologies' openness and flexibility needs to be understood as a coexistence and intersection between creative activity and exploitation. The labor of Dove consumers *is* a form of labor and, as such, is exploitative. At the same time, it is also "immaterial labor," productive of affective desires and forms of creative knowledge. Thus, neoliberal capitalism does not only make workers out of consumers, but consumption itself becomes the primary kind of labor now performed.

The campaign's repertoire of viral videos (such as "Evolution," discussed at the beginning of this essay) can be considered part of this complex process of consumer participation and immaterial labor. Since "Evolution," Dove has released "Onslaught," for instance, which depicts a torrent of media images of distorted and unrealistic femininity against a backdrop of white childish innocence. The video ends with a close-up of a young white girl's face, with a tagline reading, "Talk to your daughter before the beauty industry does." Firmly placing responsibility, and ostensible control, in the hands of the parent (and it is clear that the parent is actually the mother, as Dove advertising, including these viral videos, is targeted to women), "Onslaught" taps into circulating discourses of neoliberal individualism, where consumers are "empowered" to make choices about teaching their daughters about healthy self-esteem. Another video, "Amy," portrays a young girl who refuses to meet a boy because she has low self-esteem. Its tagline: "Amy can name twelve things wrong with her appearance. He can't name one." As a way to further individualize this ad (after all, the boy—and, by extension, masculine culture—has nothing to do with Amy's low self-esteem), the video also invites viewers to insert their name in place of "Amy," personalizing the representation and blurring the distinction between all girls who suffer from low self-esteem and the personal suffering of the individual consumer-citizen.

The Dove campaign is one example of a contemporary way of "making culture" that is wholly dependent on the brand as the context for its production. Within this context, brand strategies and management are situated not as economic principles or good business but as the affective stuff of culture. Rather than inserting brands into culture, brand managers seek to build culture around brands through emotive relationships. As the chief executive for Digital Strategy Consulting, Danny Meadows-Klue, points out, brand management in the contemporary (neoliberal) digital age is about brokering love relationships, not selling products: "Only an understanding of why media-savvy consumers tune out of classic media can create the right thinking that permits re-engagement. Only by earning the trust of their friends will brands get recommended by those friends, and only by investing time and energy in listening and building that relationship will there be a loving relationship to enjoy."[29]

Adopting the language of a marriage therapist or, perhaps more appropriately for the current era, a "life coach," this marketer argues that brand strategies need to focus on affective, authentic relationships between consumers and producers, and to build culture out of these relationships. Furthermore, these structures of feeling are coproductions with consumers, created by immaterial labor. Within brand culture, consumers produce identity, community, emotional attachments, affective practices, and relationships; brand culture within neoliberalism provides a particular kind of infrastructure for this kind of social and political behavior. As such, theorizing branding as culture allows for contextualizing the neoliberal moment as a particular transition in the development of capitalism.

Conclusion: The Compromise of Cultural Capitalism

Following Terranova, my argument here is not that our current moment represents a logical progression in consumer culture, whereby one cultural economy has plausibly transformed to the next. Rather, I am proposing that the contemporary cultural economy both embodies and materializes a different "logic of value," one that provides a fertile context for the emergence of brand culture and a particular kind of commodity activism. I try to resist overemphasizing either the incorporation of individual subjectivities by neoliberal capitalism or the autonomy of the consumer-citizen within this economy, but rather to see this dynamic as a kind of "compromise" between creative production and capitalist practices.[30]

In this light, it is important that neoliberal culture be understood as a compromise marked by tensions, slippages, and contradictions, rather than a dichotomy or binary. Such an approach disrupts the theoretical paralysis of binary thinking—as in the critique of Dove Real Beauty as hypocritical— and allows for rethinking the consumer-as-empowered-citizen, emphasizing contradictions rather than explaining them away as insignificant outliers. It should not come as a surprise, then, that within the neoliberal cultural economy, social activism is understood and experienced as a material good, as an object that has a particular exchange value within contemporary cultural capitalism. Like other identities, such as race and gender, the current manifestation of the "social activist" is managed, organized, and exchanged not simply as a commodity but as a brand, as part of culture. Like other manifestations of marketing and advertising in recent US history, political ideals, such as social justice, change, and empowerment, are marshaled within the neoliberal economy as realizable through practices of consumption and consumer citizenship.

When current identities are defined by "posts" (postfeminist, postracial, post-Fordist), older, more traditional political paradigms that mobilized social activism no longer have the same cultural or economic capital. The central subject position within neoliberalism is the enterprising individual, attached to no single institution, nation, or state politics, but working on his or her own as a cultural entrepreneur in a radically "free" market. The "activist" in neoliberal culture can be *anyone* (another of neoliberalism's utopic promises), as long as there is an unproblematic shift from "social" to "commodity" activism, and as long as brand culture supports and sustains such activism. Indeed, contemporary marketers deploy new strategies as a way to both recognize and exploit these changing identities in a shifting cultural environment, resulting in an increasingly more sophisticated and complicated exchange between the consumer and the brand.

When Unilever soap subsidiary Dove criticizes the beauty industry for damaging girls' self-esteem through a very visible, social-activist campaign funded through selling beauty products, questions of the relationship between political or individual empowerment and consumer culture seem particularly apt. Moreover, these questions are urgent in the contemporary US political and cultural context, demonstrated through a number of examples in this volume, such as new imaginings of humanitarianism, celebrity advocacy and philanthropy, and environmentalism, among other things.

It thus makes sense to think about the relationship between empowerment and consumer culture as partly a result of the contradictions within neoliberalism and to consider this relation as a particular condition of possibility. Indeed, rather than lingering on the various ways in which neoliberal brand culture is politically and culturally bankrupt, it seems to make more sense to critically interrogate the concepts that have been historically used to determine distinctions between commercial culture and political citizenship, such as "consumer" and "producer."

What is at stake in such historically informed, critical interrogation is not simply revisiting these terms to theorize what place they might occupy in a cultural debate about the making of identity. Rather, a new conceptualization of these terms and the contradictions between them is needed as a way to account for changing practices of cultural production and identity formation within a shifting economy. Moreover, such theorization illuminates the conditions of possibility that such changes might offer and the components of their making. Within brand culture, with its attendant Web 2.0 technologies for consumer-generated content and new DIY production, the "logical" outgrowths of neoliberalism's radically "free" markets are knowledge, affect, desire—the stuff of identity—as well as culture itself.

NOTES

I would like to thank Josh Kun, Travers Scott, Inna Arzumanova, Melissa Brough, Laura Portwood-Stacer, and Roopali Mukherjee for their helpful suggestions and insights on this essay.

1. "Dove Campaign for Real Beauty," http://www.dove.us/#/cfrb/.

2. There were 3 million hits on YouTube, as well as videos on the website, consumers sharing the video, etc.

3. Gary Cross, *An All-Consuming Century: Why Commercialism Won in Modern America* (New York: Columbia University Press, 2000); Lawrence Glickman, *Buying Power: A History of Consumer Activism in America* (Chicago: University of Chicago Press, 2009); Josée Johnston and Judith Taylor, "Feminist Consumerism and Fat Activists: A Comparative Study of Grassroots Activism and the Dove 'Real Beauty' Campaign," *Signs: Journal of Women in Culture and Society* 33, no. 4 (2008): 941–66; Jo Littler, *Radical Consumption: Shopping for Change in Contemporary Culture* (Berkshire, UK: Open University Press, 2009).

4. David Harvey, *A Brief History of Neoliberalism* (Oxford: Oxford University Press, 2005), 246.

5. Johnston and Taylor 2008, 229. This tension, between private desires and public obligations, has been a hallmark of citizenship for decades. It revolves revolves around the conventional notion that citizenship is a political category, represented and constituted not within the world of commerce but rather in direct opposition to those kinds of material interests. Scholars as varied as Jean-Jacques Rousseau, John Stuart Mill, Max Weber, and Jürgen Habermas have explored and supported the notion that while citizenship is ostensibly formed via the democratic process, the hopes, desires, and anxieties contained within citizenship are often realized through consumption.

6. Raymond Williams, *Resources of Hope: Culture, Democracy, Socialism* (London: Verso, 1989); see, particularly, "Culture Is Ordinary," 5–6.

7. Vicki Mayer, "My Media Studies, Fifty Years Later," *Television and New Media* 10, no. 1 (2009): 103. Advocating a neo-Marxist concept of "cultural materialism," Williams argued that "culture must be finally interpreted in relation to its underlying system of production." However, Williams disagreed with Marx in his point that "since culture and production are related, the advocacy of a different system of production is in some way a cultural directive, indicating not only a way of life but new arts and learning." Williams opposed the idea that relations of production could somehow "direct" culture, because culture is something made "by living" (Williams, 1989, 5–6).

8. Liz Moor, *The Rise of Brands* (New York: Oxford International, 2007); Celia Lury, *Brands: The Logos of the Global Economy* (London: Routledge, 2004); Inderpal Grewal, *Transnational America: Feminisms, Diasporas, Neoliberalisms* (Durham, NC: Duke University Press, 2005); Littler, 2009.

9. Moor, 2007, 1.

10. Lury, 2004, 2.

11. Lury, 2004, 7.

12. Mid-20th-century US consumer culture relied upon mass production and mass consumption, assuming an "ideal consumer" as the target for advertising and marketing. This "ideal consumer," while ostensibly inclusive of a broad demographic, was represented (through ads, products, and marketing strategies) as a white and middle-class aspirational subject-position. See Lizabeth Cohen, *A Consumers' Republic: The Politics of Mass Consumption in Postwar America* (New York: Vintage, 2003); Cross, 2000; Richard Wightman Fox and T. J. Jackson Lears, *The Culture of Consumption: Critical Essays in American History, 1880–1980* (New York: Pantheon Books, 1983). In the later 20th century, marketing techniques and strategies became more sophisticated in targeting consumers, a deregulated communications industry freed up advertisers, and the notion of "difference" occupied an increasingly visible space in media and public culture. Consumers became newly segmented into what Joseph Turow calls "primary media communities." See Joseph Turow, *Breaking Up America: Advertisers and the New Media World* (Chicago: University of Chicago Press, 1998). Eschewing the logic of the ideal, mass consumer, and enabled by narrower and more flexible practices of production, late 20th-century capitalism organized around specific niche markets, each with an identifiable boundary: upwardly mobile professionals, gays and lesbians, Latina/os, and so on. Clearly, this era of niche marketing and its subsequent fragmenting and commodifying of identities have not ended.

13. Victoria de Grazia (with Ellen Furlough), ed., *The Sex of Things: Gender and Consumption in Historical Perspective* (Berkeley: University of California Press, 1996), 275.

14. de Grazia, 1996; Susan Bordo, *Unbearable Weight: Feminism, Western Culture, and the Body* (Berkeley: University of California Press, 1993); Susan Bordo, *Twilight Zones: The Hidden Life of Cultural Images* (Berkeley: University of California Press, 1997); Lynn Spigel, *Make Room for TV: Television and the Family Ideal in Postwar America* (Chicago: University of Chicago Press, 1992).

15. de Grazia, 1996, 275.

16. Robert Goldman, Deborah Heath, and Sharon L. Smith, "Commodity Feminism," *Critical Studies in Mass Communication* 8 (1991): 333–51.

17. Anne McClintock, *Imperial Leather: Race, Gender, and Sexuality in the Colonial Contest* (London: Routledge, 1995), 208.

18. McClintock, 1995, 209.

19. Thus, cosmetics were sold to US women as accoutrements of not only femininity but also national identity: "Clothes and cosmetics helped immigrant women define themselves as 'American' and enabled them to compete in the dating game. Similarly, African American cosmetics (especially skin whiteners and hair straighteners) were advertised as 'glorifying our womanhood,' giving dignity of sorts to women stereotyped with racial and rural images." See Cross, 2000, 41.

20. Kathy Peiss, "Making Up, Making Over: Cosmetics, Consumer Culture, and Women's Identity," in *The Sex of Things: Gender and Consumption in Historical Culture*, ed. Victoria de Grazia (with Ellen Furlough) (Berkeley: University of California Press, 1996), 311–36.

21. Peiss, 1996, 331.

22. In the Toronto campaign, 51 percent of consumers voted for "Fat" in the choice between "Fat" or "Fabulous," perhaps giving even more empirical "evidence" to Dove to continue its quest for "healthy self-esteem."

23. Writing about "power femininity" in ads, Michelle Lazar characterizes this "knowledge as power" trope within contemporary marketing as an element of consumer-based empowerment: "Although the educational discourse is premised upon asymmetrical power relations between knowledgeable and authoritative experts and novices in need of guidance, empowerment in educational settings is derived from the acquisition of knowledge and skills that enable one to become self-reliant and experts in one's own right." Michelle M. Lazar, "Entitled to Consume: Postfeminist Femininity and a Culture of Post-Critique," *Discourse and Communication* 3, no. 4 (2009): 509.

24. Tiziana Terranova, "Free Labor: Producing Culture for the Digital Economy," *Social Text* 18, no. 2 (2000): 33–58.

25. Mark Andrejevic, "Watching Television without Pity," *Television and New Media* 9, no. 1 (2008): 24–46; Terranova, 2000.

26. Terranova, 2000, 38.

27. Terranova, 38–39.

28. Andrejevic, 2008.

29. Danny Meadows-Klue, "Falling in Love 2.0: Relationship Marketing for the Facebook Generation," *Journal of Direct, Data and Digital Marketing Practice* 9, no. 3 (2008): 248.

30. Terranova, 2000, 36.

3

Citizen Brand

ABC and the Do Good Turn in US Television

LAURIE OUELLETTE

> The greatest moments in life are not concerned with selfish achievement, but rather with the things we do for other people.
> Walt Disney

In 2008, the ABC network presented an ethical twist on the reality game. Instead of competing for love matches, celebrity status, or cash prizes, contestants on *Oprah's Big Give* helped the needy. Backed by Winfrey and corporate sponsors, they crisscrossed the US raising funds for causes, disseminating free food and toys, and arranging for medical care and social services while the cameras rolled. Judges evaluated the interventions, sending one player home each week until the Biggest Giver was revealed. In a tie-in promotion, ABC donated seed money to local station affiliates, challenging them to "do something big with the money, make it grow, and pay it forward to the community." TV viewers were also encouraged to use the show as a framework for performing citizenship in their own lives. To spur them on, the *Big Give* website provided resources on volunteerism and community service, including fill-in-the-blank Good Deed coupons emblazoned with the ABC logo, upon which viewers could pledge service to local schools, neighborhood parks, shelters, and soup kitchens.

The *Big Give* experiment speaks to the television industry's heightened role in postwelfare civic responsibility. From Fox's *American Idol Gives Back* to MTV's Think to Planet Green, commercial television has emerged as a visible platform for mobilizing resources and activating capacities to solve problems from homelessness to environmental destruction. While often endorsed by elected officials from the president of the US to city mayors, these initiatives enact dispersed, privatized solutions to hardships and needs. The do good turn in US television operates as an informal partnership between a supportive (but minimally involved) public sector, commercial television networks, socially responsible advertisers, private charities and nonprofit organizations, and TV viewers, who are increasingly expected to use the resources coordinated by television (and its tie-in websites) to modify their lifestyles, support causes, build communities, consume ethically, and perform volunteerism.[1]

While networks increasingly compete for ethical status, television is no longer formally regulated as a public service medium. The Telecommunications Act of 1996 entrusted the free market to oversee its contribution to civil society and political democracy. Media corporations lobbied for the legislation because it minimized ownership rules and eliminated the expectation that commercial broadcasting also serve the public interest, historically conceived as the dissemination of presumably unprofitable resources—serious news, local and national public affairs, and educational material—for informed citizenship and active participation in civic life. Yet, while the market has triumphed as a regulatory mechanism, the promise of citizenship training and civic empowerment has not entirely disappeared from US television culture. On the contrary, high-profile interventions like the *Big Give* represent the ongoing reinvention of public service—in a voluntary and commercially exploitable form.

This chapter situates the reinvention of public service within the contemporary convergence of governing and branding strategies. Taking ABC's Better Community public outreach campaign as a case study, I show how commercial television's investment in civic responsibility intersects with larger political forces, including public sector downsizing, welfare reform, and communitarian prescriptions for the renewal of American democracy. I show how parallel developments in corporate social responsibility and brand culture shape commercial initiatives to transform TV viewers into better communities and ethical citizens. As a branded *interface* to suggested civic identities and practices, ABC (which was acquired by the Disney Corporation in 1996) operates as a dominant technology of governing and citizenship—and strategically incorporates civic action into the network's business operations and brand value. While this multilayered process reveals a deepening conflation of marketing, branding, and the public interest, it would be shortsighted to dismiss the Better Community venture as a corporate ruse. ABC does not undermine the "necessary conditions for effective democratic governance"[2] due to its corporate ownership and profit-maximizing objectives, as much as it constitutes and enables what counts as civic responsibility in neoliberal democracies. For better or worse, ABC enacts a model of good government that is in synchronicity with current political rationalities and capitalizes on the results.

Better Communities and Corporate Citizens

In 2002, ABC launched its long-running Better Community public outreach campaign, with a mission of advancing the television network's standing as a corporate citizen through "community outreach efforts that serve the public interest, inform and inspire."[3] Encompassing announcements urging TV viewers to perform community service, as well as an online guide to volunteering and a slate of popular entertainment programs showcasing corporate and personal humanitarianism, the campaign positioned ABC as a socially responsible corporate citizen. More than this, it constituted ABC as a gateway to a Better Community comprising network stars, nonprofit partners, commercial sponsors, and socially conscious TV viewers who—much more than other television consumers—contribute resources (time and money) to the well-being of the communities in which they live. Why would ABC pursue what it claimed to be the "comprehensive and recognizable public service initiative" on US television in the wake of deregulatory policies? To make sense of the Better Community initiative—and the television industry's investment in civic empowerment more broadly—it is useful to trace the burgeoning and deeply intertwined currency of communitarian discourse and corporate social responsibility.

The Better Community campaign appeared in the midst of the reinvention of government in the US, an assemblage of reforms encompassing public sector downsizing, the encouragement of public-private partnerships, the outsourcing of many government services to commercial firms, and the dismantling of welfare programs.[4] ABC translated a bipartisan call for private initiative and personal responsibility as empowering alternatives to big government into fifteen-second public service announcements that doubled as station promotions, and advertising stuffed entertainment revolving around corporate giving and volunteerism. The campaign embraced the entrepreneurial zeal guiding political reform, but it also inserted the ABC television network and its viewers into communitarian solutions to the underside of unfettered capitalism. Like other examples of do good television, the Better Community campaign exemplifies an enterprising turn in governing and at the same time seeks to help overcome the consequences of a pure market logic in the civic realm.

Community is an especially popular corporate civic objective due to its positive currency and safe distance from unruly political activism or controversy. The turn to community, which is also a dominant theme in do good television, is also closely intertwined with communitarian political discourses and strategies of governing. Communitarianism is an applied political philosophy that endorses market capitalism and limited public powers but calls for additional changes to ensure the civic functionality of democratic societies. It advocates the nourishing of voluntary associations as a buffer between the downsized welfare state and the competitive self-interest found in the commercial marketplace.[5] Both the Clinton and Bush administrations adopted communitarian models of "governing through community," from the designation of community empowerment zones as an alternative to public housing programs (Clinton) to the creation of the Office of Faith-Based and Community Initiatives to "nourish dispersed religious and civil alternatives to public welfare programs" and a USA Freedom Corps Volunteer Network to mobilize citizens into "armies of compassion" (Bush). Bush also entrusted the new President's Council on National and Community Service, composed of leaders from business, entertainment, sports, the nonprofit sector, education, and media, to help the White House cultivate a stronger ethic of service and responsibility in the US. While there were crucial differences between Clinton and Bush, the point to be made here is that community has become an objective of governing across political regimes. This matters for our purposes for two reasons: First, good communities (like good citizens) are not born but made—constituted through policies, political discourses, and cultural technologies such as television. Second, as Nikolas Rose persuasively contends, community has become "another word for citizenship" that stresses civic duties rather than collective entitlements. Rose sees the uptake of communitarianism as a substitute for a diminishing social contract—an intervention that softens the "harshest dimensions of neo-capitalist restructuring" by encouraging citizens to serve associations (neighborhoods, localities, social networks, families) that are "decidedly private and which more or less absolve the state of responsibility for society."[6]

In the US, communitarianism is closely associated with prominent scholar and political consultant Amitai Etzioni.[7] In his many books, speeches, and ongoing work with the Institute for Communitarian Studies at George Washington University, Etzioni promotes an understanding of community as a counterbalance to a model of society created in the image of the "marketplace, in which self-serving individuals compete with one another."[8] Communities, he contends, also offset the need for public oversight by reinforcing a voluntary moral order rooted in "traditional values" of respectability, responsibility, and independence. Conceived as dispersed, self-managed ethical zones, community poses an alternative not only to the welfare state but also to the model of democracy associated with broadcast regulation and earlier interpretations of the public interest in television. As Rose points out, community as conceived by Etzioni and other influential thinkers offers a way to "regenerate society" that comes not from "law, information, reason, or deliberative democracy" but from moral "dialogue and action" within voluntary associations.[9] As we shall see, a similar assumption orients ABC's campaign to revitalize community service and volunteerism (and bolster its own brand identity).

While Etzioni naturalizes the space of community, he concedes that citizens *must be trained* to "participate in communitarian society." Even those who have "acquired virtue" will require ongoing guidance, "for if left to their own devices . . . [they] gradually lose much of their commitment to values."[10] What Rose calls technologies of community have proliferated since the 1990s, offering tutelage and instruction. This is partly a response to widely circulating reports of declining volunteerism, everyday philanthropy, and civic engagement in the US. Robert Putnam's influential study *Bowling Alone* lamented the collapse of voluntary associations, indicating that few contemporary Americans demonstrate the civic propensities that Alexis de Tocqueville credited with the "capacity to make democracy work."[11] By the mid-1990s, barely one American in three reported any charitable giving in the previous month, and fewer than two in five claimed even "occasional religious giving," according to Putnam's study.[12] These trends paralleled an equally sharp reduction in participation in community institutions, from lodges to parent-teacher associations.[13] As Rose points out, the "decline of community" ascribed to these trends was also held responsible for a slew of civic problems, from "drugs, crime and alienation, to family breakdown and the loss of good neighborliness."[14] For Putnam (who penned Bush's 2001 inaugural speech), any attempt to reinvent government also needed to "revitalize" community and its subjects.

While communitarianism gained currency, corporate social responsibility was also actively encouraged as a dimension of governmental reform. Both Clinton and Bush called on the corporate sector to partner in social programs and fill gaps left by the divested welfare state. As Andrew Barry argues, the market's willingness to take on responsibility for ethical problems is not surprising. In an era when "direct state control has declined," he explains, corporations are increasingly expected to "perform the job of government at a distance."[15] Yet, the rise of cause marketing, corporate philanthropy, and other manifestations of what Barry calls ethical capitalism are only viable to the extent that they are also profitable. The age of paternalistic philanthropy, exemplified by Andrew Carnegie's view of wealth as a "sacred trust, which its possessor was bound to administer for the good of the community," passed some time ago.[16] In 1970, Milton Friedman, a leading figure of the Chicago school of neoliberalism, unapologetically declared in the *New York Times*, "The social responsibility of business is to increase profits."[17] Nonetheless, corporations have increasingly embraced objectives (fundraising for cures, promoting recycling, citizenship training) that blur boundaries between public and private, governing and profiteering. According to business historian David Vogel, this development is not only the outcome of public sector downsizing and government at a distance. As the entrepreneurial spirit was reforming the welfare state, many corporations were discovering a lucrative "market for virtue." Today, says Vogel, corporate social responsibility is approached not as an unprofitable duty but as the key to successful profit maximization.[18]

In his genealogy of corporate social responsibility, Vogel argues that contemporary advocates of ethical capitalism have basically accepted "Friedman's position that the primary responsibility of companies is to create wealth for their shareholders"—with an important twist: in order for companies to maximize profit, he explains, the prevailing assumption is that "they must now act virtuously."[19] In other words, social responsibility is enacted less as a paternalistic duty than as a competitive business strategy: "Never before has the claim that corporate virtue can and should be profitable enjoyed so much currency or influence," Vogel writes.[20] The new tendency to approach social responsibility as an instrument of profitability is the outcome of the neoliberal reforms, including deregulation and expanded entrepreneurialism, that Friedman and his colleagues promoted, and that spawned a perceived need for greater corporate involvement in ethical issues and civic affairs. As Vogel explains, if the midcentury firms "popularly depicted in John Kenneth Galbraith's *New Industrial State* could afford to support objectives only tangentially linked to its business objectives . . . the world in which these corporations existed has disappeared in the US thanks to concentration of ownership, increased competition, threats of takeovers."[21] In a postwelfare, free market economy, he contends, value creation must drive *all* corporate strategy. This includes the television industry's efforts to revitalize public service in profitable terms that engage TV viewers in solutions to civic problems.

The concept of the citizen brand, which has revolutionized marketing in recent years, takes this a step further by placing corporations and consumer culture at the center of governing and citizenship. In his book *Citizen Brand: 10 Commandments Transforming Brand Culture in a Consumer Democracy* (2002), Mark Gobé argues that corporations that wish to increase profits will have to distance themselves from the greed and exploitation associated with deregulated global capitalism. One way of doing so, he suggests, is to integrate do good activities into business plans and branding strategies so that an image of trust and ethics can be built on a "real dedication to being part of human solutions around the world."[22] In his manual *Citizen Brands: Putting Society at the Heart of Your Business* (2003), Michael Willmott agrees that citizenship must "be a part of branding," and explains how the public interest can be harnessed as a form of market intelligence.[23] As one example, he suggests that public support for community (bolstered by the policies and discourses discussed earlier) can be appropriated as an objective of corporate citizenship and channeled into "economic success."[24]

The Better Community campaign exemplifies the ethical turn in capitalism, presented not as an obligation (which might imply public oversight) but as ABC's *choice* to advance an empowering civic agenda. ABC is positioned at the center of communitarian strategies for activating citizens and buffering the consequences of privatization and welfare reform. Public outreach entails channeling the demands being placed on individuals and communities into the ethical value of the ABC network. It is not coincidental that the Better Community project is overseen entirely by ABC Corporate Initiatives, for its approach to doing good is much more compatible with new directions in marketing and branding than were earlier (unrealized) public service ideals emphasizing rational debate and an informed citizenry.

Citizen Disney and the Rebranding of ABC

The Disney Corporation, the parent corporation of ABC, is a prime example of the multilayered use of community as a technology of governing, a strategic business practice, and a branding strategy. The Disney Corporation, the largest media conglomerate in the world, characterizes itself as a good neighbor visibly committed to social responsibility (exemplified by employee volunteer programs and corporate giving) and humanitarian causes—particularly community and the environment. Disney has diffused these commitments across its corporate holdings, including film studios, theme parks, television networks, and cable channels.[25] The Disney-owned ESPN channel incorporates volunteerism and community service into its operations, enticing employees and "sports enthusiasts" at home to make a difference by volunteering on behalf of nonprofit organizations. The (now defunct) SOAPNet partnered with volunteer events in Hollywood and sponsored community outreach programs in public schools, using soap opera clips to promote family, responsibility, and communication skills. The Disney-ABC Television Group, which oversees the Disney Channel and ABC, is also dedicated to "serving and inspiring individuals and communities through a variety of public service initiatives and outreach programs." Disney-ABC claims that it "proudly supports non-profit organizations in their endeavors to make the world a better place," while its television channels—with their capacity to reach millions of people—provide "ideal platforms to inspire viewers to drive positive change in their communities."[26]

Disney's investment in community and volunteerism is related to the reinvention of government. Disney was a corporate partner in the Bush White House's efforts to encourage volunteerism as a solution to postwelfare needs and problems. Disney also sponsored the National Conference on Volunteering and Service organized by the Corporation for National Community Service, the Points of Light Foundation, and the USA Freedom Corps. At the 2005 meeting, leaders from government and the corporate sector met to devise strategies for developing volunteer service (a term used to describe everything from corporate giving to bake sales) to meet America's "pressing social needs." The responsibilities bestowed upon corporations and individual citizens were evident by the keynote speeches: US Department of Health and Human Services secretary Mike Leavitt lectured on the importance of "economic goodness," and the closing remarks were delivered by Mark Victor Hansen, best-selling author of the Christian self-help book *Chicken Soup for the Soul*.[27] It is telling, but not surprising, that culture industries and popular media figured heavily in the brainstorming session. Although communitarians (including Etzioni and Putnam) condemn mass media as a factor in the decline of community, television and the web are also recognized as useful instruments for retraining citizens and rebuilding voluntary associations independently of big government. ABC's Better Community campaign is one such technology, operating at a distance from the state to constitute responsibility for postwelfare society as a corporate and community affair.

ABC has inserted itself into the communitarian space between the uncaring market and so-called welfare dependency. The question remains: If corporate social responsibility is now practiced as a profit-making endeavor, as Vogel suggests, how does the Better Community campaign fuel ABC's and Disney's coffers? To understand how valuable commitments to ethical business and community building have become for the cultural industries, it is worth juxtaposing the current approach to public service with the "all-business" mentality unleashed by broadcast deregulation. While Disney has always billed itself as an all-American company committed to traditional values, the media mergers and takeovers of the 1980s led all conglomerates to an intensified focus on the bottom line. Within an increasingly competitive industrial climate, former Disney CEO Michael Eisner confessed in a 1981 memo, "We have no obligation to make history; we have no obligation to make art; we have no obligation to make a statement; to make money is our only objective."[28] Sounding a lot like Milton Friedman a decade earlier, Eisner acknowledged that the company's primary, indeed sole, purpose was to maximize profits for shareholders. As late as 1997, the ABC television network (recently purchased by Disney) owned up to a similar sentiment with its TV is Good branding campaign. Mocking any notion that television should serve a purpose higher than producing wealth, the spots proudly positioned ABC as a venue for the hedonistic consumption of trivial entertainment. Pitting TV viewers seeking pleasure and escape against the concerns of do good reformers, the advertisements offered tongue-in-cheek advice such as "Life is short. Watch TV" and "Don't worry, you've got billions of brain cells."

ABC's attempt to brand the right to consume television with no redeeming attributes was short-lived. In 2002, the network switched gears dramatically with what it called the most visible public service campaign on television. Branded as ABC—A Better Community, the campaign generated more than 100 public service announcements to date, in which ABC stars urge TV viewers to "make a difference" in their communities. Early in the campaign, the talent read quotations by famous historical figures in order to situate ABC within a recognizable genealogy of ethical activity and public service. Interspersed with pitches for automobiles, mouthwash, and diet soda were reminders that: *"You make a living by what you get, but you make a life by what you give"* (Winston Churchill); *"Everyone has the power for greatness . . . because greatness is determined by service"* (Dr. Martin Luther King Jr.); *"No man can sincerely help another without helping himself"* (Ralph Waldo Emerson); *"The best way to find yourself . . . is to lose yourself in the service of others"* (Mahatma Gandhi); and *"The greatest moments in life are not concerned with selfish achievement, but rather with the things we do for other people"* (Walt Disney).

Visually framed by the ABC Better Community logo, accompanied by inspirational music and ending with a call to action (including a visit to the ABC website), the spots linked ABC to an iconic pantheon of civic leadership. Within the logic of the campaign, the political differences between entrepreneurs like Disney and activists like King were insignificant; what mattered was their shared commitment to doing good—a moral disposition to which the ABC audience should aspire. Once ABC had established its ethical credibility, the inspirational passages were dropped and well-known

ABC stars such as George Lopez (*The George Lopez Show*), Nicollette Sheridan (*Desperate Housewives*), and Evangeline Lilly *(Lost)* urged TV viewers to take specific actions, like becoming a mentor or cleaning up a neighborhood park. The stars took over as civic tutors in the new promotions, guiding the conduct of individuals while also constituting ABC as a Better Community on the basis of values presumably shared by executives, talent, and audiences. While the initial spots had selectively linked civic progress to the legacy of political figures like King, the announcements that followed disassociated good citizenship from any reminder of grassroots activism or critique. What was radical about the campaign, however, was its aggressive attempt to move TV viewers away from their sets, into civic life. Breaking commercial television's associations with leisure, domesticity, and passive consumption, it recast the ABC audience as an active community of unselfish, civically responsible people. The imagined viewer was addressed as an ethical subject who, with gentle reminders and practical advice, could make a difference in the world outside commercial television. In this way the public service campaign provides what Etzioni calls the training required to "restrain impulses," "delay gratification," and balance "pleasure and living up to one's moral commitments."[29]

In 2006, ABC relaunched the Better Community initiative with much fanfare. The renewed commitment to community service provided the occasion for a new round of publicity kicked off by a special announcement from actress Geena Davis. Davis, who portrayed the first female president of the US on ABC's (now-canceled) drama *Commander-in-Chief*, addressed the audience during a special network showing of *The Ten Commandments*. Drawing civic credibility from her television character and a moral compass from the biblical film, she reiterated the ABC network's unique contributions to community service and volunteerism. Davis also reminded viewers of their crucial role in realizing the network's mission by making a difference in the communities in which they live. Here as before, the Better Community was doubly constituted as an imagined community whose membership involved consuming ABC, and as the outcome of suggested civic actions. Carried out across multiple sites, these actions supported the communitarian turn in government while also providing coveted ethical value to the ABC brand.

The profitability of corporate social responsibility and community is realized in the generation of brand identity and value. The stakes are high for a mass television network in the age of cultural fragmentation and niche marketing. As one handbook on the television business explains, "In a world with dozens and eventually hundreds of television channels, those with the most clearly differentiated brands would be the ones most likely to succeed."[30] ABC combines the concept of the citizen brand with the brand community to differentiate the network's compassion and civic relevance. "Brand community" is a relatively new term used by market researchers to describe a "specialized, non-geographically bound community, based on a structured set of social relationships among admirers of a brand."[31] Like other communities, brand communities are believed to possess "a shared consciousness, rituals and traditions, and a sense of moral responsibility."[32] The Better Community campaign envisions the mass audience as a brand community composed of ABC viewers, each of whom exercises ethical dispositions and capacities within existing institutions (schools, hospitals, charities) and spaces (neighborhoods, parks, municipalities). Although this ethical activity takes place outside television culture, it can only be realized through the ABC brand, which activates and rewards action with affirmation and belonging. ABC operates as what Celia Lury calls a branded interface—not only to the consumption of television but to the duties and practices of contemporary citizenship.[33] TV is no longer good in the self-interested sense evoked by the earlier ABC campaign. ABC is the gateway for civic obligations in the double service of the "community" and the Better Community brand.

Civic Entertainment and Branded Governance

ABC also mobilized its entertainment programming for the Better Community cause. Pro-social themes of philanthropy, volunteerism, and community service were integrated into existing ABC programs, and new series revolving around such activities were launched. In 2003, a story line was developed for *All My Children* in which the soap opera characters volunteered for the faith-based organization Habitat for Humanity, while the actors volunteered for a real-life Habitat project in the Bronx. ABC's prime-time reality entertainment lineup has been especially integral to the Better Community brand. ABC pioneered what it calls a transformational alternative to the self-promoting and scheming that initially defined the genre. The focus of many ABC reality programs is overcoming hardships and problems. *Miracle Workers* provided medical care to the seriously ill and uninsured; *The Scholar* awarded a college scholarship to the most deserving contestant; and *Extreme Makeover Home Edition* partners with Sears, the Sears American Dream Foundation, local businesses, and a rotating cast of volunteers to help families revamp dilapidated homes. The first US television program since the 1950s to intervene in the lives of the needy on a continuing basis, *Home*

Edition operates with minimal production costs (sponsors donate goods in exchange for integrating their products into the interventions, and the labor required to make over the home is donated). The show urges the audience to extend its do good mission by volunteering for the nonprofit agencies profiled on the ABC Better Community website. Like the public service announcements, *Home Edition* constitutes viewers as an integral dimension of the program's mission of building a "better community, one family, one house, one donation at a time."[34]

Home Edition and other ABC reality programs stitch the network into existing resources of privatized care. Another way of putting this is that ABC offloads much of the cost and labor of public service onto sponsors, nonprofits, and TV viewers. The do good mission of shows like *Home Edition* depends on free volunteer labor and the goodwill of corporate sponsors like Sears. Sponsors donate goods and services (which are integrated into the programs) to needy families in exchange for a powerful new way of connecting with TV viewers in the age of zapping and new technologies—an ethical version of what Henry Jenkins calls affective economics.[35] ABC also depends on the ethical authority and ongoing work of existing charities and nonprofit agencies, including Home Aid, American Red Cross, Toys for Tots, the Better Business Bureau, Boys and Girls Clubs of America, Keep American Beautiful, and the Make-a-Wish Foundation. These partnerships are publicized by *Home Edition* and profiled in depth on the Better Community website, and it is through them that ABC viewers are to actualize their capacities as ethical citizens. Besides consolidating information about ABC's transformational programs, the site also serves as a more detailed gateway to suggested forms of civic action. Visitors can learn about the agencies and causes that ABC supports, and find how-to resources and direct links to volunteer clearinghouses (including those created by the Bush administration). Affiliated sponsors and their good deeds are also recognized. In these ways, the website helps connect the ABC television network with its Better Community partners and viewers and offloads the burden of public service onto them.[36]

More than this, the website complements the on-air promotions and transformational programming by facilitating viewer agency and channeling ethical surplus into the ABC brand. It enables the convergence of television branding and "governing through freedom," defined in Foucault's sense of the conduct of conduct. "To govern humans is not to crush their capacity to act, but to acknowledge it and to utilize it for particular ends," says Rose of liberal rule.[37] Under neoliberal conditions, the imperative to govern ourselves through our own choices and initiatives has intensified—as have dispersed technologies (such as do good campaigns) for activating our capacities and steering them toward desired outcomes (such as community). According to Adam Arvidsson, contemporary brand culture is similar to the extent that consumers are conceived as agents whose autonomous activities can be steered toward the creation of value. If "government is about the political constitution of life forms," branding achieves this through the "provision of particular ambiences that frame and partially anticipate the agency of consumers,"[38] he explains. Contrary to theories of advertising as false consciousness, Arvidsson sees brands as productive "platforms for action" that are increasingly "inserted into the social" in order to "program the freedom of consumers to evolve in particular directions."[39] From this perspective, the civic-themed ABC Better Community brand can be seen as a platform for guiding the freedom of TV viewers in their roles as citizens as well as television consumers.

Branding can take up political and biopolitical objectives, as is the case with ABC. However, brand management is ultimately concerned with "controlling, pre-structuring and monitoring what people do with brands, so that what these practices do adds to its value," Arvidsson explains.[40] With socially responsible brands especially, this entails ensuring that the "production of a common social world on the part of consumers" proceeds in ways that *enhance brand value*. To ensure this, brand managers use techniques similar to the processes of citizenship training Rose describes: "One does not so much give orders or shape actions according to a given norm, as much as one works from below, by providing an ambience in which freedom is likely to evolve in particular ways."[41] Branding is not identical to governing in Foucault's biopolitical sense, however. What is different is that the conduct of conduct is undertaken in the first instance to generate value (profit). Such value derives not from the manufacture of goods but from the surplus that consumers produce in their engagement with the brand, Arvidsson contends. Just as public officials call on ethical citizens to provide voluntary civic labor, brand managers enlist the productive capacities of consumers—and intervene in "such a way as to make such capacities generate value." For Arvidsson, the brand becomes not only a governing device but also an instrument for channeling the work of consumers and brand communities (making meanings, crafting lifestyles, interacting with each other) into a "hyper-socialized, de-territorialized factory."[42]

In the context of the Better Community campaign, any distinction between governing and branding is collapsed. ABC brands an ethical disposition and suggested mode of civic conduct, not a product. To create this intangible commodity, it must move TV viewers beyond a passive engagement with the text (ABC programs) to the investments and actions that produce brand value. Because the value of the Better Community campaign is linked to the civic good, this means that performing one's duty as a citizen within the ABC interface also produces an ethical surplus that can be recuperated as brand value. This is not to suggest that going online to learn about volunteerism when prompted to do so by a public service announcement or *Home Edition,* or contacting a nonprofit partner or performing community service, are less than real activities. It simply means that the resources and "ambience" supporting these actions is provided by ABC and used to generate viewer loyalty. ABC conducts our dispersed ethical activity and sells it back to us as membership in a Better Community united not by nation or social contract but by a commercial television network. In becoming (or thinking about becoming) citizens who choose to "make a difference" in their communities, TV viewers are also lending their energies to the production of ABC as a do good brand.

This is not an entirely new phenomenon: Disney, for example, has a long history of interactive branding. In the 1950s, Christopher Anderson notes, the corporation mobilized the ABC Disneyland program to encourage TV viewers to also visit the company's theme park: "Walt identified the program with the park in order to create an inhabitable text, one that would never be complete for a television-viewing family until they had . . . made a pilgrimage to the park itself. A trip to Disneyland—using the conceptual map provided by the program—offered the family viewer a chance to perform in the Disneyland narrative, to provide unity and closure through personal experience, to witness the 'aura' to which television's reproductive apparatus could only allude."[43] The innovation introduced by the ABC Better Community campaign is the need for TV viewers to complete the "inhabitable" text in ways that involve ongoing community action (facilitated by digital technologies). It extends the brand further into an emergent form of social life in which consumers are conceived as citizens who perform their duties within the productive ambience of the ABC brand.

Brand Communities and Exclusions of Citizenship

While I have focused on the convergence of governing and branding strategies, I conclude by probing the contradictions of ABC's emergence as a citizen brand. Rather than stating the obvious—that ABC (in tandem with Disney) exploits a communitarian ethic for commercial gain—I want to address the hierarchies of inclusion and exclusion associated with collapsing boundaries of citizenship, commercial television, and brand culture. I do this by way of two examples. The first is an episode from the debut season of *Home Edition* involving African American community activist and Watts resident Alice Harris. The episode begins as the *Extreme Makeover: Home Edition* bus rolls into Watts to rebuild Harris's home, which has been destroyed in a flood. As the camera zooms in on a pair of designer sneakers hanging from telephone wires and the music strikes a low chord, host Ty Pennington explains the impoverished, mostly black Los Angeles neighborhood's association with crime and riots. The community here is suggested to be far less virtuous and capable than the middle-class (and presumably white) ABC audience.

Harris, on the other hand, is presented as the bearer of the ethical responsibility that ABC seeks to enact. She has been chosen for the home makeover due to her lifelong efforts to bring literacy programs, shelters, meal programs, and community organizations to Watts. Praised by public officials (including the mayor of Los Angeles and California senator Dianne Feinstein) and shown in photographs with Bill Clinton, Harris is situated within communitarian discourse and the culture of volunteerism—despite her long struggle to reform the public welfare system from the vantage point of its subjects. As Rose points out, the concept of community as a civic duty has displaced a more radical genealogy rooted in the struggles of subordinated populations to construct self-managed alternatives to the disciplinary state.[44] Harris is part of this radical genealogy, but her activism cannot be valued within the interlocking governing and commercial logics at work on the program.

The constitution of a Better Community is limited to ethical activities that produce surplus value for ABC and its socially responsible partners. The extent to which these value-generating activities correspond to political discourses and reforms speaks to the alignment of governing, business, and branding. This is the context in which the shiny Sears trucks arrive with donated merchandise and volunteer service personnel to assist neighbors with damaged appliances, while the *Home Edition* crew delivers computers to the community center and spruces up the basketball court. These gifts relieve the public sector of any responsibility in the aftermath of the flood, yet it is also understood that the charity is only temporary. While neighbors are shown milling about and gathering to applaud the "reveal," they have no role in these helping activities. Watts is the object of volunteerism; the poor neighborhood evokes compassion and guidance but is not situated as part of the ABC brand community. This is further emphasized when the crew installs security cameras in Harris's revamped home so she can "watch over" her community at a safe distance. As Rose points out, the authoritarian side of communitarianism is intensified community policing and crime control;

the jubilance with which the home security system is presented to Harris suggests that these control mechanisms—even more than volunteerism and other forms of community service—are especially needed in Watts.

The coding of suggested civic capacities as predominantly white and middle-class is also revealed on the Better Community website. Like ABC's public service announcements and do good–themed entertainment, the website addresses individuals with the resources (time, money) to participate in good citizenship and community as defined by the network. The systemic social inequalities that make it difficult for disadvantaged groups to perform this selective interpretation of civic action make it virtually impossible for TV viewers lacking value-generating capacities to fully participate in the Better Community brand. The website does not allow Better Community members to identify as disempowered or disenfranchised. There are no resources available for those seeking assistance for themselves, rather than opportunities to help "others." Thus, the site makes middle-class privilege (and the consumer value it implies) a condition of belonging to the merging political and consumer order branded by ABC.

TV viewers who do not use the site as a gateway to voluntary service (actual or imagined) are denied ethical status as well as brand membership. This was made particularly clear when the Better Community message board was unexpectedly taken over by people who clogged the forums with urgent appeals for help. Perhaps denied by the formal application process at work on *Home Edition* and other transformational shows, the posters shared harrowing stories of unmet health, housing, and income needs and requested donations directly from ABC viewers. Challenging the limits of communitarianism and corporate social responsibility, the posts rendered the consequences of the collapsing social contract visible and seemingly unresolvable. In so doing, the uninvited (and unanswered) posts called ABC's self-appointed role as an interface to civic responsibility—and its ethical brand value—into question. Not surprisingly, the forums were removed.

What seems most urgent are the striking similarities between the active consumers cultivated by brand managers and the active citizens called into being by strategies of governing through community. Just as the ABC network enlists TV viewers to build a citizen brand, political regimes since the 1990s have called on ethical citizens and communities to produce alternatives to public welfare. The Better Community campaign conjoins these developments, and profits from them. In so doing, it set the stage for a surge of branded do good television ventures, with their own hierarchies of participation.

NOTES

1. This chapter draws from my essay "Do Good TV," *Flow* 3, no. 2 (2006). An earlier version was presented at the 2007 meeting of the Society for Cinema and Media Studies in Philadelphia.

2. Robert McChesney, *Rich Media, Poor Democracy* (New York: New Press, 2000), xi.

3. ABC Better Community website, http://abc.go.com/site/a-better-community/ organizations.

4. For a more detailed analysis of television's relationship to the reinvention of government, see Laurie Ouellette and James Hay, *Better Living through Reality TV: Television and Post-welfare Citizenship* (Malden, MA: Blackwell, 2008).

5. Nikolas Rose, *Powers of Freedom: Reframing Political Thought* (Cambridge: Cambridge University Press, 1999). According to Rose, "In the institution of community, a sector is brought into existence whose vectors and forces can be mobilized, enrolled, deployed in novel programs and techniques which encourage and harness active practices of self-management and identity construction, of personal ethics and collective allegiances. I term this government through community" (176). One major difference between the Clinton and Bush administrations is that Bush placed more emphasis on religious institutions and the moral dimensions of "compassionate conservativism."

6. Rose quoted in Gerard Delanty, *Community* (London: Routledge, 2000), 89.

7. Etzioni's output is enormous. His model of communitarianism is developed in a number of pamphlets, journalistic articles, and books, including *The Moral Dimension: Toward a New Economics* (New York: New Press, 1990); *The Spirit of Community* (New York: Touchstone Books, 1994); *The New Golden Rule: Community and Morality in a Democratic Society* (New York: Basic Books, 1998); and *The Common Good* (Bristol: Polity Press, 2004). Etzioni founded and leads the Institute for Communitarian Policy Studies and the Communitarian Network, and publishes the journal *Responsive Community*. His website is http://www.gwu.edu/~ccps/.

8. Etzioni, 1990, xi.

9. Rose, 1999, 183. For a critique of the moralizing tendencies and gender, racial, and cultural politics of communitarianism, see Mark Reinhardt, "The Song Remains the Same: Communitarian's Cultural Politics," in *Cultural Studies and Political Theory*, ed. Jodi Dean (Ithaca: Cornell University Press, 2000), 95–114; and Miranda Joseph, *Against the Romance of Community* (Minneapolis: University of Minnesota Press, 2002).

10. Etzioni, 1998, 187.

11. Putnam paraphrased in Rose, 1999, 180. See also Robert Putnam, *Bowling Alone: The Collapse and Revival of American Community* (New York: Simon and Schuster, 2001).

12. Putnam, 2001, 126.

13. Putnam, 2001, 116–33.

14. Rose, 1999, 181.

15. Andrew Barry, "Ethical Capitalism," in *Global Governmentality*, ed. Wendy Larner and William Walters (London: Sage, 2004), 202.

16. Carnegie quoted in Putnam, 2001, 117.

17. Milton Friedman, "The Social Responsibility of Business Is to Increase Its Profits," *New York Times Magazine*, September 13, 1970, 32–33, 122–26. See also James Arnt Aune, "How to Read Milton Friedman: Corporate Social Responsibility and Today's Capital-

isms," in *The Debate over Corporate Social Responsibility*, ed. Steve May, George Cheney, and Juliet Roper (Oxford: Oxford University Press, 2007), 207–18. For more on the Chicago school of neoliberalism, see Michel Foucault, *The Birth of Biopolitics: Lectures at the College de France, 1978–1979* (New York: Palgrave Macmillan, 2008).

18. David Vogel, *The Market for Virtue: The Potential and Limits of Corporate Social Responsibility* (Washington, DC: Brookings Institution Press, 2005).

19. Vogel, 2005, 26.

20. Vogel, 2005, 19.

21. Vogel, 2005, 25.

22. Mark Gobé, *Citizen Brand: 10 Commandments for Transforming Brand Culture in a Consumer Democracy* (New York: Allworth Press, 2002), xvii.

23. Michael Willmott, *Citizen Brands: Putting Society at the Heart of Your Business* (New York: Wiley, 2003), 233.

24. Willmott, 2003, 4, 27. The Disney Corporation follows this trend by focusing on community and environmentality. Since this chapter was written, the ABC Better Community campaign has also integrated more environmental themes into its focus on volunteerism and community involvement.

25. "Disney Now Largest Media Company," *Huffington Post*, August 1, 2009, http://www. huffingtonpost.com/2009/04/01/disney-now-the-largest-me_n_181670.html; Walt Disney Corporation, 2008 Corporate Social Responsibility Report, http://disney.go.com/crreport/ community/responsibilityandimpact.html. The company identifies its communitarian aims as follows: "Since the earliest days of The Walt Disney Company, we've aimed to be a positive and productive member of the communities in which we live and work." Disney's role in public-private partnerships and strategies of governing is also emphasized: "Disney provides expertise to develop solutions to key challenges in the public sphere. Disney Imagineers are active in creating new visions for the use of public spaces such as children's hospitals and schools. In 2008, Walt Disney Imagineering lent its creative expertise to the US government and the Trust for the National Mall to improve the visitor experience at the National Mall in Washington, DC. Disney Imagineers reviewed potential improvements to facilities, horticulture and movement of people. To support public diplomacy efforts, Disney created a video entitled 'Welcome: Portraits of America' that was given to the US government to create a more welcoming experience for travelers to the country. The video is currently shown at US embassies, consulates and airports and aboard some flights arriving in the country. Disney has also lent expertise to address queue management, customer service and signage for government agencies that serve the public."

26. Disney-ABC Group Corporate Press Site, http://www.disneyabctv.com/community. shtml.

27. Corporation for National and Community Service, "HHS Secretary Leavitt Touts 'Economics of Goodness' at Closing Session of National Volunteer Conference," Press Release, August 8, 2005, http://www.nationalservice.gov/about/newsroom/releases_detail. asp?tbl_pr_id=167.

28. Eisner quoted in James R. Stewart, *DisneyWar* (New York: Simon and Schuster, 2006), 32.

29. Etzioni, 1990, 45. Some of the on-air public service announcements can be viewed online at the ABC Better Community website, http://abc.go.com/abettercommunity/ index?pn=index.

30. Howard Blumenthal and Oliver Goodenough, *This Business of Television* (New York: Billboard Books, 2006), 159.

31. Albert M. Muñoz Jr. and Thomas C. O'Guinn, "Brand Community," *Journal of Consumer Research* 27, no. 4 (2001): 412–32.

32. Muñoz and O'Guinn, 2001, 412.

33. Celia Lury, *Brands: The Logos of the Global Economy* (London: Routledge, 2004). See particularly "The Interface of the Brand," 48–73.

34. ABC Better Community Website, Show Outreach, *Extreme Makeover Home Edition*, http://abc.go.com/abettercommunity/index?pn=emhe.

35. Henry Jenkins, *Convergence Culture: When Old and New Media Collide* (New York: NYU Press, 2006).

36. See the ABC Better Community website for a complete list of the network's partners.

37. Rose, 1999, 4. For an introduction to the literature on governmentality, see Michel Foucault, "Governmentality," in *The Foucault Effect: Studies in Governmentality*, ed. Graham Burchell, Colin Gordon, and Peter Miller (Chicago: University of Chicago Press, 1991), 87–104. Scholars who have developed a Foucauldian approach to governmentality include Colin Gordon, "Governmental Rationality: An Introduction," in *The Foucault Effect*, 1–54; Graham Burchell, "Liberal Government and Techniques of the Self," in *Foucault and Political Reason: Liberalism, Neo-liberalism and Rationalities of Government*, ed. Andrew Barry, Thomas Osborne, and Nikolas Rose (Chicago: University of Chicago Press, 1996), 19–36; Nikolas Rose, "Governing 'Advanced' Liberal Democracies," in *Foucault and Political Reason*, 37–64; Barbara Cruikshank, *The Will to Empower: Democratic Citizens and Other Subjects* (Ithaca: Cornell University Press, 1999); and Mitchell Dean, *Governmentality: Power and Rule in Modern Society* (Thousand Oaks, CA: Sage, 1999).

38. Adam Arvidsson, *Brands: Meaning and Value in Media Culture* (London: Routledge, 2006), 74.

39. Arvidsson, 2006, 74.

40. Arvidsson, 2006, 74, 82.

41. Rose, 1999, 170.

42. Arvidsson, 2006, 82.

43. Christopher Anderson, *Hollywood TV: The Studio System in the 1950s* (Austin: University of Texas Press, 1994), 152–53. See also J. P. Telotte, *Disney TV* (Detroit: Wayne State University Press, 2004).

44. Rose, 1999, 170.

4

Good Housekeeping

Green Products and Consumer Activism

JO LITTLER

"Green products" in many ways seem to embody what this book terms "commodity activism" par excellence. Every year more products labeled as "green" hit the shelves, raising questions about the extent to which environmental awareness is changing the quality of objects and services for the greater or greener good, and to what extent environmental anxieties are merely (and ironically) being seized upon and channeled into encouraging us to buy more and more stuff. Furthermore, the extent to which such products can be understood to be "environmentally friendly" or as exemplary of corporate greenwash is often notoriously fraught and subject to vigorous contestation. (To take but one example, the British Advertising Standards Association recently ruled that ads by car manufacturer Lexus and petrochemical giant Shell should be banned, as they both misled the public with their green claims.)[1]

This chapter explores green consumption as a form of commodity activism in a number of ways. First, it contextualizes green consumption in the context of both historical changes to consumer culture and the environmental movement. Second, it offers an overview of key theoretical paradigms through which "green products" either have been, or might be, conceptualized, including "green governmentality," "productive democracy," and "cultural ecology." Third, it considers some of the contradictions of the green commodity—that deeply ambiguous agent of activism—by focusing on one particular product: the nappy. This example is used to tease out and navigate through the historical, environmental, and theoretical paradigms in the earlier section. To do this, it highlights the role of cultural and media discourse in the construction of what "green commodities" mean today by drawing from specific examples, including contemporary popular fiction aimed at mothers (or "henlit") in which such commodities have a persistent presence, alongside the theories of Felix Guattari expressed in *The Three Ecologies*, which, I argue, can help theorize the relationship between such discourse and other social and ecological aspects of environmentalism and consumption. In doing so, the chapter aims to move beyond simply stating that the terrain is "complex," and to move further toward an understanding of which particular aspects of green products are worth buying and which aspects are themselves worth disposing of.

Green Products: Some Contexts

To understand the contemporary expansion in the production, branding, and selling of "green products," we need to have a sense of significant shifts that have taken place in two main areas: first, in environmentalism and its surrounding politics, and second, in the nature of contemporary consumer capitalism (phenomena that are also in a number of ways intimately connected).

One key context for the expansion of "green" products has been the emergence of the fragmented niche markets of post-Fordism. The shift, roughly from the 1970s, from "producer-led" to "consumer-led" manufacturing, from class-based demographic research to increasingly complex forms of lifestyle branding, the use of emotional selling points, and the expansion of spatial and sensory marketing techniques, has been widely documented in cultural studies and the social sciences.[2] As Luc Boltanski and Eve Chiapello have shown, "alternative" and bohemian values were themselves used to fuel the culture of late or post-Fordist capitalism.[3] The proliferation of "alternative" and green products and sensibilities in the 1970s was by the close of the decade seized upon and turned into commercial opportunities, spawning megabrands like the Body Shop and Celestial Seasonings tea, a process Thomas Frank terms "the conquest of cool."[4] Corporations have since this time channeled ethical consumption in ever more specific lifestyle niches for a variety of interest groups, moving toward the highly variegated paradigm of "mass specialization" known in the business sector as the "long tail" model.[5] In other words, we now have a very eclectic marketplace where you can buy hyperexploited goods or extremely sound goods depending on your education, mood, and the weight of your wallet.

In addition, green consumption, just like the wider field of ethical consumption in which it can be located, has expanded after the rise of the new Right from the 1970s and of so-called free-market neoliberal ideologies. The reorganization of global trade rules and the erosion of public provision in favor of corporate interests led to a widening gap between rich and poor both within and across nations. This is the background against which many of ethical consumption's initiatives have mushroomed, including fair-trade and antisweatshop organizations like No Sweat and American Apparel.[6] The expansion of free market production under neoliberalism facilitated the production of vaster quantities of goods—through, for example, the increase in poorly paid and sweatshop labor in export-processing zones and in "disposable" fashion and toys.[7] This expansion in the sheer *quantity* of goods used by wealthier consumers has been variously termed "affluenza," "overconsumption," and "turbo consumption."[8] The US sociologist Juliet Schor, for example, has calculated that in 2003 the average American bought fifty-seven pieces of clothing whereas in 1991 he or she bought thirty-four.[9] Green products exist in this context in two ways: first, as rejoinders to overconsumption (as in the jute "bag for life" designed to replace numerous plastic bags) and, second, in that some "green" products have themselves been produced using cheap overseas labor. In the UK in 2007 there was a brief media storm over Anya Hindmarch's "ethical" product "I'm not a plastic bag," which was discovered to have been imported from China, where it was produced without the use of fair-trade or organic materials.[10]

The expansion of green products has also been facilitated by technological changes. Relevant issues here include forms of digitalization and transportation that have allowed "just-in-time" flexible production to become a global phenomenon, meaning that, for example, consumer trends can be commissioned by a toy or clothing company from cheap production sources halfway around the globe. It is against such extensive air miles that many green products position themselves (e.g., the local organic vegetable box), and, again, it can also be out of such technology that they emerge (e.g., a Fuzzi Bunz reusable nappy produced in the US and sold in Britain).

Second, the expansion in green production has also been reliant on the rise of the information society, as through faster and more graphic media technologies it has become easier to report on environmental degradation and pollution, whether through images of polar bears on icebergs in *Vanity Fair*, reports about extreme weather in newspapers, or eco-blockbuster documentaries like *An Inconvenient Truth* and *The 11th Hour*.[11] Third, new forms of technological production have been developed as eco-*solutions*, such as advanced designs of photovoltaic solar panel or solar-powered telephone chargers.

The other—and most prominent—set of key contextual factors explaining the emergence of the green product are those that might broadly be grouped under the rubric of "environmental changes." This itself is a wide, multifaceted, and often interconnected group of issues spanning pollution, biotechnology, climate change, and the depletion of natural resources. Both non–genetically modified products and the meteoric global rise of organic food reflect a widespread anxiety about the extent to which industrialized countries have become overindustrialized. The problem of running out of natural resources to use for energy—namely, oil, coal, and gas—has started to stimulate forms of consumption that are less dependent on nonrenewable energy.[12] These include seasonal food that can be grown without heated greenhouses and local produce that uses fewer food miles, and switching to renewable forms of power (like wind or solar), as well as spawning some deeply environmentally problematic alternatives like biofuel, which through deforestation creates as much damage as it seeks to address.[13]

Finally, there is climate change. Whatever you may think about climate change, it is increasingly harder to avoid thinking and feeling about it at all as global warming has become mainstreamed as an issue. While relatively little of sufficient or extensive significance has at the time of this writing been done about it at the level of policy, climate change *denial*, a public relations practice largely funded by ExxonMobil and its sponsored subsidiaries, has now arguably peaked.[14] Anxieties about climate change are clearly being mobilized through a number of green products, which are marketed as ways to cut down on carbon dioxide production to "save" or "help" the planet, from bags for life to "eco" radios and calculators. Obviously this discourse of "buying to help save the planet" can interconnect these various themes in multiple ways: for example, electric cars and cycling are often promoted as addressing issues of both peak oil and climate change.

These, then, are some of the key contexts for the contemporary emergence and expansion of the green product. And yet there are many different ways of understanding or interpreting the significance of such products' emergence. In the next section, I bring together some of these divergent perspectives and distinctions, which I group under the rubrics of "green governmentality," "productive democracy," and "cultural ecology."

Theorizing Green Products: From "Green Governmentality" to Grassroots Democracy

The cultural geographer Noel Castree recently argued that Western environmentalism is, today, "a movement of paradoxes: it appears to exert real societal influence, whilst in practice being mostly ineffectual."[15] Castree continues that the environmental movement no longer dominates discourse on the environment, which instead has been "co-opted to the cause of a specifically liberal, market-led form of environmental management in key western states."[16] Castree's concern about who has the most power over environmental discourse come as part of his survey of the shifting fortunes of the environmental movement, and his aim is to find ways to help a progressive left/radical environmental agenda regain power over both the discourse and the movement. However, his diagnosis of the neoliberal co-optation of environmental discourse is one shared by a number of other writers. Tim Forsyth and Zoe Young have argued, for example, that we are in "a new green order" where politicians announce that debate over climate change should begin, but that the answers are all sewn up:

> There seems to be a consensus among global elites about where to start (be afraid, be very afraid . . . . but always trust the government), how to address the challenge (change development patterns in the South to "offset" carbon emissions produced by business as usual in the North), and who is responsible (mainly you and me). Real doubts and arguments are suppressed while market friendly "solutions" are served up on a nice, glossy plate.[17]

In these terms, people's fears are channeled into one set of neoliberal solutions. The individual is burdened with an overwhelming, rather than partial responsibility for change—what Foucauldians call "responsibilization."

Such arguments are compatible with what Timothy Luke once termed "green governmentality," a condition in which state environmental policy and discourse are preoccupied with the "conduct of conduct" of individuals within that system. While, importantly, it is feasible for "responsibilization" of the individual to occur under a more social democratic state model, Luke's prescient analysis, from 1999, is concerned with how it functions as part of a profoundly pro-corporate set of Clintonite/Gore-ite policies, or, in other words, as a neoliberal state strategy. For Luke, environmental discourse is being deployed through strategies of governmentality to regulate public behavior while at the same time being used as fuel for both corporate competitiveness and discourses of economic growth, which is fundamentally incompatible with being green.[18] What I am calling "green governmentality" positions can clearly, then, have different politics to them, in that they are, for example, able to accentuate the historicity of the environmental movement[19] or polemicize and dismiss it.[20] Used with sensitivity to context, and alongside other tools, they can act as both a crucial argument and powerful methodology. Used badly, they can work to support antienvironmentalism or to pompously dismiss grassroots environmentalism as little more than false consciousness.

A second constellation of interpretative positions is one I will here term "productive democracy," in which the power of ethical consumption to *change* cultural and economic systems is emphasized. This term is borrowed from Robin Murray's typically cogent conceptualization of the act of recycling as a kind of "productive democracy": noting that the public is not paid to recycle, but that people regularly press to be able to do it more, he argues that this is an area of enormous democratic power and potential.[21] While Murray is talking about recycling rather than the formation of green products, his term is a useful means of interpreting the contemporary clamor for green goods. Crucially, "productive democracy" is a position that can cross the political spectrum. From one particular pro-corporate, economically right-wing perspective, for example, green products can make money and save the world. This is the kind of perspective to be found in the battery of business books that discuss ways of greening your product, such as *Green to Gold: How Smart Companies Use Environmental Strategy to Innovate, Create Value, and Build Competitive Advantage*.[22] But equally, for many left-wing anticapitalists, the development of green products can also be perceived as necessary to a healthy political, social, and environmental system. The 2009 European Election Manifesto of the UK's Green Party, for instance, explicitly critiqued privatization and economic liberalization while supporting the production of green products as part of their "Green New Deal."[23]

The *enthusiasm* with which greener products are being demanded and sought after is the key insight of the "productive democracy" position. It is a position that recognizes the importance of cultural discourse: of how people's interests, inclinations, and desires play an important role in shaping the present. At the same time, however, any "productive democracy" argument can only avoid a celebratory individualism by locating its analysis in relation to larger political systems.[24] For example, when enthusiasm for green products is adopted by and routed through large *corporations*—where increasing shareholder profit, usually by shifting increasing numbers of units, is necessarily the primary motive for business—the end result is often likely to be environmentally problematic. By contrast, the encouragement of green products through campaigning for changes to the type of products available through *regulation* (by, for example, outlawing deeply un-green products such as patio heaters, or refrigerators emitting certain amounts of carbon dioxide), or through cooperatives—which do not prioritize profits for a few but rather pool wealth and resources—are actions that participate in very different economies of value.

Green governmentality approaches therefore tend to interpret green products from a somewhat "top-down" perspective (with the top being the state), whereas "productive democracy" approaches tend to interpret green products by privileging "bottom-up" systems of people power. A third approach is to borrow from the work of Felix Guattari on cultural ecology.[25] Best known for his theoretical work with Deleuze, in later life Guattari was particularly interested in the intersections between environmentalism and philosophy (or "ecosophy") and stood as a green parliamentary candidate in France. Guattari discussed how we are constantly confronting a "nagging paradox," as we have

> on the one hand the continuous development of new techno-scientific means to potentially resolve the dominant ecological issues and reinstate socially useful activities on the surface of the planet, and, on the other hand, the inability of organized social forces and constituted subjective formations to take hold of these resources in order to make them work.[26]

In other words, humans have the resources to deal with the problems: we just have not yet been able to get it together to deal with it. In *The Three Ecologies* Guattari shows how any attempts to cut through these paradoxes need to work through three different formations or "ecologies"—environmental, social, and mental—arguing that these realms need to be conceptualized together, and that discrepancies across them are damaging. As I have attempted to show elsewhere, this can be a useful tool to help pick apart some of the problems of green consumption.[27] Drawing from *The Three Ecologies* can help us highlight the contradictions that exist around green products. For example, green consumption can be consumed as a middle- or upper-class practice to ramify social divides; it can exist as an isolated act; buying more green goods can ironically mean *increased* consumption; a corporation can produce a few green lines while also producing deeply environmentally harmful ones (or "partial greening"); green marketing can be used to update a company's image while the products remain unchanged; or through all-out greenwashing a company can use green branding to try to hide a destructive environmental record.

Importantly, Guattari's work emphasizes political solutions as well as contradictions, and here we might gesture toward how they can be addressed. So, for example, the problem of greenwashing can be addressed through much tighter governmental regulation, in which corporations are held *accountable* to the public (as in "corporate social accountability") rather than letting them try to be *responsible for* the public (as in the corporate push for "corporate social responsibility").[28] This also necessitates "mental" shifts in the way we think about corporate behavior and shifts in "social" ecologies in terms of the extent of the power we grant to corporations, in order to change environmental ecologies.

Guattari's terms, then, are useful as they show how we need to bring psychological, social, and environmental ecologies together. They are potentially very capacious in terms of what they allow us to discuss. They can also, I think, help us understand, and be able to deploy, theories of green governmentality and productive democracy in a more effective and nuanced fashion. In the next section, I will attempt to illustrate this by focusing on one particular example: the nappy.

Nappy Wars

Nappies are an interesting area to focus on here for a number of reasons. They are a product that is as close to a "need" as any, and yet they involve a large number of permutations in terms of mode, style, and price. Because the nappy is seen as a domestic product, which is significant in terms of its environmental impact, it is a subject on the front line of many an article and judgment about environmental lifestyle changes it is possible to make to "help the environment." The image of the waste mountain of 4,000 to 6,000 nonbiodegradable nappies that an average child using disposables will get through in his or her lifetime, for example, is regularly conjured up by environmental campaigners and journalists.[29] Being a product for new babies, the nappy connects both to the question of overpopulation and to a variety of narratives about "new beginnings" and "the future"—including the future of "the planet." In addition, new identities and roles of parenthood also bring their own specific shape and weight to the table, meaning that the subject can be freighted with all kinds of discursive significance, particularly for the various strata of the middle classes who can afford the money and psychological space to mull over the issue of what to buy and why.

It is against this backdrop that certain types of nappy are being positioned as radical environmental alternatives for the self-aware purchasing parent. The next section highlights a few of the divergent positions over nappies and environmentalism—what we might term "the nappy wars"—in order to interpret the different forms of "commodity activism" they seem to offer by bringing together the theories previously discussed. These positions include, first, the response of large corporations to "eco-nappies"; second, the nappy as activist tool and environmental object fetish; and, third, the discursive backlash to commodity activism.

Green Wipeouts

The rise of the disposable nappy since the 1960s and 1970s has in the present climate of increasing anxiety over excess carbon dioxide production become something of a topical discussion point.[30] In the UK, for example, according to an independent report for *Ethical Consumer*, 90 percent of the nappies used are not washable, nappies form 2 to 3 percent of household waste, and the emissions produced are the equivalent of 98,600 cars being driven 12,000 miles every year.[31] Cloth nappies, which today exist both in their earlier incarnation as a plain piece of fabric to be tied with a safety pin and in a multitude of new designs (with snaps, Velcro fastenings, and removable pads; or made from bamboo or hemp, for example), are often presented in such features as a much more environmentally friendly alternative. This is primarily because they can be reused (on the same child or on more than one child), thus producing far less landfill and carbon dioxide emissions (although they often also reduce the number of chemicals, bleach, plastics, and perfumes in use). More recently, the largely biodegradable or "environmentally friendly" disposable such as Moltex-Oko, Tushies, and Nature nappies have gained popularity as a bridge between these two systems.[32]

The nappy climate is therefore one in which individual middle-class consumers are beginning to be "responsibilized" into taking responsibility for the environmental impact of their child's waste by changing their own consumption habits. The question of eco-responsibility through nappy purchasing is overwhelmingly being left to and encouraged as an *individual* matter. In one important respect what is also most striking in this context is just how *little* this process has become ingrained, given that nonenvironmental disposable nappies, particularly Pampers (Proctor and Gamble) and Huggies (Kimberly Clark) still overwhelmingly dominate the UK and US markets. Both are companies with bad environmental records, being regularly listed in the top 100 polluting companies in the US; Kimberly Clark has for several years been campaigned against by Greenpeace for its destruction of Canadian forests.[33] If this demonstrates that green governmentality is being activated as a mechanism to deal with this environmental issue, it also shows something of how "the environmental option" is minimized as a lifestyle option for the few as large corporations use a battery of strategies to keep their resolutely nonenvironmental products mainstream: or what we might call "green wipeout."

Let us look at two examples of such a cornering of the marketplace. All mothers who are in National Health Service hospitals in the UK today receive a folder after birth containing a variety of free samples and money-off coupons. Such corporate incursions into the public sector are new and part of the broader neoliberal system of privatization of public space documented by, for example, David Harvey and Dexter Whitfield.[34] All these samples, promotional leaflets, and coupons are from large corporations; the nappy sample in 2008, when I received it, was from Pampers. This means that even while local councils in the UK aim through a money-off scheme to encourage its residents to use reusable nappies, this message, which does not appear in the pack, is not circulated or promoted to all new mothers. In fact, it is directly contradicted by the ubiquitous presence of profoundly nonenvironmental corporate messages that new mothers receive after the birth of their child.

To take a second example, a number of smaller companies have pioneered the development of the "green" disposable nappy in Europe, notably the brands Moltex Oko, Tushies, and Nature nappies, with the latter two being the only predominantly biodegradable disposable nappies currently on sale in the UK. Nature nappies, made by the Scandinavian company Naty, have over the past few years gained a greater toehold in the European market, having been sold in the UK in the large supermarkets Sainsburys and Asda alongside specialist retailers. In 2008 Sainsburys removed Nature nappies from its shelves and replaced them with its own brand of "green" nappy, Eco, prompting an outcry from Nature-loving parents. As one post by "Amateur Eco Dad" on a parental discussion board put it, "Sainsbury's claims are really woolly—they claim the nappies 'minimise plastic use'—and have a 'reduced impact absorbent core'—but that still doesn't mean that that plastic use or impact is anyway near acceptable. Just that it's less of an impact than before."[35] Sainsburys, so the allegations ran, had used the product of a small pioneering company effectively as market research, only to co-opt its consumer base and replace it with its own in-house brand when the product proved successful. Notably, Eco nappies, while marketed as "green," are not biodegradable like Nature nappies; its "green" claims are considerably thinner in substance.

Clearly it has been far easier for corporations to gain profit from selling disposable nappies over and over again rather than reusables. So far the widespread launch of the green nappy by major corporations is itself in its infancy. To adopt Guattari's emphasis on possible solutions,[36] we might say that without appropriate regulation—such as against advertising for disposable nappies in the public sector (or indeed anywhere); tightening up "green" claims and the minimum environmental requirements for disposables—the economic muscle of such corporations in a neoliberal climate is being used, despite the large amount of media and public interest in the subject, to lever out green or greener products from the marketplace.

Green Commodity Activism . . . or Object Fetishism?

Yet corporate attempts to wipe out pioneering green products are not the only position in the contemporary cultural ecology of the nappy. Both the emergence of the biodegradable nappies mentioned earlier and the existence and expansion of reusable nappies can be understood as examples of what we might term "green commodity activism." Reusable and green nappies are products that tend not to use large-scale above-the-line (paid-for) advertising, except for print advertisements in specialist journals and magazines. They are instead heavily promoted through word of mouth: through discussions, references in parenting books, website searches, numerous media articles on parenting or on making household changes to "help the environment," or talks given at prenatal classes, for example. These features alone do not do enough to warrant the moniker of "green commodity activism" given that they are all routes that many contemporary viral and guerrilla marketers and PR companies are aiming to head down.[37] But rather than these techniques being engineered by specialist PR companies, it is instead predominantly parents who do the viral marketing and who often set themselves up as retailers for various "green" nappy products, promoting these products (again) through word of mouth and notice boards.

These products, circulating in such promotional and distributional networks, might be understood not only as "green commodity activism" but also as forms of "productive democracy" at work. Parents and prenatal class leaders predominantly promote such products not because they get paid for doing so but because they believe in them as products that they think will "help the environment" by producing less waste, and which will help "offset" some of the immense carbon dioxide output of their offspring. (There is often an interesting relationship between guilt and the therapeutic power of green consumer activism at work here.) Their great strength lies in the richness of these local networks. But clearly these networks do not exist completely "outside" capitalism. The nappies might sometimes be distributed by co-ops, but they are mainly produced by for-profit companies, albeit small ones with predominantly good environmental records.[38] As such they exist in the complex and contradictory zone of ethical shopping. They offer more progressive alternatives to those provided by Kimberly Clark and Proctor and Gamble, but the "ecologies" both of their production (in that they are not cooperatives) and in the wider social area of regulation (in that, for example, the minimum environmental standards for nappies are so lax) means that their existence as progressive green products is precarious.

Furthermore, reusable nappies can be thought of as having problematic "ecologies" in other ways. They are cheaper than disposable nappies over a baby's lifetime, but there is more initial outlay, putting them out of reach of parents from low-income backgrounds. While the richness of their promotional and distributive networks comes from their intense viral marketing, this very factor can put them out of reach of those people who are for whatever social or cultural reasons outside of these contact zones. In the UK, for example, reusable nappies are often associated with white middle-class, middle-aged women. Furthermore, the reusable nappy may perhaps at times come to be focused on in isolation as a virtuous environmental object: to become, in an analogous way to the "bag for life," a kind of green fetish, overfocused upon while other areas (like the regulation of corporate pollution) are ignored and receive somewhat less public and media attention. In these terms, we might see how they not only work as a form of productive democracy but are simultaneously drawn into the zone of green governmentality.[39]

The Backlash against Commodity Activism

So we have considered the issue of green commodity activism from a number of angles, including the contexts for their expansion and the ways they can be interpreted. We have applied this to our case study of the nappy, to view the problems blocking the green activist commodity from its very emergence alongside the problems in its current existence. In this last section, I turn to the next issue confronting the green activist commodity: the backlash against it.

One place we can see this backlash against both environmentalism and the green activist commodity at work is in a specific type of social/mental ecology: the new branch of popular fiction aimed at mothers, which is often called "henlit" (as in a "grown-up-and-nested" version of "chicklit"). The extent to which environmentalism in general is ridiculed in henlit is remarkable. In these novels, anyone interested or involved in "natural birth," breastfeeding beyond a few weeks, or the National Childbirth Trust is roundly demonized, and "organic" is positioned as being the consumer choice of cranks and weirdos. There is nearly always a character who "represents" an environmental position among the mother-heroine's new friends, which tend to fall into three or four stock types (alpha, yummy, sane friend, and eco-loon).

The eco-loon figure is always presented as extremely drab, dogmatic about breastfeeding, socially incompetent, and physically unattractive. In Polly Williams's novel *The Rise and Fall of a Yummy Mummy*, for example, eco-mother Michelle is portrayed as an "extreme lactivist" whose breast "can only be described as 'an udder'" and who drinks her own breast milk herself as well as giving it to her child.[40] (Eco-mothers are without fail drawn as characters who can only evangelically sermonize about breastfeeding and castigate other women unfairly.)[41] In Jane Green's *Babyville*, one mother is shocked to find out that another gives organic food to her children, because until then she had "looked so . . . *normal*."[42]

The habits and appearance of eco-practitioners are thus often exaggerated into grotesque, comic figures whom we are invited to laugh at. In *Shopaholic and Baby* the eco-female is Jess, an environmentalist, anticonsumerist, and even (horror of horrors) an academic. Jess brings her endearing and lovable label-queen sister (the mother-heroine) some already-used rags out of which she is going to make reusable baby wipes and a copy of the magazine *Frugal Baby*, which features "pictures of babies dressed in old flour sacks."[43] The environmental position is located as one that is unhygienic, sour-faced, and ridiculous. It is notable that the now widespread practice of buying biodegradeable baby wipes does not feature in the novel, as that would not be able to be so roundly derided. Similarly, the triumphant big scene finale of *I Don't Know How She Does It* features a group of other women getting retribution on a former sexist male colleague by inciting him into a ridiculous investment opportunity: the biodegradable nappy.[44] The fact that there are nappies on the market that are largely biodegradable and produced using recycled materials is roundly ignored, enabling an ecological project to be positioned as both economically unsustainable and slightly insane.

Crucially, however, these characters are not lower-class women who cannot afford environmental products but middle-class mothers who aspire above their social station. The relationship to ecology and environmentalism in these novels is therefore primarily one of disavowal. Such disavowals of environmentalism are, moreover, congruent with encouragement and incitement of consumerism: both of buying more and more objects, and ensuring that these objects are new, not secondhand; corporate, not cooperative; intensively produced, not organic. This, in other words, is a backlash against green commodity activism. If it indicates both the disavowal and distancing of certain groups of people toward environmentalism, it also indicates the condition of struggle in which the green product finds itself in the marketplace because of its relatively marginal status.

The social life of a green product as a form of "commodity activism" is a complex one. It operates in a field of contradictory consumption, in a world in which we are increasingly encouraged to address environmental, social, and political concerns through consumption, or to "shop for change." The issues facing its actual *emergence* into the marketplace and its *reception*, or "later-life," are distinct and variegated. The green product may act as a fetish, only serving the needs of a small group of people; it may mark the emergence of a liberating form of grassroots democracy-from-below; or it may act as a gross instance of corporate "greenwash." It can be used both to extend environmental, social, and mental equalities and to limit them: to "damage" as well as "heal."

To navigate this zone, and these divergent positions, the theoretical tools of productive democracy, green governmentality, and cultural ecologies are useful. They can help us see how just neoliberal culture both enables the *very partial* emergence of progressive products and simultaneously *cuts off* the possibilities for their full emergence and more widespread use. They can also help show how what is most progressive about green commodity activism is when it can be used to push—through social, environmental, and mental ecologies—toward wider equalities: whether to regulate corporate behavior, to change psychological expectations, or to push beyond green capitalism into green cooperativism.

NOTES

1. See Advertising Standards Authority, *Environmental Claims in Advertising: Is Green a Grey Area? 2008*, http://www.asa.org.uk, accessed May 2009.

2. Robert Bocock, *Consumption* (London: Routledge, 1993); Mike Featherstone, *Consumer Culture and Postmodernism* (London: Sage, 1991); Yiannis Gabriel and Tim Lang, *The Unmanageable Consumer: Contemporary Consumption and Its Fragmentations* (London: Sage, 1995); Celia Lury, *Consumer Culture* (Cambridge: Polity Press, 1996); Celia Lury, *Brands: The Logos of the Global Economy* (London: Routledge, 2004); Steven Miles, *Consumerism: As a Way of Life* (London: Sage, 1998); Liz Moor, *The Rise of Brands* (Oxford: Berg, 2007); Mica Nava, Andrew Blake, Iain McRury, and Barry Richards, eds., *Buy This Book: Studies in Advertising and Consumption* (London: Routledge, 1997).

3. Luc Boltanski and Eve Chiapello, *The New Spirit of Capitalism* (London: Verso, 2006).

4. Thomas Frank, *The Conquest of Cool: Business Culture, Counterculture and the Rise of Hip Consumerism* (Chicago: University of Chicago Press, 1997). See also Sam Binkley, *Getting Loose* (Durham, NC: Duke University Press, 2008).

5. Chris Anderson, *The Long Tail: Why the Future of Business Is Selling Less of More* (New York: Hyperion, 2006).

6. Fair trade has its roots in both 1950s Christian imperialism and the anticolonial movements of the 1960s, but it only really boomed and became codified with the fair-trade mark in the 1980s, to compensate for the inequalities of global trade.

7. Naomi Klein, *No Logo: Taking Aim at the Brand Bullies* (London: Flamingo, 2000); Andrew Ross, *No Sweat: Fashion, Free Trade and the Rights of Garment Workers* (London: Verso, 1997).

8. The expansion in the quantity of goods consumed globally also needs to be related to the rise in the global population. The relationship between consumerism and the global population expansion is a subject around which care needs to be taken, particularly given that consumption has been used, historically, to channel fears about the power of those groups who are new to practicing it and who by virtue of practicing it have increased power. See Rachel Bowlby, *Shopping with Freud* (London: Routledge, 1993); Andreas Huyssen, *After the Great Divide: Modernism, Mass Culture and Postmodernism* (Bloomington: Indiana University Press, 1987); Mica Nava, "Modernity's Disavowal," in *Modern Times*, ed. Mica Nava and Alan O'Shea (London: Routledge, 1996), 38–76. Just as there were moral panics over the consumption habits of white women throughout the 19th and turn of the 20th century (who were, as Andreas Hussyen put it, "knocking at the gates of power") and over newly affluent teenagers of the 1950s, more recently there is sometimes a racialized panic today about Chinese and Indian shoppers buying too much. However, it is equally possible and necessary for the consequences of the energy production of an expanding population to be discussed in terms that are resoundingly anti-imperialist.

9. Jo Littler, "Tackling Turbo Consumption: An Interview with Juliet Schor," *Soundings* 34 (2006): 45–55.

10. Jo Littler, *Radical Consumption: Shopping for Change in Contemporary Culture* (Buckingham: Open University Press, 2009), 103.

11. Maxwell Boykoff and Michael Goodman, "Conspicuous Redemption: Promises and Perils of Celebrity Involvement in Climate Change," *Geoforum* 40 (2009): 395–406; Lyn Thomas, "Alternative Realities: Downshifting Narratives in Contemporary Lifestyle Television," *Cultural Studies* 22, no. 5 (2008): 680–99; Gill Branston, "The Planet at the End of the World: 'Event' Cinema and the Representability of Climate Change," *New Review of Film and Television Studies* 5, no. 2 (2007): 211–29.

12. Andrew Simms, *Ecological Debt: The Health of the Planet and the Wealth of Nations* (London: Pluto, 2005), 24–26.

13. George Monbiot, *Heat: How We Can Stop the Planet Burning* (London: Penguin, 2007), 157–61.

14. Monbiot, 2007, 157–61.

15. Noel Castree, "The Future of Environmentalism," *Soundings* 34 (2006): 12.

16. Castree, 2006, 12.

17. Tim Forsyth and Zoe Young, "Climate Change CO2lonialism," *Mute* 2, no. 5 (2007): 29.

18. Timothy W. Luke, "Environmentality as Green Governmentality," in *Discourses of the Environment*, ed. Éric Darier (Oxford: Blackwell, 1999), 121–51.

19. Castree, 2006, 12.

20. Forsyth and Young, 2007, 28–35.

21. Robin Murray, *Creating Wealth from Waste* (London: Demos, 1999).

22. Daniel C. Esty and Andrew S. Winston, *Green to Gold: How Smart Companies Use Environmental Strategy to Innovate, Create Value, and Build Competitive Advantage* (Hoboken, NJ: Wiley, 2009).

23. "Green Party: It's the Economy, Stupid!" http://www.greenparty.org.uk/news/2009-05-14-launch.html.

24. Murray, both an academic political economist and coordinator of fair-trade projects, manages to do this with considerable verve and integrity.

25. Felix Guattari, *The Three Ecologies*, trans. Ian Pindar and Paul Sutton (London: Continuum, [1989] 2000).

26. Guattari, [1989] 2000, 31.

27. Littler, 2009, 92–115.

28. CORE, "The Corporate Responsibility Coalition" (2009), http://www.corporate-responsibility.org; Littler, 2009, 50–69.

29. See, for example, Nick Rosen, "Are You an Eco-Wimp or a Green Warrior?" *Times*, August 11, 2005.

30. Leo Hickman, "It Won't Wash," *Guardian*, May 20, 2005; Lyn Thomas, "Alternative Realities: Downshifting Narratives in Contemporary Lifestyle Television," *Cultural Studies* 22, no. 5 (2008): 680–99.

31. "The Hidden Contents of Nappies," *Ethical Consumer*, November/December 2007, 26–48; Karen McVeigh, "UK's First Nappy Recycling Plant," *Guardian*, April 24, 2008.

32. I have not drawn on the notorious 2005 report by the UK Environmental Agency, given that as a report it was discredited soon after publication (even by the Environmental Agency itself, which has since pledged to redo it). Contradicting nearly all other environmental science reports on the subject (aside from those sponsored by Kimberly Clark and Proctor and Gamble), the findings of this report were relayed by environment minister Ben Bradshaw in the House of Commons as meaning that there was little significant difference in environmental impact between disposable and reusable nappies. A brief storm of media publicity followed, most of which highlighted how the report was based on an extremely small sample of people who used reusables—in many parts of the report, the results of this survey were based on the habits of *only two* people—and who apparently reused them in a very particular way: by always doing a ninety-degree boil wash, tumble drying, even *ironing* them. See Channel Four News, "Fact Check: Rash Verdict on Nappies," July 16, 2007, http://www.channel4.com/news/articles/society/environment/factcheck+rash+verdict+on+nappies/603782. Given that a large proportion of people using reusables do so for environmental reasons, washing on a low temperature, air drying, and never ironing, this struck a large number of journalists as rather odd, even while the report was seized upon with glee by the antienvironmental and anti-PC lobby. A number of both some features and independent counterreports followed contradicting the EA advice, some suggesting that this strange result bore an uncanny resemblance to the disposable nappy industry's own propoganda and questioning the vested interests of those compiling the report. See Hickman, 2005.

33. "The Hidden Contents of Nappies," 2007, 38–40, 43–45.

34. David Harvey, *A Brief History of Neoliberalism* (Oxford: Oxford University Press, 2005); Dexter Whitfield, *Public Services or Corporate Welfare* (London: Pluto, 2001).

35. Sainsbury's, http://www.sainsburys.co.uk/YOURIDEAS/forums/ShowThread.aspx?PostID=10282&PageIndex=2.

36. Guattari, [1989] 2000.

37. See Liz Moor, *The Rise of Brands* (Oxford: Berg, 2007).

38. "The Hidden Contents of Nappies," 2007.

39. If we follow Guattari's emphasis on imagining solutions, one example of how this situation might change exists in the grants that are being given to new parents in the UK by many local county councils to subsidize their purchase of resusable nappies. If such an initiative were rolled out on a wider basis and publicized more heavily, it would help address the classed nature of the reusable nappy consumer. Similarly, if local nappy laundry services—of which there are many in the UK—were run and promoted by councils, this would help address the mental ecologies blocking their more widespread use, given that for many parents disposables are used simply to gain extra time. And if reusable nappy users campaigned for greater regulation in the nappy sector, in terms of what was allowed to exist in the market at all—or if the regulations themselves were simply tightened—this would prevent it becoming simply a green fetish.

40. Polly Williams, *The Rise and Fall of a Yummy Mummy* (London: Sphere, 2006), 56–57.

41. Williams, 2006, 56.

42. Jane Green, *Babyville* (London: Penguin, 2001), 45, emphasis in original.

43. Sophie Kinsella, *Shopaholic and Baby* (London: Bantam Press, 2007), 28, 70.

44. Allison Pearson, *I Don't Know How She Does It* (London: Vintage, 2003).

PART TWO

Celebrity, Commodity, Citizenship

As the liberal welfare state and its apparatuses of social justice are battered by populist and legal assaults, and as the legitimacy of and resources for public programs wither within the cultural imaginary, celebrities and privatized philanthropies within a "nonprofit industrial complex" have gradually taken their place assuming responsibility for persons who, within the terms of neoliberalism, are called to pull themselves up by their proverbial bootstraps. Social action in the neoliberal era is, thus, characterized by the increasing presence of Hollywood celebrities, pop icons, and corporate moguls who have stepped in where the state used to be, proliferating privatized forms of welfare and redistribution.

If, as the essays in the previous part of this volume have suggested, cultural resistance in the current moment is characterized by a necessary embeddedness within institutions and discourses of the market, the chapters collected here in the second part offer careful readings of political paradoxes introduced by commodification and celebrity within cases of such "marketized" cultural resistance. Unpacking the terms of an uneasy "truce" between circulating paeans to bootstraps individualism and free market entrepreneurialism, on the one hand, and political interventions geared to global social justice packaged and performed by celebrities, on the other, these essays centrally explore a range of ethical and strategic tensions that mark instances of commodity activism in the neoliberal moment.

To these ends, the authors in this part consider, for example, what our analyses of neoliberal citizenship miss when we read screen star Brad Pitt's rebuilding campaigns in post-Katrina New Orleans simply as a diverting—and profitable—spectacle. What account of Pitt's celebrity activism might we make given that his presence in storm-ravaged New Orleans champions solutions to state-sanctioned disregard and displacement of "suffering Others" that are nevertheless fully invested in commodity capitalism and discourses of celebrity? How should we unpack strident critiques of global capital when they emanate from the hypercommodified performative repertoires of hip-hop culture? What is the civic impact of media moguls who combine neoliberal entrepreneurial savvy and "postracial" opportunism in their efforts to proliferate media representations of marginalized Others? How and for whom does screen siren Angelina Jolie's ambassadorial philanthropy work?

Engaging this range of questions, the chapters in this part substantiate the claim that commodity activism, as a historico-cultural phenomenon, defies ready generalizations. Powerful reminders of the commonplace of contradiction within hegemonic discourses of the neoliberal age, these analyses, moreover, offer us the means to rethink traditional models of activism and philanthropy and Left assumptions about the dialectics of resistance. Pursuing recalibrations taking shape within modes of civic intervention in the historical context of global capital and neoliberalism, the essays in this part illuminate the ways that social action orchestrated, performed, and circulated by celebrities may be transforming cultural imaginaries of what it means to "do" citizenship at the present moment. Bringing into relief a dappled terrain of emergent subjectivities—citizens and consumers, activists and entrepreneurs, celebrities and agitators—these essays work to highlight political dilemmas raised by shifts in what counts as "citizenship," "marginality," and "democratic resistance."

Exploring these tensions, this part of the book opens with Kevin Fox Gotham, who examines the collision of commodification, celebrity, and citizenship as they were brought into relief in the aftermath of Hurricane Katrina that devastated the Gulf Coast of the US. Gotham examines the role of celebrity activism in the spectacularization of disaster, a process by which, as he puts it, tragic events and catastrophes are reduced to profit-making opportunities and consumption-based entertainment experiences. Closely reading screen star Brad Pitt's "Make It Right" campaign as a major site of such spectacularization, Gotham reveals how Pitt's celebrity advocacy in the rebuilding effort in New Orleans, while clearly framed within and enriched by corporatized and consumption-based market interests, has nevertheless also managed to build a social movement that has influenced the national political agenda by focusing public attention on entrenched class and race inequities brought to light by the storm.

Next, Roopali Mukherjee's essay offers an interpretive reading of the politics and aesthetics of "Diamonds (Are from Sierra Leone)," a much-lauded single by hip-hop superstar Kanye West that highlights human rights atrocities fueled by the global trade in African "blood diamonds." For Mukherjee, West's single and the music video that accompanies it centrally underscore the commonplace of contradiction, the messy push and pull of autonomy and subjugation, when political work is embedded within, and thus defined by, commodity culture. Engaging the showy celebrity of materialist "bling" cultures of hip-hop and the promise of political critique that lurks within them, the essay explores the terms of a racial politics embedded within West's single to reveal how neoliberal citizens actualize their political subjectivities from *within* circuits of consumption and exchange. Mukherjee argues, moreover, that such modes of consumer citizenship, despite their failings and myopias, are neither easily nor always written off as inauthentic or opportunistic.

Isabel Molina-Guzmán's essay follows in this line, exploring Mexican American screen actress and television producer Salma Hayek's media productions as, on the one hand, they animate and deploy commercialized discourses of identity and authenticity, and, on the other, offer clear instances of political intervention from the cultural margins. Exploring the tensions between cultural celebrity and political voice, Molina-Guzmán focuses on the ways that Hayek's dual claims to Latina and Mexican cultural authenticities work to commodify Latinidad while simultaneously enabling political interventions geared toward media visibility for Latina/os and entrepreneurial autonomy over such representations. For Molina-Guzmán, Hayek's self-conscious promotion of cultural authenticities typifies the paradoxes of commodity activism in that such plays of authenticity engage in a crucial, if somewhat blunted, recuperative politics, realigning identity politics and ethnic struggle with commercialized and marketized global media discourses of the moment.

Alison Trope expands on these paradoxes of celebrity activism in her contribution, with a focus on screen icon and global philanthropist Angelina Jolie. Contextualizing Jolie's endeavors within long-standing traditions of privatized philanthropy and circulating mythologies of the white "maternal missionary figure," Trope troubles the knee-jerk skepticism that Hollywood philanthropy typically elicits, as well as the terms of reductive moral critiques deployed within public discourses to dismiss Jolie. Even as celebrity activists straddle the line between altruism and self-promotion, harnessing their philanthropic-activist image to "give back" while commodifying and branding themselves to evermore profitable ends, Trope's analysis reminds us that Jolie's image, like those of her star philanthropic peers, does in fact bear forcefully on social causes, carrying "marked and marketable weight" in modeling personal acts of generosity and philanthropy among the public at large.

Finally, focusing on linkages between visual culture and commodity activism, Melissa Brough explores humanitarian work against global suffering that is marketed using popular cultural spectacles, within which media celebrities, performing the "humanitarian donor-as-consumer," urge their audiences toward the "conspicuous consumption of humanitarianism." Brough's analysis focuses on Invisible Children, Inc., one of the most innovative and lucrative new media–driven humanitarian campaigns, tracing the role of visual images in constructing both beneficiary and donor identities within contemporary narratives of Western humanitarianism. Reading shifts in visual rhetorics from a realist to a postmodern, youth-oriented pop culture aesthetic, Brough suggests that humanitarian visual culture increasingly proliferates neoliberal constructions of donors-as-consumers that remain grounded within the logics of consumer capitalism and popular cultural cultures of glamorous celebrity. Serving centrally to construct the "sympathy-worthiness" of humanitarianism's distant beneficiaries, such campaigns cater to the changing aesthetics of Western donors, holding "compassion fatigue" at bay while anesthetizing our encounters with global structural inequalities that are significant forces in engendering humanitarian crises in the world.

5

Make It Right?

Brad Pitt, Post-Katrina Rebuilding,
and the Spectacularization of Disaster

KEVIN FOX GOTHAM

In today's entertainment-saturated world, the notion of "spectacle" has become a key concept in the social sciences, arts, and humanities even though scholars contest its meaning and societal effects. Spectacle refers to the dominance of amusement, leisure, and tourism in the organization and marketing of cities as entertainment destinations.[1] Casinos, shopping malls, sports stadiums, and theme parks are the most visible spatial manifestations of spectacle and signal the centrality of dramatic public displays and commodity images in everyday life.[2] Closely related to the production of spectacular spaces is the emergence and proliferation of sports spectacles like the Olympics and the Super Bowl, political spectacles like the Monica Lewinsky scandal and the O. J. Simpson "megaspectacle,"[3] and military spectacles like the War on Terrorism and the Iraq War.[4] In an era of intense capitalist competition, mainstream corporate media process events, information, and knowledge in the form of media spectacle to attract audiences and advertising dollars. In addition, the increased interpenetration of entertainment and other realms of society—for example, "infotainment" (information and entertainment), "edutainment" (education and entertainment), and "charitainment" (the use of celebrities to persuade consumers to donate to charities), and so on—is indicative of the ways in which entertainment codes increasingly permeate contemporary society and culture.[5] Overall, the growth of research on spectacle reflects growing awareness among diverse scholars that we have entered a new era of commodity production defined by the production and consumption of entertaining and spectacular imagery.[6]

This chapter examines the role of celebrity activism in the spectacularization of disaster, using a study of the recovery and rebuilding of New Orleans since Hurricane Katrina. The spectacularization of disaster is a process by which tragic events and catastrophes are reduced to profit-making opportunities and consumption-based entertainment experiences. Naomi Klein describes the idea of exploiting crisis and disaster as the modus operandi of "disaster capitalism," a term that reflects the use and dominance of "free market" ideology and policies to manipulate and control disaster-shocked people and countries.[7] Specifically, this chapter analyzes Brad Pitt's "Make It Right" (MIR) campaign as a major site of spectacularization to highlight both progressive and negative features of the post-Katrina rebuilding process. Pitt's MIR campaign uses celebrity-oriented entertainment to highlight social problems, draw attention to the positives of sustainable development, and leverage investment to build green affordable housing for victims of Hurricane Katrina. As a strategy of political advocacy, MIR embraces spectacle and entertainment to popularize New Orleans's plight and frame urban recovery and rebuilding as consumable entertainment. As an example of the spectacularization of disaster, Pitt's effort involves the use of celebrities to provide an entertainment-based incentive to donate time and money, mobilize volunteers to assist in rebuilding post-Katrina New Orleans, and communicate a political message in person (through photo ops), on television, or online.

My goal in this chapter is to point to the limitations and contradictions of constructing and producing disaster-as-spectacle via celebrity activism. As a major spectacle, the MIR campaign reflects the spread of celebrity activism to the field of disaster recovery and rebuilding.[8] In recent decades, Hollywood celebrities have helped propel issues like global warming and climate change, hunger and starvation, disease and famine to the top of the political agenda in many countries.[9] As a catalyst of social transformation, celebrity activism both reflects and challenges existing social structures and organization. Celebrity activism can dramatize social issues, and expand and reinforce openings and possibilities for actors to use commodified symbols and spectacular imagery for positive and progressive ends, including launching radical critique that exposes the reality of inequality and the deprivations of social policy. Jerry Lewis's Labor Day Telethon, Angelina Jolie's campaigns for the UN Refugee Agency, and Bono's launch of Product RED in 2006 have garnered media and scholarly attention on the impact and influence of celebrities in raising public awareness about particular issues. Just as there are multiple actors involved in the production of celebrity, audiences can play an active role in the construction and interpretation of celebrity.[10] As a site of struggle and conflict over status and cultural symbols, celebrity activism represents a complex, multifaceted reality, a mixture of repressive and resistant qualities that we should analyze in terms of the dialectical concern with conflict and contradiction. Thus, rather than celebrating or condemning celebrity activism, it makes more sense to identify contradictions and tensions, and situate current trends and novel happenings within larger social, economic, and cultural transformations. Following Ferris, "celebrity can be problematized without being pathologized."[11]

Brad Pitt's "Make It Right" Campaign

Since the Hurricane Katrina disaster on August 29, 2005, scholars and researchers have assailed the government response to the catastrophe and condemned the sluggishness of the rebuilding effort in New Orleans and along the Gulf Coast.[12] For critics, the anemic and lethargic rebuilding process is due to a number of factors, including bureaucratic inefficiencies, the Iraq War in siphoning resources for recovery efforts, and institutional fragmentation that impedes coordination among the public and private sectors in delivering resources and stimulating recovery.[13] Others maintain that a long history of government-induced and government-sanctioned racial discrimination and segregation is the culprit as a plethora of failed social policies have exacerbated inequality and poverty in post-Katrina New Orleans.[14] Still others argue that the neoliberal reliance on market-centered tax subsidies, deductions, and exemptions rather than public outlays is responsible for the slowness of rebuilding.[15] Overall, Hurricane Katrina has created new political fissures and incited debates over whether cities are now less safe from natural disasters, terrorist attacks, and major epidemics. The barrage of critical commentary unleashed by Katrina suggests a future of intense scholarly debate and research on postdisaster recovery, rebuilding, and public policy.

Brad Pitt's "Make It Right" campaign opens a new frontier in postdisaster urban recovery by combining star power and celebrity advocacy to attract media attention and investment to help rebuild the Lower Ninth Ward neighborhood in New Orleans. Hurricane Katrina has rallied many celebrities, including Harry Connick Jr. and Scarlett Johansson, but Pitt's campaign has been the only one to build a foundation to leverage and combine corporate donations, architecture firms, and merchandising opportunities to help rebuild a major section of New Orleans. The mission of the MIR Foundation is to redevelop the Lower Ninth Ward by building a neighborhood of high-quality, affordable, and environmentally conscious homes that reflect and promote sustainable development. Launched in December 2007, MIR began by commissioning designs for an initial 150 low-cost homes from thirteen prominent architecture firms. Construction began on the first homes in early 2008. The houses have many flood-protection features, including some with foundations that can float, roof patios for hurricane and flood relief, and innovative recycling and energy-generating installations to reduce costs. The goal of the MIR Foundation is to build homes that "recreate and nurture the unique culture and spirit of the Ninth Ward, which symbolize[s] the soul of New Orleans." According to Pitt, "A New Orleans rebuilt without the Ninth Ward would never be whole."[16] As of March 2009, MIR had constructed ninety homes.[17]

According to MIR promotional materials, when Pitt visited the Lower Ninth Ward after the Hurricane Katrina disaster, neighborhood residents told him that "while the terrible crisis had exposed their vulnerability, Katrina had also created an opportunity: to build something better than what had existed before."[18] Having listened to one former resident's plea to help "make this right," Pitt was supposedly inspired to name the project "Make It Right." Pitt's MIR campaign includes fourteen local, national, and international world-renowned architecture firms (table 5.1). Along with these firms and a coalition of nonprofit organizations, the MIR Foundation seeks donations, corporate sponsors, and seed capital to catalyze neighborhood redevelopment. While Pitt is the celebrity spokesperson for the MIR Foundation, he is by no means the primary auteur though he does play an authorial role as a visionary director due to the collaborative aspect of the MIR design and rebuilding process. Much of the planning takes place among the designers and planners who work within the architecture firms that make up the foundation. Pitt asks foundations, corporations, and individuals to contribute to the project by adopting one house, several houses, or a portion of a house through the project website, makeitrightnola.org. "You can adopt a tankless water heater or a solar panel or a tree or a low-flush toilet," according to Pitt. "You can give it to someone for Christmas . . . instead of another sweater."[19]

The MIR Foundation presents Brad Pitt as a new authority on urban disaster rebuilding, an urban planning expert who is sought after by architecture firms and other organizations in New Orleans and elsewhere. According to Pitt, Hurricane Katrina "illuminated the brutal truth that there's a portion of our society that we're not looking after, that we are marginalizing. And that shouldn't be."[20] In his vision, the new home dwellers will no longer be "getting the crap materials that give your kids asthma, increase your health bills. They're not getting the cheap appliances that are going to run up your bills and keep that burden on you. It's a respectful way to treat people [and] this to me is a social justice issue."[21] In short, the MIR Foundation and Pitt's advocacy efforts aim to raise global awareness of the plight of the Ninth Ward, propel

TABLE 5.1

Local, National, and International Architecture Firms Involved in Make It Right

Local	
Billes Architects	New Orleans, LA
Eskew Dumez Ripple	New Orleans, LA
Concordia	New Orleans, LA
Trahan Architects	Baton Rouge, LA
John Williams Architects	New Orleans, LA
National	
BNIM	Houston, TX
Kieran Timberlake	Philadelphia, PA
Morphosis	Santa Monica, CA
Pugh + Scarpa	Santa Monica, CA
International	
Adjaye Architects	London, England
Constructs	Accra, Ghana
GRAFT	Berlin, Germany
MVRDV	Rotterdam, Holland
Shigeru Ban Architects	Tokyo, Japan

Source: MIR Foundation. http://www.makeitrightnola.org/index.php/building_green/
meet_the_architects/

postdisaster recovery to the top of the political agenda, and attract funding and investment using a star-power strategy of activism and philanthropy.

At the same time, MIR also reflects a desire to expand merchandising opportunities and consumption-based entertainment experiences. The MIR Foundation website encourages people to "make it right" by purchasing shirts, hats, caps, bags, and posters that contain the signature "9" to show support for the Ninth Ward. The merchandise reflects the MIR mission, and consumers are encouraged to purchase these items as representations of "forward thinking green products." Rebuilding celebrities such as entertainer Ellen DeGeneres and the New Orleans Saints coach Sean Payton invite people to donate to their "Team Sponsored Home" to help build homes for displaced families. DeGeneres and Payton supply the "cool quotient"[22] and promote celebrity advocacy as a vehicle of urban "recovery" and "rebuilding." Cross-promotional activities with *American Idol*, architecture and construction firms, and *The Ellen DeGeneres Show* aim to create a series of tie-ins or associative chains to facilitate brand alignment and brand extension, the ultimate goal of which is to produce and expand the commodity sign and form. The implication of these developments is that spectacle-enhancing strategies such as advertising, marketing, public relations, promotion, and branding inexorably permeate the MIR Foundation and campaign to the extent that tragic events, catastrophes, and the overall Katrina disaster become major profit-making opportunities.

Overall, we can view the MIR campaign as an extension of the commodification process that defines neoliberal capitalism and a major indicator of the blurring boundaries between entertainment and tragic events. As an object and vehicle of consumption, the MIR campaign expresses and validates consumer culture through merchandising opportunities, product endorsements, and cross-promotional activities.[23] The impulse toward merchandising and star-powered activism uses the logic of spectacle to construct and present urban "recovery" and "rebuilding" as drama, image, story, and entertaining display. Consequently, the public is invited and encouraged to view New Orleans and the Hurricane Katrina tragedy as narrative, spectacle, and "infotainment," in which information and entertainment inexorably merge. These points suggest that in the neoliberal era, the codes of entertainment increasingly shape the form, style, and appearance of activism, and political advocacy in turn becomes more cinematic and spectacular, in the sense of Guy Debord's concept of the spectacle.[24] Just as spectacle is a culture of celebrity that provides dominant role models and icons of fashion, look, and personality, celebrity activism reflects and reinforces the extension of the logic of commodified entertainment to urban disaster.

A Spectacle of Pink

Brad Pitt's MIR effort incorporates the logic of spectacle and dramatic presentation to transform the Ninth Ward from a devastated space of flooded homes into a vibrant community of homeowners. One early promotional effort, launched in December 2007, encouraged donors to sponsor symbolic pink houses as metaphors of hope, opportunity, and community rebuilding. The "Pink Project," according to the MIR website, is a "hybrid of art, architecture, cinema and media" that is "an informational, commemorative, communication tool which raises awareness and activates individual participation to heal local wounds in need of global aid." Working with the international architecture firm GRAFT (Berlin), Pitt and the MIR Foundation "merge film and architecture" into a presentation that can bring immediate global attention to New Orleans and the Lower Ninth Ward neighborhood. The Pink Project suggests that the image of pink houses will "create emotive storyboards containing perspectives rich with history and memories."[25] At the installation's commencement in December 2007, the components of each house were arranged like a tangram puzzle. Over the next five weeks of fundraising, sponsors and individual donors supplied the money to reassemble the pink placeholders to symbolize the construction of 150 real homes on 429 "volumes"—small-scale model homes scattered throughout fourteen square blocks. Donations registered "the effects of a collective consciousness," and 150 house volumes were standing on the site by the end of January 2008. The final week of the installation showcased a site with reassembled house volumes representing the rebuilding of the neighborhood. At night the site is lit with 350 lights focusing on specific pink volumes. The base volumes are configured into houses each week, the exterior lights moved inside the pink house to create a soft glowing lantern effect. In addition, the spectacle contains 1,000 candles, commemorating the lives that were lost to the storm.

Pink, a symbol rich with the promise of homes that will be constructed for the community of the Lower Ninth, resonates with an immediate and cogent message: "They have not been forgotten." As the promotion from the MIR website tells us:

> The simple legibility of the pink monopoly house reassembled from smaller individual components intentionally focuses attention on a problem of manageable scale, allowing the individual to physically participate in the installation through donations. Contributions become incorporated into the built environment through architectural assembly. In this, there is a transformation from an individual American Dream into a collective one. Real beauty arises from harnessing the power of global awareness and global helplessness and providing an outlet. Pink is an opportunity to interact meaningfully with the world by rebuilding a torn cultural fabric.[26]

For Pitt, pink is a color that symbolizes hope and renewal, promises transformation and empowerment, and commands collective action and political mobilization. "Through the immediate potency of the spectacle, aided by local and global media," pink attempts to disassociate itself from the negative images and connotations of past failures. Pink "generates an armature robust

5.1. Pink Project. Week Five. http://www.makeitrightnola.org/index.php/media/
image_archive/Feature_The_Pink_Project/#.

enough to enable the outpouring of individuals into a collective effort striving for positive change—reversing the diaspora and bringing people home."[27]

One major limitation of using spectacles to dramatize and convey New
Orleans's plight (as well as other social problems and political issues) is that
by their nature, spectacles are focused around consumption and entertainment, not politics and broad societal transformation. While celebrity activists may address important inequalities and social justice concerns, they
typically do not question the commodification process or call for collective
mobilization to challenge the exploitation of wage laborers within the entertainment sector. Though some audience members may be receptive to whatever political objectives celebrity advocates are supporting, many prefer the
titillating performance or celebrity-oriented information and will resist educational or political messages meant to sway public opinion.

In addition, the commodification process that defines the MIR campaign
constrains and limits which individuals and groups can be legitimate participants in the rebuilding process. That is, "participation" in the rebuilding
effort is contingent on one's status as a "donor" and "consumer." Disaster-as-
spectacle constitutes people as consumers and uses advertising and marketing to exploit consumer desires to rebuild the Lower Ninth War for profit

and economic gain. One cannot participate and help the MIR in revitalizing the Lower Ninth Ward unless one embraces the logic of entertaining spectacle as a vehicle of urban rebuilding. In this respect, the marketing of disaster-as-spectacle becomes an overt and intentional avenue of capitalist accumulation with tie-ins with the buying and selling of other products. The various actors and organized interests that market disaster recovery and rebuilding give people a choice of goods and services to consume. Yet what they seek to limit, if not eliminate, is the participation of nonconsumers in helping to rebuild the Lower Ninth Ward and New Orleans.

Celebrity Activism as Social Critique

We can view Brad Pitt's MIR Foundation as part of an emerging strategy of political advocacy for New Orleans spawned by a feeble federal response to the Hurricane Katrina disaster and made possible by the growing force of spectacle and entertainment in culture and society. Neoliberal policies and regulatory strategies applied to New Orleans, including the emphasis on privatization of disaster response services, deregulation, and generous tax subsidies to corporations to rebuild the region, dovetail with the spectacularization of disaster.[28] Like his speeches after 9/11, President Bush called for national unity in the face of tragedy and promised that the federal government would lead a "comprehensive recovery effort" as part of a "sustained federal commitment to our fellow citizens along the Gulf Coast."[29] In a globally televised speech from Jackson Square in the French Quarter on September 15, 2005, President Bush promised to do "what it takes" to rebuild the Gulf Coast.[30] In practical terms, a catastrophe of the size and scope of Katrina demanded a commensurate response, a national rebuilding effort. For Louisiana lieutenant governor Mitch Landrieu, Hurricane Katrina was an "American tragedy that requires a full-hearted America response."[31]

But for those who have followed the tragedy, there has been no "American response," no organized national effort, and no unified coordination to deal with the misfortune that has followed the catastrophe. Despite billions of dollars spent for disaster preparedness since 9/11, the various government agencies, officials, and other authorities were not prepared to work with each other during and after the Katrina disaster. Conflicting signals between local and federal agencies paralyzed relief efforts and have slowed long-term recovery. The catastrophe of Katrina necessitated well-planned government action, a strengthened safety net, and innovative forms of policy. What the nation expected was a comprehensive national policy on disaster recovery that laid out a clear path of revitalization and rebuilding for New Orleans and the Gulf Coast. Such a policy could have articulated shared problems and suggested collective solutions that the nation as a whole could follow when future disasters strike. What the nation received, however, was a fragmented decision-making process, a heavy deference to and blind reliance on the nonprofit and private sectors, incessant reports of fraud and waste, and deep mistrust for public action.[32]

Thus, what shocked the world about Katrina was not the hurricane but the response. Much of the government's response to Katrina has been to deny the extent of human vulnerability, blame the victims (the residents of New Orleans), obfuscate the social causes of the disaster, and conceal the consequences of the displacement and devastation. Both Republican and Democratic leaders assailed President Bush for his failure to mention ongoing efforts to rebuild after Hurricane Katrina in his January 2007 State of the Union Address. The omission incensed people in hard-hit New Orleans and the Gulf Coast region and was criticized by Louisiana's Republican senator David Vitter and other politicians. "I guess the pains of the hurricane are yesterday's news in Washington," Louisiana Governor Kathleen Blanco said after Bush's speech. "But for us it's still very real, very real, and it's something that we live every single day."[33]

Since the disaster, a major ideological struggle has been under way to conceal the problem of Katrina, to transform it into a special problem for a subgroup of people, and thereby to disconnect it from the systemic factors that deepened the destructive impact of the storm. Specifically, we can interpret Bush's rhetorical reticence as a calculated and tactical attempt to neutralize the outrage that the image of destruction and displacement produces in those who see it. Rather than address Katrina as a fundamental problem of US society and neoliberal policy, the dominant reaction has been to treat New Orleans and the Gulf Coast as a set of isolated problems to be dealt with as charity cases or subjects of piecemeal and ad hoc attention. Insofar as possible, government officials seek to define Katrina's destruction as a problem of individuals rather as a societal problem created by economic and political arrangements.

Overall, the big question facing New Orleans and other future cities that experience a major disaster is, can celebrity activism be an effective vehicle for urban rebuilding? The success of neighborhood recovery hinges on the extent to which Brad Pitt can create an enduring institutional effort to rebuild the Lower Ninth Ward neighborhood—through a synergy of local, national, and international architecture firms and through lasting political changes in urban disaster assistance. On the one hand, celebrity activism can raise important issues, expose people to previously submerged social problems, generate millions of dollars for humanitarian relief efforts, and encourage targeted groups to mobilize around important opportunities for political change. On the other hand, critics argue that it is debatable whether celebrity activism can solve social problems or have a transformative impact on society.[34] Thrall et al. have argued that celebrities can make important political statements on specific issues that can have impact, but they do not steer the policy debate, and their influence on politics is weak.[35]

Yet when we examine the different aspects of MIR, we find that the foundation is not only an institution of urban rebuilding but a vehicle of political activism and criticism. Two points are relevant. First, the MIR campaign, like many other activist organizations, draws attention to the racially unequal impacts of the collapse of the Army Corps of Engineers' levee system and the importance of addressing racially inequalities as a major element of sustainable development. Second, the MIR campaign exposes the incompetence and dysfunction of government agencies such as the Army Corps of Engineers and the Federal Emergency Management Administration (FEMA). This is not to imply that without MIR there is no sustained and convincing critique of FEMA and federal policy. The point is that MIR offers an additional point of critique that supports and bolsters both grassroots and global critiques of the neoliberalization of government services over the last decades. In the end, MIR opens a discursive space for criticism of dominant institutions but also encourages planners, architects, and urban researchers to discuss and debate future policies and planning strategies to create more democratic, egalitarian, and sustainable metropolitan areas. Perhaps Make It Right and other organizations like it should be considered successful if political leaders reshape and develop new comprehensive policies and practices not only to rebuild cities affected by disaster but to defend and protect cities from future disasters.

Analyzing celebrity activism as conflictual and contradictory focuses attention on the ways in which individuals and groups can campaign against marginalization and use celebrity status and entertainment to further resistant agendas. While on one level celebrity activism reflects the trends toward the commodification of life, it can also open opportunities for people to engage in critical reflection and political mobilization. Pitt's celebrity activism proffers an implicit social critique of the federal disaster relief effort in New Orleans—a response to government ineffectiveness, limited private sector investment, and scattershot urban recovery efforts. Pitt's appearances on *Larry King Live*, *The Today Show*, *The Oprah Winfrey Show*, and *Charlie Rose* suffice as major venues for political advocacy and critical dialogue about the causes and consequences of social inequality, social injustice, and continuing marginalization in US society. Using money, media, and a desire for progressive social change, Pitt and his allies in the MIR effort have helped raise mass awareness and exposed people around the world to the lethargic government response to the Hurricane Katrina disaster and the problems of coordinating different policies and government action to encourage urban rebuilding. Through lobbying efforts and meetings with elected officials, Pitt has pressured individual leaders and governments to take action against poverty and inequality in post-Katrina New Orleans.

More important, Pitt's MIR represents an extension of "charitainment" whereby active celebrities methodically and strategically communicate political messages and solicit donations not only through video entertainment channels but also through websites, digital media, and other sophisticated communication technologies. In this sense, we can view the different individuals and organizations in Pitt's MIR Foundation—for example, celebrities, architecture firms, corporate sponsors, and donors—as a multifaceted political pressure group to convince political leaders and policy makers to formulate and implement new policies to remedy urban vulnerability and promote sustainable development.

Finally, as a form of social critique, Pitt's MIR campaign uses the discourse of commodification and entertainment to open up and help nurture a new form of political activism that can connect and mobilize otherwise disparate groups and interests. Critics have argued that celebrities depoliticize social issues and discourage broad-based political mobilization because they do not question the powerful interests, social structures, and processes that legitimize the status quo.[36] Instead, as I have argued and demonstrated in this chapter, Brad Pitt's MIR Foundation has been a major force in directing money and resources into the Lower Ninth Ward through concerted and organized fundraising efforts and strategic political lobbying. Unlike individuals engaged in conventional activism (sit-ins, direct protest, community organizing), celebrities can make direct appeals to powerful leaders to sponsor and effect progressive social change. Furthermore, celebrities can use their fame and talents to raise funds and advocate for important issues regarding equality, democracy, and dignity. While celebrities have long been involved in activism and political advocacy, Pitt's MIR is novel because it encompasses a variety of organizations, including architecture firms, corporations, and nonprofits, to support a new model for rebuilding neighborhoods and cities affected by disasters. These points suggest that MIR could become the prototype for a new kind of celebrity activism that transcends single-issue agendas and merges celebrity, corporate firms and networks, and grassroots organizations to catalyze social transformation.

Conclusion

I have argued that Brad Pitt's MIR Foundation and campaign are an instance of the spectacularization of disaster whereby tragic events and catastrophes are framed and interpreted as profit-making opportunities and consumption-based entertainment experiences. While most research on entertainment and spectacle has condemned celebrity and star-powered advocacy as a pathological manifestation of the commodification process, I contend that celebrity activism is fraught with tensions and contradictions. Pitt's celebrity advocacy has been important for building a social movement infrastructure based on individual and corporate donations, grassroots campaigning, and wooing other celebrities to support the rebuilding effort in New Orleans. On balance, Pitt's campaign has become an important mechanism for targeting donors and attracting audiences using entertainment-oriented information and merchandising opportunities. In the short term, MIR has raised millions of dollars to build new homes in the Ninth Ward, encouraged different groups and interests to mobilize, and helped draw public attention to a major issue. With the aid of media reporters and outlets, Pitt has helped influence the national political agenda through access to congressional legislators. One may wonder if the plight of New Orleans would have attracted as much press (or remained in the press) without the assistance of a prominent Hollywood entertainer and his foundation.

Over the long term, however, it is difficult to know whether MIR will be effective in transforming federal disaster policy, steering political debate, and promoting sustainable development as an expedient to reducing vulnerability to disasters. Scholars of social activism have suggested that celebrity advocacy is essentially a form of entertainment-oriented mobilization that operates outside the formal policy process to seek attention, dramatize social problems, and popularize issues.[37] Different political interest groups turn to Hollywood because they believe celebrities have tremendous power to attract attention from the news media and to connect important social issues with famous people. In the end, Brad Pitt's star-powered strategy raises more questions than answers: Looking beyond the recent past and present, what will be the long-term impact of the MIR Foundation on the Ninth Ward and New Orleans? Will Pitt's celebrity advocacy affect public opinion, alter political debate, and transform social policy? What will be the indicators and measures of "recovery" and "rebuilding" for New Orleans and the Ninth Ward? Will Pitt's effort help the public view the damage and destruction caused by Hurricane Katrina as national social problems or, instead, as local issues being promoted by a celebrity? Will Brad Pitt and MIR promote new political alliances and synergies between the private and public sectors to revolutionize the ways in which government and industry respond to disasters and rebuild cities?

NOTES

1. Kevin Fox Gotham, "Marketing Mardi Gras: Commodification, Spectacle, and the Political Economy of Tourism in New Orleans," *Urban Studies* 39, no. 10 (2002): 1735–56; Kevin Fox Gotham, "Fast Spectacle: Reflections on Hurricane Katrina and the Contradictions of Spectacle," *Fast Capitalism* 2, no. 2 (2007a): 126–67; Kevin Fox Gotham, "(Re) Branding the Big Easy: Tourism Rebuilding in Post-Katrina New Orleans," *Urban Affairs Review* 42, no. 6 (2007b): 823–50; Kevin Fox Gotham, "Critical Theory and Katrina: Disaster, Spectacle, and Immanent Critique," *City: Analysis of Urban Trends, Culture, Theory, Policy, Action* 11, no. 1 (2007c): 81–99.

2. Paul Chatterton and Robert Hollands, *Urban Nightscapes: Youth Cultures, Pleasure Spaces, and Corporate Power* (New York: Routledge, 2003); Mark Gottdiener, ed., *New Forms of Consumption: Consumers, Culture, and Commodification* (Lanham, MD: Rowman and Littlefield, 2000); Mark Gottdiener, *Theming of America: Dreams, Visions and Commercial Spaces*, 2nd ed. (New York: Westview Press, 2001); George Ritzer, *Enchanting a Disenchanted World: Revolutionizing the Means of Consumption*, 3rd ed. (New York: Pine Forge Press, 2007).

3. Douglas Kellner, *Media Spectacle* (New York: Routledge, 2003).

4. Retort [Iain Boal, T. J. Clark, Joseph Matthews, and Michael Watts], *Afflicted Powers: Capital and Spectacle in a New Age of War* (London: Verso, 2005); Julian Stallabrass, "Spectacle and Terror," *New Left Review* 37 (2006): 87–106.

5. James Pontiewozik, "The Year of Charitainment," *Time*, December 19, 2005, http://www.time.com/time/magazine/article/0,9171,1142281,00.html; Chris Rojek, *Celebrity* (London: Reaktion Books, 2001); John Urry, *The Tourist Gaze*, 2nd ed. (Thousand Oaks, CA: Sage, 2002).

6. In his classic book, *The Society of the Spectacle*, Guy Debord argued that the spectacle is a system of social control, a tool of depoliticization and massification that relegates subjects passive to societal manipulation and thereby obscures the nature and effects of capitalism's power and deprivations. See Guy Debord, *The Society of the Spectacle*, trans. Donald Nicholson-Smith (New York: Zone Books, 1994). In this Debordian conception, the mobilization of spectacle works to mask and disguise the social conflicts and contradictions of capitalist development and thereby shifts attention away from pressing social inequalities and problems through the production of entertainment and consumption. On the other hand, spectacles can be highly contested and publicly controversial. In producing spectacles around controversial social issues, different political and economic actors and organized interests can involuntarily provide an arena through which people can challenge and debate major social problems. Spectacles can display inequalities and reveal submerged social problems that can, in turn, breed oppositional political agendas and movements dedicated to challenging the status quo. See Kevin Fox Gotham and Dan Krier, "From Culture

Industry to the Society of the Spectacle: Critical Theory and the Situationist International,"
Current Perspectives in Social Theory 25 (2008): 155–92; Gotham, 2007a; Gotham, 2007b.
Such a conception challenges the long-standing Debordian argument that spectacles and
spectacular imagery "seduce" and "distract" people using the machinations of advertis-
ing and commodified media culture. For examples and overviews, see Jean Baudrillard,
Simulations (New York: Semiotext(e), 1983); Jean Baudrillard, "Consumer Society," in *Jean
Baudrillard: Selected Writings*, ed. Mark Poster (Stanford, CA: Stanford University Press,
1988), 29–56; Zygmunt Bauman, *Intimations of Postmodernity* (New York: Routledge, 1992).
Far from stifling political dissent, spectacles can establish a discursive space in which people
can contest the social divisions and injustices that pervade US society.

7. Naomi Klein, *The Shock Doctrine: The Rise of Disaster Capitalism* (New York: Henry
Holt, 2008).

8. Over the course of the 20th century, celebrity activism has covered many occupa-
tions, career fields, and institutions including religion and politics. Today, celebrity activism is recognized and replicated across the globe as the "celebrity-industrial complex"
now supplies a constant supply of celebrity participation in political causes, social justice
issues, and the electoral process itself. Celebrities such as Bob Geldof, Susan Sarandon,
and Sean Penn, among others, have been involved in activist causes, including global
poverty and health, climate change, antiwar campaigns, and so on. Others such as Ronald
Reagan, Arnold Schwarzenegger, and Jesse Ventura have used their fame to move into the
electoral process itself and become politicians, thus blurring the lines between celebrity
and politics. Murray Milner notes that celebrity is a distinctive form of status in part
because it matches the vast scale of modern social organizations and the commodification of mass communications. See Murray Milner, "Celebrity Culture as a Status System,"
Hedgehog Review 7 (2005): 66–77; Maureen Orth, *The Importance of Being Famous: Behind
the Scenes of the Celebrity-Industrial Complex* (New York: Henry Holt, 2004).

9. For critical overviews, see David S. Meyer and Joshua Gamson, "The Challenge of
Cultural Elites: Celebrities and Social Movements," *Sociological Inquiry* 62, no. 2 (1995):
181–206; A. Trevor Thrall et al., "Star Power: Celebrity Advocacy and the Evolution of the
Public Sphere," *International Journal of Press/Politics* 13, no. 4 (2008): 362–85; Darrell M.
West and John Orman, *Celebrity Politics* (Upper Saddle River, NJ: Prentice Hall, 2003).
One way of testing whether celebrity activism has been growing is to examine the connection between national news media coverage, celebrity, and activism. I traced *New York
Times* coverage of celebrity activism from 1970 to 2009 and looked at how often the words
"celebrity" and "activism" appeared in stories as a rough proxy for the level of media
coverage of celebrities and activism. In the 1970s, the *New York Times* published 15 articles
mentioning celebrities and activism. This coverage increased to 20 articles during the
1980s and 53 during the 1990s. From 2000 to March 2009, the *New York Times* published
129 articles that included "activism" and "celebrity" in the text. Though this measure of
celebrity activism is rough, these figures show increased news coverage of celebrities and
activism. To be fair, it is difficult to know whether celebrity activism is really increasing
or whether news media are increasing their coverage of celebrities. It may be that rising
celebrity advocacy (and news coverage of it) reflects the growing importance of activism,
collective action, and political mobilization surrounding different social problems and
issues. As coverage of different social issues and problems increases, celebrities are more
likely to become active and therefore get more news coverage as well.

10. Rosemary J. Coombe, "The Celebrity Image and Cultural Identity: Publicity Rights and the Subaltern Politics of Gender," *Discourse* 14 (1992): 59–88; Tyler Cowen, *What Price Fame?* (Cambridge: Harvard University Press, 2000); Richard Dyer, *Heavenly Bodies: Film Stars and Society* (London: Routledge, 1986); Joshua Gamson, *Claims to Fame: Celebrity in Contemporary America* (Berkeley: University of California Press, 1994).

11. Kerry O. Ferris, "The Sociology of Celebrity," *Sociology Compass* 1, no. 1 (2007): 381.

12. As the deadliest and most destructive disaster in US history, Hurricane Katrina caused more than 1,000 deaths and catastrophic property damage along the Mississippi and Alabama coasts. Approximately 90,000 square miles of the Gulf Coast region were designated as federal disaster areas, an area almost as large as the UK. In New Orleans, Katrina flooded 80 percent of the city, including 228,000 occupied housing units (45 percent of the metropolitan total) and more than 12,000 business establishments (41 percent of the metropolitan area's total businesses). Katrina forced the evacuation of hundreds of thousands of residents from southern Louisiana and Mississippi, including nearly everyone living in New Orleans and surrounding suburbs. In the weeks after the storm roared ashore on August 29, 2005, the Federal Emergency Management Administration (FEMA) distributed aid to more than 700,000 households, including 1.5 million people directly affected by the storm. All told, 1.1 million people, 86 percent of the metropolitan population, lived in areas that were in some way affected by Katrina, through either flooding or other forms of damage. See Mark Muro et al., *New Orleans after the Storm: Lessons from the Past, a Plan for the Future* (Washington, DC: Brookings Institution Metropolitan Policy Program, October 2005).

13. Gotham, 2007a; Gotham, 2007b; Gotham, 2007c.

14. Peter Dreier, "Katrina and Power in America," *Urban Affairs Review* 41, no. 4 (2006): 528–49.

15. Meredith M. Stead, "Implementing Disaster Relief through Tax Expenditures: An Assessment of the Katrina Emergency Tax Relief Measures," *New York University Law Journal* 86, no. 6 (2006): 2158–91; Robert P. Stoker and Michael J. Rich, *Lessons and Limits: Tax Incentives and Rebuilding the Gulf Coast after Katrina* (Washington, DC: Brookings Institution Press, 2006).

16. "Make It Right," www.makeitrightnola.org.

17. Katy Reckdahl, "Pitt's First Post-Katrina Houses Near Completion," *Toronto Star*, August 30, 2008, H12.

18. "Make It Right" website.

19. Robin Pogrebin, "Brad Pitt Commissions Designs for New Orleans," *New York Times*, December 3, 2007.

20. Andrew Gumbel, "After Katrina: The House That Brad Built: Failed by Their Government, Forgotten by the Insurance Industry, the People of New Orleans' Lower 9th Ward Finally Have a Hero to Help Rebuild Their Shattered Lives," *Independent*, December 2007, 1.

21. Michelle Krupa, "Brad Pitt Busy Making It Right in the Lower 9," *Times-Picayune*, December 2, 2007, 1.

22. Lisa Ann Richey and Stefano Ponte, "Better (Red) Than Dead? Celebrities, Consumption and International Aid," *Third World Quarterly* 29, no. 4 (2008): 711–29.

23. Neal Gabler, *Life: The Movie: How Entertainment Conquered Reality* (New York: Vintage, 1999); Milner, 2005; Todd Gitlin, "The Culture of Celebrity," *Dissent* 45, no. 3 (1998): 81–83; Wendy Kaminer, "Get a Life: Illusions of Self-Invention," *Hedgehog Review* 7,

no. 1 (2005): 47–58; P. David Marshall, *Celebrity and Power: Fame in Contemporary Culture* (Minneapolis: University of Minnesota Press, 1997); Neil Postman, *Amusing Ourselves to Death* (New York: Viking, 1984); Richard Schickel, *Intimate Strangers: The Culture of Celebrity* (Garden City, NY: Doubleday, 1986).

24. See Debord, 1994.

25. "Make It Right," http://www.makeitrightnola.org/mir_SUB. php?section=pink&page=main.

26. "Make It Right" website.

27. "Make It Right" website.

28. Kevin Fox Gotham and Miriam Greenberg, "From 9/11 to 8/29: Post-Disaster Recovery and Rebuilding in New York and New Orleans," *Social Forces* 87, no. 2 (2008): 1037–62.

29. "President Outlines Hurricane Katrina Relief Efforts," August 31, 2005, http://www. whitehouse.gov/news/releases/2005/08/20050831-3.html; "President Addresses Nation, Discusses Hurricane Katrina Relief Efforts," September 5, 2005, http://www.whitehouse. gov/news/releases/2005/09/20050903.html.

30. CNN.com, "Bush: We Will Do What It Takes" (September 15, 2005), http://www. cnn.com/2005/POLITICS/09/15/bush.transcript (accessed October 20, 2010).

31. Mitch Landrieu, "Lieutenant Governor Landrieu Address to Louisiana Tourism and Promotion Association," Speech in Lake Charles, Louisiana (January 18, 2006), http://www.crt.state.la.us/DocumentArchive/tourism/2006_01_18_LTPA_SPEECH.pdf (accessed October 20, 2010).

32. Gotham and Greenberg, 2008; Chester Hartman and Gregory D. Squires, eds., *There Is No Such Thing as a Natural Disaster: Race, Class, and Hurricane Katrina* (New York: Routledge, 2006); David Brunsma, David Overfelt, and J. Steven Picou, eds., *The Sociology of Katrina: Perspectives on a Modern Catastrophe* (Lanham, MD: Rowman and Littlefield, 2007).

33. "Blanco Rips Bush on State of Union Address: Louisiana Governor Says Speech Proves Hurricanes Are 'Yesterday's News,'" Associated Press News Release (January 24, 2007), http://www.msnbc.msn.com/id/16796461.

34. Gabler, 2005.

35. Thrall et al., 2008

36. Gabler, 1999; Chris Rojek, *Celebrity* (London: Reaktion Books, 2001).

37. Gamson, 1994; Thrall et al., 2008.

—————————————————————————————————— 6 ——

Diamonds (Are from Sierra Leone)

Bling and the Promise of Consumer Citizenship

————— ROOPALI MUKHERJEE ——————————————————

People ask me how we wearing diamonds
When there's little kids in Sierra Leone
Losing arms for crying while they mining

Talib Kweli

"Bling" is the terminology used from a hip-hop song and is
being used at the forefront to speak about diamonds. So why
can't hip-hop be at the forefront of the change?

Kareem Edouard

Late in the summer of 2005, hip-hop superstar Kanye West released
his highly anticipated second album, *Late Registration*.[1] Among the songs
on the album, West unveiled the music video for the single "Diamonds (Are
from Sierra Leone)" that offers a stylized indictment of human rights atrocities fueled by the global trade in African "blood diamonds." Raising thorny
issues about child soldiers, slave labor, and the culpability of the global diamond industry within these conditions, West's video appeared in the midst
of a surge of Western interest in the "conflict diamond" trade and its humanitarian costs.

In a resolution adopted in December 2000, the United Nations defines
conflict diamonds as "diamonds that originate from areas controlled by
forces or factions opposed to legitimate and internationally recognized
governments, and [which] are used to fund military action in opposition
to those governments, or in contravention of the decisions of the Security
Council."[2] Author Greg Campbell explains that these gems, often referred
to as "blood diamonds," are mined in Central and West African war zones
including Angola, Liberia, Ivory Coast, Sierra Leone, the Democratic Repub-

lic of Congo, and the Republic of Congo.[3] Sold illegally to finance insurgencies, war efforts, and warlord activities, the trade in blood diamonds drew international attention when reports emerged that these armies routinely and forcibly conscripted African children as soldiers and slave laborers.[4] Over a decade of war in Sierra Leone, an estimated 50,000 civilians perished, 20,000 were deliberately maimed, many having their hands hacked off by rebel militias, and more than 2 million—one or more than one out of every three Sierra Leoneans—suffered displacement.[5] Nearly a decade after the civil war ended, as many as 200,000 child soldiers remain in Africa.[6]

The World Diamond Council—funded by major players in the global diamond trade including De Beers, the largest player in the industry that sources 40 percent of the world's diamonds, all from Africa—estimated that at the height of the atrocities in the late 1990s, conflict diamonds represented approximately 4 percent of the world's diamond production. Since then, the council claimed, transnational agreements like the Kimberley Process,[7] under which members agree to monitoring and certification protocols to track and authenticate gemstones from mine to retail outlet, had worked to reduce the trade in blood diamonds to less than 1 percent of the yearly $60 billion industry.

Opposing these claims, human rights organizations like Global Witness and Amnesty International have criticized the Kimberley Process as ineffective and corrupt.[8] According to Bonnie Abaunza, director of Amnesty International USA's Artists for Amnesty program, "More than $23 million in blood diamonds is currently being smuggled into the United States and international markets."[9] Similarly, United Nations investigators reported that, as late as 2006, rebels in Ivory Coast had smuggled millions of dollars worth of diamonds into the world market through Ghana and Mali, where illicit stones are mixed in with—and thus rendered untraceable among—certified diamonds.[10] Initiatives to strengthen the Kimberley Process, promulgated at the organization's annual plenary meeting in Botswana in 2006, confirmed claims that the transborder certification system was marred by loopholes, haphazard and underresourced enforcement, and a thriving smuggling trade.[11]

What Is This "Resistance" in Black Cultural Resistance?

Starting in the year 2000, a series of small- and big-budget films began to appear that focused on the global trade in diamonds, drawing attention to the ways that Western demand for these gems is implicated in wartime atrocities in Africa. Notable among these, Sierra Leonean filmmaker Sorious Samura's *Cry Freetown* (2000) traces human rights repercussions of the trade in illicit diamonds, focusing on the plight of conscripted child soldiers and displaced and maimed civilians during the eleven-year civil war in Sierra Leone. In his more recent *Blood on a Stone* (2006), Samura reveals flaws in the Kimberley Process, embarking on a journey to show how easily uncertified diamonds can be smuggled out of Sierra Leone to New York, where nine out of ten merchants were willing to buy the illicit stones.[12]

Hollywood productions in recent years, including prime-time television episodes,[13] feature documentaries produced by National Geographic and the History Channel,[14] and big-budget motion pictures like the James Bond feature *Die Another Day* (Lee Tamahori, 2002), Lions Gate Films' *Lord of War* (Andrew Niccol, 2005), and most recently, Warner Brothers' *Blood Diamond* (Edward Zwick, 2006), likewise, highlight Western complicities with repressions that mark the diamond trade.[15]

Within this milieu, African American filmmaker Kareem Edouard's powerful short, *Bling: Consequences and Repercussions* (2005), featuring hip-hop icon Chuck D as narrator, and Raquel Cepeda's ninety-minute documentary *Bling: A Planet Rock* (2006), coproduced by VH1's Rock Docs franchise and the United Nations Development Program, juxtapose the evolution of "bling" cultures of hip-hop that indulge showy spectacles of diamond jewels and accessories as markers of African American empowerment and materialist triumph against the devastating impact of the diamond trade on impoverished Africans.

A central segment of Cepeda's documentary features a traveling contingent of hip-hop artists including Paul Wall, Raekwon of the Wu-Tang Clan, and reggaeton star Tego Calderon, who, at the filmmaker's invitation, visit diamond mines in the Kono district in northeastern Sierra Leone, neighboring villages dependent on their livelihood from the diamond trade, and refugee, child soldier, and amputee camps around Freetown, the nation's capital. Moved to tears by the poverty and abjection they witness, the artists promise to use the power and influence of hip-hop to promote awareness about the diamond trade and "conscientious consumerism" among the hip-hop community.[16]

Kanye West's "Diamonds (Are from Sierra Leone)" emerged within this context together with singles by other high-profile hip-hop stars like Talib Kweli ("Going Hard," 2005), Nas ("Shine On 'Em," 2006), Lupe Fiasco ("Conflict Diamonds," 2006), and British artists Kubus and BangBang ("Conflict Diamonds," 2007) that sought to raise awareness "not just about innocent lives being taken in the Western African country of Sierra Leone, nor . . .about the way the reins of the diamond industry are held by one particular diamond digger . . . but that hip-hop is allowing itself literally to be pimped out to further the continuation of such atrocities."[17]

Hip-hop's "diamond obsession" illuminates peculiarly cruel ironies. Symbols of status within draconian hierarchies of consumer culture, diamonds retain a unique currency within the performative repertoires of American culture generally, and hip-hop in particular. One measure of the scale of this market, retail sales of diamonds have steadily increased in the US in recent years, from a little over $26 billion in 2000 to more than $33 billion in 2005. Today, Americans buy roughly half of all diamonds traded in the world.[18]

As African Americans indulge showy displays of diamond jewels to signal, and perhaps exaggerate, their cultural rank and social power, these spectacles curry favor within material cultures that have for decades excluded blacks and derided their acquisitive aspirations on racist grounds.[19] Scholars agree that African Americans, not unlike other citizens within what Lizabeth Cohen terms the "Consumers' Republic,"[20] historically projected politicized aspirations onto commodities, placing great conviction in the capacity of material possessions to make their humanity visible. Commodity consumption emerged as a symbolic means to claim and assert full personhood, and as these efforts were met with white ridicule and violent censure, black rituals of luxury consumption took shape as crucial sites for racialized battles over who would count as fully and truly "American."[21]

Within contemporary culture, the consumption of luxury goods by hip-hop artists and the emulation of these habits by the black working classes,[22] likewise, signify a pleasurable consolation prize. While the election of Barack Obama to the US presidency forces reformulations of the coordinates at which racial history and black political subjectivity meet, African Americans have for generations been forced to the outskirts of civil and political society, and, as Michael Hanchard argues, remain, for the most part, limited to vantage points ill suited to direct political engagement.[23] Thus, the fetishized currency of diamonds within black popular culture, while it feeds structures of global inequity that oppress and dehumanize Africans half a world away, simultaneously writes a late chapter in the tortuous saga of the performance of black political subjectivity through commodity consumption.

Hip-hop artists lamenting the trade in blood diamonds, like rappers moved to tears in Cepeda's documentary, offer us glimpses of the ironic confluences between hip-hop's ethical inclinations and promise as an agent of political change, on the one hand, and the ambiguities, on the other, of popular cultural forms that are thoroughly commodified and thus potentially evacuated of their political power. In each instance, hip-hop artists, leveraging branded public personae and profitable artistic repertoires, illuminate the paradoxes of popular cultural genres that are both "socially conscious" and branded commodities themselves.

Such commodified forms of political voice raise a series of questions for scholars interested in parsing the meanings and implications of contemporary social activism within neoliberal hegemonies of the late capitalist moment. Ruth Wilson Gilmore, among others, has noted that the dismantling of the liberal welfare state over the past thirty years—ushered in by the rise of corporatization and market fundamentalisms encapsulated under the aegis of neoliberalism—has produced a "shadow state" populated by privatized philanthropies within a "nonprofit industrial complex" who are left to take responsibility for persons who would otherwise be abandoned.[24]

For some, such growing reliance upon privatized resources fuels what Arundhati Roy has termed the "NGO-ization" of social activism, whose structural incentives cannot but skew toward careerist activists, milquetoast reforms, and, ultimately, the preservation of the status quo—first world hegemonies, free market capitalism, and the unregulated concentration of wealth.[25] For others, however, these shifts reveal transformations in modes of citizenship, a continuation of politics by other means. Here, as "civic citizens" are refashioned ever more forcefully into "consumer-citizens," traditional civic responsibilities—contributing to the general good of the nation as well as prodding government to protect the rights, safety, and fair treatment of citizens—are increasingly expressed and actualized through circuits of commodity consumption and exchange.[26]

Thus, against larger concerns about the "end of politics," anxieties based on a dim view of the consequences of shifts marking how we "do" citizenship at the present moment, this essay claims centrally that activist efforts by hip-hop artists against blood diamonds, while they may indeed be marred by ethical contingencies and political complicities, offer a useful case to unpack the terms of broad shifts reshaping modes of cultural resistance at the current moment. Urging us against sweeping dismissals of commodified modes of social activism, these efforts are neither easily nor always written off as simply inauthentic or opportunistic. Instead, they reveal the ironic promise of political action borne out of neoliberalism itself. Highlighting the lurking constancy of contradiction within hegemonic discourses, these instances of activism allow us to trace how neoliberal citizens actualize their political subjectivities, not through rejections of commodity culture but, rather, from *within* circuits of consumption and exchange.

Exemplifying these trends, Kanye West's decision to take a public stand on issues raised by the global trade in diamonds is not uncharacteristic of the artist's emerging oeuvre. Recognized by music critics as operating "far outside rap's usual strictures . . . the only mainstream rapper willing to tackle politics"[27] and "a brilliant social commentator unafraid to tackle [sensitive] subjects,"[28] West's music has lamented the blunting of black political militancy by drug use ("Crack Music," 2005), the impact of class inequities on US health care ("Roses," 2005), and the scourge of AIDS, which West claims he "knows the government administered" within black communities ("Heard 'Em Say," 2005). In perhaps the most widely viewed of his public outbursts, West's political voice found an attentive audience when the artist stepped off script during an appearance on "A Concert for Hurricane Relief," NBC's nationally televised benefit for victims of Katrina in September 2005, to denounce the president's appallingly feeble relief efforts, saying, "George Bush doesn't care about black people."[29]

Likewise, casting a critical eye inward upon black culture, West has equated "drug dealing and hip-hop as bootstrap ghetto enterprises: 'Now the former slaves trade hooks for Grammys / This dark diction has become America's addiction'" ("Crack Music," 2005),[30] and bemoaned "materialism in black culture: 'Couldn't afford a car / So she named her daughter Alexus'" ("All Falls Down," 2004).[31] And urging political solidarity between black and gay struggles for civil rights, the artist spurred tabloid speculation about his own sexuality after he lashed out at the scourge of homophobia within hip-hop culture in an August 2005 appearance on the MTV special "All Eyes on Kanye West."

Moreover, as is nearly de rigueur among front liners in hip-hop today, West leads a number of philanthropic initiatives. The Kanye West Foundation, renamed the Dr. Donda West Foundation in 2008 after the untimely death of his mother, for instance, serves as an educational nonprofit that works to decrease school dropout rates among black and Latino youth.[32] West is also a regular performer at fundraisers and benefit concerts, including "Live 8" in July 2005[33] and "Live Earth" in July 2007.[34] West also serves as celebrity sponsor for grassroots organizations like the Millions More Movement and 100 Black Men of America and has worked in recent years to assist young Iraq War veterans struggling through debt and post-traumatic stress disorders.[35] His charitable contributions—in excess of $450,000 since 2003— ranked him fifth among the top ten black celebrity philanthropists of 2007.[36]

By Left progressive standards that imagine "a complete shift in the pattern of ownership, the expansion of the rights of labor, and the democratization of the relations of production within U.S. society,"[37] West's political voice signifies, at best, a modest intervention. Part of the general trend toward privatized safety nets necessitated by the withering of the welfare state, the artist exemplifies the limits of political action in the neoliberal era. However, complicating our view of what it means to "resist" at the present moment, political critiques of the kind that West offers are not reducible to ideological complicity alone. Instead, they articulate the civic potential—at once racially defined and politically accountable—that lurks *within* commercialized black public discourses. Offering glimpses of how race is implicated within strategies of consumer citizenship, these efforts illuminate the ironic promise of political action when hip-hop stars manage to effect social change despite— or, perhaps, as a consequence of—their embeddedness within hypercommoditized cultures of bling. Key for our purposes here, these critiques force recalibrations of what counts as "politics," illuminating the promise of political reappropriations of consumerism and enterprise, unpacking how contemporary modes of consumer citizenship manage to reinvent eviscerating apparatuses of care and community.

In the remainder of this chapter, I offer an interpretive reading of the politics and aesthetics of West's "Diamonds (Are from Sierra Leone)" and the music video for the single[38] to parse the terms of a racial politics borne out of these contradictions of the neoliberal moment. In other words, this analysis is intended to underscore, above all, the commonplace of contradiction, the messy push and pull of autonomy and subjugation, when political work is embedded within, and thus defined by, circuits of commodity consumption and exchange.

The Case of the Diamond Ditty
The Global South Comes North

Directed by famed hip-hop video artist Hype Williams, the music video for "Diamonds," shot entirely in black-and-white, opens with a tracking shot of a dimly lit mineshaft. Moving slowly up roughly laid skip rails, the camera catches sweaty children bent over, digging in the heat of serpentine drifts underground. Staring bleakly into the camera, the children wear faces of lost innocence as an armed overseer barks orders at them. Primitive pickaxes, lamps, and a fraying lithograph of a gas-masked rescuer who arrives too late to save a fallen miner suggest crude and perilous working conditions. A male voice-over intones in an African accent:

We work in the diamond rivers from sunrise to sunset. Under the watchful eyes of soldiers, everyday we fear for our lives. Some of us were enslaved by rebels and forced to kill our own families for diamonds. We are the children of the blood diamonds.

Recirculating familiar signifiers of African suffering—emaciated children ravaged by circumstance, hapless victims of cruelty and injustice, "Diamonds" begins by regurgitating clichéd tropes of faraway horrors, muddled tragedies that blight distant lands, contrasting "their" agony against "our" fortunes. Reminiscent of infomercials for charities, popular during the 1980s and 1990s, that featured Western celebrity spokespersons surrounded by abject brown or black children urging viewers to "sponsor a child for as little as thirty cents a day," "Diamonds" replays familiar cadences of African misery and American magnanimity, isolating the global South as unyielding scene of human tragedy.

Unlike the "sponsor-a-child" infomercials, however, "Diamonds" opens with the caption "Little is known of Sierra Leone / And how it connects to the diamonds we own." Thus, from its start, the video implicates Western demand for African gems within circumstances of hyperexploitation that mark the global trade in diamonds. Refusing its audience the comfort of Western innocence, "Diamonds" suggests instead that the fetishized market in diamonds in the US may be a crucial factor enabling the brutalization of African children. Against the grain of established tropes that construct global economic inequities as "organic" or "natural," West's video hints at vested politico-economic interests that rely upon neocolonial conditions of global exploitation and injustice, conditions that necessitate the systemic impoverishment of the global South to guarantee the enrichment of the North.

Western culpability within these inequities is literally wrought in blood in one scene where a young white couple, watched stonily by one of the African children, convulses in horror as a diamond engagement ring oozes blood after the woman has accepted the jewel and the proposal it symbolizes. Puncturing the magical aura of the diamond engagement ring—which, as De Beers has constructed it, best serves its symbolic function when a man spends the equivalent of three monthly paychecks on it—the scene casts a Macbethian curse on consumptive tokens of romantic love and commitment. The marriage proposal and the engagement ring that vouches for its sincerity, entrenched rituals of heteronormative culture, are thus confronted by the bloody price they exact from faraway workers.

Likewise, scenes of patrician privilege that feature white patrons at an upscale diamond boutique are disrupted as the largest, and presumably most expensive, of the store's gems is held out for perusal by the skinny dark arm of an unseen African child. As one of the attending suit-clad salesmen leans in to take the jewel from the child's fingers, he wears a look of caution and embarrassment, anxious about the revelation that the child's presence threatens. A range of crimes are implicated throughout: certainly, the barbarous rampages of African rebels and impotence of African state authorities but, equally, the greedy collusions of Western traders and willed innocence of Western consumers.

"Diamonds," thus, repeatedly and jarringly inserts hyperexploited African workers within rituals and spaces of privileged Western consumerism. Connecting conspicuous consumption in the global North with exploitative relations of production in the global South, the video centrally disturbs the willed innocence of northern privilege as well as the mythic naturalization of southern poverty. West's audience who, one assumes, knows little of Sierra Leone, is thus forced to consider its role, both active and enabling, within vile secrets of circuits of global trade and neocolonialism.

Global Brotherhoods

As West originally wrote it,[39] "Diamonds" was an ode to Roc-a-fella, the record label owned by hip-hop mogul Shawn "Jay-Z" Carter that produces West's music, and which uses as its logo the image and hand sign of "The Roc," a kite-shaped diamond formed by joining both hands at the tips of the thumbs and index fingers. In the original version, West raps: "When I speak of diamonds in this song / It ain't about the ones that be glowin' / I'm talkin' bout Roc-a-Fella my home." The single, moreover, prominently samples the Shirley Bassey theme "Diamonds Are Forever" created in 1971 for the James Bond movie of the same name, in which diamonds are better than men or love because they can be counted on to "never lie," to "never leave in the night."[40] Thus, in its first writing, "Diamonds" began as a call to brotherhood among Roc-a-fella artists, suggesting that, like diamonds, Roc-a-fella is "forever," a family that will never lie, never leave you in the night.

As a number of scholars writing about black political culture have noted in recent years, the post–civil rights era is marked by a return to masculinist brotherhoods that marked black cultural nationalisms of the 1970s but now fuse in paradoxical ways with stances of a hypercommoditized blackness that celebrate entrepreneurial individualism, corporate capitalism, and materialist pleasure.[41] Revealing what Greg Tate has termed the "quantum paradox" of hip-hop, internal tensions that enable and accommodate a "range of black ideologies from the most anti-white to the most pro-capitalist without ever having to account for the contradiction,"[42] "Diamonds" emerges in step with political celebrations of what Todd Boyd calls the "new H.N.I.C. (Head Negroes In Charge)"[43] and of the hip-hop brotherhoods they craft, enraced and gendered solidarities that serve as crucibles for political consciousness.

"Diamonds" offers a keen example of the conscientizing work of such brotherhoods. In an interview for *MTV News*, West explains that while he was recording the single, he heard about conflict diamonds and "kids getting killed [and] amputated in West Africa." The artist explained:

> Mark Romanek, the director who [designed the video for] Jay's *99 Problems*, and Q-Tip [lead rapper in the iconic 1990s hip-hop group A Tribe Called Quest] both brought up blood diamonds. They said, "That's what I think about when I hear diamonds. I think about kids getting killed, getting amputated in West Africa." And Q-Tip's like, "Sierra Leone," and I'm like, "Where?" And I remember him spelling it out for me and me looking on the Internet and finding out more.[44]

We find a lucid moment of political conscience emerging from hip-hop brotherhoods here, fraternities that work as knowledge networks for activist strategies that, in this case, underscore the urgency of cementing a transcontinental bond of "brothers-in-arms" across the global North and South.

At one point in the video, as West calls out his allegiance to his Roc-a-fella brotherhood by gesturing the hand sign of "The Roc," a child worker follows, half a world away, moving her hands from her panning basket in shoulder-deep waters to furtively form the Roc-a-fella logo with her fingers. As coded signs of membership within the Roc-a-fella brotherhood serve metaphorically to construct belonging within the fraternity of racial globality,[45] the child rejects one diamond for another, casting off her subjugation for the promise of solidarity.

In several scenes, we see West and the African children working together to disrupt the civility and decorum of consumptive rituals in the West. In the final rescue sequence, for example, as West drives a vintage Gullwing Mercedes through the window of a diamond boutique, disrupting an ongoing transaction inside, the children help his efforts along, directing him from the backseat and helping him up to his feet after the impact of the crash. As West and the freed children scramble away from the scene, the familial bond they enact underscores the promissory power of global racial solidarities as alliances of mutual advantage.

Reminiscent of calls for pan-African unity articulated by cultural nationalists from Marcus Garvey to Malcolm X, the video claims common cause for black Americans with Africans struggling against injustice and oppression. While they may not be enacted everywhere in the same way, these conditions nevertheless brutalize and dehumanize, providing openings for racial solidarities even if they are always "coalitional, contingent, and performative."[46] In this light, "Diamonds" serves equally as a cautionary tale against black American collusion with globalized neocolonialisms. Demanding Western, and particularly black American, political solidarity against practices of transnational trade that exploit "brothers" and "sisters" in the global South, the video articulates a racial critique of African American cultural habits of internalized colonization and acquiescence. Black American solidarities with African diamond workers, thus, emerge not only as a way to "save" hyperexploited African workers but also as a means to shake off African American compliance with hegemonic hierarchies of Western material cultures and, simultaneously, to resuscitate the political force of hip-hop.

Between Civic Citizens and Consumer Citizens

Substantiating the ways in which modes of consumer citizenship may be reshaping what Paul Gilroy calls "hetero-ethnic and transnational resistance movements,"[47] "Diamonds" enacts the terms of broad transformations in modes of citizenship and cultural resistance. Defined by, and thus contained within, circuits of commodity exchange, texts like "Diamonds" complicate— and trouble—post–civil rights claims about the "end of black politics," shifts that entail the evisceration of black political leadership, the collapse of black political subjectivities, and the "selling out" of black political conscience.[48]

At the same time, texts like "Diamonds" pointedly reaffirm the marginality of grassroots politics premised on Marcusian "absolute refusal,"[49] the obscurity, in other words, of a subaltern politics that stands outside and apart from institutions of neoliberal power. Thus, cultural interventions of the sort that "Diamonds" epitomizes reveal the muddled force and consequence of "commodity activism" as it attempts to reappropriate neoliberal consumerism and entrepreneurialism to activist ends.

The video offers several moments of provocation exemplifying these contradictions. For one, West's attack on the diamond industry may be surprising given that the star is an icon within the giddy spectacles of bling culture.[50] If, like others within the world of hip-hop, West's engagement with the brand aesthetics of bling appears to contradict his political stand against blood diamonds, it may be significant that the star learned about the horrors of the trade within the cultural milieu of bling, a milieu often written off as narcissistic and pathological. Thus, "Diamonds" offers a keen example of cultural resistance— replete with contradiction and paradox—that emerges from *within* neoliberal hegemonies of entrepreneurial individualism and materialist pleasure.

Likewise, the final rescue in "Diamonds" is orchestrated by converting a vintage luxury automobile, an iconic symbol of status within the emulative cultures of conspicuous consumption, into a weapon of militant disruption, ramming it headfirst into the genteel civility of the diamond boutique. Striking one mode of consumerism using totems of another, the scene is laden with contradiction: the anticapitalist protest that finds its resistive voice through iconic consumerism. These aesthetic choices may indeed point to contemporary infirmities within black political consciousness for they privilege individualized heroism over grassroots action, and consumerist militancy over structural change. But they point equally to openings, ever present within hegemonic discourses, reminding us that civic politics in the neoliberal era, far from being vitiated by them, may be enabled by, and nurtured within, modes of consumer citizenship.

Over the course of their endeavors, moreover, while the children literally smash Western capitalism and, with guile and cunning, manage to scurry away victorious, West moves effortlessly from aiding the militant strike to enacting a hypercommoditized blackness characteristic of the new H.N.I.C. His performance makes a pointed refusal to choose between "race man" and "corporate mogul," between "political ally" and "the man" himself. Throughout, West performs the persona of the iconic hip-hop mogul, a category that includes highly successful black entrepreneurs like Shawn "Jay-Z" Carter, Sean "P. Diddy" Combs, and Russell Simmons, with flamboyance and careful orchestration. As markers of long-sought civil rights dreams of black control over black wealth, the ascension of hip-hop moguls to corporate boardrooms and their unprecedented entrepreneurial autonomy speak in multiple tongues. On the one hand, as Christopher Holmes Smith has argued, the hip-hop mogul serves as a quintessentially neoliberal icon, a visual signifier of the "good life" who reinforces the idea that consumerism and personal enrichment are viable and sufficient modes of black political subjectivity.[51] On the other hand, as West's political choices in "Diamonds" and elsewhere suggest, the hip-hop mogul may also serve subversive ends, opening hegemonic standards of neoliberal entrepreneurialism to reappropriation and political repossession. Thus, as he appears in "Diamonds," West functions as an agitator, a galvanizer of racial sentiment who is also, as it turns out, fully invested with the neoliberal credibility of the hip-hop mogul. Here again, giddy icons of consumer and entrepreneurial culture are found, in vexed contradiction, as resistive voices for anticolonial and anticapitalist protest.

Finally, as the video ends, it closes with the caption "Please purchase conflict-free diamonds." Urging individualized action as a redemptive response to global suffering, "Diamonds" is thus, in one sense, a typical text within recent media attention on blood diamonds, ultimately advocating little beyond "conscientious consumerism."[52] So doing, "Diamonds" champions political strategies that bear little in common with political activists across the world who are engaged in anticapitalist struggles for solidarity against the labor practices of multinational corporations, unfair international trade practices across the global North and South, and World Bank and IMF structural reforms that are instrumental in enabling the conditions for human rights atrocities in impoverished developing nations.

Thus, even as it traces its political genealogy to the civil unrest of the sixties that urged African Americans to politicize their consumptive choices by withdrawing support from businesses that dehumanized black consumers and workers, West's intervention is nevertheless wholly neoliberal. Defined by circuits of commodity consumption and enterprise, it refuses a subaltern politics outside and apart from institutions of neoliberal power.

This entrenchment, as is evidenced by this analysis, illuminates both the limits and the promise of civic action in the neoliberal era. For even as modes of consumer citizenship remain stymied by their limitations and myopias, they nevertheless manage to disrupt, attack, and stir. The willed innocence of Western habits of consumerism, the hypocritical decorum of rituals of Western materialism, the galvanizing promise of global racial alliance, and the call to politicize material culture—to buy and boycott with a conscience—each is deployed to critical effect in West's work. More than evidence for the failings of black political action in the neoliberal moment, each is an instance of the spaces that neoliberalism leaves open, spaces within which reside opportunities, however impoverished they may appear, to craft social activism within the terms of neoliberal consumer citizenship.

NOTES

1. A follow-up to his debut release, *The College Dropout*, and second in a three-part series, *Late Registration* spurred both cheers and jeers. Some hailed the album as "an undeniable triumph," a "more ambitious, superbly crafted follow-up," and "the year's most accomplished rap album." See Rob Sheffield, "Kanye West: Late Registration," *Rolling Stone*, August 25, 2005, http://www.rollingstone.com/artists/kanyewest/albums/

album/7569017/review/7583389/late_registration; Robert Hilburn, "West Connects with Heart and Sophistication," *Los Angeles Times*, August 28, 2005, E36; Sean Fennessey, "Kanye West: Late Registration," *Pitchfork*, August 28, 2005, http://pitchfork.com/reviews/albums/8768-late-registration/. Others grumbled, however, that the album was "as ornate and bloated as West's ego," and West himself "a few credits short of graduating to the next level." See Jon Caramanica, "Kanye West, 'Late Registration,'" *Spin*, August 30, 2005, http://www.spin.com/reviews/kanye-west-late-registration-roc-felladef-jam; Jozen Cummings, "Kanye West: Late Registration," *Pop Matters*, August 30, 2005, http://www.popmatters.com/music/reviews/w/westkanye-lateregistration2.shtml.

Naysayers notwithstanding, the album rose to the top of the Billboard 200 chart within weeks of its release and earned eight Grammy nominations, including the prestigious Album of the Year award. At the Grammy ceremonies on February 8, 2006, West won three awards—Best Rap Album for *Late Registration*, Best Rap Song for the single "Diamonds (Are from Sierra Leone)," and Best Rap Solo Performance for "Gold Digger," both featured on the album. By April 2006, *Late Registration* had sold 3 million copies worldwide (http://www.billboard.com/bbcom/index.jsp).

2. UN General Assembly, Conflict Diamonds: Resolution A/RES/55/56, December 1, 2000, http://www.un.org/peace/africa/Diamond.html; United Nations, March 21, 2001, "Conflict Diamonds" (New York: United Nations Department of Public Information, March 21, 2001).

3. Greg Campbell, *Blood Diamonds: Tracing the Deadly Path of the World's Most Precious Gems* (Boulder, CO: Westview Press, 2002). Africa produces an estimated 65 percent of the world's diamonds. See Mireya Navarro, "Diamonds Are for Never?" *New York Times*, December 14, 2006, G1.

4. Janine Roberts, *Glitter and Greed: The Secret World of the Diamond Cartel* (New York: Disinformation Company, 2007); Tom Zoellner, *The Heartless Stone: A Journey through the World of Diamonds, Deceit, and Desire* (New York: Picador, 2006).

5. Christopher Wyrod, "Sierra Leone: A Vote for Better Governance," *Journal of Democracy* 19, no. 1 (2008): 70–83.

6. Elizabeth Snead, "Crystallizing Opinion," *Los Angeles Times*, October 10, 2006, E1. By the mid-2000s, a number of novels and nonfiction exposés had been published for Western audiences that narrated wrenching tales of African child soldiers—boys, and sometimes girls, orphaned in conflict or stolen by rebel militias from their families and drugged, brutalized, and humiliated into committing horrific acts of violence against civilians. Uzodinma Iweala's acclaimed *Beasts of No Nation* (New York: HarperCollins, 2005) and Ahmadou Kourouma's *Allah Is Not Obliged*, trans. Frank Wynne (New York: First Anchor Press, 2007, originally published Paris: Editions de Seuil, 2000) appeared alongside memoirs by child soldiers themselves. Notable among the latter are China Keitetsi's *Child Soldier* (Johannesberg: Jacada Media, 2005), the tale of a Ugandan girl soldier conscripted into the rebel forces of the National Resistance Army during in the 1970s, Dave Eggers's *What Is the What* (San Francisco: McSweeney's, 2006), a nonfiction novel written in collaboration with Valentino Achak Deng, one of the so-called lost boys of Sudan, and Sierra Leonean Ishmael Beah's *A Long Way Gone* (New York: Sarah Crichton Books, 2007), sold in the US by the coffee mega-retailer Starbucks, which organized a national reading tour for the author and marketed the book as the introductory feature for its book club. Along similar lines, *God Grew Tired of Us: The Lost Boys of Sudan* (Chris-

topher Quinn and Tommy Walker, 2006), a documentary featuring screen stars Brad Pitt as executive producer and Nicole Kidman as narrator, describes the life stories of Ishmael Beah, Achak Deng, and others among the "lost boys." Recalling Luis Mandoki's *Innocent Voices* (2004), a film that describes the plight of child soldiers during the civil war in El Salvador, *God Grew Tired* won the Grand Jury and Audience awards for Best Documentary at the Sundance Film Festival in 2006. See Jason Cowley, "Why We Have Fallen for Africa's Lost Boys," *Observer*, April 29, 2007, 4; Sister Rose Pacatte, "The Roots of Bling: 'Blood Diamond' and 'Blood on a Stone,'" *The Tidings*, December 15, 2006 http://www.the-tidings.com/2006/1215/blood_text.htm.

7. Diamond industry executives, concerned about the economic impact of negative public perceptions, joined forces with national governments and the United Nations in 2003 to require certification and monitoring of global diamond production and trade. Introduced by United Nations Resolution 55/56, the Kimberley Process Certification Scheme requires all participating nations to certify that any diamond originating from within its borders does not finance a rebel group or other entity seeking to overthrow a UN-recognized government, that every diamond export be accompanied by a Kimberley Process certificate, and that no diamond is imported from, or exported to, a nonmember of the scheme. This three-step plan serves to ensure a chain of countries that deal exclusively with nonconflict diamonds. Seventy-one nations are signatories to the Kimberley Process, although the agreement functions as a "soft law," that is, it is not legally binding on the participating countries. See Barbara Harlow, "The 'Kimberley Process': Literary Gems, Civil Wars, and Historical Resources," *CR: The New Centennial Review* 3 (2003): 219–40; http://www.kimberleyprocess.com/. The agreement remains marred by governments and the industry failing repeatedly to act against gross violations. See Daniel Howden, "Exclusive: The Return of Blood Diamonds," *Independent*, June 25, 2009, http://news.independentminds.livejournal.com/323411o.html.

8. Austin Merrill, "Jewel of Denial: Will Hollywood's Latest Cause Put African Diamonds on Ice?" *RadarOnline*, December, 2006, http://www.radaronline.com/features/2006/12/jewel_of_denial_1-print.html; Snead, 2006.

9. Scott Bowles, "'Blood Diamond' in the Rough," *USA Today*, December 4, 2006, 1D.

10. Merrill, 2006; Robinson, 2006.

11. Robinson, 2006; Vivienne Walt, "Diamonds Aren't Forever," *Fortune*, December 7, 2006, http://money.cnn.com.magazines/fortune/fortune_archive/2006/12/11/83955442/?postversion=2006112806.

12. Pacatte, 2006.

13. These include an episode of the prime-time NBC crime drama *Law & Order* entitled "Soldier of Fortune" (Richard Dobbs, 2001).

14. These include National Geographic's *Diamonds of War: Africa's Blood Diamonds* (2003) and the History Channel's *Blood Diamonds* (2007).

15. The World Diamond Council reportedly spent $15 million in a campaign designed by the public relations film Sitrick and Company to counter the message of the film *Blood Diamonds*. Full-page newspaper advertisements detailed measures diamond producers have taken to end the flow of conflict diamonds, and retailers in the US were encouraged to educate themselves about the issue. An industry website, www.diamondfacts.org, was set up to provide detail on the value of diamond mining for national economies in Africa showcasing local schools, roads, and clean water facilities funded by profits from

the trade. The council also urged director Edward Zwick to acknowledge the success of the Kimberley Process in the script or end credits, which he declined to do. Nikki Finke, "Blood from Stones," *LA Weekly*, November 2, 2006 http://www.laweekly.com/2006-11-02/news/blood-from-stones/; Simon Robinson, "Hollywood Plays Rough with Diamonds," *Time*, November 20, 2006, http://www.time.com/time/magazine/article/0,9171,1561151,00.html; Snead, 2006, E1; T. L. Stanley, "Gem Sellers Launch Blitz against 'Blood Diamond,'" *Advertising Age* 77, no. 50 (2006): 12. Closer to the film's release date, journalist Nikki Finke reported what some termed a "smear campaign" by the World Diamond Council against the film, which included fabricated stories about Warner Brothers having reneged on a promise to provide prosthetic limbs to orphaned African teenage and child amputees who appeared as extras in the film.

16. Angus Batey, "The Death of Bling," *Times,* January 20, 2007, 21; "Film Explores Connection between Hip-Hop, 'Blood Diamonds,'" *US Fed News*, June 13, 2007; "Hip-Hop Artists Examine Diamond Trade in Sierra Leone for Upcoming VH1 Rock Doc.," *PR NewsWire US*, January 11, 2007.

17. Melanie J. Cornish, "The New-Age Minstrel (interview with Kareem Edouard)," *NobodySmiling.com*, 2008, http://www.nobodysmiling.com/hiphop/interview/85516.php.

18. Valli Herman, "Diamonds Have More Best Friends Than Ever," *Los Angeles Times*, December 8, 2006, E18; Parija A. Kavilanz, "Jewelers Sweat a 'Blood Diamond' Holiday," *CNNMoney.com*, September 11, 2006; Navarro, 2006.

19. Jason Chambers, "Equal in Every Way: African Americans, Consumption and Materialism from Reconstruction to the Civil Rights Movement," *Advertising and Society Review* 7, no. 1 (2006); Elizabeth Chin, *Purchasing Power: Black Kids and American Consumer Culture* (Minneapolis: University of Minnesota Press, 2001); Lawrence B. Glickman, "Introduction: Born to Shop? Consumer History and American History," in *Consumer Society in American History: A Reader*, ed. Lawrence B. Glickman (Ithaca: Cornell University Press, 1999), 1–14; Grace Elizabeth Hale, *Making Whiteness: The Culture of Segregation in the South, 1890–1940* (New York: Vintage, 1999); Robert E. Weems Jr., *Desegregating the Dollar: African American Consumerism in the Twentieth Century* (New York: NYU Press, 1998); Bobby M. Wilson, "Race in Commodity Exchange and Consumption: Separate but Equal," *Annals of the Association of American Geographers* 95, no. 3 (2005): 587–606.

20. Lizabeth Cohen, *A Consumers' Republic: The Politics of Mass Consumption in Postwar America* (New York: Knopf, 2003).

21. Chambers, 2006; Paul R. Mullins, *Race and Affluence: An Archaeology of African America and Consumer Culture* (New York: Kluwer Academic/Plenum, 1999), 189.

22. Consumer statistics and scholarly analyses alike reveal considerable effort on the part of working-class black youth to conspicuously consume in ways that attempt to emulate the glitzy performative buying power of black popular cultural icons. National statistics suggest that black teens between the ages of twelve and nineteen spend more on clothing, fine jewelry, computer software, and athletic footwear relative to such patterns among all other teenagers. See*African American Market in the U.S.* (New York: Packaged Facts, 2008); Robert Brown and Ruth Washton, *The U.S. African-American Market*, 5th ed (New York: Packaged Facts, 2004); Magazine Publishers of America, *African American/ Black Market Profile* (New York: Magazine Publishers of America Information Center, 2008). Such buying, Elizabeth Chin explains, offers black youth a means to refute cultural reproaches that stem from their class and race disadvantages and, as Jason Chambers

shows, is traced to long-established preferences among African Americans for brand-name products and chain stores, preferences that took shape historically as coping strategies to assure some measure of quality in products and customer service in the face of discriminatory treatment at the hands of white retailers. See Chambers, 2006; Chin, 2001.

23. Michael Hanchard, "Cultural Politics and Black Public Intellectuals," *Social Text* 13, no. 3 (1996): 95.

24. Nicole P. Marwell, "Privatizing the Welfare State: Nonprofit Community-Based Organizations as Political Actors," *American Sociological Review* 69, no. 2 (2004): 265–91; Jiannbin Lee Shiao, *Identifying Talent, Institutionalizing Diversity: Race and Philanthropy in Post–Civil Rights America* (Durham, NC: Duke University Press, 2005); Ruth Wilson Gilmore, "In the Shadow of the Shadow State," in *The Revolution Will Not Be Funded: Beyond the Non-profit Industrial Complex*, ed. INCITE! Women of Color Against Violence (Boston: South End Press, 2007), 41–52.

25. Christine E. Ahn, "Democratizing American Philanthropy," in *The Revolution Will Not Be Funded: Beyond the Non-profit Industrial Complex*, ed. INCITE! Women of Color Against Violence (Boston: South End Press, 2007), 63–76; Alejandro Bendaña, "NGOs and Social Movements: A North/South Divide?" Civil Society and Social Movements Programme (paper no. 22, June 2006), United Nations Research Institute for Social Development; Jeanine Plant, "Forget the Foundations," *In These Times*, July 4, 2007, http://www.inthesetimes.com/article/3229/forget_the_foundations/; Arundhati Roy, "Public Power in the Age of Empire" (speech presented at the American Sociological Association, San Francisco, August 16, 2004, http://www.democracynow.org/2004/8/23/public_power_in_the_age_of_empire/.

26. Cohen, 2003; Anne M. Cronin, *Advertising and Consumer Citizenship: Gender, Images and Rights* (London: Routledge, 2000); Néstor García Canclini, *Consumers and Citizens: Globalization and Multicultural Conflicts*, trans. George Yúdice (Minneapolis: University of Minnesota Press, 2001); George Yúdice, "The Vicissitudes of Civil Society," *Social Text* 14, no. 4 (1995): 1–25.

27. Alexis Petridis, "Where Egos Dare," *Guardian*, August 19, 2005, 17.

28. Kitty Empire, "Review: Releases: West, Life—with a Difference," *Observer*, February 15, 2004, 14.

29. Video of West's entire speech may be found at "George Bush Doesn't Care about Black People," September 5, 2005, www.youtube.com.

30. Jon Pareles, "A Producer in Another Star Turn," *New York Times*, August 29, 2005, E4.

31. Empire, 2004, 14.

32. http://www.drdondawestfoundation.org/the_foundation.html.

33. Organized in July 2005, Live 8 convened a series of worldwide concerts to pressure world leaders to "make poverty history." The stated aims of the concert included demands for dropping the debt of the world's poorest nations, increasing and improving aid, and negotiating fair-trade rules in the interest of poorer countries.

34. Live Earth, similarly, organized a series of concurrent worldwide concerts to initiate a three-year campaign to combat climate change.

35. "Kanye West and 'Choose or Lose' Give Young Veterans a Surprise 'Homecoming,'" *MTV News*, July 21, 2008, http://www.mtv.com/news/articles/1591258/20080721/west_kanye.jhtml.

36. www.BlackGivesBack.com.

37. Manning Marable, "History and Black Consciousness: The Political Culture of Black America," *Monthly Review: An Independent Socialist Magazine* 47, no. 3 (1995): 84.

38. The music video that this chapter focuses on is properly read among a larger context of political or "message" hip-hop and activist-themed music videos that has emanated from hip-hop since its inception. Gil Scott-Heron's *The Revolution Will Not Be Televised* (1974), Grandmaster Flash and the Fabulous Five's *The Message* (1982), N.W.A's *Fuck tha Police* (1988), Public Enemy's *Fight the Power* (1995), Immortal Technique's *Voices of the Voiceless* (2009), and Talib Kwali's *Papers, Please* (2010) each takes its charge as "the CNN of the street," combining social commentary and ghetto testimony, gritty reality as well as playful fantasy. A considerable scholarly literature is available on the political valences of hip-hop, including, notably, Yvonne Bynoe, *Stand and Deliver: Political Activism, Leadership and Hip Hop Culture* (Berkeley: Soft Skull Press, 2004); Murray Forman and Mark Anthony Neal, eds., *That's the Joint: The Hip-Hop Studies Reader* (New York: Routledge, 2004); Robin D. G. Kelley, *Yo' Mama's Disfunktional: Fighting the Culture Wars in Urban America* (Boston: Beacon Press, 1997); Yusuf Nuruddin and Victor Wallis, eds., "Special Issue: Hip Hop, Race, and Cultural Politics," *Socialism and Democracy* 18, no. 2 (2004); and Trisha Rose, *Black Noise: Rap Music and Black Culture in Contemporary America* (Hanover, NH: Wesleyan University Press of New England, 1994).

39. Visual images used in music videos do not always reflect the lyrical content of singles on which they may be based. Indeed, the narratives and aesthetics of music videos may deviate substantially from the songs on which they are based, producing visual representations that may be unrelated to the lyrics or musical affect of the song. Kanye West's music video for "Diamonds" is a case in point, and, as this analysis shows, shifts across lyrical narratives and video images can sometimes offer glimpses of shifting political strategies as artists take a single from the recording studio to the soundstage.

40. In the 1971 original, diamonds are forever because even "when love's gone, they'll luster on" (lyrics by Don Black, music by John Barry). Echoing themes from Broadway songwriter Jule Styne's iconic "Diamonds Are a Girl's Best Friend," famously performed by Marilyn Monroe in *Gentlemen Prefer Blondes* (Howard Hawks, 1953), Bassey's 1971 classic enjoys a place of prominence among pop feminist anthems that celebrate female sisterhoods as networks of counterknowledges about strategies for independence from patriarchal love as a means to female empowerment, what in more recent times has been termed "girl or pussy power." Thus, perhaps inadvertently, "Diamonds" echoes themes of tongue-in-cheek defiance from an earlier era, underscoring the urgency of subaltern solidarities for economic emancipation, and the abiding exigency of guile and cunning as preferred "weapons of the weak" (James C. Scott, *Weapons of the Weak: Everyday Forms of Peasant Resistance* (New Haven: Yale University Press, 1985).

41. Darryl Dickson-Carr, *The Columbia Guide to Contemporary African American Fiction* (New York: Columbia University Press, 2005); Nelson George, *Post-soul Nation: The Explosive, Contradictory, Triumphant, and Tragic 1980s as Experienced by African Americans (Previously Known as Blacks and Before That Negroes)* (New York: Viking, 2004); Eddie S.Glaude Jr., *In a Shade of Blue: Pragmatism and the Politics of Black America* (Chicago: University of Chicago Press, 2007); Bambi Haggins, *Laughing Mad: The Black Comic Persona in Post-soul America* (New Brunswick, NJ: Rutgers University Press, 2007); Keith M.

Salma Hayek's Celebrity Activism

Constructing Race, Ethnicity, and Gender as Mainstream Global Commodities

ISABEL MOLINA-GUZMÁN

> They hadn't noticed there were 38 million Latinos in the U.S., an important market. They were quite stupid businesswise.
>
> Salma Hayek, 2007

Mexican-born telenovela star Salma Hayek first crossed the cinematic border between Mexico and the US in 1995 when she appeared in her first Hollywood film as a gunslinging, sultry bookstore owner and Antonio Bandera's spitfire love interest in Latino director Robert Rodriguez's *Desperado*. For the next four years, such as in this 2004 interview with *Latina* magazine, the role Hayek humorously refers to in interviews as the "bikini girl" defined her Hollywood career.[1] From *54* (1998) to *Wild Wild West* (1999), Hayek was more often than not depicted wearing as little clothing as possible. After years of playing one-dimensional English-language roles in front of the camera, Hayek decided to transform Hollywood through her production and directorial work behind the camera. Ten years after her arrival in Los Angeles, Hayek would establish her first production company, Ventanarosa (pink window); coproduce and star in the award-winning art-house film *Frida* (2002), for which she earned an Academy Award nomination for best actress; produce and star in her first television movie, *In the Time of the Butterflies* (2001); cofound her second production company, Ventanazul (blue window, 2007); and coproduce and guest star in the international hit television program *Ugly Betty* (2006–10). What is particularly interesting about Hayek is not that she founded two of the first production companies to specialize in US Latinos and Latin American audiences, films, and television programs, but the complex and sometimes contradictory narratives of identity she publicly circulates to stake claim to her right to represent and be represented in the mainstream media.[2]

51. Christopher Holmes Smith, "'I Don't Like to Dream about Getting Paid': Representations of Social Mobility and the Hip-Hop Mogul," *Social Text* 21, no. 4 (2003): 71.

52. Here, the argument goes, if consumers in the US educate themselves about the gems they buy, asking questions of retailers and demanding certificates of provenance for each stone, the global supply of illicit diamonds would find no demand.

Salma Hayek's Celebrity Activism

Constructing Race, Ethnicity, and Gender
as Mainstream Global Commodities

ISABEL MOLINA-GUZMÁN

> They hadn't noticed there were 38 million Latinos in the U.S., an
> important market. They were quite stupid businesswise.
>
> Salma Hayek, 2007

Mexican-born telenovela star Salma Hayek first crossed the cinematic border between Mexico and the US in 1995 when she appeared in her
first Hollywood film as a gunslinging, sultry bookstore owner and Antonio
Bandera's spitfire love interest in Latino director Robert Rodriguez's *Desperado*. For the next four years, such as in this 2004 interview with *Latina* magazine, the role Hayek humorously refers to in interviews as the "bikini girl"
defined her Hollywood career.[1] From *54* (1998) to *Wild Wild West* (1999),
Hayek was more often than not depicted wearing as little clothing as possible. After years of playing one-dimensional English-language roles in front
of the camera, Hayek decided to transform Hollywood through her production and directorial work behind the camera. Ten years after her arrival in
Los Angeles, Hayek would establish her first production company, Ventanarosa (pink window); coproduce and star in the award-winning art-house
film *Frida* (2002), for which she earned an Academy Award nomination for
best actress; produce and star in her first television movie, *In the Time of
the Butterflies* (2001); cofound her second production company, Ventanazul
(blue window, 2007); and coproduce and guest star in the international hit
television program *Ugly Betty* (2006–10). What is particularly interesting
about Hayek is not that she founded two of the first production companies
to specialize in US Latinos and Latin American audiences, films, and television programs, but the complex and sometimes contradictory narratives of
identity she publicly circulates to stake claim to her right to represent and be
represented in the mainstream media.[2]

36. www.BlackGivesBack.com.

37. Manning Marable, "History and Black Consciousness: The Political Culture of Black America," *Monthly Review: An Independent Socialist Magazine* 47, no. 3 (1995): 84.

38. The music video that this chapter focuses on is properly read among a larger context of political or "message" hip-hop and activist-themed music videos that has emanated from hip-hop since its inception. Gil Scott-Heron's *The Revolution Will Not Be Televised* (1974), Grandmaster Flash and the Fabulous Five's *The Message* (1982), N.W.A's *Fuck tha Police* (1988), Public Enemy's *Fight the Power* (1995), Immortal Technique's *Voices of the Voiceless* (2009), and Talib Kwali's *Papers, Please* (2010) each takes its charge as "the CNN of the street," combining social commentary and ghetto testimony, gritty reality as well as playful fantasy. A considerable scholarly literature is available on the political valences of hip-hop, including, notably, Yvonne Bynoe, *Stand and Deliver: Political Activism, Leadership and Hip Hop Culture* (Berkeley: Soft Skull Press, 2004); Murray Forman and Mark Anthony Neal, eds., *That's the Joint: The Hip-Hop Studies Reader* (New York: Routledge, 2004); Robin D. G. Kelley, *Yo' Mama's Disfunktional: Fighting the Culture Wars in Urban America* (Boston: Beacon Press, 1997); Yusuf Nuruddin and Victor Wallis, eds., "Special Issue: Hip Hop, Race, and Cultural Politics," *Socialism and Democracy* 18, no. 2 (2004); and Trisha Rose, *Black Noise: Rap Music and Black Culture in Contemporary America* (Hanover, NH: Wesleyan University Press of New England, 1994).

39. Visual images used in music videos do not always reflect the lyrical content of singles on which they may be based. Indeed, the narratives and aesthetics of music videos may deviate substantially from the songs on which they are based, producing visual representations that may be unrelated to the lyrics or musical affect of the song. Kanye West's music video for "Diamonds" is a case in point, and, as this analysis shows, shifts across lyrical narratives and video images can sometimes offer glimpses of shifting political strategies as artists take a single from the recording studio to the soundstage.

40. In the 1971 original, diamonds are forever because even "when love's gone, they'll luster on" (lyrics by Don Black, music by John Barry). Echoing themes from Broadway songwriter Jule Styne's iconic "Diamonds Are a Girl's Best Friend," famously performed by Marilyn Monroe in *Gentlemen Prefer Blondes* (Howard Hawks, 1953), Bassey's 1971 classic enjoys a place of prominence among pop feminist anthems that celebrate female sisterhoods as networks of counterknowledges about strategies for independence from patriarchal love as a means to female empowerment, what in more recent times has been termed "girl or pussy power." Thus, perhaps inadvertently, "Diamonds" echoes themes of tongue-in-cheek defiance from an earlier era, underscoring the urgency of subaltern solidarities for economic emancipation, and the abiding exigency of guile and cunning as preferred "weapons of the weak" (James C. Scott, *Weapons of the Weak: Everyday Forms of Peasant Resistance* (New Haven: Yale University Press, 1985).

41. Darryl Dickson-Carr, *The Columbia Guide to Contemporary African American Fiction* (New York: Columbia University Press, 2005); Nelson George, *Post-soul Nation: The Explosive, Contradictory, Triumphant, and Tragic 1980s as Experienced by African Americans (Previously Known as Blacks and Before That Negroes)* (New York: Viking, 2004); Eddie S.Glaude Jr., *In a Shade of Blue: Pragmatism and the Politics of Black America* (Chicago: University of Chicago Press, 2007); Bambi Haggins, *Laughing Mad: The Black Comic Persona in Post-soul America* (New Brunswick, NJ: Rutgers University Press, 2007); Keith M.

Harris, "'Untitled': D'Angelo and the Visualization of the Black Male Body," *Wide Angle* 21, no. 4 (1998): 62–83; Richard Iton, *In Search of the Black Fantastic: Politics and Popular Culture in the Post–Civil Rights Era* (Oxford: Oxford University Press, 2008); Mark Anthony Neal, *Soul Babies: Black Popular Culture and the Post-soul Aesthetic* (New York: Routledge, 2002); Tommie Shelby, *We Who Are Dark: The Philosophical Foundations of Black Solidarity* (Cambridge: Harvard University Press, 2005); Greg Tate, *Flyboy in the Buttermilk: Essays on Contemporary America* (New York: Simon and Schuster, 1992).

42. Greg Tate, *Everything but the Burden: What White People Are Taking from Black Culture* (New York: Broadway, 2003).

43. Todd Boyd, *The New H.N.I.C. (Head Niggas In Charge): The Death of Civil Rights and the Reign of Hip Hop* (New York: NYU Press, 2003).

44. Kanye West, "All Eyes on Kanye West: Interview with Sway," *MTV News*, August 2005, http://www.mtv.com/bands/w/west_kanye/news_feature_081805/index3.jhtml.

45. Kamari Maxine Clarke and Deborah A. Thomas, eds., *Globalization and Race: Transformations in the Cultural Production of Blackness* (Durham, NC: Duke University Press, 2006).

46. Kamala Vishweswaran, "Race and the Culture of Anthropology," *American Anthropologist* 100, no. 1 (1998): 77.

47. Paul Gilroy, *Against Race: Imagining Political Culture beyond the Color Line* (Cambridge: Harvard University Press, 2000).

48. Houston A. Baker, *Betrayal: How Black Intellectuals Have Abandoned the Ideals of the Civil Rights Era* (New York: Columbia University Press, 2008); Bill Cosby and Alvin F. Poussaint, *Come on People: On the Path from Victims to Victors* (Nashville: Thomas Nelson, 2007); Michael C. Dawson, *Black Visions: The Roots of Contemporary African-American Political Ideologies* (Chicago: University of Chicago Press, 2003); Michael Eric Dyson, *The Michael Eric Dyson Reader* (New York: BasicCivitas, 2004); Norman Kelley, *The Head Negro in Charge Syndrome: The Dead End of Black Politics* (New York: Nation Books, 2004); Kelley, 1997; Bakari Kitwana, *The Hip Hop Generation: Young Blacks and the Crisis in African American Culture* (New York: BasicCivitas, 2003); Marable, 1995; Steve Perry, *Man Up! Nobody Is Coming to Save Us* (Mayfield Heights, OH: Renegade, 2006); Adolph Reed Jr., "What Are the Drums Saying, Booker? The Current Crisis of the Black Intellectual," *Village Voice*, April 11, 1995, 31–36; Tavis Smiley, ed., *The Covenant with Black America* (Chicago: Third World Press, 2006); Juan Williams, *Enough: The Phony Leaders, Dead-End Movements, and Culture of Failure That Are Undermining Black America—and What We Can Do about it* (New York: Three Rivers, 2007).

49. Herbert Marcuse, *One Dimensional Man: Studies in the Ideology of Advanced Industrial Society* (Boston: Beacon Press, 1964).

50. The latest of these contradictions emerged with news that the artist recently had diamonds permanently inserted to replace the bottom row of his teeth. When asked why at his appearance on *The Ellen DeGeneres Show* on October 19, 2010, West explained that he "just thought the diamonds were cooler." See Lisa Robinson, "Hot Tracks: Kanye West Opens up to Lisa Robinson," *Vanity Fair*, November 2010, http://www.vanityfair.com/culture/features/2010/11/kanye-201011; Shari Weiss, "Kanye West Teeth: Rapper Shows Off His Permanent Diamond and Gold Chompers," *Daily News*, October 20, 2010, http://www.nydailynews.com/gossip/2010/10/20/2010-10-20_what_a_shiny_smile_kanye_west_shows_off_diamond_and_gold_teeth.html#ixzz17k9chodK.

I analyze Hayek's interviews with the media to understand how she positions herself as a cultural activist and her production companies as privileged ethnic commodities. The media narratives Hayek circulates in her bid to intervene in mainstream cultural productions are illustrative of the ideological tensions surrounding the desire by transnational, multiethnic, and racially hybrid communities to represent themselves and be represented. As a cultural activist, Hayek advocates for increased and more complex roles for Latina/o, Latin American, and Spanish actors, as well as more nuanced productions by and about Latina/os and Latin America.[3] Indeed, Australia's *Herald Sun* once described Hayek's desire to start her own production companies as fulfilling "her ambition to open 'a back door into Hollywood' for actors who until now have concealed their Hispanic identity."[4] What is at stake in the journalistic framing of Hayek's work is how "Hispanic" is being deployed and which "Hispanics" are being let in through the "back door" via Hayek's cultural advocacy. An analysis of the public stories Hayek tells about her motivations for engaging in production and development illustrates the complexities surrounding definitions of Latina/o identity and the desire by mainstream media to commodify Latinidad for global profits.

On one level Hayek's intervention speaks to the culture of invisibility that has historically surrounded Latina/o and Latin American actors in film, television, and advertising.[5] Latina/o actors who have been most successful, such as Anthony Quinn, Raquel Welch, and Cameron Diaz, often desire or are required to pass for non-Latina/o and white. Angharad Valdivia documents how actors who cannot pass for non-Latina/o white because of either classed or racialized linguistic accents or physicality, such as Rosie Perez, are relegated to stereotypical secondary roles if they are cast in roles at all.[6] More recently the success of Zoë Zaldaña, who has popularly played the role of the alien other in *Avatar* (2009) and *Star Trek* (2009) or the black love interest in *Guess Who* (2005), illustrates the dynamics of colorism and phenotype for Latina actors whose blackness often limits the type of Hollywood roles available to them. Hayek's activism is thus both cultural and political, as Stuart Hall, building on Antonio Gramsci, suggests that the representational within contemporary capitalist democracies is indicative of status, power, and social hierarchies.[7]

Given Hollywood's disinterested history in ethnic and racial minorities and the narrowcasting that often surrounds American Indian, black, Latina/o, and Asian actors, it is not surprising that Hayek would become such a powerful advocate for diversifying both the means of production and the productions themselves. *Latina* magazine, one of the most successful magazines targeted at young educated and professional Latinas living in the

US, recognized the significance of Hayek's work as cultural activist when they named her top "on the list of 10 daring, dazzling Latinas who rocked" in 2004. Driven by her goal (and perhaps self-motivated need) to "open a back door" and increase Hollywood access for Latina/o actors, Hayek, however, tests the limits and possibilities of activism through the mainstream cultural spheres. In other words, she simultaneously opens the representational doors to Latina/o and Latin American actors and stories, yet carefully patrols the borders of ethnic authenticity through the stories she tells to maintain her authority as cultural producer. This is particularly ironic given Hayek's own complex identity—including her ethnic heritage as both Lebanese and Mexican; fluid transnational identity as a Mexican and US citizen; and conflicted relationship to US racial formations and racialized US Latina/o identity.

Thus Hayek's commodity activism, in the form of cultural interventions in the global mainstream media, illustrates the processes of symbolic colonization and symbolic ruptures at play in the commodification of Latinidad.[8] Symbolic colonization arises from the ideological processes inherent in media practices that help produce constructions of Latinidad as stable, fixed, homogeneous, and globally commodifiable. Building on my collaborative research with Angharad Valdivia, I define Latinidad as a social construct that is shaped by external forces, such as the census, marketing, advertising, news, and popular culture. So external force shapes how Latinidad is commodified and understood by audiences, and yet the signifiers of Latinidad are equally central to how people who identify as Latina/o stake claim to social, cultural, and political visibility. Symbolic colonization is produced through the storytelling mechanisms in news, film, and television narratives through which ethnic and racial difference is made safe, familiar, and valuable via its difference from and relationship to dominant norms. However, Hayek engages the storytelling mechanisms that contribute to the symbolic colonization of Latinidad to market herself and her production companies, and yet her complicated identity challenges popular media discourses about US ethnic and racial difference. The fluid national, cultural, and ethnic heritages of public figures, such as Salma Hayek, are never quite fully assimilated or socially accepted. It is the inability to fully categorize them within US discourses about ethnicity and race that I call symbolic ruptures. Similarly, an examination of tabloid coverage of Jennifer Lopez illustrates how she is celebrated for her global marketability and simultaneously disciplined for her desire to disturb US ethnic and racial categories.[9] While both women embrace their identities as multicultural symbols of ethnic minority success in the US, they must navigate the ethnic and racial borders carefully by occupying an ambiguous space within the US racial binary. Through positioning herself as an authority on Latinidad, Hayek participates in the symbolic colonization of Latinidad through the reproduction of dominant norms that homogenize Latina/o identity as gendered, racialized, foreign, exotic, and consumable. At the same time Hayek's work as a producer and actor destabilizes dominant media discourses about Latinidad by demanding increased visibility, as well as more complex stories that symbolically rupture or potentially fragment the commodification of difference.[10]

Throughout the past twenty years, growing interest in advertising, marketing, and media production geared toward the US Latina and Latin American market created a unique opening for Hayek to position herself as a cultural expert and use her authority to exert cultural and economic influence in Hollywood. According to the latest US census figures, Latina/os now number more than 55 million and make up more than 16 percent of the population, and Latinas are now the largest ethnic and racial minority group among women under the age of thirty-four.[11] In Latin America, for example, combining the populations of just three major centers of cultural production (Mexico, Argentina, and Brazil) yields a potential audience of almost 350 million people.[12] Consequently, Latina/os inside and Latin Americans outside the US are a large and lucrative global market. As I have argued elsewhere, the desire for synergistic programming, the success of cross-promotional strategies such as dual-language programming, and global media integration are encouraging the development of shows and entertainment personalities that can easily move across multiple audience demographics.[13] Latinas in particular are central to media industry efforts to use sexuality, ethnic difference, racial ambiguity, and multicultural accents to sell products and programming to global audiences.[14]

Consequently, Hayek presents a rich opportunity for exploring cultural activism as a form of commodity activism. By analyzing journalistic profiles and media interviews with the actor, I explore the language and stories she tells about herself, her work as cultural activist, and her status as a global commodity. Specifically, I examine forty-nine stories published from 1999 to 2007 in US and international newspapers, magazines, and news broadcasts, as well as published transcripts from interviews with journalists conducted in 2002–3.[15] Analyzing published accounts about Hayek provides an opportunity to problematize public discourses about the commodification of Latinidad, even those discourses circulated in the interest of expanding media representations.

Commodity Activism and the Global Mainstream Media

Citizenship in contemporary neoliberal society is intricately linked with the politics of cultural representations or the "right to be represented" within mainstream and alternative media spaces.[16] Nevertheless, as postcolonial queer theorist May Joseph argues, the desire for cultural visibility is fluid and sometimes contradictory. Individuals within a community are defined by intersectional identities that shift according to context, social space, and time such that the representational "is a contingent process, a state of becoming that is strategic in its solidarities with multiple publics as they negotiate simultaneous identifications within various political communities."[17] For instance, differences in transnational migration and racial, ethnic, national, sexual, and class identities within one demographic group, such as US Asians or US Latinos, fragment the process of representation and representational struggles to gain cultural and political legitimacy. Thus, representational advocacy must continually negotiate the intersecting vectors of identity and the power dynamics and social hierarchies embedded in cultural performances, especially performances circulated through the global mainstream media.

Contemporary articulations of citizenship must also be negotiated within the context of a neoliberal society that blurs the line between political representation and consumption. Although writing within the context of Asian American literature, Viet Thanh Nguyen eloquently summarizes the vexed neoliberal relationship between citizen and consumer:

> Thus the contemporary Asian American identity that has allowed Asian Americans to participate in American politics—frequently as an anticapitalist force—has now also become a thing, a commodity, to be marketed and consumed. While Asian American political identity has enabled political resistance against racism and capitalist exploitation, Asian American cultural identity in the present moment furthers the aims of capitalism because Asian American cultural identity—an Asian American *lifestyle*—is both commodity and a market at the same time.[18]

In her book on Latina/o politics, marketing, and culture, Arlene Dávila postures a similar assessment of the category Hispanic or Latina/o where discourses about Latinidad have enabled the formations of political coalitions and the highly profitable marketing of Latina/o identity.[19] Within the context of neoliberalism, citizen and consumer are converged, ultimately drawing into question the limits and possibilities of gaining cultural and political legitimacy through mainstream media representations. Hayek's public discourse about her identity and desire to open the representational space for Latina/os and Latin Americans presents an opportunity to think through the neoliberal tensions that exists between the desire for visibility in mainstream media productions by marginalized groups and the economic, social, and cultural demands for the commodification of ethnic, racial, gender, and sexual Others by audiences.

Situated within a Marxist framework, the process of commodification makes invisible the exploitative social and labor relations that produce the commodity.[20] For instance, as Roopali Mukherjee documents in her essay in this volume, the economic and physical violence surrounding the mining of diamonds is erased through advertising campaigns that focus on the iconic status of the gem as a symbol of heterosexual fidelity and romance, making them safer and more desirable to consume. Applying Marx to discussions of communication, Vincent Mosco argues that the value of media commodities in the global marketplace must then be understood in terms of the ideological needs and desires the commodity fulfills as well as its ability to maximize profits.[21] In the case of Latinidad, much like the phenomenon that surrounds the commodification of black culture, it is the authentic production of an exotic but desirable difference that fulfills both ideological and economic demands.

Indeed, writing about the commodification of black male friendship in the infamous "Whassup Budweiser" television advertising campaign, Eric King Watts and Mark P. Orbe suggest that the commodification of ethnic and racial people is defined by the discourse of "spectacular consumption," where the effective and marketable consumption of difference is determined by an ideologically safe performance of ethnic and racial authenticity.[22] For instance, the Budweiser commercials celebrated the authenticity of the phrase "whassup" as part of urban black male vernacular and made it globally consumable through use of humor. The use of the writer's real-life black male friends partaking in everyday activities produced the aura of marketable authenticity, while the buffoonish dialogue and actions undercut the potential subversiveness of dignified representations of black male friendship. Similarly, engaging the mainstream media to intervene in the cultural landscape surrounding Latinidad requires Hayek to participate in the discourse of spectacular consumption. She must circulate a media discourse about herself that reinforces her privileged authority as an authentic Latina/Mexicana to produce media texts that both colonize and rupture media representations of Latinidad.

As both actor and media producer Hayek functions as a commodity, com-modifier, and commodity activist whose labor in front of and behind the camera contributes to the ideological and economic elements of the spec-tacular consumption of Latina/o identity. She thus stands at the intersection of symbolic colonization and symbolic rupture. Hayek's self-acknowledged role as commodity activist is informed by a keen understanding of the eco-nomics surrounding the global media marketability of Latina/o identity and the ways her cultural labor provides unprecedented cultural visibility to a politically, culturally, and socially marginalized people, especially in the anti-immigration context of the 21st century. Because the commodification of Latina/o identity must negotiate the contours of a heterogeneous Latina/o ethnoracial difference, Hayek carefully mediates and controls a commer-cially viable identity narrative that reifies her status as "ethnically authentic" while producing media stories that are universally familiar and comfortable.

The Spectacular Production of Latina Authenticity

Central to Hayek's role as a commodity activist and expert authority on Latina/o production is the circulation of media stories that reinforce her ethnic authenticity. By framing herself as more authentically Latina and Latin American than other actors or producers, Hayek utilizes her Mexican nationality and US citizenship to create a privileged space from which to speak about Latinidad. For example, in an interview with *Daily Variety* about Ventanarosa, Hayek explains her unique value:

> I started out doing TV, and I know the Spanish TV market very well. . . .
> I have a lot of ideas for shows that are commercial and high-quality, that
> can raise the level of Spanish-language TV. And I have access to talent in
> Mexico that nobody knows about.[23]

Hayek's acting in Mexican telenovelas is used as the evidence for her cul-tural expertise and media authority. While telenovelas are by far the most successful and profitable programming of mainstream Spanish-language media, few would argue that they are usually the highest-quality programs. Yet by virtue of her upbringing in Mexico and her telenovela career during the late 1980s and early 1990s, Hayek claims authority and unique knowl-edge over Spanish-language productions. Her status as a Spanish speaker and Mexican telenovela actor provides her with insider industry knowl-edge that others presumably do not have. In other words, Hayek suggests that because she speaks Spanish and grew up in Mexico, her productions will be more "true" or "real" for US Latino and Latin American audiences and therefore more globally commodifiable. She produces a privileged space for herself and her production companies by creating an authenticity discourse grounded in language and nationality. Hayek would go on to effectively foreground this discourse of authenticity in claiming the right to produce and star in the biopic about Frida Kahlo's life.[24]

The discourse of authenticity based on Hayek's biographical information is also circulated in the trade press by her production staff. In a 1999 *Daily Variety* report on the decision by Ricka Fisher (former Disney Telefilms vice president) to accept the presidency of Ventanarosa films, Fisher emphasized the embodied authenticity of Hayek:

> "Salma has a remarkable energy, and remarkable storytelling insights," said Fisher, noting that Hayek already has an international following. "We are taking advantage of the company's knowledge of the Latino marketplace as there is a great deal of attention being paid to that explosion right now, but that's not our only criteria."[25]

Hayek's celebrity status and personal knowledge about Latin America, which presumably extends to the US Latina/o market, is the basis of the companies' expertise and special status within the media industry. Although the economically wealthy and multiethnic Hayek had been living in the US for only a few years at the time of the interview, her identity as a woman born and raised in Mexico provides her company with advantageous knowledge about the "Latino marketplace" across the globe.

Within publicity stories about the production companies, Hayek and then Ventanarosa's director of development José Tamez, a former Televisa telenovela writer, characterize themselves (and are effectively framed by journalists) as embodying unique knowledge that can better represent and speak to Latina/o-themed projects for the English- and Spanish-language mainstream audience. Their narrative is similar to the discourse of Latin American advertising professionals working for US Latina/o marketing companies.[26] The privileging of Hayek and Tamez, their upbringing and development in Mexico, and professional experiences within Mexico City–based media reinforce the privileging of authenticity based on Latin America culture and signifying practices. Latin American cultural elites are therefore able to function as cultural spokespersons for both US Latina/o and Latin American audiences. The ability of Latin American media producers to define the representational landscape of global Latinidad elides the ethnic, racial, and class diversity of these populations. As wealthy, educated, professional Mexicans, their Latin American subjectivity sets the cultural agenda by which Latina/o voices are heard, what type of stories about US Latina/os and Latin Americans will be told, and what signifying practices are culturally authentic and socially appropriate for conveying Latina/o and Latin American identity on television and in films. Interestingly, Hayek's class and citizenship status actually came under contestation by Mexican and Mexican American activists protesting *Frida* for its erasure of Kahlo's Marxist politics to commodify Mexican culture for global consumption.[27] By pointing out the particularity of Hayek's and Tamez's identities, I do not wish to place a value judgment on the validity of their perspectives as Latin Americans. Rather, I seek to acknowledge and contextualize Hayek's and Tamez's status and perspectives both in Mexico and in the US as particular to their wealth, class, ethnic, and citizenship status. Though both Hayek and Tamez immigrated to the US as adults, they are rarely located by the anti-Latina/o immigration discourse. Because narratives of authenticity carry within them hierarchical implications of identity and social status, Hayek's privileging of herself as the "authentic" Latina voice to globally represent Latinidad must be carefully interrogated.[28]

Due to the diversity within Latinidad, claiming authenticity to speak on behalf of economically, nationally, racially, and ethnically distinct transnational Latina/o communities is complicated. Indeed, Hayek's production agreements reflect the difficulty in staking a claim to represent Latinidad on a global level. Ventanarosa Productions, which coproduced *Frida* and developed the global television hit *Ugly Betty*, also has arrangements with Miramax, Colombia TriStar TV, and NBC-owned Telemundo network for English, Spanish, and bilingual programming. Most Ventanarosa projects have been geared toward reaching the bilingual and Spanish-language market in the US through Telemundo. However, Ventanarosa's most successful projects have been *Ugly Betty* and *Frida*, both English-language productions. Looking to make further inroads into the more lucrative English-language market, Hayek's film production arm, Ventanazul, has marked a much more explicit global mission. Summarizing the goals of Ventanazul in a *Daily Variety* 2007 interview, Hayek said, "I think we are the only company right now whose sole mission is to specialize in two things: 1) appealing to the Latin market and 2) taking a Latin story or a Latin talent and appealing to the global market."[29] Relying on Hayek's status as a Mexican woman and therefore authentic Latin American and expert in Latinidad, Hayek's production companies strive to commodify Latinidad both within and outside the US. As of 2010 Ventanazul had one low-budget English-language romantic comedy in development through its production partnership with MGM starring the native-Spanish speaker Hayek.[30] Hayek has actually starred in all but a few of the productions by her companies, drawing into question the companies' role as a star vehicle for the actor as opposed to opening up access to other Latina/o and Latin American actors. Nevertheless, the production agreements of both of Hayek's companies reflect a broad and global reach that, based on a discourse of authenticity, she alone can embody.

The Possibilities and Limitations of Latina Commodity Activism

To effectively and profitably commodify Latinidad, Hayek must carefully discipline authenticity to maintain the border against trespasses by other US Latina/o actors and producers. Her conscious use of the word "Latin" as opposed to the more racialized label "Latina/o" is another example of Hayek's asserting an authenticity border that foregrounds "Latin" American over US Latina/o identity and consequently privileges her identity status over others. Although Hayek carefully cultivates her identity as a Mexican actor and producer as the source of her authenticity, she also circulates media narratives that allow her access to US Latinidad. In particular, Hayek's stories of racism, discrimination, and racialized othering circulated in media interviews invoke a public performance of identity that positions her as authentic within US racial formations. Through these discourses Hayek reinforces a connection to US Latina/o audiences and markets, gaining access to both US and Latin American–based productions.

Controlling access to both English- and Spanish-language productions demands that she position herself as an authentic transnational ethnic body that understands the US racial experiences but maintains her true cultural connection to Mexico. Mexican, Latin American, and "Latin," only Hayek uniquely can give voice to previously marginalized US Latina/o and Latin American groups. She is simultaneously of and not-of the US, allowing her a bilingual, bicultural, binational location from which to advocate for the increased media visibility of herself and others. In the final section, I analyze the double-edged sword of Hayek's authenticity discourses by outlining the potentially transformative narratives Hayek uses to define her cultural labor and the limits of those same narratives.

"No Good Parts for Brown Girls in Hollywood"

Throughout news coverage and interviews about her production efforts, Hayek consistently mobilizes stories about xenophobia, racism, and racial discrimination to reinforce the authenticity of her status as a US-based Latina cultural producer. Recounting her personal confrontations with racial and ethnic discrimination in the US allows Hayek to frame her life story as unique, politically relevant, and similar to those of other US Latina/os. For example, a story on Hayek that was part of *Daily Variety*'s 2007 "Women's Impact Report" opened with:

> "They laughed when I came here," recalls Salma Hayek. "They said, 'You're never going to be an actress. You're Mexican.'" That was before her Oscar nomination (for playing the title role in "Frida"), before her Emmy win (for directing "The Maldonado Miracle") and before "Ugly Betty" collected two Golden Globes earlier this year.[31]

In this news article, Hayek's success is connected not to her cultural expertise in Mexico but to her ability to overcome racism and racial discrimination within Hollywood. Her Mexican identity and Spanish accent become evidence of her US authenticity through serving as authentic proof of overcoming racial barriers in the US. Accounts about racism and racial discrimination within Hollywood circulated through the mainstream media further affirm the political significance of Hayek's production work, such as in this 2003 interview with Stone Phillips on *Dateline NBC*:

> HAYEK: They [Hollywood directors] said things like, you know, "With your accent it makes sense to cast you as a maid, but a maid wouldn't look like the way you look."
> PHILLIPS: So your accent fit the stereotype, but your appearance did not.
> HAYEK: Exactly. "How can I play a successful woman? I have an accent." There are so many successful people with accents in America. Hello, wake up! Look around. It's not all white bread. There's textures and colors in this country, and I don't know why Hollywood is so afraid of it.[32]

Within this interview segment Hayek effectively uses her experience of discrimination to locate herself as a racialized member of the US. In tension with media stories about her authentic Latin American perspective, Hayek's stories about her professional media experience in Mexico are replaced by narratives foregrounding her shared racialized reality in the US. In a profile with London's *Evening Standard*, she shared other examples of the racial discrimination she has faced when interviewing with a Hollywood studio executive: "You can never be a leading lady because we can't take the risk of you opening your mouth and people thinking of their maids—because that's what you sound like."[33] These stories of racial discrimination reinforce the importance of Hayek's work as a commodity activist and her unique status as an authentic voice and representative for US Latinas/o identity and media stories.

Hayek's cultural campaign for social justice through narratives of US racism and Hollywood racial discrimination apparently resonated with entertainment journalists around the world, as is evident in headlines such as "Salma Hayek Is Changing the Way Hollywood Views the Latin World" and an article that begins, "Salma Hayek hasn't forgotten her Mexican roots and neither have blinkered casting agents in the United States. As her summer blockbuster *Wild Wild West* is released she tells Brian Pendreigh how she fought back."[34] The journalistic framing of her story as a Mexican immigrant overcoming Hollywood typecasting taps into familiar and compelling discourses of ethnic and racial identity and the struggle for civil rights in the US. For instance, in an interview with Australia's *Herald Sun*, Hayek draws an interesting contrast that further highlights the importance of her production work: "Hayek, who recalls a time when there were signs in shabby Los Angeles hotels that read 'No Mexicans or animals,' is also to get close to $100 million a year from a Hollywood studio to make films for America's increasingly influential Latino audiences."[35] Although it is unlikely that Hayek ever stayed in shabby Los Angeles hotels, the implicit allegiance with Mexican and Latina/o experiences of discrimination is clear. Hayek's most explicit assertions of racism and discrimination occur in media interviews outside the US, specifically Australia and England. While Hayek does invoke her experiences with discrimination in Hollywood interviews with the US media, such as interviews on *NBC Dateline* and *The Oprah Winfrey Show*, she rarely calls it racism—perhaps sensitive to the negative publicity such comments might provoke by US media outlets and white audiences, especially in the anti-immigration context of the past decade.

In her early Hollywood roles, Hayek argues, her Mexican identity and accent often racialized her as working-class and nonwhite, which resulted in highly sexualized, one-dimensional "bikini girl" roles.[36] In a 1999 interview with the *Boston Globe*, Hayek explained the type of industry discrimination she faced:

But coming from a Spanish-speaking background put me out of the running for every role except prostitutes and maids, to the point where people would see my name and picture and would want to meet me, then they would realize I was Mexican and would send me away.[37]

Indeed, a quick scan of roles Hayek performed before the 1999 creation of Ventanarosa certainly illustrates the racialized typecasting culture she faced. In *Dusk Till Dawn* (1996) she played a vampiric erotic dancer; in *54* (1998) she played a bisexual swinger studio girl; and in *Wild Wild West* (1999) she spends most of the movie wearing lingerie. In a 2002 interview with the *Toronto Sun*, Hayek criticized the sexualization of these early roles: "On *Wild Wild West*, I was never comfortable one day (wearing a low-cut outfit). I was ashamed to come out of the trailer every time, every time. Sometimes, it is easier to be naked with honesty."[38] Explaining the hypersexualized nature of her early roles, Hayek argues that her Mexican national origin in combination with her Spanish-accented English placed her outside whiteness and limited her access to more complex and less stereotypical roles than other Latina actors, such as Jennifer Lopez, once again privileging her discourse of identity as more authentic than others.

"The Mex Factor"

For Hayek, the discrimination she faced in Hollywood and the stereotypical roles she was offered as a consequence serve as proof of the need for her production companies as important representational interventions and commodities in the global mainstream media. However, to claim her privileged status as cultural spokeswoman for US Latina/os and Latin Americans, Hayek must engage in a complicated identity discourse that locates her as simultaneously and uniquely Mexican and US Latina. Her stories about racial discrimination locate Hayek's authenticity within a specific US space, and stories of cultural expertise depend on Hayek's position within Mexico. She must therefore patrol the border of authenticity in the US and in Mexico. Foregrounding her experience of racial discrimination in the US to justify her right to produce movies such as *Frida*, she must also emphasize her roots and identity in Mexico as the source of her representational privilege in Latin America. In this 1999 interview with England's *Birmingham Post*, Hayek explains her representational motivations:

I'm creating my own projects so I can choose parts that are closer to me. If Hollywood won't give me what I want, I'm at a place where I can supply them for myself. . . . There are a lot of things about my roots that are unknown to the world and there are a lot of wrong images. I'd like to change that.[39]

She deftly moves between stories about the need to provide access for actors who face racialized discrimination in the US to arguments about the need for socially respectable representations of and about Latin America. Achieving representational visibility for Mexico is a political act—even if that visibility, as in the case of *Frida*, depends on the spectacular consumption and symbolic colonization of authentic Mexican identity through mainstream media vehicles.[40]

Hayek's commercial interests and motivations are usually left out of most articles about the actor and her production company. Instead, journalists emphasize the actor's more emotionally authentic intellectual and political desires, ignoring the market implications of her success, such as in this London *Guardian* story: "But Hayek is more than just a pretty bottom. She is aware of her image as Hollywood's sexy Latina and she talks passionately, and convincingly, about being a sex symbol and the need for movies of humanity and dignity."[41] Interconnecting the way the representation is both commercial and political, Hayek's endeavors as a commodity activist are framed as intellectual and political. Most profiles about the actor similarly draw attention to her intelligence and articulateness while foregrounding her sexualized body and identity, thereby benefiting from the spectacular consumption of Latinidad even as they seek to disrupt it, as this *Birmingham Post* headline illustrates: "A Seriously Sultry Star."[42] Although Hayek often foregrounds the economic imperatives of her production companies in the trade press, she carefully focuses on the ethical dimensions of her labor in the mainstream commercial media by highlighting her battles with US racism and the need for dignified representations of Latinidad in the global mainstream media.

To Be or Not to Be Latina

Hayek's discourse of authenticity is dependent on maintaining her cultural authority through the construction of her Mexican identity as more culturally legitimate and essentially different from other US Latina actors and producers, in particular Jennifer Lopez. Language, linguistic accents, and the racial discrimination of Mexican immigrants in the US play a critical role in maintaining the border for authenticity and unique authority to represent both US Latina/os and Latin Americans. In describing Telemundo network's production deal with Hayek, then president Peter Tortorici explained:

> This is a great example of how we can combine the strength of the two companies to attract people who can work in both languages and cultures. . . . I was enormously impressed with [Hayek's] skills and enthusiasm. She blew me away. So many of these deals are nothing more than announcements, but I'm convinced she's a serious player.[43]

Tortorici reifies Hayek's identity discourse by engaging in the argument that her production efforts are unique and significant because she is one of the few producers who can authentically represent Mexicans and US Latina/os. Of course the source of Hayek's authenticity, her Mexican identity, has not deterred her from representing or producing stories about the cultures and identities of others. Hayek maintains a rigid definition about who can be and represent Latin American or US Latina/o based on national origin and language, but she opens up representational access for herself. For instance, in *In the Time of the Butterflies*, she plays a Dominican activist, and in *Ugly Betty* she produces a story about a second-generation US Mexican woman who cannot speak Spanish. Carefully crafting the borders of authenticity, she creates a space for her productions that is impossible for others to occupy.

Not surprisingly, Hayek has spent much time defining herself and her production work against that of US-born Puerto Rican Jennifer Lopez, so much so that the media began circulating stories about a bitter feud between the women. Focusing on the racial discrimination that surrounds linguistic accents in Hollywood, Hayek more often than not aligns herself with Spanish Europeans Penélope Cruz and Antonio Banderas because of their shared accent. Engaging in a story of "who's more discriminated," as in this 1999 interview with Australia's *Courier Mail*, Hayek differentiates between herself and Lopez:

> Of her supposed animosity towards Jennifer Lopez, she says "That's bull—! It's just two of us (Hispanic women stars) and I wish there were more." She has noted in interviews that Lopez is American-born, while Hayek, of course, still has that accent, so has had less of a range of roles on offer, until now.[44]

In a similar article in *el Andar* on the battle between Hayek and Lopez to make a movie about Frida Kahlo's life, Hayek argued that Lopez's "Spanish is very bad. . . . [N]ow it's very convenient, because when she has to be Latin, she's

Latin."[45] Hayek uses Spanish fluency and the identity label "Latin" to market herself and her production company as more authentic than other US Latinas, even though the movie *Frida* was actually produced in English in the US.

Perhaps in recognition of the industry's continued interest in one of the fastest-growing media markets in the US, Hayek appears to be rethinking how she marks the border of authentic US Latinidad. In a 2007 interview with *Marie Claire*, Hayek shared:

> I started out in Hollywood at the same time as Jennifer Lopez. Before us, Latinas only had roles that were part of the backdrop, as the maid or the prostitute. We changed that. Of course, you're always looking for those Meryl Streep parts, but I am grateful for the things I did. Look at where we are now: sixteen Oscar nominations for films by Mexican directors this year [and four wins].[46]

While still privileging her ethnic specificity as Mexican, she locates her trajectory alongside the "shared" trajectory of Jennifer Lopez, who also began by playing highly stereotypical Latina roles. Implicitly acknowledging the environment of racial typecasting and racial discrimination that defined both women's early career, Hayek engages in a more collective discourse by describing herself and Lopez as "us, Latinas." Reversing her public rejection of the label "Latina" and her decade-long contention that the women had little in common, Hayek is once again redefining the discourse of identity and authenticity she utilizes to claim representational space in the US Latina/o market.

Conclusion

The financial and critical success of Hayek's production companies depends on the commodifiable production of ethnic authenticity and universally appealing story lines that captivate multiple audiences regardless of age, gender, race, nationality, and language. The tensions embedded in Hayek's public stories about the production ideals of her companies and her most successful production projects to date (*Frida*, *Ugly Betty*) illustrate the global tension between the spectacular consumption of ethnic and racial authenticity and the demand for consumable difference inherent in the media discourses that produce symbolic colonization. Hayek's public discourse of Latina and Mexican authenticity illustrates the limits of her commodity activism, in particular how she negotiates the market demands for Latinidad and the safe consumption of difference.

Hayek's dependence on identity narratives to achieve representational visibility and complexity exemplify the difficulty of symbolically rupturing representational discourses of Latinidad through the global mainstream media. Hayek's cultural intervention is dependent on her ability to successfully commodify herself as an authentic Latina who has the authority to control the discourse about Latinidad for global consumption. However, her public discourse about identity, culture, and media representation inherently disciplines Latinidad by reproducing an exclusionary discourse about who falls under the ethnoracial category of Latinidad and under what cultural and political conditions. It is a discourse of authenticity based on language and national origin and one in which she has relaxed the markers of authenticity more recently in attempts to situate herself within the map of US Latina/o producers by being more inclusive of other US Latina/o actors and producers.

Hayek's project of commodity activism demands more and more complex representations of Latina/os and Latin Americans, thereby symbolically rupturing the dominant media discourse about Latinidad by redefining the global media landscape. Engaging in interventions through the mainstream media, however, raises questions about the limits and possibilities of a form of commodity activism inherently dependent on the global mainstream commodification of women and ethnic and racial minorities. In particular, Hayek participates in the symbolic colonization of Latinidad by enforcing the borders of authenticity through the privileging of her Latin American identity and personal experiences with US racial discrimination. Hayek's commodity activism is therefore dependent on reinforcing a narrow construction of who has the right to represent Latinidad and under what forms. The cultural and political project of expanding representations through the global mainstream media is constrained by the demands of spectacular consumption that desires authentic difference but only under acceptable terms. In Hayek's case she must circulate stories that reaffirm her authenticity by privileging her Latin American identity and producing television and cinematic stories that circulate safe and consumable stories about Latina difference. *Frida* and *Ugly Betty* globally succeed because they reinforce the dominant narrative of Latinidad as familiar and exotic, as feminine and hypersexualized, as safely outside of the US racial binary. Despite the limitations of the identity discourses by which Hayek can intervene culturally in the global media landscape, it cannot be denied that her film and television productions do provide moments of symbolic ruptures for audiences who celebrate the increased visibility of Latinidad and more nuanced representations about Latina/o lives and experiences, whether those experiences are grounded in the terrain of the US, Latin American, or the transnational imaginary.

1. "Mujeres of the Year," *Latina*, December, 2004.

2. Jennifer Lopez's production company, Nuyorican Productions, came on the scene two years later and has yet to field a major movie or television hit. It produced *El Cantante* (2006), *Bordertown* (2006), and *Feel the Noise* (2007), which combined earned US$22.7 million worldwide. *Bordertown*, Box Office Mojo, http://www.boxofficemojo.com/movies/ id=bordertown.htm (accessed May 5, 2010); *El Cantante*, Box Office Mojo, http://www. boxofficemojo.com/movies/?id=elcantante.htm (accessed May 5, 2010); *Feel the Noise*, Box Office Mojo, http://www.boxofficemojo.com/movies/?id=feelthenoise.htm (accessed May 5, 2010).

3. Building on the comparative and interdisciplinary tradition of Latina/o studies, this chapter uses the term "Latina/o" when discussing potential positions of commonality among US descendants from Mexico, the Spanish Caribbean, and Central and South America. Because "Latino" is a Spanish-language derivative of a masculine noun, the term "Latina/o" is used as a more gender-inclusive term to describe the community. Otherwise, when the analysis centers on a specific national group or when the terms are used by participants, the chapter uses nationality-specific terms such as "Chicana/o" or the Spanish-language term *Mexicana/o*. Furthermore, Silvio Torres-Saillant suggests, Latinidad is an ethnoracial identity that is both ethnically located and racially informed in the US and as such must constantly negotiate its relationship to whiteness and blackness and the tension between ethnic specificity and panethnicity. Because the term "Latina/o" is used in the US as a panethnic demographic label to subsume immigrants and nonimmigrants from more than twenty-six countries of origin spanning the Spanish Caribbean and Latin America, conflicting interests across racial categories, nationalities, linguistic backgrounds, and citizenship exist uncomfortably within one marketable category. Silvio Torres-Saillant, "Inventing the Race: Latinos and the Ethnoracial Pentagon," *Latino Studies* 1, no. 1 (2003): 123–51.

4. Darren Devlyn and John Harlow, "The Mex Factor: Salma Hayek Is Changing the Way Hollywood Views the Latin World," *Herald Sun* (Melbourne), May 23, 2007. The quotation for this chapter's epigraph also comes from this article.

5. Myra Mendible, ed., *From Bananas to Buttocks: The Latina Body in Popular Film and Culture* (Austin: University of Texas Press, 2007); Charles Ramírez Berg, *Latino Images in Film: Stereotypes, Subversion, Resistance* (Austin: University of Texas Press, 2002); Clara Rodriguez, *Latin Looks: Images of Latinas and Latinos in the U.S. Media* (Boulder, CO: Westview Press, 1997).

6. Angharad N. Valdivia, "Stereotype or Transgression? Rosie Perez in Hollywood Film," *Sociological Quarterly* 39, no. 3 (1998): 393–408.

7. Stuart Hall, "Gramsci's Relevance for the Study of Race and Ethnicity," *Journal of Communication Inquiry*, 10, no. 2 (1986): 5–27.

8. For a more thorough discussion of the concepts of symbolic colonization and symbolic ruptures, see Isabel Molina-Guzmán, *Dangerous Curves: Latina Bodies in the Media* (New York: NYU Press, 2010).

9. For a more thorough discussion of Lopez, see Molina-Guzmán, 2010.

10. For a more thorough discussion of the concepts of symbolic colonization and symbolic ruptures, see Molina-Guzmán, 2010.

11. US Bureau of the Census, *Hispanic or Latino Origin by Specific Origin* (Washington, DC: U.S. Bureau of the Census, 2007), http://factfinder.census.gov/servlet/DTTable?_bm=y&-geo_id=01000US&-ds_name=ACS_2007_3YR_G00_&-redoLog=false&-mt_name=ACS_2007_3YR_G2000_B03001 (accessed May 5, 2010).

12. UN Population Division, *World Population Prospects: The 2008 Revision*, http://esa.un.org/unpp/index.asp (accessed May 7, 2010).

13. Molina-Guzmán, 2010.

14. Myra Mendible, "Introduction: Embodying Latinidad: An Overview," in Mendible, 2007, 1–28; Isabel Molina-Guzmán, "Mediating Frida: Negotiating Discourses of Latina/o Authenticity in Global Media Representations of Ethnic Identity," *Critical Studies in Media Communication* 23, no. 3 (2006): 232–51.

15. All the accounts were collected through the LexisNexis online database and retrieved on February 2, 2009.

16. Toby Miller, *Cultural Citizenship: Cosmopolitanism, Consumerism, and Television in a Neoliberal Age* (Philadelphia: Temple University Press, 2007).

17. May Joseph, "Transatlantic Inscriptions: Desire, Diaspora, and Cultural Citizenship," in *Talking Visions: Multicultural Feminism in a Transnational Age*, ed. Ella Shohat (Cambridge: MIT Press, 1998), 357–66.

18. Viet Thanh Nguyen, *Race and Resistance: Literature and Politics in Asian America* (New York: Oxford University Press, 2002), 9.

19. Arlene Dávila, *Latino Spin* (New York: NYU Press, 2009).

20. Karl Marx, *Das Kapital*, vol. 1 (London: Penguin, 1976), 320–31.

21. Vincent Mosco, *The Political Economy of Communication* (Thousand Oaks, CA: Sage, 2009).

22. Eric King Watts and Mark P. Orbe, "The Spectacular Consumption of 'True' African American Culture: 'Whassup' with the Budweiser Guys?" *Critical Studies in Media Communication* 19, no. 1 (2002): 4.

23. Jenny Hontz, "Hayek Has 2-Yr./2-Tongue Deal with Col, Telemundo," *Daily Variety*, January 21, 1999.

24. Molina-Guzmán, 2006, 232–51.

25. Cynthia Littleton, "Hayek Banner Taps Fisher Prez," *Daily Variety*, June 15, 1999.

26. Arlene Dávila, *Latinos, Inc.: The Marketing and Making of a People* (Berkeley: University of California Press, 2001).

27. See Molina-Guzmán, 2010.

28. Authenticity is often used by the hegemonic class to discipline the most vulnerable of populations. For a postcolonial critique of authenticity, see Gareth Griffiths, "The Myth of Authenticity," in *The Post-colonial Studies Reader*, ed. Bill Ashcroft, Gareth Griffiths, and Helen Tiffin (London: Routledge, 1995), 237–41.

29. Peter Debruge, "Salma Hayek," *Daily Variety*, August 2, 2007.

30. Debruge, 2007; *Untitled Nicolás López Project*, IMDb, 2010, http://www.imdb.com/title/tt1067581/ (accessed May 5, 2010).

31. Debruge, 2007.

32. Stone Phillips, "Salma Hayek Discusses Her Career and Latinos in Hollywood," *Dateline NBC*, March 7, 2003.

33. Tim Cooper, "How Leading Lady Salma Turned Tide against Racism in Hollywood," *Evening Standard* (London), January 10, 2003.

34. Devlyn and Harlow, 2007; Brian Pendreigh, "'I Said, I'm a Big Shot Now and I Want a Bigger Part,'" *Guardian* (London), July 7, 1999.

35. Devlyn and Harlow, 2007.

36. Michael Quintanilla, "Having Her Say," *Latina*, December 2004, cover image.

37. Jay Carr, "Savvy Salma Hayek: Star of 'Wild Wild West' Doesn't Take No for an Answer When It Comes to Her Career Moves," *Boston Globe*, June 27, 1999.

38. Bruce Kirkland, "Hayek's Work of Art: Film's Long Journey Could End with a Statue on Oscar Night," *Toronto Sun*, October 27, 2002.

39. Jeff Hayward, "A Seriously Sultry Star," *Birmingham Post*, August 18, 1999.

40. For a more in-depth discussion of the movie *Frida*, see Molina-Guzmán, 2006.

41. Pendreigh, 1999.

42. Hayward, 1999.

43. Hontz, 1999.

44. Helen Barlow, "One of the Boys," *Courier Mail* (Queensland, Australia), August 14, 1999.

45. Julia Reynolds, "Las Dos Fridas: Hollywood's Long, Slow Race to Make the Definitive Frida Kahlo Film," *el Andar*, Summer 2001, 38–41.

46. Julia Savacool, "Salma Hayek: Hot Mama!" *Marie Claire*, May 2007, http://www.marieclaire.com/celebrity-lifestyle/celebrities/interviews/salma-hayek (accessed June 29, 2011).

8

Mother Angelina

Hollywood Philanthropy Personified

ALISON TROPE

Angelina Jolie sets the scene. Over a sea of provocative and heart-wrenching images of hardship and disease, she intones: "Extreme poverty means not having enough food to feed your family; walking long distances barefoot to collect safe water to drink; hospitals overflowing with patients suffering from diseases that should be preventable." These images and words introduce a 2005 video diary produced and aired on MTV in which Jolie accompanies UN adviser and economist Dr. Jeffrey Sachs on a trip to Africa. The video not only serves as documentary witness and record of indigenous problems but also sends a message to a Western audience, more specifically an audience of youthful MTV viewers and future activists. Jolie pauses dramatically after the introduction to signal blame while also laying the ground-work for future philanthropy and activism by directly addressing the MTV viewer: "Rich nations have seen fit to look away from extreme poverty. But do you know that we can wipe it off our planet in just twenty years?"

Jolie's participation no doubt played a pivotal role in MTV's decision to produce and air this video and further contributes to the video's ongoing life on a variety of Internet sites. Jolie has cachet with MTV's audience and therefore can harness the network as a site to disseminate information and instigate action. As an actor with box office draw, Jolie also depends on this same audience to sustain her career and her stardom. The relationship between star, philanthropic cause, and audience is therefore complicated. Indeed, this relationship signals a debate over and an attempt to assess the personal motives, altruism, and cultural authority of Jolie and her philan-thropic peers in Hollywood. Media outlets, political pundits, and celebrity watchers both praise and target such Hollywood philanthropists, celebrat-ing the potential of star power while derisively criticizing the work as com-mercially tainted "celanthropy," method-giving, "charitainment," and mor-alistic posing. Such mixed readings of Hollywood philanthropists and their motives complicate the terrain of celebrity giving and its potential impact. In light of much recent scholarship and popular press around corporate giving as well as Hollywood-giving (the latter notably featured since 1998 in special issues of the *Hollywood Reporter* and *Variety*), it is nonetheless worth considering the personae that get constructed in this giving process and the rhetoric, praise, and criticism that get mobilized to this end. In particular, I am interested in exploring the ways in which the association with giving changes not only the star but also the way the star, as a commodity *and* an individual with a specific gender and racial identity, potentially changes public perception of the cause.

It is important to rethink the way celebrities, consumers, and corporations can "give back." It seems prudent, in turn, to rethink traditional models of philanthropy, the historic and contemporary landscape of philanthropic causes, and the assumptions about philanthropists themselves within a neoliberal and global economic context. Indeed, just as foundations increasingly take on business models and corporations think strategically about giving, Hollywood stars can personify philanthropy, serving as philanthropic models and conduits for their respective causes. While we cannot dismiss the crossover between star and philanthropy completely, it is clearly a model we cannot naively embrace and celebrate. Thinking about the conjunction of Hollywood and philanthropy offers insight into historical and contemporary imperatives of the star system, as well as the ways in which a neoliberal economic paradigm (and its associated reform strategies) potentially impacts traditional models of charity.

In her essay "Neoliberal Legacies: Planned Giving and the New Philanthropy," Mary-Beth Raddon argues that "neoliberal discourse exalts a mode of citizenship defined by personal acts of generosity," by setting up an overly simplistic opposition, if not a hierarchy, between those who give and those who receive.[1] This opposition valorizes acts of donating and fundraising at the expense of what Raddon calls more "normative" and "collectivist orientations to civic virtue," such as "paying taxes, social movement activism, artistic and cultural creation, and the everyday work of caring for people within households and neighborhoods."[2] The Hollywood philanthropist potentially plays a more problematic role in this opposition compared with other philanthropists. While firmly situated on the giving end, Hollywood philanthropist-activists like Jolie do not necessarily obviate the collectivist orientations to which Raddon alludes. In the roles they play both on and off screen, stars can serve as role models, potentially spurring activism and political engagement. Strategically harnessing the role model status, many Hollywood philanthropists, in fact, directly align their artistic and cultural output with the causes they support. As P. David. Marshall explains in his book *Celebrity and Power*, the star that engages in philanthropic acts carefully crafts and "demonstrates a subjectivity that goes beyond the self to the conception of selflessness and public leadership."[3] Such an alignment neatly satisfies the star's necessary negotiation of public and private personae and yet also potentially and problematically blurs the line between altruism, self-promotion, and self-preservation.

The popular discourse and press surrounding Angelina Jolie's philanthropic work provide a rich and contested picture of the alignment between star and cause. Jolie, therefore, offers a significant case study. While she is frequently praised and even deemed saintly by a popular press that likens her to Mother Theresa and historical Hollywood philanthropist Audrey Hepburn, Jolie's philanthropic work, like that of many of her celebrity peers, also has been viewed with great skepticism, foregrounding a key question circulating around Jolie and her celebrity peers: Do celebrity philanthropists and social activists harness their status and cachet to benefit others, or do they use the philanthropic-activist image to benefit and brand themselves? In other words, is the star's philanthropy strategic and insular, as is the case with much corporate giving, or is it altruistic? Can it be both? And, more important perhaps, can we ever truly assess the line between the two? These questions are difficult, if not impossible, to answer in any clear or concrete way. Like the some 68,000 foundations that currently exist in the US, the celebrity philanthropist must negotiate and balance individual autonomy with public accountability.[4] Some celebrities have handled this balance with more acuity than others.[5] Given a star's required integration of public and private personae, Jolie is in a unique position to achieve this balance.

Investigating this balancing act requires examining not only each celebrity and cause individually but also the star and charitable work within a historical and economic frame. Angelina Jolie's philanthropic efforts, therefore, must be contextualized within the economic imperatives of the star system as they intersect with a host of other factors including her personal life, her on-screen roles, her testimonials and interviews, her construction in and by the popular press, as well as her interactions with specific policy makers and reformers (some of whom embrace a decidedly neoliberal agenda).

Angelina Jolie radiates Hollywood stardom. As of December 2008, she was named the highest-paid actress in Hollywood, and she is regularly featured in entertainment magazines as well as tabloids (especially since the public disclosure of her relationship with the equally high-profile Brad Pitt and the adoption and birth of their many offspring).[6] At the same time, since taking on the post of goodwill ambassador for the United Nations High Commission for Refugees (UNHCR) in 2001, she has made more than twenty-five site visits to poverty-stricken third world regions, documented her observations, spoken out in public forums to political figures, including former secretary of state Condoleezza Rice, and in 2007 was invited to join the prestigious Council on Foreign Relations (a think tank whose former members include Henry Kissinger and Alan Greenspan). Most important, for many skeptical of celebrity philanthropy, Jolie also has donated much of her own money (up to one-third of her income by some estimates) to the wide range of causes she supports.[7] In the end, it is this very literal financial contribution that distinguishes her from many of her peers as a philanthropic star. As this essay contends, Jolie's philanthropic work must be viewed both within a long-standing tradition of private philanthropy and Hollywood philanthropy that is in dialogue with, if not setting the stage for, our contemporary neoliberal moment during which the opposition of public and private often takes center stage. Her endeavors further must be situated in terms of the role gender has played in the history of both of these philanthropic and public-private contexts. Using a comparative and historical frame, then, this essay works to trouble the knee-jerk skepticism surrounding Hollywood philanthropy, rethink the reductive moral critique used to lambaste Jolie, and contemplate the ways in which gender and a maternal ideal get mobilized in the context of her humanitarian efforts.

Hollywood Philanthropy and History

The history of Hollywood philanthropy and activism dating from the late 1910s and continuing throughout the 20th century offers a broad and elastic context for the study of contemporary stars such as Angelina Jolie. While a neoliberal frame offers an important window to explain the changing landscape and strategies within contemporary philanthropy and activism, particularly in a global context, the history of Hollywood philanthropy helps situate the act of giving as a key component of the star system, if not the Hollywood industry more broadly.

As stars became central to Hollywood's industrial structure in the late 1910s and early 1920s, a star's daily life and off-screen persona became central to the development of a star "system." Fan magazines and the burgeoning studios of this period worked to produce stars as unique commodities, framing a star's activities, proclivities, and personality traits in such a way that they enhanced the star's on-screen persona and cemented the star's most attractive attributes. The story of a star's background and rise to fame often revolved around a conventional and familiar narrative of transformation (from humble beginnings to Hollywood fame, from rags to riches). Many of these foundational stories also relied on tales of good fortune and discoveries. These narratives functioned, in large part, to make the star attainable and approachable to the audience, making the public persona take on a private dimension. A star's power to identify and cultivate a connection with the audience was and continues to be the underlying foundation of the star system as developed by the Hollywood studios and their publicity machines.[8]

Given this history, it is not surprising that charity work, philanthropy, and activism would figure into the off-screen narratives of some of the earliest stars. Indeed, as the star system developed, individuals frequently used their celebrity status as a platform to discuss politics and air their personal views on subjects such as women's suffrage and war.[9] Mary Pickford, one of the most well known silent film stars, played a significant role in campaigning for Liberty Bonds during World War I and was instrumental in the foundation of two entities designed to support actors in need, the Motion Picture Relief Fund and later the Motion Picture Country Home. Pickford's star persona, the innocent and childlike "Little Mary," complemented such philanthropic endeavors and no doubt added to her star power and public reach. Hollywood moguls of the classical era also engaged in philanthropic outreach in an attempt to emulate the gentile aristocracy as well as wealthy East Coast Jews, according to film historian Neal Gabler. Throughout the 1930s and beyond, Hollywood moguls consistently gave to Jewish organizations and causes. Gabler contends that for these moguls, "philanthropy was a mark, as well as an expectation of status."[10] Therefore, while philanthropic efforts during this early Hollywood period may have been motivated by altruism among stars and other Hollywood players, such historical Hollywood giving often was tinged with more base motives tied to self-preservation and legitimacy. The fact that the star's philanthropic deeds are generally disclosed, if not well known to the public, further complicates a clear interpretation of intent.

Stars, even if genuinely invested in a cause, are reminded of the symbolic and, in turn, commercial value of giving and encouraged to pursue public displays of charity and altruism by their handlers. Marlene Dietrich's agent Charles Feldman, for example, pointed to the public profile and cachet garnered by her work for troops during World War II, claiming, "The entire industry is cognizant of your efforts."[11] Many contemporary stars hire philanthropic advisers or organizations that recommend particular causes aligned with and designed to further their persona and image. In his overview of contemporary celebrity, P. David Marshall discusses this rising political consultancy business that aids celebrities in choosing appropriate and relevant social causes, arguing that connections between stars and charities can add value to the star by underscoring "the possible connotations of depth, intelligence, and commitment to his or her public persona."[12]

The philanthropic star, therefore, clearly functions within a system of exchange, in which charitable acts have the potential to impact status, public perception, and persona. Despite the different components of exchange, Hollywood philanthropy in many respects historically runs parallel to traditional aristocratic giving as well as corporate giving. The traditional elite philanthropist, the corporation, and the star each gain some value, whether economic, cultural, or symbolic, through the act of giving. As Teresa Odendahl argues in her critique of the philanthropic elite, "Public relations discourse on philanthropy was originally framed by the wealthy people it would benefit."[13] At the same time, it is worth noting that the value accrued by the star in the context of philanthropic giving suggests a more complicated discursive arena. Many of the elite Odendahl describes use their giving not only as a means to accrue status but also to paternalistically flaunt their own cultural capital and expertise. Angelina Jolie and many of her celebrity philanthropist peers take a decidedly different approach, strategically framing their causes more humbly either in terms of autobiography and personal passion or as a learning experience. In order to function within the star system, in fact, the cause must be situated as decidedly personal and, as in the case with Jolie, intimately tied to her identity as an actress, wife, and mother. Jolie does not simply sit on a board of trustees or write checks to select causes, though many in Hollywood exercise this mode of philanthropy.

Jolie, among a small cadre of her celebrity peers, sets herself apart. As a global icon, she can more easily leverage her star power in the international arena and engage in what I call "action giving"; she is there, in the trenches, making site visits, talking to refugees. Most important for her star status, she is photographed doing all of this and publicly discusses her personal impressions and experiences. This visibility is key to both the cause and Jolie's stardom and further distinguishes her in many ways from philanthropic stars of Hollywood's golden age. In addition to posting journals of her site visits, the UNHCR website, like the "Think MTV" website, further cements the association between star and philanthropic systems by featuring a link to Jolie's biography as actress (focusing on her films and accolades) beside a link to her biography as humanitarian. Jolie seems acutely aware of the necessary juxtaposition, even exploiting it to the benefit of her star persona and her philanthropic causes. According to some sources, coverage of Jolie's personal life in the media often contractually hinges on coverage of her charity work. Jolie's philanthropic adviser, Trevor Nielson, validates the connection, disingenuously eliding Jolie's potential motives tied to her role as star: "If Angie can use the interest and redirect it, she wants to do that."[14]

Narratives of Transformation: Rewriting the Star through Philanthropy

Part of the skepticism around Angelina Jolie, like many of her star peers involved in charity, stems not only from her celebrity status and motives but also from her knowledge and understanding of the issues at hand. For Jolie, the skepticism is even more pointed, as it stems directly from her well-documented troubled, highly sexualized, if not perverse, tabloid past. The tabloid tales most famously included a passionate open-mouthed kiss with her brother at the 2000 Oscar telecast and marriage soon thereafter to Billy Bob Thornton, whose blood she wore in a vial around her neck. During this period, she was widely described as a wild child with a penchant for bondage, sexual experimentation, and drugs.

It was soon after these tabloid spectacles that, in 2001, Jolie transformed. Reportedly moved by a script about refugees and other news reports and books detailing the magnitude of a global refugee problem, Jolie called the UN and asked how she could help. By her own account, she effused, "You might think I'm crazy. . . . I'm an actress. I just want to learn. I don't want to go with the press."[15] She subsequently volunteered and after a lengthy "audition" began serving as goodwill ambassador for the UN High Commission for Refugees, funding her own visits to witness atrocities in some twenty countries including the Ivory Coast, Sierra Leone, Tanzania, Cambodia, Sudan, Thailand, Jordan, Sri Lanka, Kosovo, Ecuador, and Pakistan and donating $1 million to aid Afghan refugees in 2001 alone.[16]

From the outset, Angelina Jolie's involvement with the UN was not widely played up in the popular press. If we believe her accounts, she did not seek out publicity to document her early trips to Africa with the UNHCR. The UN also may have justifiably shown trepidation in its initial dealings with Jolie given her past. Much of the initial press around Jolie's involvement, imbued with skepticism and sarcasm, framed her early UN volunteer work as yet another unpredictable maneuver—one that was perhaps self-indulgent or motivated by publicity. Frequent references were made to her bad-girl, sex-crazed past and her use of crisp long-sleeved white blouses to calculatedly cover her tattoos.

In the face of such public scrutiny and criticism, Jolie consistently framed her UNHCR experiences as a process of self-discovery, one that made her a better person and allowed her not to focus so much on her own problems. Refusing her own commodity status, she explained: "Anyone who's identified with me by feeling alone or a bit crazy should know that I've figured it out. . . . Get outside yourself. Get outside your environment. Do something for other people."[17] In March 2002, Jolie seemed to take her own advice, making a more drastic and permanent move to adopt a son from a Cambodian orphanage whom she had first seen the previous November on one of her goodwill trips. This single act played a pivotal role in shifting the public focus from Jolie as sex fiend to mother, from narcissist to nurturer. She subsequently continued to pursue her humanitarian goals, split from Thornton that summer, and took sole custody of her son Maddox.

Throughout this period of transition from bad girl to humanitarian, images in the press depict a serene, pensive Jolie with child—her own as well as the needy victims of the third world nations she visits. Photos of Jolie further depict a decidedly deglamorized star image, wearing a headband for a *Today Show* interview or trekking without makeup through the back roads of rural Kenya. The glamour, in turn, was muted and reserved for the red carpet and, from 2005 to 2008, for her stint as spokesmodel for the conservative and traditional clothing line St. John Knits. The choice of St. John, moving away from Jolie's previous predilection for a goth-punk aesthetic or even couture Armani, marked another deliberate softening of her image, not to mention an augmented aura of respectability, substance, and class. This aura became valuable, no doubt, when speaking before business leaders in Davos, Switzerland, at the World Economic Forum or at a Capitol Hill press conference for the Global Business Coalition on HIV/AIDS in 2005. As Jolie commented in June 2006, "Take that punk in me to Washington and I fight for something important."[18]

Jolie's transformed persona clearly corresponds with P. David Marshall's description of the philanthropic star that consciously crafts an image of selfless, public leader.[19] Jolie claimed to have abandoned her publicist and instead aligned herself with Trevor Neilson. Neilson is currently president of the Global Philanthropy Group and adviser to many executives, politicians, and celebrities. He formerly served as philanthropic consultant for the Endeavor Group, executive director for the Global Business Coalition on

HIV/AIDS and the Bill and Melinda Gates Foundation, and arguably still plays a publicity role for Jolie. In addition to Neilson, Jolie also keeps company with Jeffrey Sachs, whose titles include professor of health and policy management, director of Columbia University's Earth Institute, director of the United Nations Millennium Project, and president and cofounder of Millennium Promise. These seemingly strange bedfellows, alongside Pitt and her children, round out and legitimate Jolie's persona as philanthropist, glamorous star, and mother, keeping at bay the sex symbol image and the scandal associated with the breakup of Pitt and ex-wife Jennifer Aniston.

In interviews, Jolie has tended to distance herself from Hollywood stardom and excess, taking on a self-deprecating, even guilty tone. With CNN's Anderson Cooper, Jolie claimed, "I have a stupid income for what I do for a living."[20] In journals kept during her various UN missions, Jolie often self-consciously references her privileged and pampered lifestyle. These journals, which are available on the UNHCR website as well as in a book published by Simon and Schuster in 2003, entitled *Notes from My Travels*, are peppered with concrete information, statistics, and background on given regions. Just as her personae of star, philanthropist, and mother coalesce in the popular media, the hard facts about each region are intertwined with atmospheric descriptions of the landscape, the real people and suffering Jolie encounters. This calculated blend of public and private, of cause and personal experience demonstrates Jolie's adept harnessing of her own star image. The journals take a largely apolitical stance, pairing an admiration for native languages and cultures and an appreciation for the human condition while accentuating the refugees' innocence and victimization. Jolie's self-reflexive musings, laced with astonishment, frequently comment on the limited and biased news coverage of the regions she is visiting. Such criticism further parallels her apparent frustration over her own admittedly limited education. (She frequently refers to her lack of college education.) The naïveté and acknowledged ignorance permeating Jolie's journals make them accessible, but, more important, strategically make her accessible.

It would be easy to create a neat cause-effect argument explaining Jolie's desire and motive to join the ranks of philanthropic causes and adopt children from third world nations. Indeed, much media coverage of Jolie has taken on this argument, rewriting her past as a series of mistakes, mishaps, and subsequent discovery, climaxing in a social, political, and maternal epiphany during her time in Cambodia. Like many stars whose images similarly have been fueled and shaped by elaborate publicity and public relations mechanisms, Jolie's persona has become the product of a narrative of transformation; she

8.1. UNHCR goodwill ambassador Angelina Jolie sits and speaks with Sudanese women who have just crossed the border into Tine, Chad, after fleeing fighting in the Darfur region of Sudan, June 2004, UNHCR, E. Parsons.

becomes a do-gooder and crusader, on a rescue mission that has real-world sociopolitical implications. Of course this narrative is too simple, and while there may be some truth in it and the assumptions made about her motives, it is nonetheless worth considering the broader implications of her stardom and her motherhood on the image and realities of private philanthropy.

Marshaling the Maternal: The Personal Is Political

In addition to her philanthropic work, Jolie's transformation as star and public persona is intimately tied to her role as mother. The connotations and value tied to Jolie's maternal image manifest themselves both in her role as UNHCR goodwill ambassador and real-life mother and, more significantly, in the intersection of these public and private personae—an intersection that was perfectly captured in her famed 2006 postpartum sit down with CNN's Anderson Cooper, entitled "Angelina Jolie: Her Mission and Motherhood."

In tying Jolie's personal life so closely with her politics and philanthropic work, Cooper's interview reproduced a gender-infused narrative common in the history of both Western philanthropy and Hollywood philanthropy.

Historically, the ideals and everyday work of philanthropy neatly have adhered to the prescribed domestic and nurturing roles historically assigned to white women. Both middle-class reformers and their elite counterparts have taken on such maternal leanings. While the actual monetary source may have remained largely in men's hands, white women often played a symbolic "lady bountiful" role by interfacing with the public and the charitable cause, thereby gaining "cultural prestige," particularly in elite circles.[21] And while such roles may seem retrograde, as Odendahl argues, the gendering of the female philanthropist is not confined to history, appearing in many ways "frozen in a previous time period."[22] Contemporary philanthropy, in many ways, remains a feminine arena, dedicated to helping those in need as well as nurturing those institutions that will enhance the public and build its cultural capital. Gender plays a key role in defining not only the figure of the philanthropist but also the narratives and images constructed around the philanthropic work.[23]

Given the significance placed on imagery and narratives of transformation in the making of Hollywood stars, it is worth considering the role gender plays in framing Hollywood philanthropists such as Jolie. From the outset, the media consistently have framed Jolie's humanitarian efforts with her gender, in the causes she supports, but more pointedly in the images and words tied to her visits with refugees, particularly children. These images not only document her maternal leanings, thereby highlighting her gender; they further situate Jolie as a specifically white figure of salvation. Her femininity and whiteness, therefore, significantly intertwine, calling forth images of civility and purity, and historically reverberating in the context of American reform movements as well as European colonialism.

Within celebrity philanthropic circles, children's charities tend to outnumber other popular causes, making the white maternal missionary figure fairly commonplace. Stars such as Audrey Hepburn, Mia Farrow, Marlo Thomas, and even former *All in the Family* cast member Sally Struthers have tied their names and images firmly to causes that involve children in need. This is not to say that nonwhite celebrities have not also engaged in this kind of philanthropic work, especially in the contemporary era. However, the media attention generated by the star status of figures such as Jolie and Hepburn before her clearly surpasses many of their peers, reaffirming the implicit power of whiteness and femininity in certain philanthropic endeavors.

It is Hepburn, as both star and philanthropist, whom Jolie mostly closely incarnates and is often compared to. Lauded for her classic beauty and regal yet approachable persona, Hepburn embodied many ideal star qualities. In

8.2. UNHCR goodwill ambassador Angelina Jolie jokes with Afghan children in the refugee camp of Katcha Ghari on the edge of the Pakistani city of Pehawar, May 2005. UNHCR, J. Redden.

her role as goodwill ambassador for the United Nations International Children's Emergency Fund (UNICEF), Hepburn, like Jolie, traveled to many war-torn and poverty-stricken zones around the world, testified before Congress, and spoke publicly on behalf of the organization. On these missions, the media frequently captured images of Hepburn directly interacting with, physically surrounded by, and selflessly caring for children in need.

Children have played a central role in Angelina Jolie's philanthropic image as well. In many ways, children have figured centrally in her transformation from sexually perverse bad girl to legitimate and safe childbearing figure. Jolie frequently wove her newfound maternal leanings into stories about both her philanthropic work and her acting, again deliberately merging her public and private personae. On her first trip to Tanzania, she reportedly distributed baby formula to new mothers at a refugee camp. At an Olympic Aid forum in February 2002, sitting amid world leaders such as Archbishop Desmond Tutu and Prime Minister Gro Brundtland of Norway, a teary-eyed Jolie told the story of two young African children who had recently witnessed the murder of their parents. Such maternal leanings were compounded by the adoption of Maddox, a decision Jolie directly linked to what she read, and later witnessed at refugee camps, particularly the first time she saw a child die. Taking cues from Jolie, who claimed the adoption changed her life, the popular press hyperbolically suggested that Maddox *transformed* her, *turned her around*, and *"saved"* her.[24] The interviews she did following the adoption focused on a softer, gentler, more sincere, even celibate Angelina Jolie—one safely consumed by a virtuous combination of motherhood and missions.

During press for the release of the second *Tomb Raider* installation in 2003, Jolie further alluded to her maternal longings, linking them directly to her acting: in order to summon tears for a scene, she purportedly imagined extending her hand to an anonymous child. It was also in 2003, after her divorce from Thornton, when the spectacle and taboo of her sexually charged past became decidedly muted in the press. Jolie received not only more positive press touting her philanthropic work and maternal instincts but also attention from more legitimate outlets outside the realm of typical entertainment magazines and tabloids.

Aside from the tabloid fodder surrounding her relationship with Pitt, much of the popular press on Jolie since her taking on the UNHCR post tends to downplay her star status or, at least, juxtapose the glamorous actress image alongside the earthy missionary and natural mother. Pitt's philanthropic partnership aids in shifting the focus away from sex and scandal. While their romantic relationship and sexual chemistry definitely take center stage in much popular press, the regular reporting on their commitment to causes highlights the value and significance of their philanthropic work and activism. In turn, Jolie and Pitt's stardom intimately intertwines the personal and the political. The juxtaposition of on-screen and off-screen roles adheres to the historical construction of stars discussed by Hollywood historians such as Richard Dyer and Richard DeCordova,[25] among others. In Jolie's case, it also adheres to what has become a more recent media "genre"—the celebrity mom profile.

Taking the lead from historians Dyer and DeCordova, P. David Marshall discusses the "homology" between on-screen and off-screen celebrity lives and the consistency required in the construction and maintenance of successful star portraits. Jolie's role in the 2003 film *Beyond Borders* and her portrayal of Marianne Pearl in *A Mighty Heart* (2007) closely parallel her humanitarian interests and work in war-torn third world regions and therefore function to solidify her goodwill image. Her voice work for animated features such as *Kung Fu Panda* and *Shark Tale* further ties Jolie to the family film market, deliberately underscoring values, particularly maternal ones, outside of her film work.

Like many of her celebrity mother peers, Jolie's image subscribes to the tenets of what Susan Douglas and Meredith Michaels have dubbed the "new momism."[26] For Douglas and Michaels, the "new momism" functions on two primary levels. Motherhood becomes the primary feature in defining a woman's femininity, if not her identity. And, especially for celebrity moms, motherhood is salvation. Both of these facets seamlessly operate within a star's highly constructed narrative of transformation. With references tying motherhood to salvation coming up frequently not only in the popular press around Jolie but also in her own words, it is clear that her image consciously is brokered on the ideology of "new momism." At the same time, in comparison to other examples of celebrity moms discussed by Douglas and Michaels dating from the 1980s, Jolie's blatant disregard for grandeur in the raising of her children is noteworthy. Her adopted children are orphans from disease-infested and conflict-ridden third world regions. While they may dress in hip clothes and sport mohawks, luxury and excessive monetary doting are not part of the child-rearing image Jolie offers the public. Rather, Jolie's "new momism" revolves around a grounding in nature, world travel, and exposure to other cultures, an earthiness that is decidedly anti-Hollywood and aligns itself very neatly with Jolie's philanthropic work and globetrotting goodwill.

Jolie has rewritten herself both figuratively and literally, removing the tattoos that previously celebrated her love and perverse attraction for Thornton, while adding others that mark a maternal love in designating the longitude and latitude of the sties where her children were born. In addition to her work with the UNHCR, she also has devoted time and money to projects in these sites: Cambodia, Ethiopia, Namibia, and Vietnam. Her involvement and special projects in these particular countries, such as the Maddox Jolie-Pitt Project and the Maddox Chivan Children's Center, reveal the direct intersection of her public and private roles. And, like all celebrity moms, who balance the public role of celebrity with the private role of mother, Jolie is allowed, if not required, to balance her maternal desire with a healthy amount of sex appeal.

Quick Fixes and Flash

Such intersection of the public and private has not been totally immune from criticism. In 2006, as she and Pitt prepared for the birth of their daughter Shiloh in Namibia, they were criticized as celebrity colonialists for pressuring the government to impose a ban on foreign journalists from entering the country. In many circles, Jolie's interview with CNN's Cooper stirred more

ANGELINA JOLIE

Notes from My Travels

VISITS WITH REFUGEES IN AFRICA,
CAMBODIA, PAKISTAN, AND ECUADOR

8.3. Notes from *My Travels* book cover.

controversy, revealing what can happen in a not so carefully constructed public relations opportunity. Referring to Africans monolithically as a "tribal" people, for many, smacked of colonialism, putting Jolie's whiteness in high relief despite her efforts to frame the label in semihistorical context.[27] Her description of indigenous cultures that "just recently learned to govern themselves" unknowingly set a condescending tone. Her maternal leanings sounded ironically paternal as she went on to optimistically herald African attempts to self-govern: "But there are also pockets where they're really trying to pull themselves together. And we need to be there to really support them at that time, to help them to understand how better to govern. It really is a work in progress. It's not just going to happen overnight."[28] Finally, in discussing the decision making around adopting their next child, Jolie responded that it would be "another boy, another girl, which country, which race would fit best with the kids." Such a pithy response supported additional criticism of Jolie's motives for adoption, citing the use of her children as props or accessories who conveniently serve as mediators with the general media-watching public as well as the third world nations she visits on a regular basis. Jolie as typical Western missionary, therefore, is not always an attractive image. As Paul Tiyambe Zeleza argues, Jolie's self-indulgent missionary stance is primarily "exoticism, not enlightenment."[29]

Such criticism against Jolie must be framed, however, as part of a broader discourse within economic and development policy circles that attacks not only celebrities but also other nongovernmental organizations (NGOs), global corporations, and humanitarian groups. Much of the critique around these potential humanitarian and aid organizations, activists, and philanthropists revolves around the approach to aid. Accused of jumping on an "aid-and-trade bandwagon," these groups typically are condemned for relying on quick-fix approaches and neoliberal reform strategies rather than attending to entrenched and systemic problems.[30] Jolie's adviser Jeffrey Sachs has been the target of such criticism. While he is a world-renowned and heavily credentialed economist, some of his peers who share an expertise in the economics of developing regions view his approach as simplistic and potentially harmful. A 2006 article in the *World Policy Journal* claims that Sachs and his counterpart Thomas Friedman base their arguments on unproven myths and do a disservice to the public by propagating easy fixes in best-selling books. According to the authors, while Sachs and Friedman are articulate, learned globetrotting pundits, they have "hijacked the development debate."[31]

Given Jolie's prominent position as celebrity philanthropist and her deference to Sachs, we might say the same about her. A star like Jolie certainly has the power to highjack a cause or debate and present a one-sided, biased picture. A star's persona, in fact, largely relies on an ability to craft and perpetuate simple, familiar, and easy-to-digest imagery and product for the public. As more and more stars seek out philanthropic and activist roles, their knowledge and motives come under media and public scrutiny. Such scrutiny certainly is justified; however, for many Hollywood philanthropists, with public and private lives blurred, motives, in particular, remain difficult to assess in any definitive way. If Jolie follows Sachs, does she deserve criticism simply because she is a star or because she is someone who, like Sachs, may have a controversial outlook on third world aid? Jolie's star status will remain inextricably tied to her particular views on refugees and third world poverty, as well as the humanitarian endeavors she takes on. Consciously or not, Jolie deploys a star identity. Some may argue that Jolie, as a public figure with potential impact, has a responsibility to act on informed opinions, that she should be held accountable for her views and actions. By all accounts, Jolie fulfills this responsibility. Nonetheless, Jolie's potential highjacking of a cause is noteworthy as her star power potentially eclipses not only her mentor Sachs but also the cause itself.

In our contemporary media-saturated and consumer-driven landscape, Hollywood philanthropy and activism clearly cannot be dismissed. Furthermore, with philanthropy and philanthropic projects receiving growing attention in mainstream media circles, it is important to note a shift in the typical philanthropic persona, away from the limited ranks of Rockefellers and Carnegies and toward a more open system that includes corporate and Hollywood citizenry of all sorts.[32] The social capital and actual capital possessed by these philanthropic newcomers, including Jolie, is real and significant, though nonetheless burdened by historical gender, race, and class connotations. In addition to the money Jolie personally has donated, her star image serves as a conduit, attracting fans and other media- and celebrity-watchers to her work. The impact is real and even measurable. Organizations such as UNICEF, the World Food Program, and the UNHCR have attempted, however loosely, to quantify the power of their celebrity advocates by gauging donations and website traffic following celebrity appearances on *The Oprah Winfrey Show* and CNN and in *People* magazine. After Jolie's interview with Anderson Cooper, for example, the UNHCR claimed to have received a spike in donations totaling more than half a million dollars.[33]

While Jolie may encourage individuals to follow in her philanthropic footsteps, it is unclear whether or not she can encourage those same individuals to follow her path of self-education and self-improvement, and further, whether she has real, measurable impact on the corporate and public sectors. Did those who donated to the UNHCR after the Jolie-Cooper interview read her journals or any other information on the UNHCR website? Had they read Sachs or Friedman or researched any other views on the politics of aid? Do the government leaders and diplomats that Jolie has met change their views or policies based on the arguments she presents? It seems likely that most who donate to the UNHCR or other Jolie causes simply followed Jolie because of who she is, because of her star status, her compelling presentation of a cause, and a desire to identify with her. The same could be said perhaps for politicians and diplomats, some of whom might be equally starstruck. In addition to assessing and addressing the potential impact of Hollywood philanthropy, therefore, it is also important to take into account the ways in which rhetoric and media images deployed around stars such as Jolie complicate the nature and quality of their impact. The quick fix of star power provided by media outlets MTV, CNN, *Oprah*, and *People* magazine may stimulate donations, but it also may breed other quick fixes based on watered-down understandings of social, political, and economic issues. The image and star persona have the potential to overtake and obfuscate the cause, as well as inadvertently silence or marginalize other voices and alternative perspectives.

The path to change and progress is a complex one, particularly when celebrities, corporations, and products become part of the equation. A neoliberal paradigm potentially breeds and proliferates this new and thorny landscape of giving, but as this essay suggests, the Hollywood philanthropist's role is not necessarily new. Nor is the scrutiny of spurious motives new to discussion of stars, or philanthropists for that matter. The line between altruism and self-promotion, between philanthropy and celebrity, between enlightenment and exoticism will always be debated and difficult to discern. This difficulty was true in Mary Pickford's time as it is for Angelina Jolie today, though played out on a decidedly different global industrial playing field. Rather than focusing on a star's motives, it seems prudent to consider the ways in which the star's image can impact the cause, both historically and in a neoliberal context of personal giving. Jolie, like her star philanthropic peers, plays a key role in modeling personal acts of generosity and philanthropy to the public at large. Further, she directly calls on her viewing public to follow her lead, as she suggests in her MTV video diary: to look at extreme poverty, and to believe that it can be wiped off the planet in twenty years. This prediction likely betrays Jolie's overinvestment in the mentorship of Jeffrey Sachs, yet as spoken by Angelina Jolie, the star, it has a marked and marketable weight that cannot be ignored.

NOTES

1. Mary-Beth Raddon, "Neoliberal Legacies: Planned Giving and the New Philanthropy," *Studies in Political Economy* 81 (2008): 42. See also Samantha King, *Pink Ribbons Inc.: Breast Cancer and the Politics of Philanthropy* (Minneapolis: University of Minnesota Press, 2006).

2. P. David Marshall, *Celebrity and Power: Fame in Contemporary Culture* (Minneapolis: University of Minnesota Press, 1997), 110.

3. Marshall, 1997.

4. Joel L. Fleishman, *The Foundation: A Great American Secret: How Private Wealth Is Changing the World* (New York: Public Affairs, 2007), xiv.

5. Andrew Cooper discusses several examples of poor celebrity role models who have worked as spokespeople on behalf of the UN, including Sophia Loren and ex–Spice Girl Geri Halliwell. Andrew Cooper, *Celebrity Diplomacy* (Boulder, CO: Paradigm, 2008), 15–35.

6. "Women in Entertainment Power 100 List," *Hollywood Reporter*, December 5, 2008. This status reflects the trade publication's annual ranking of influential female executives in Hollywood. Rankings reflect professional achievements, company role, financial and green-light responsibility, and force of personality. In the case of actresses, it specifically reflects the amount of pay they can garner per film in any given year. See http://www.hollywoodreporter.com/hr/features/womeninentertainment/celebrity-gallery.jsp?profileID=12337.

7. "Time 100 Power Givers," *Time*, April 27, 2007. Jolie and Pitt gave $4 million each to their joint foundation in 2006 according to federal tax returns released in 2008. They gave $1 million each to Doctors Without Borders and Global AIDS Alliance. Other donations in smaller amounts went to causes tied to their onscreen and off-screen lives. Namibia Red Cross Action Program (the site of daughter Shiloh's birth), the Daniel Pearl Foundation (Jolie played the widow Marianne Pearl in the film *A Mighty Heart*), and Global Green USA, among others, with the foundation's expenses totaling a mere $27,000. See also the *Chronicle of Philanthropy*, March 24, 2008. In November 2008, Trevor Neilson told the *New York Times* that additional grants of $2 million for an AIDS clinic in Ethiopia and $2.6 million to Make It Right, an organization devoted to rebuilding New Orleans, as well as $500,000 to groups focused on helping Iraqi schoolchildren were made by the Jolie-Pitt Foundation. In addition to donations to the fund made by Jolie and Pitt themselves, the Jolie-Pitt Foundation is also the entity that collects and distributes monies received from the sale of photos of Jolie, Pitt, and their children. See also Brooks Barnes, "Angelina Jolie's Carefully Orchestrated Image," *New York Times*, November 21, 2008.

8. Marshall, 1997.

9. Richard DeCordova, *Picture Personalities: The Emergence of the Star System in America* (Urbana: University of Illinois Press, 1990), 110.

10. Neal Gabler, *An Empire of Their Own: How the Jews Invented Hollywood* (New York: Crown, 1988), 288–91. See also Steven Carr, *Hollywood and Anti-Semitism: A Cultural History Up to World War II* (New York: Cambridge University Press, 2001), 194–95. Some of this giving was tied to weeding out or combating anti-Semitism, according to Carr.

11. Tom Kemper, *Hidden Talent: The Emergence of Hollywood Agents* (Berkeley: University of California Press, 2009), 229.

12. Marshall, 1997, 110.

13. Teresa Odendahl, *When Charity Begins at Home: Generosity and Self-Interest among the Philanthropic Elite* (New York: Basic Books, 1990), 16.

14. Barnes, 2008.

15. "Interview: Angelina Jolie Discusses Her Work with the United Nations High Commissioner for Refugees," *Weekend Edition* (Washington, DC), October 25, 2003.

16. UNHCR website, http://www.unhcr.org/cgi-bin/texis/vtx/help?id=3f94ff664 (accessed March 29, 2009). Cooper and others frame the UN trial as an "audition," with Cooper specifically situating it in relation to some of the problematic UN goodwill ambassador choices of the recent past.

17. J. D. Heyman, "Women of the Year 2001: Angelina Jolie—Far Reaching Out," *Us Weekly*, December 10, 2001, 48.

18. Saabira Chaudhuri, "Hollywood's Most Influential Celebrity Activists," *Forbes*, November 22, 2006.

19. See Marshall, 2007.

20. Alessandra Stanley, "The Jolie Interview: The Humble Star and Eager Newsman," *New York Times*, June 22, 2006.

21. Odendahl, 1990, 116.

22. Odendahl, 1990. It is also noteworthy that the majority of jobs in the charitable sector, some 70 percent, are held by women. See Raddon, 2008, 41.

23. The same can be said of the "diplomat" label also used in relation to celebrity philanthropists and activists. Diplomacy, arguably, reads as feminine because it implies a more talk-centered, nonaggressive approach.

24. Michelle Tauber, "And Baby Makes Two," *People*, August 4, 2003, http://www.people.com/people/archive/article/0,,20140693,00.html.

25. DeCordova, 1990.

26. Susan J. Douglas and Meredith Michaels, *The Mommy Myth: The Idealization of Motherhood and How It Has Undermined Women* (New York: Free Press, 2004).

27. Paul Zeleza, "Angelina Jolie Discovers Africa," June 21, 2006, http://zeleza.com/blogging/u-s-affairs/angelina-jolie-discovers-africa (accessed March 3, 2007).

28. http://transcripts.cnn.com/TRANSCRIPTS/0606/20/acd.01.html.

29. Zeleza, 2006.

30. Robin Broad and John Cavanagh, "The Hijacking of the Development Debate: How Friedman and Sachs Got It Wrong," *World Policy Journal*, Summer 2006, 21–30.

31. Broad and Cavanagh, 2006, 21–30.

32. Odendahl notes the "well-recognized 'turnstile' between posts in government, large nonprofits and business," reflecting the often incestuous crossover between philanthropy and politics. Odendahl, 1990, 54.

33. Nora Boustany, "Hollywood Stars Find an Audience for Social Causes," *Washington Post*, June 10, 2007.

9

"Fair Vanity"

The Visual Culture of Humanitarianism in the Age of Commodity Activism

MELISSA M. BROUGH

We're on a mission; put Uganda deep inside your mind.
It needs attention and a dance to make it sparkle and shine.
They're in bad times.
We got to shake it up and break it up. We'll end the war without a gun.
We're not qualified.
We need to congregate and demonstrate so one day we can celebrate.
We are here to change the world!

These are the opening lyrics of *Global Night Commute: A Musical to Believe In*, a seven-minute spoof—with a serious twist—of the 1986 Disney film *Captain EO* that featured Michael Jackson singing "We Are Here to Change the World."[1] Directed by Francis Ford Coppola, the original short musical was created for a now-defunct Walt Disney World attraction at the Epcot theme park. In this 2006 video remake streaming on YouTube, the three young American founders of the nonprofit organization Invisible Children—and throngs of break-dancing youth—perform a technicolor musical of intertextual, hipster bliss. The video culminates in choreographed demonstrations in the streets to bring peace to Uganda. The video was part of a campaign "to make a visual call to end night commuting in northern Uganda," which mobilized more than 80,000 youth in April 2006 to sleep overnight in parks in 126 cities across the US.[2] This "musical to believe in" is *Captain EO* meets *We Are the World* meets Disney's *High School Musical*, and it is part of the changing face of American humanitarianism.

The last four decades have witnessed the dramatic growth of the nongovernmental, nonprofit sector in the US and internationally.[3] Together with increasing intrasector competition and the adoption of new media tech-

9.1. *Global Night Commute* campaign poster. Courtesy of Invisible Children, Inc.

nologies, this proliferation has fueled the niche marketing and branding of humanitarian organizations[4] and made visual images of humanitarianism increasingly pervasive in US (and global) culture.[5] As commodity activism grows, so too does humanitarian consumption, fueled by and marketed through an increasingly prolific, complex visual culture.

Until recently, the visual culture of Western humanitarianism was heavily entrenched in an iconography of suffering, most often conveyed through a realist aesthetic. Today, factors including neoliberal consumer culture, the professionalization of humanitarian communications, and Web 2.0 social networking are shaping new forms of humanitarian visual culture and, to varying degrees, new content.[6] The spectacle of suffering—a spectacle typically produced to construct the "sympathy-worthiness" of humanitarianism's beneficiaries—is increasingly paired with pop culture spectacle. The earnestness of "real" portrayals of suffering is being matched with—or even supplanted by—more lighthearted, postmodern pastiche and youth culture aesthetics, and glamorized or playful representations of the humanitarian *donor-as-consumer*. Cause-branded clothing lets us wear our humanitarian identity on our sleeve or wristband, and we can now collect our causes as Facebook "friends," amassing philanthropic social capital. Are these signs of ever more exploitative humanitarian spectacle for American consumption, or of a refreshingly honest philanthropy that does not hide its innate narcissism? Does the "conspicuous consumption" of humanitarianism anesthetize our encounter with structural inequalities, or is it giving rise to creative forms of entrepreneurial activism and mobilizing a new generation of cosmopolitans?

In this chapter I consider visual media produced within the humanitarian sector, focusing in particular on Invisible Children, Inc. (IC) as one of the most innovative and lucrative new media–driven humanitarian campaigns and an exemplary case of some of the shifts in the contemporary visual culture of Western humanitarianism. I begin with a discussion of the relevance of visual culture and the work it performs in the field of Western humanitarianism, tracing the role of visual images in constructing both "beneficiary" and "donor" identities within the humanitarian narrative.[7] I argue that there has been a growing emphasis on the identity of the donor in recent years, in tandem with the shift from a realist to a postmodern, youth-oriented, pop culture aesthetic. These shifts are not absolute, nor are they without historical precedent; but tracing them offers a heuristic for understanding the changing terrain of the visual culture of humanitarianism and its implications in the contemporary era. Both the generative and the counterproductive potential of the conspicuous production and consumption of humanitarian media in the US are considered.

Visual Culture and Western Humanitarianism

Being a spectator of calamities taking place in another country is a quint-essential modern experience. (Susan Sontag, *Regarding the Pain of Others*)

The visual culture of humanitarianism is most productively understood as a visual *economy*, facilitating certain material practices (economic, political, technological, social, cultural, institutional, etc.) that have significant geopolitical implications.[8] For example, the Western humanitarian narrative and its visual culture have, throughout modern history, been imbricated in the material practices of Christian evangelism, colonialism, Cold War politics, international development, neocolonialism, neoliberalism, and commodity capitalism.[9] A groundswell of humanitarianism—the basis of its modern form—arose in the late 18th century, embedded within the broader bourgeois, liberal "civilizing process" occurring at the center and periphery of Western colonialist empires.[10] Anne McClintock argued that the production of a certain visual culture was instrumental in reconciling Enlightenment thinking (i.e., individual liberty and scientific rationalism) with this imperial project.[11] Colonial discourse depended upon the visual construction of narratives of primitivism and civilization in which the Western "self" was reified as civilized and the non-Western "Other" as primitive and in need of paternal rule or saving. Representations of the distant, "primitive," "uncivilized," or suffering Other thus served as teleological signifiers of Western "progress," helping to legitimate discourses and practices of colonialism, capitalism, and early humanitarianism.[12] Visual technologies like photography, advertising, museums, and exhibitions such as the world's fair enabled the display of colonial ethnography in what McClintock called "the commodity display of progress."[13] The result was a regime of representation that infantilized (and simultaneously commodified) the non-Western Other—particularly the dark-skinned African Other—through an evolutionary trope of the "Family of Man" in which "native" was conflated with "child."[14] It implied a paternal dependency that continues to undergird Western discourses of humanitarianism and development, and set a precedent for contemporary humanitarian commodity spectacle and consumption.

Particularly since the Christian missions of the 19th century, the visual culture of humanitarianism has developed a certain iconography, or set of recognizable tropes, that communicates key elements of the humanitarian narrative.[15] Leshu Torchin contends that "the evangelical legacy produced missions that provided the transnational infrastructure for sharing visual testimony and administering aid and offered an instrumental iconography of suffering."[16] This iconography—or "mobilizing aesthetics"—was critical; humanitarian projects require the visual articulation of *need*, as well as the *solution* to obtain political legitimacy and funding, paralleling the persuasive strategy of commercial advertising.

For much of the 20th century, humanitarian discourse was largely embedded within the Cold War narrative of the expansion of liberal—and later neoliberal—modernization and development, which discursively figured Western powers as guarantors of freedom, progress, peace, and poverty reduction while constructing the "third world" as needing protection and development.[17] An aesthetic of realism characterized the construction of the humanitarian beneficiary.[18] Enabled by the development of visual mass media technologies, photography and documentary film in particular,[19] the realist aesthetics and the earnestness of much of 20th-century humanitarian discourse implied, falsely, a philanthropic space outside of the marketplace of cultural consumption.

In the 18th century, the emerging English middle class's newfound *distance* from physical discomfort was one of the conditions that enabled the rise of modern humanitarianism; images of suffering, while evoking "spectatorial sympathy," also functioned to reaffirm the distance one had attained from such suffering.[20] By the 20th century, however, the vast majority of the visual artifacts of American humanitarianism were produced with the intent of bringing distant, "real" human suffering *closer* to the American public-as-donor—just close enough so that one could possess the image, as evidence of their philanthropic contribution. For example, photographs of sponsored children have served as a common tool for donor cultivation, used by organizations like World Vision and Save the Children.[21]

Despite the fact that documentary photography and video remain the predominant genres of visual representation of humanitarian organizations' work and beneficiaries, the commitment to a realist aesthetic has notably diminished.[22] It has been eclipsed by the full integration of corporate brand culture and humanitarianism. The niche branding of identities and lifestyles characteristic of commodity capitalism now includes the branding and consumption of humanitarian projects—and the humanitarian identity—as *products*.[23] In addition to your cause-of-choice wristband, you can signal your humanitarianism by slapping down your RED American Express credit card to purchase your Product RED Converse sneakers. The ultimate commodity fetishization—and distanciation from suffering—is achieved; instead of the image of a person in need, we purchase a sneaker reflecting our philanthropic identity. All of this speaks to the symbiotic relationship between Western modernity/postmodernity, humanitarianism, and capitalism, a relationship fueled by the productive, seemingly dialectical tensions between *realism and spectacle* and *proximity and distance* to human suffering produced in large part through visual culture.

The Donor, the Beneficiary, and the Humanitarian Narrative

Lilie Chouliaraki calls the symbolic politics of humanitarian media and its ability to spur action, the "mediation of suffering." She sees the news media in particular—broadcasting stories of crises worldwide via satellite—as "agents of cosmopolitan imagination."[24] Margaret McLagan has also analyzed the ways in which the spectacle of suffering circulates through mass media platforms, working to establish "witnessing publics" that can be mobilized as advocates or donors.[25] The majority of this literature has sought to understand how media representations of humanitarianism's potential beneficiaries work to elicit active responses from viewers.

Lynn Fujiwara, for example, has analyzed how "people categories" such as *refugee* have been "constructed to carry moral and emotional meanings to gain the 'sympathy-worthiness' that may result in some form of social change."[26] Much of this discursive production has occurred through the use of visual stereotypes, "victim frames,"[27] and other essentializing modes of depicting "third world–looking people."[28] In a sector that is highly vulnerable to fundraising pressures, those responsible for producing visual representations of humanitarian need often find themselves in a double bind, juggling the fiscal pressure to mark beneficiaries as helpless victims in order to raise funds for programs that aim to empower these very same beneficiaries. Maintaining the dignity of beneficiaries while exploiting the representation of their very disempowerment is one of the primary discursive struggles within the sector, waged largely through visual representation.

The majority of scholarship on humanitarian visual culture thus focuses on the construction of the beneficiary.[29] Less attended to, but increasingly significant, is how the identity of the Western *donor* is constructed through visual media. Narratives of distant humanitarian crises also play a critical role in the constitution of *American* subjecthood, as selfless and powerful donor, activist, paternal figure, or savior. Rosemary Hicks and Jodi Eichler-Levine offer the recent example of the Save Darfur Coalition's discursive justification for American intervention in Darfur, showing how activists in the US "demonstrated their Americanness by assuming the identities of powerful saviors."[30] Humanitarian donors, by "evoking their powers as Americans to 'save,'" may reaffirm "collective narratives of national identity"[31] and American exceptionalism.[32] Analyzing the social construction of the American donor is particularly relevant in the age of commodity activism, as the American public is increasingly asked to *buy* into humanitarianism and adopt it as part of their individual and collective consumer identities.

It is perhaps not surprising, then, that the earnestness of 20th-century depictions of humanitarian need is giving way to a trend toward "fair vanity"—a phrase proposed by pop star Bono in the first-ever "Africa Issue" of the American fashion and culture magazine *Vanity Fair*. Bono's stated strategy, as coeditor of the issue, is an explicit exercise in the fetishization of Africa: "I want people to see the adventure of Africa . . .to bring some sex appeal to the idea of wanting to change the world."[33] This is not only a fetishizing of the "needy" other but also the construction of the sex appeal of America-as-donor/consumer. Fair vanity, it seems, is not only about stylized and commodified philanthropy; it is also about adventure and spectacle. This is perhaps being most stunningly illustrated by the producers behind the "musical to believe in."

Invisible Children: A New Model and Mobilizing Aesthetic?

Jason Russell, Bobby Bailey, and Laren Poole founded Invisible Children in 2004 as recent University of Southern California graduates, after completing their documentary film *Invisible Children: Rough Cut*.[34] Only four years later, IC had ninety staff running development programs in Uganda and thirty US staff who, significantly, were almost exclusively under the age of thirty. In 2005 they raised more than $300,000; by 2008 revenue growth reached over $10 million.[35] At the time of this writing 2,098 US school clubs were registered to support IC projects in eleven Ugandan schools.[36] And as is increasingly popular in the commercial sector, IC utilizes user-generated content from its supporters to help collectively envision and market its mission, through Web 2.0 sites like Myspace, YouTube, and Facebook.

IC itself has produced two documentaries, several short videos (including music and dance videos), podcasts, and the graphically striking book *Global Night Commute: The Making of a Revolution* and is producing a feature film about its experiences "discovering an unseen war" in Uganda. The high production quality and style flaunt many postmodern trappings:

nostalgic aesthetics, self-deprecating humor, intertextuality, pastiche, and camp. IC's campaign is multimedia and multiplatform and exhibits transmedia storytelling on a level matched by few, if any, humanitarian organizations to date.[37]

Creative storytelling through visual media is at the core of the organization's dual mission to be "both an innovative media-based organization" (i.e., a production company) and a humanitarian/development nongovernmental organization.[38] Approximately 50 percent of its programming budget is therefore spent on media and event production, largely in the US, with the stated goal of bringing "awareness to the situation and promoting international support of the peace process taking place."[39] IC refers to these production activities as the "Movement" component of the organization (as opposed to its direct aid and development work), which uses stories and images to connect to and mobilize US youth to support its projects in Uganda. This in turn produces content for more stories, creating a circular process of humanitarian media production.[40]

The IC Movement encourages innovative fundraising, activist, and lobbying techniques just as zealously as it solicits donations, if not more so. Through organized competitions, IC challenges its student clubs to be entrepreneurial and creative in their fundraising strategies; participants have grown and shaved mustaches, convinced their teachers to shave their heads if a fundraising goal was met (a "shave it to save it" campaign), and landed "floks" of plastic pink flamingos in neighbors' yards that were subsequently removed for a donation. Club members document these tactics on video and upload and share them on YouTube. IC is seen as a leader in innovative uses of Web 2.0 platforms for nonprofit campaigning; its strategies have included an exclusive, semisecret online social network called the "Vanguard" for young IC supporters wanting "a deeper experience."[41] Given its remarkable fundraising success, unprecedented US student mobilization for Uganda,[42] cutting-edge uses of Web 2.0 media tools, and unconventionally large proportion of its budget allocated to media production, IC's claim that it has "redefined the concept of humanitarian work" as a "new brand of charity" may not be entirely unwarranted.[43]

In IC's media, emphasis is placed on the American donor/activist as much as, if not more than, IC's beneficiaries. Invisible Children's videos unapologetically embrace the opportunity for personal growth offered by entrepreneurial participation in the humanitarian adventure. IC sends the winners of high school fundraising competitions, organized through an online social networking site, to Uganda to visit the schools and camps of internally dis-

9.2. Book cover courtesy of Invisible Children, Inc.

placed communities that their funds support. This is the topic of IC's second documentary, *Go*,[44] which follows three US high school students' experiences in Uganda. The factors responsible for the internally displaced person (IDP) camp—including the Ugandan government's discursive framing of the conflict to justify mass, forced displacement[45]—go unquestioned by the students, at least on camera. Instead, the IDP camp serves as the setting for their emotional adventure into a dangerous unknown in an attempt to "save" the Africans from themselves, echoing—indeed regurgitating—familiar missionary and colonialist narratives. This is exemplified when one of the American teenage girls seemingly saves a young Ugandan woman by convincing her to continue taking her HIV medications; a resolution that, the film suggests, would not have come to pass had it not been for the American teenager. At the same time, the American humanitarian is "saved" as a kind of virtuous, redemptive being.

IC cofounder Bobby Bailey sets the tone of *Go*'s filmic journey, in which the audience sees Uganda through the eyes of the American teens. From his seat on the back of a motorcycle cruising through the streets of Kampala, Bailey turns to the camera and says: "Welcome. This is *your* adventure." A safari-esque sequence of the students traveling through Uganda atop buses and motorcycles, interspersed with elephant and alligator sightings, precedes their journey into the IDP camp. The sequence plays like an adventure travel advertisement, and the effect is a sense that this is, ultimately, about disaster tourism and its function in constructing the Western humanitarian experience, or what Alexandra Schultheis calls "humanitarian autobiographies."[46]

The youths' discourses of personal growth in *Go* overtly express what more "adult" humanitarians have been less willing to acknowledge: that, at its core, the humanitarian experience is one of finding oneself through the encounter with the (suffering) Other—in a sense, a process of mutual saving. Upon return to the US, the young American from the wealthiest of the participating schools reflects, "I thought I was gonna go [to Uganda] and like help them and change their world. . . . I thought I was going to be changing them. But coming back it's like, it was the complete opposite, like I feel like I took so much more from it than they ever could."[47] This complements the voice-over that concludes the students' adventures in Africa: "Some people are born into privilege. But privilege is relative. And what we've really been given is a responsibility to give back—human to human. We all come from somewhere, but that's not what life's about. Think instead of where you can GO."[48] Such discourse in the film reaches a level of candidness rarely exhibited by humanitarian organizations. And yet, the contradictions, tensions, structural inequalities, and systemic violence underlying the crisis in northern Uganda are largely obfuscated by an insistence on the narrative of the young humanitarian, a narrative that is squarely situated within the dehistoricizing, neoliberal discourse of entrepreneurialism (e.g., think of "where you can go" as opposed to where you came from, historically).

IC's media has thus relied upon discursive and visual strategies that function to dehistoricize, essentialize, and exoticize Africa. For example, essentialized "African children" (an insert title repeated multiple times in IC's first documentary) are decontextualized from the specificities of culture, language, political economy, and history. The deployment of the generic "African children" harkens back to the "Family of Man" trope and implies a paternalistic relationship while erasing African (adult) agency. IC's *Rough Cut* does not explore the ways in which Ugandans are addressing these challenges themselves, enabling the narrative to privilege the salvational role of the American protagonists. Instead of a film that explores child soldiers as "indicators of global inequalities that would require structural changes to rectify," a narrative of youthful humanitarian adventure is offered for the Western viewer's consumption.[49]

Like many nonprofits today, Invisible Children sells merchandise such as Ugandan-made bracelets to raise funds; these are accompanied by short films about the lives of individual Ugandan children, harkening back to World Vision's and Save the Children's child sponsorship packages.[50] Yet these products—or "merch," as IC calls them—are just one part of what the organization has branded as a hip, life-changing experience for young do-gooders. The Invisible Children lifestyle includes tours across the US in IC buses led by IC "roadies," who travel with rock bands and hold screenings at high schools and colleges across the country. As Jason Russell explains, these young humanitarians

> want to really continue to do it as a lifestyle. It's a paradigm shift that they've had and they want more. . . .We've had hundreds of people who have gone in [*sic*] Northern Uganda to visit the Invisible Children. And many have stayed and not come home because they want to see a better future for these kids.[51]

The echo of earlier civilizing projects is not faint, but is pop-culturized and combined with the cultivation of an entrepreneurial community of youth activists drawn to the adventures of life "on tour."

The IC Movement is, however, expanding the modes of participation in the international humanitarian sphere, traditionally dominated by elite philanthropists, for a younger American public.[52] This is one way in which IC's pop culture tactics appear to be generative. Further, IC's approach may contain the potential to change the nature of these donors' relationships to their beneficiaries. Zine Magubane suggests the use of Johannes Fabian's theorizing on the potential of *coevalness* to interrogate contemporary practices of American philanthropy.[53] Fabian, critiquing anthropological discourse, argued that "whatever objectivity we can hope to attain must be founded in intersubjectivity." He utilized the concept of coevalness to suggest that in order "to knowingly be in each other's presence we must somehow share each other's past."[54] Invisible Children's practice of bringing youth to Africa to change their perspectives, and the resulting production of humanitarian narratives, might be done in such a way as to establish American and Ugandan youth as "coevals." This, in essence, appears to be one of IC's goals, and scenes throughout the documentaries of the youth sharing their personal histories and discovering commonalities suggest this as a real possibility—at least for the winners of IC's competitions and, perhaps vicariously, their young audiences. We see the American and Ugandan teen girls doing their makeup together and talking about boys, and the boys beatboxing together. The stereotypically gendered nature of these "coeval" moments aside, they function narratively to "humanize" the Ugandan protagonists for an American audience and create moments of identification, albeit on American cultural terms and largely dehistoricized. Crucially, Fabian's conceptualization of coevalness requires that "*both parties* must be recognized as knowers as well as known."[55]

The narrative of mutual saving, insofar as it is a self-aware one that acknowledges the inherent power differential in the relationship between donor and beneficiary, may also contain the possibility of coeval identification or intersubjectivity. A recent IC campaign speaks directly to this potential. The campaign was called "The Rescue of Joseph Kony's Child Soldiers" and had the slogan "Abduct yourself to free the abducted." Like the 2006 Global Night Commute, IC mobilized thousands of youth across the US (and some internationally) to advocate for the release of the Lord's Resistance Army's child soldiers and an end to the conflict.[56] The concept of The Rescue was to secure local, national, and international media coverage by staging a public "abduction" of IC's protesters, who would then be "rescued" if and when a "mogul" (celebrity, state governor, or a member of Congress or their representative) made a public statement of support and media coverage was secured. In this way, as in the Global Night Commute, participants embodied the role of the victim in order to become the savior—a physical enactment of the process of mutual saving.

9.3. The Rescue campaign, Washington, D.C., April 2009. Courtesy of Invisible Children, Inc.

These campaigns involve a degree of participatory spectacle unparalleled in the humanitarian sector. Popular participation is a key component of Stephen Duncombe's conceptualization of *ethical spectacle* as an activist tactic: the collective, carnivalesque, self-reflexive enactment of a social change "dream," performed as a spectacle but tied to real material goals and actions.[57] In his formulation, the public must participate as coproducers, much like IC's Global Night Commute and The Rescue events. A strength of the participatory model for the production of humanitarian visual culture is that the conscious experience of performing spectacle could cultivate a more self-reflexive, critical practice of visual production and consumption.[58] IC's events signal the generative potential—and youth appeal—of collaborative spectacle. Yet on the whole, the production and packaging of IC's media and events to date limit this potential for coevalness or "ethical spectacle" to meaningfully challenge existing power dynamics; conventional discourses of the relations between Africa and the West, and the role of humanitarian aid in helping to maintain these relations, remain intact.

Perhaps the most glaring example of this problem is IC's strategy to market *Go*. Three special DVD packages of the film for purchase contained a "golden ticket" that could be redeemed for a free trip to Uganda. The reference to Roald Dahl's children's novel *Charlie and the Chocolate Factory* was quite intentional though painfully unironic. At the time of this writing, the first two golden tickets had been found; a video of the first winner, an ecstatic young ticket holder from Salt Lake City, Utah, was posted on IC's website, replete with the sound track and font from the title sequence of the original 1971 film adaptation of the novel.[59] If metaphors help construct our cultural realities, we must ask ourselves, *what* is IC's "chocolate factory" producing? The answer seems to be humanitarian adventure and consumption, reminiscent of the imperial adventure marketed and consumed in the 19th century.

Such problems with IC's media were part of my motivation for writing about the contemporary visual culture of humanitarianism, yet some of its most recent media project a more self-reflective and critical humanitarian discourse. In *Go*, some of the shortcomings of IC's first documentary are rectified; the Ugandan government's role in the forced displacement of the Acholi population is at least referenced (though not interrogated), and the perspectives of some African experts are included. And while I was writing this chapter in 2009, IC released a short fundraising video that addresses the discourse I was interrogating. *TRI 2009* briefly narrates the problematic history of Western humanitarianism in order to position IC's approach in contrast to this history, as one that is based on listening, activism, creativity, and perhaps even coevalness: "We decided to go out and listen instead. *Really* listen. And the needs of the needy soon became the desires of friends. . . . But it did not end there; our once self-righteous charity invasion was transformed into an inclusive and ferocious quest for justice."[60] An area for future analysis is the extent to which these discursive shifts have become consistent across IC's media, how this may change the humanitarian identities they are cultivating, and whether and how these discursive shifts translate into changes in their material practices in Uganda.

Conclusion

The combination of the proliferation of humanitarian visual culture and the neoliberal construction of donors-as-consumers suggests that the power of humanitarian public opinion, increasingly expressed via consumption, may be growing; the geopolitical implications of this remain uncertain but not inconsequential. Does "fair vanity" run the risk of catering too heavily to the whims and fashion trends of potential donors, or might it lead, as IC is endeavoring to do, to the cultivation of a broader, more cosmopolitan (and generous) humanitarian public?

Market forces and the production of visual media have been key to the construction of humanitarianism throughout its modern history. The historical and political contexts of Western humanitarianism, however, are conventionally obfuscated in order to sell the humanitarian identity to donors, resulting in the production of a decontextualized, ahistorical visual culture and discourse. The question thus is whether fair vanity and the pop-culturization of humanitarianism primarily serve to anesthetize or obfuscate structural inequalities, or whether they contain other generative potentials for social change. Further, *what*—and *whose*—social change we are talking about must continually be interrogated.[61]

Invisible Children's media are bold, beautiful, and captivating the minds of tens of thousands of American youth. They are creating a space for idealism that works within the context of postmodernism and neoliberalism, which is precisely its promise and its peril. Radically reconfiguring humanitarianism will likely require the innovative vision of youth, from both the global North *and* South; it will undoubtedly require a re-visioning that moves beyond the tropes that have historically produced and maintained the West's hegemonic relationship with the subaltern Other, allowing for the articulation of different discourses and logics.

"Fair vanity" may prove to be a more self-aware humanitarian culture that acknowledges self-interest and personal discovery in the encounter with the other. If a turn from realist to postmodern, youthful aesthetics signals a turn away from mimesis-as-earnestness, this may create space for image producers in the humanitarian sector to escape the double bind that requires the portrayal of suffering and victimhood to establish the humanitarian narrative and renders beneficiaries powerless. Yet while the focus on constructing the identity of the donor may offer an escape from the challenges of representing difference and suffering, it remains grounded within the logic of neoliberal consumer capitalism and identity branding. It is thus critical to acknowledge that the pop-culturizing of humanitarianism and its open consumption may further subject the sector to market pressures and steer much-needed resources toward media production (rather than beneficiaries) in an effort to cater to the ever-changing aesthetic and technological trends of US donors and to evade "compassion fatigue." Understanding the nature of this constraint on humanitarian organizations' communication processes and how it drives their visual economy necessitates ongoing analysis of the political economy behind humanitarian media.[62]

The shift in emphasis on the discursive production of the beneficiary to that of the donor, in tandem with a turn from realism to a youth-culture-inspired, postmodern aesthetics, is certainly not absolute and has historical predecessors. Yet this heuristic is useful in that it prompts us to question what is at stake in how the humanitarian narrative is constructed, and helps identify critical areas for analysis of its contemporary visual culture. The relationship between the "prosumer" (producer *and* consumer of user-generated content) and humanitarian consumption is one such area that requires further analysis. The goal of these critical exercises should not be solely academic; the humanitarian sector should continue to cultivate, in *practice*—and, perhaps, in play—a self-critical discursive environment characterized by greater accountability, humility, privileging of local knowledge and solutions, and which works to challenge the relations of power between donors and beneficiaries.

As a former employee in the humanitarian sector, I am well aware that an academic critique will not alleviate the very real material circumstances and structural violence that afflict humanitarianism's so-called beneficiaries. My intention is not to denounce humanitarianism as simply a veneer for geopolitical manipulation but rather to make the point that the cultural and political field of humanitarianism is a complex and rightfully contested one, and that its visual economy plays a determining role in material relations and outcomes. The goal is to help make visible the ways in which popular consciousness of this structural violence (partly responsible for creating the need for such a sector in the first place) is curtailed under the pressures of the visual economy of humanitarianism in the US.

NOTES

1. I am grateful to the editors, Alexandra Juhasz, Curtis Marez, Inna Arzumanova, and Zhan Li for their insightful feedback on earlier versions of this chapter. I am also indebted to Invisible Children for providing the images for inclusion in this chapter.

2. Invisible Children, http://www.invisiblechildren.com (accessed December 7, 2008). Children living in the internally displaced person (IDP) camps in northern Uganda who walk to town centers nightly to avoid capture by the Lord's Resistance Army (LRA) are referred to as "night commuters." Some cite the subsequent reduction in night commuting as evidence of the campaign's success; see Susan Resnick West, "Invisible Children: A Case Study" (working paper, Annenberg School for Communication, University of Southern California, 2008).

The video "A Musical to Believe In" can be viewed at http://www.youtube.com/watch?v=N6QWdVD4zsc.

3. D. Robert DeChaine, *Global Humanitarianism: NGOs and the Crafting of Community* (Lanham, MD: Lexington Books, 2005); Kirsten A. Gronbjerg and Laurie Paarlberg, "Community Variations in the Size and Scope of the Nonprofit Sector: Theory and Pre-

liminary Findings," *Nonprofit and Voluntary Sector Quarterly* 30, no. 4 (2001): 684–706; Kathryn Sikkink and Jackie Smith, "Infrastructures for Change: Transnational Organiza-tions, 1953–93," in *Restructuring World Politics: Transnational Social Movements, Networks, and Norms*, ed. Sanjeev Khagram, James V. Riker, and Kathryn Sikkink (Minneapolis: University of Minnesota Press, 2002), 24–44.

4. Margaret McLagan, "Circuits of Suffering," *Political and Legal Anthropology Review* 28, no. 2 (2005): 223–39; Lilie Chouliaraki, "Distant Suffering in the Media," Professor Lilie Chouliaraki Inaugural Public Lecture, London School of Economics (February 27, 2008); Inderpal Grewal, *Transnational America: Feminisms, Diasporas, Neoliberalisms* (Durham, NC: Duke University Press, 2005).

5. I use the term "humanitarianism" broadly throughout this chapter to include philan-thropically funded sectors concerned not only with crisis response but also with alleviat-ing poverty and violence. Development, human rights, and humanitarian discourses are closely related and often interdependent; for a relevant discussion of the relationship between human rights and humanitarian discourses, see Grewal, 2005. For a discussion of some of the distinctions between these sectors, see Paul Harvey and Jeremy Lind, "Dependency and Humanitarian Relief: A Critical Analysis," *HPG Report—Humanitarian Policy Group*, no. 19 (2005): ii–50.

6. Margaret McLagan, "Principles, Publicity, and Politics: Notes on Human Rights Media," *American Anthropologist* 105, no. 3 (2003): 605–12; Chouliaraki, 2008.

7. The term "beneficiary" refers here to the recipient(s) of humanitarian aid. It is one of the discursive mechanisms of the humanitarian sector that has the effect of obfuscating the negative impacts that may also result (however inadvertently) from humanitarian aid or interventions; however, I use the term in this chapter to be consistent with the sector's terminology.

8. Fuyuki Kurasawa, "Perilous Light: On the Visual Representation of Distant Suffer-ing," *Cultural Shifts* (public lecture at the Institute of Political Economy, Carleton Univer-sity, March 28, 2008); David Campbell, "Geopolitics and Visuality: Sighting the Darfur Conflict," *Political Geography* 26, no. 4 (2007): 357–82; Deborah Poole, *Vision, Race, and Modernity: A Visual Economy of the Andean Image World* (Princeton: Princeton University Press, 1997).

9. Kiri Gurd, "Connections and Complicities: Reflections on Epistemology, Violence, and Humanitarian Aid," *Journal of International Women's Studies* 7, no. 3 (2006): 24–42; Adam Branch, "Against Humanitarian Impunity: Rethinking Responsibility for Dis-placement and Disaster in Northern Uganda," *Journal of Intervention and Statebuilding* 2, no. 2 (2008): 151–73; Rosemary Hicks and Jodi Eichler-Levine, "'As Americans against Genocide': The Crisis in Darfur and Interreligious Political Activism," *American Quarterly* 59, no. 3 (2007): 711–35; Alex de Waal, "War Games," *Index on Censorship* 36, no. 4 (2007): 6–11. For more detailed histories of Western humanitarianism, see Karen Halttunen, "Humanitarianism and the Pornography of Pain in Anglo-American Culture," *American Historical Review* (1995): 303–34; Mario Klarer, "Humanitarian Pornography," *New Literary History* 36 (2005): 559–87; Thomas L. Haskell, "Capitalism and the Origins of the Humani-tarian Sensibility, Part 1," *American Historical Review* 90, no. 2 (1985): 339–61; DeChaine, 2005; Richard A. Wilson and Richard D. Brown, *Humanitarianism and Suffering: The Mobilization of Empathy* (New York: Cambridge University Press, 2008).

10. Halttunen, 1995; Haskell, 1985.

11. McClintock writes, "To meet the 'scientific' standards set by the natural historians and empiricists of the eighteenth century, a visual paradigm was needed to display evolutionary progress as a measurable spectacle. The exemplary figure that emerged was the evolutionary family Tree of Man . . . racial hierarchy and historical progress became the fait accompolis of nature. . . .Imperial intervention could thus be figured as a linear, nonrevolutionary progression that naturally contained hierarchy within unity: paternal fathers ruling benignly over immature children." Anne McClintock, *Imperial Leather: Race, Gender and Sexuality in the Colonial Context* (New York: Routledge, 1995), 37–38, 45.

12. See also Tony Bennett, "The Exhibitionary Complex," in *The Nineteenth-Century Visual Culture Reader*, ed. Vanessa R. Schwartz and Jeannene M. Przyblski (New York: Routledge, 2004), 117–29; Haskell, 1985.

13. McClintock, 1995, 44.

14. McClintock, 1995, 38.

15. Kurasawa, 2008.

16. Leshu Torchin, "Ravished Armenia: Visual Media, Humanitarian Advocacy, and the Formation of Witnessing Publics," *American Anthropologist* 108, no. 1 (2006): 214.

17. Anne Orford, "Muscular Humanitarianism: Reading the Narratives of the New Interventionism," *European Journal of International Law* 10, no. 4 (1999): 679–711; Gurd, 2006; Arturo Escobar, *Encountering Development: The Making and Un-making of the Third World* (Princeton: Princeton University Press, 1995); Grewal, 2005.

18. Torchin's analysis of the 1919 film *Ravished Armenia* shows how a realist aesthetic was advanced to produce the humanitarian narrative and mobilize donors for the Near East Relief campaign.

19. Kurasawa, 2008; Torchin, 2006.

20. Halttunen, 1995, 309.

21. While this form of commodification of human suffering is possibly the most explicit insofar as the literal image of the beneficiary is exchanged, the commodification of images of humanitarianism's beneficiaries predates the 20th century. See Magubane, 2008; McLagan, 2005. Perhaps as evidence of the waning cultural resonance of humanitarian earnestness, the practice of child sponsorship is now widely parodied within pop culture entertainment. For example, *About Schmidt* (2002), *The Simpsons*, "Blame It on Lisa" (2002, season 13, episode 15), and *South Park*, "Starvin' Marvin" (1997; season 1, episode 9).

22. See McLagan, 2003, regarding this shift in human rights media.

23. Sarah Banet-Weiser and Charlotte Lapsansky, "RED Is the New Black: Brand Culture, Consumer Citizenship and Political Possibility," *International Journal of Communication* 2 (2008): 1248–68.

24. Chouliaraki, 2008, 5; Lilie Chouliaraki, "The Mediation of Suffering and the Vision of a Cosmopolitan Public," *Television & New Media* 9, no. 5 (2008): 371.

25. McLagan, 2003; McLagan, 2005.

26. Lynn H. Fujiwara, "Immigrant Rights Are Human Rights: The Reframing of Immigrant Entitlement and Welfare," *Social Problems* 52, no. 1 (2005): 81; see also Donileen R. Loseke, "Constructing Conditions, People, Morality, and Emotion: Expanding the Agenda of Constructionism," in *Constructionist Controversies: Issues in Social Problems Theory*, ed. Gale Miller and James Holstein (New York: Aldine, 1993), 207–16. People categories are also key discursive components of international human rights legal frameworks. "Refugee," for example, catalyzes a mandate for international response that the category of "internally displaced person" does not.

27. The *victim frame* is a widely recognized media frame. See Robert Benford and David Snow, "Framing Processes and Social Movements: An Overview and Assessment," *Annual Review of Sociology* 26 (2000): 611–39. It is based on "the archetypical role of the innocent victim . . ..Victimizing people is a dramaturgic technique." Baldwin Van Gorp, "Where Is the Frame? Victims and Intruders in the Belgian Press Coverage of the Asylum Issue," *European Journal of Communication* 20, no. 4 (2005): 489.

28. Ghassan Hage, *White Nation: Fantasies of White Supremacy in a Multicultural Society* (New York: Routledge, 2000).

29. See also Terence Wright, "Moving Images: The Media Representation of Refugees," *Visual Studies* 17, no. 1 (2002): 53–66; Liisa H. Malkki, "Speechless Emissaries: Refugees, Humanitarianism, and Dehistoricization," in *Siting Culture: The Shifting Anthropological Object*, ed. Karen Fog Olwig and Kirsten Hastrup (London: Routledge, 1997), 223–54; Campbell, 2007; Escobar, 1995.

30. Hicks and Eichler-Levine, 2007, 712.

31. Hicks and Eichler-Levine, 2007, 711.

32. de Waal, 2007.

33. "Bono Guest-Edits Vanity Fair," http://youtube.com/watch?v=v34u3KSnKSE (accessed December 7, 2008). Bono is also cofounder of Product RED; the One Campaign, an advocacy organization to fight poverty particularly in Africa; and Debt, AIDS, Trade in Africa (DATA).

34. *Invisible Children: Rough Cut*, directed by Jason Russell, Bobby Bailey, and Laren Poole (2004, Invisible Children, Inc.).

35. Resnick West, 2008.

36. Invisible Children, http://s4s.invisiblechildren.com (accessed June 11, 2009).

37. Henry Jenkins has popularized the concept of transmedia (also known as crossmedia or multiplatform) storytelling as "a process where integral elements of a fiction get dispersed systematically across multiple delivery channels for the purpose of creating a unified and coordinated entertainment experience." See Henry Jenkins, "Transmedia Storytelling 101," last modified March 22, 2007, http://www.henryjenkins.org/2007/03/transmedia_storytelling_101.html (accessed March 6, 2009).

38. Resnick West, 2008, 1.

39. Invisible Children, "Frequently Asked Questions," http://www.invisiblechildren.com/about/faq/ (accessed March 2009).

40. Resnick West, 2008.

41. Resnick West, 2008, 4.

42. Resnick-West, 2008.

43. Invisible Children, http://www.invisiblechildren.com/ (accessed March 2009).

44. *Go*, directed by Jason Russell, Bobby Bailey, and Laren Poole (2008, Invisible Children, Inc.)

45. Adam Branch has argued that the Ugandan government's discursive framing, which was largely adopted by the UN, obfuscated the underlying power struggle; the government-induced displacement was framed as a "result of LRA violence, not government violence," and was "re-framed as a purely humanitarian problem to be solved by foreign aid agencies." See Branch, 2008, 157. Further, he argues, the presence of humanitarian aid convinced many people to remain in the camps, yet the aid was not sufficient to meet their needs and in fact *created* a humanitarian crisis. In his account, the Ugandan case

exemplifies the symbiotic relationship between militarization and humanitarian intervention. Chris Dolan and Lucy Hovil support Branch's argument, although they view certain responses from the UN Security Council and the UN High Commissioner for Refugees as having challenged the Ugandan government's policies of militarization and encampment. Chris Dolan and Lucy Hovil, "Humanitarian Protection in Uganda: A Trojan Horse?," HPG Background Paper (London: ODI, 2006).

46. Alexandra Schultheis, "African Child Soldiers and Humanitarian Consumption," *Peace Review* 20, no. 1 (2008): 36.

47. *Go*, 2008.

48. *Go*, 2008.

49. Schulteis, 2008.

50. Invisible Children has also run a sponsorship program. See http://www.invisible-children.com/theMission/the_education_program (accessed June 11, 2009).

51. From an interview with Jason Russell by David Puente (Perspectives, ABC News Now, March 1, 2007). This migration of American youth to small communities in northern Uganda has yielded some problematic results, straining resources and relations. IC's website now reads, "As we've developed as an organization, we've seen how a large influx of people without a pre-planned purpose can be detrimental to a small community." "Invisible Children," http://www.invisiblechildren.com/about/faq/ (accessed March 2009).

52. Nearly 80 percent of IC's donations in 2009 were of twenty dollars or less (Invisible Children, http://blog.invisiblechildren.com/2009/11/move-over-bill-and-warren-im-poor-but-awesome/, accessed December 2009). Extensive demographic statistics on IC's supporters were not available at the time of this writing, but a 2009 online survey of IC's recurring donors found that more than 76 percent were female and nearly 47 percent were between the ages of twenty and twenty-five. See Invisible Children, "Recurring Donor Survey Results Report, " 2009.

However, IC's director of public and media relations Jedidiah Jenkins noted that, overall, the demographics of IC's youth supporters are not as diverse as the organization would like (J. Jenkins, unpublished interview by Sangita Shreshtova, 2009).

53. Zine Magubane, "The (Product) Red Man's Burden: Charity, Celebrity, and the Contradictions of Coevalness," *Journal of Pan African Studies* 2, no. 6 (2008): 102.1–102.25.

54. Johannes Fabian, "The Other Revisited: Critical Afterthoughts," *Anthropological Theory* 6, no. 2 (2006): 142, 145.

55. Fabian, 2006, 146, emphasis added.

56. Much of this mobilization was accomplished using the online social networking tools Facebook and YouTube. A similar IC event in 2007, called "Displace Me," was instrumental in securing the US State Department appointment of a senior adviser to focus on the peace talks in northern Uganda. See http://www.invisiblechildren.com/ (accessed March 2009).

57. Stephen Duncombe, *Dream: Re-imagining Progressive Politics in an Age of Fantasy* (New York: New Press, 2007).

58. See Campbell, 2007, for another discussion of the relevance of conscious performance to the production of humanitarian media and discourse. See also Melissa Brough, "Invisible Children: Participatory Culture and Humanitarian Spectacle," last modified February 26, 2010, http://sites.google.com/site/participatorydemocracyproject/case-studies/invisible-children.

59. "The First Golden Ticket Has Been Found," http://www.invisiblechildren.com/media/videos/ (accessed March 2009).

60. Invisible Children, "Give Peace a TRI," YouTube video, March 20, 2009, http://www.youtube.com/watch?v=XFI7q6uPjs8&feature=channel (accessed June 8, 2009).

61. Robert Chambers, *Whose Reality Counts? Putting the First Last* (London: Intermediate Technologies, 1997); Escobar, 1995.

62. Kurasawa, 2008; see also Simon Cottle, "Global Humanitarianism and the Changing Aid-Media Field," *Journalism Studies* 8, no. 6 (2007): 862–78.

PART THREE

Community, Movements, Politics

In 2010, a new Levi's billboard campaign featured "workers" from the steel belt town of Braddock, Pennsylvania, engaged in various poses of industrial labor using the slogan "We Are All Workers." What does it mean that such an iconic slogan from the history of the American labor movement is harnessed as corporate advertising? Against nostalgic laments that "there are no more movements," this part takes seriously the political meanings of such instances of corporate appropriation. Contributors to part 3 of this volume locate the emergence of commodity activism within the context of American social movements and the historical relations between activist politics and consumer practices. Illuminating shifts in discourses of "democracy" and democratic citizenship, this part explores the ways in which contemporary social action is being retooled to accommodate individual self-interest as the primary mobilizing modality of engagement. The Consumers' Republic, by these logics, remains the context for political participation as political agency is evermore ensconced within discourses of the market.

Among its conceptual objectives, this collection has sought to explore politico-economic and cultural adjustments that not only are redefining the practices and priorities of social activism but also circulating imaginaries of resistance, solidarity, and civic community in the neoliberal era. If, as our contributors in the previous two parts have noted, transformations in modes of activism—shifts that entail complex imbrications of branding, commodification, celebrity, and consumerism—have ushered in a range of ethical tensions in how we "do" citizenship and in what counts as "politics" at the present moment, the essays we present in this third and final part of the book centrally engage the implications of neoliberal ideologies for political formations, grassroots solidarities, and the equivocal promise of "community" as site of political redress and retrenchment.

As corporations and media celebrities lead efforts to "save Darfur," "fight AIDS," and "reNew Orleans," the essays in this third and final part focus on the implications of such commodified social activism for the "grassroots" and the sustainability and impact of political formations that emanate upward from civic communities. Authors in this part centrally explore the relations between politics and community as they shift under the discursive influences of neoliberalism. Thus, the chapters collected here consider from different perspectives, for example, the ways in which health and food have been incorporated into a broader governmentality, one that often connects the health of a nation with the health of individuals by encouraging commodity activism as civic duty; the way that feminist communities with a focus on the sex-positive retail industry can articulate progressive politics; the checkered influences of community coalitions as media policy is gradually yoked to the logics of commodification; and the various complications that arise when corporate social responsibility is charged to attract "hard-to-reach" communities of color.

We begin with a chapter by Samantha King that offers an analysis of the rise of corporate-sponsored "thons"—health-focused public events—walks, runs, rides, and so on, that bring masses of people together to raise funds to help combat chronic and terminal illnesses. King suggests that thons and the participant communities that cohere around them underscore the emergence of health as a neoliberal "supervalue" and serve as significant performative sites where physical well-being is conflated with virtuous citizenship. As responsibility for health comes to figure prominently in measures of proper citizenship, and as consumer-oriented philanthropy becomes the preferred mode through which to demonstrate responsibility to others, physical activity–based fundraisers represent a potent site for disciplining citizens to conformity with a variety of neoliberal values—self-control, civic responsibility, family management, and so on. Analyzing the microdynamics of power within the 2004 Avon Walk for Breast Cancer in Boston, King reveals how the thon, as a site that privileges consumption in the name of social change, has emerged as a key vehicle in the contemporary conflation of citizenship, social action, and consumerism.

In their chapter, Josée Johnston and Kate Cairns lay the historical groundwork for the rise of commodity activism through a focus on the politics of food. Charting tensions associated with what the authors term "eating for change," Johnston and Cairns examine particular histories, subjectivities, and forms of collective action that are imagined and enacted across sites of food politics. In the contemporary context of market dominance and state retreat, subcultures of "foodies," the production and distribution of local and/or organic food, and, more generally, the "food movement" offer a case to unpack tensions within these politics. Challenging ready bifurcations across celebrations and excoriations of contemporary "eating for change" campaigns, Johnston and Cairns argue that such reductive analyses of power vis-à-vis agency obscure possibilities for collective action within the politics of food.

Next, drawing insights from an ethnographic study, Lynn Comella situates the feminist-owned sex toy industry as a kind of social activism characterized by ambivalence about consumption *as* politics. Comella argues that feminist sex toy stores have created a context in which consumerism can lead to progressive sexual politics. Pointing out what is increasingly clear about commodity activism, Comella makes the case that all commodities do not carry the same political and social possibilities, and thus, not all "commodity activism" can be understood within a generalized framework. "Sex positive retailers" do not sell products alone; they also trade in ideology and political practices that enable sexual empowerment for women, empowerment that, within the contemporary cultural and political economy, is characterized by ambivalence about consumer capitalism.

In the next chapter, John McMurria examines shifts in how various advocacy communities have organized for and against the emergence of pay-TV—television delivery systems that require viewers to pay a fee for particular programs. As free over-the-air broadcast TV gives way to greater levels of pay-TV, McMurria finds evidence of increasing commodification in the logics of broadcast regulation as community and consumer coalitions fall in line with industry discourses that treat television programs as products bought and sold in the marketplace, and audiences themselves as commodities that are traded for profit between networks and their advertisers.

Comparing three cases—citizen responses to the emergence of pay-TV in the US in the 1950s and 1960s, recent deliberations over US regulations to require cable operators to offer subscribers the choice to purchase channels individually on an à la carte basis rather than in preset packages, and, finally, the 2008 cable and satellite TV regulatory reforms in Canada—McMurria maps how coalitions of community-based organizations variously championed and contested discourses of commodification within policy debates over pay-TV. As television's long-held public interest mandates are gradually edged out as untenable and perhaps unnecessary, McMurria highlights discursive, strategic, and structural shifts in accepted models of public service broadcasting, revealing the implications for communities and politics when citizen responses to pay-TV themselves become embedded within the logics of commodification and marketization.

In the final essay, Mari Castañeda troubles distinctions between social responsibility and marketing through her focus on "hard-to-reach communities;" specifically, Latina/o communities in the US that have been both exploited for their consumerism and vilified as the "wrong" kind of citizens. Questioning assumptions of social marketers that behavioral changes can be marketed as products, Castañeda looks at the health and domestic violence campaigns of Avon and Verizon and their impact on Latina/o communities and laborers. Revealing a marked ambivalence on the part of Latina/o communities concerning the intersections between consumption and politics, Castañeda maps out a complicated terrain of policy, health, and institutionalized racism to argue that while commodity activism (such as buying a Pink Ribbon lipstick from Avon to help raise awareness in Latina/o communities about breast cancer) does provide an important context for public education on issues that have historically remained cloistered in these communities, this kind of action sidesteps key infrastructural and intersectional frameworks that need to be addressed in order to adequately address health and domestic violence issues among communities of color in the US.

───────────────────────────────────── 10 ─────

Civic Fitness

The Body Politics of Commodity Activism

───── SAMANTHA KING ──────────────────────────

The past three decades have witnessed an exponential growth in physical activity–based fundraising events, or "thons." During this time, all the major health foundations in the US began to stage national networks of charitable walks, runs, and rides. Their efforts have included the Relay for Life and Making Strides Against Breast Cancer (American Cancer Society); Jump Rope for Heart and Hoops for Heart (American Heart Association); the Asthma Walk (American Lung Association); the Late Night Walk and Team in Training (Leukemia and Lymphoma Society); March for Babies (March of Dimes); and the Race for the Cure and the Breast Cancer 3-Day (Susan G. Komen for the Cure). In the same era, local foundations, schools, and hospitals have created a multitude of similar but smaller events. Moreover, at least one corporation, Avon, has joined the trend with the founding in 1998 of its Breast Cancer 3-Day, a sixty-mile walk.

Competition among businesses that specialize in creating and managing thons, and among their charitable partners, is intense. Organizations thus strive to introduce a steady flow of fresh gimmicks, and in some instances new categories of disease, with the intent of improving their market share of consumer-activists eager to do their part. In 2009, for example, four Canadian cities hosted the Underwear Affair, in which entrants walked or ran in their underclothes to raise money for "cancers below the waist."[1] Breast cancer is the chosen cause for the 15,000 participants in the annual Playtex MoonWalk, who stroll through the streets of London, England, in their bras.[2] For individuals with deeper pockets and a desire to mesh philanthropic activity with adventure tourism, Across the Divide, a company specializing in "exceptional worldwide challenges," organizes charitable treks to locations such as the Great Wall of China and the Everest base camp.[3]

The high overhead cost of staging these events and the relatively small sums of money they generate means that for the most part their appeal has

───────────────────────────────────── 10 ─────

| 199

little to do with their fundraising potential. As a 2007 study notes: "Without question, special events seem to be an extremely inefficient way of raising contributions."[4] Corporations and foundations counter such observations with the argument that regardless of their financial limitations, thons raise awareness of their target causes, cultivate potential donors, and build name recognition for the recipient organizations. Because the vast majority of events generate funds for health charities, their supporters also point to the health-promoting potential of large groups of people participating in physical activity for a worthy cause.

In a historical moment in which the discursive connections between physical well-being and virtuous citizenship have intensified (the panic around the so-called obesity epidemic being perhaps the most prominent example of this articulation), the latter claim lends itself to critique, but not to easy dismissal. Indeed, it is this dimension of the thon that forms the focus of my essay. I am particularly concerned with probing the resonance of the thon in the context of what Robert Crawford has identified as the emergence of health as a "supervalue" under neoliberalism[5]—that is, as a lens through which a variety of other values (e.g., discipline, civic responsibility, family) are filtered. I argue that as self-responsibility for health has come to figure prominently in measures of proper citizenship, and as consumer-oriented philanthropy has become the preferred mode through which to demonstrate responsibility to others, physical activity–based fundraisers represent a potent site for the celebration and recirculation of dominant norms and values. Moreover, as a site where consumption occurs both in the name of social change ("pay this entry fee, buy this T-shirt, and a cure for breast cancer will be found!") and as a commodity in itself (i.e., an item that corporations and foundations compete over in the philanthropic marketplace), I suggest that the thon represents a key vehicle in the contemporary conflation of social action with consumerism.

My analysis begins with a discussion of the preeminence of health in the US at the present historical conjuncture, with a particular focus on the fitness boom. I then move to a consideration of the relationship between the rise of neoliberalism and the contemporary preoccupation with philanthropy. The history of the thon I offer here centers on the moral resonances of health, shifts in the relationship between the state and the private sector under neoliberalism, and the transformation of the philanthropic and nonprofit industries. The final part of the essay focuses on field research conducted at the 2004 Avon Walk for Breast Cancer in Boston, Massachusetts.

By focusing on the microdynamics of power that characterize the walk, I seek to illustrate how such events are not simply metaphors for neoliberal values but tools that work to differentiate productive from unproductive bodies, deserving from undeserving recipients, and proper from improper citizens.

Neoliberalism and the Rise of Health as a Supervalue

The last three decades in the US have been characterized by a significant increase in the importance of health in everyday life.[6] Although what counts as health and how it should be achieved are highly contested, there is general agreement across the political spectrum that health is a necessary and worthy goal. Michel Foucault's work on biopower[7] has been particularly helpful in explaining the longer history of health as a social imperative. He points to the emergence, in the 18th and 19th centuries, of a form of power in which the health of the population became a particular concern of governmental institutions, practices, and discourses. Through mechanisms of surveillance (e.g., statistical research) that are internalized by individual subjects, the utility, appearance, and relationship of the self to the body become constantly visible and subject to normalization and conformity. Of course, how precisely health is defined, measured, or produced and resisted varies considerably across time and space. Crawford highlights some of the following factors as key to the emergence of health as a supervalue in the present moment: The substantial resources—institutional and individual, public and private— devoted to securing the health of the population; the expansion of health professions, the numbers of workers who populate their ranks, and the goods and services they offer; extensive media coverage of health; and the ascendance of the Internet as both an exhaustive source of expertise about medical problems and a primary medium of support and information sharing for e-patients.[8] In this context, Crawford argues, health is not a topic of interest confined to those who are ill or to the professionals who care for them but is instead a primary subject of conversation, especially in middle-class social networks. Disease causation, illness prevention, and wellness strategies have become central points of common interest, the subject of complex forms of lay knowledge, and key to the discourses through which contemporary identities are shaped and performed. This is not to suggest that such commitment to health translates into progressive social change, even if it is widely understood as a "good thing." As Eberhard Wenzel explains:

We are able to observe almost an obsession with them [health and the environment], as if individual changes in ways of life—important for the individual and significant for the culture though they may be—possessed the power to overthrow a system of economic relations that aims at growth in numerical terms rather than at development, enabling society to sustain its specific modes of private and public interaction.[9]

In other words, the fashioning of healthy identities, like other aspects of the preoccupation with the fit body, is molded by and generative of moral judgments that reflect the dominant political norms of contemporary neoliberal capitalism.

In the context of neoliberalism: "Personal responsibility for health is widely considered the sine qua non of individual autonomy and good citizenship."[10] According to Crawford, subjects "come to define themselves in part by how well they succeed or fail in adopting healthy practices and by the qualities of character or personality believed to support healthy behaviors."[11] Although the ability of individuals to act upon health discourses is acutely shaped by their access to material and cultural capital with class, race, and gender resonances, such constraints become largely invisible under the normalizing logic of health as a supervalue. Ill health thus comes to be seen as a choice, as a reflection of a lack of hard work and bodily dedication.

Of key importance to my analysis is Crawford's suggestion that the "new health consciousness" that gained ascendancy in the 1970s and 1980s was not simply reflective of the emergence of neoliberalism but in fact played a decisive role in the formation of this mode of organizing political and economic life.[12] A widespread awakening to environmental dangers and the effects of smoking was particularly important in producing concerns about "lifestyle" hazards, an interest in changing risk behaviors, and a new "take-charge" discourse of personal responsibility for health.[13] Thus, although corporations and government officials with a political and economic stake in a turn away from collectivism and regulation mobilized ideologies of individual responsibility to live healthily and stay in shape,[14] these ideologies also grew out of middle-class beliefs that the body offered a route to personal renewal and a secure future.

The turn to "working out" on the part of millions of previously sedentary, mostly middle- and upper-class Americans and the concomitant appearance of numerous new fitness-related products on the market were defining features of the emergence of health as a supervalue. Sociologists of sport have argued that the fitness boom of the 1980s represented a way to reinforce the prevailing ideology of Reaganism, which blamed the effects of a brutal economic downturn and pervasive social inequalities on the alleged individual inadequacies and familial dysfunction of the lower classes, especially poor blacks, while simultaneously celebrating individualism and free will.[15] As sedentary behavior and illegal drug use became twin evils of the moment, "Just Do It" and "Just Say No" emerged as mutually reinforcing imperatives of this period.[16] In sum, self-betterment and quality of life through healthy consumption became the normative codes of conduct and therefore that by which bodies were judged, celebrated, or condemned.[17] This relationship was induced not simply by the marketing and consumption of fitness products; instead, it was a strategy of neoliberal governmentality. Individuals were rewarded for adopting—or penalized for failing to adopt—strategies for biological self-betterment by networks of government that sought to reduce health costs by educating the public against bodily neglect and promoting the body as a locus of pleasure, self-expression, and personal fulfillment.[18]

Although other factors were also at play and indeed intersected with health discourses (e.g., the decline of organized labor, the racialized and gendered politics of the war on drugs, and so on), individual liability for health "played a decisive role" in the ascendance of personal responsibility over collective responsibility.[19] Crawford offers two reasons for this claim: First, the preoccupation with the healthy body became a model for what individual responsibility or lack thereof would differentially grant. In other words, health consciousness operated as "an embodied replication of individual responsibility for economic well-being."[20] Second, the emergence of "healthism," a term coined by Crawford in an earlier essay, contributed to the middle classes turning away from the movement for national health insurance in the late 1970s and opened the way for subsequent neoliberal attacks on the welfare state.[21] He writes: "What has become clear in hindsight is that individual responsibility for health, although not without challenge, proved to be particularly effective in establishing the 'common sense' of neoliberalism's essential tenets."[22] Among these was the idea that "virtuous citizens"—that is, those who looked after themselves—were unfairly burdened by paying taxes to provide medical care for those individuals who lacked appropriate bodily discipline. And efforts to centralize public control over health care played into anxieties over "big government," as the 1993 Clinton effort showed. In this context, fundraising tools that capitalized on the idea of exercise as a sign of healthy citizenship and which produced active rather than armchair philanthropists, and philanthropists rather than taxpayers, proved particularly appealing.

The abandonment of the ideal of collective and public responsibility for health, however historically tenuous it was in the US context, thus paved the way for commodity activisms to emerge. In the case of breast cancer, the late 1970s to the early 1990s were marked by the emergence of local, and later national, activism devoted to increased government spending on research, widened access to mammography, and regulation of surgical practices. The disease, in this context, was widely understood as a public responsibility appropriately responded to with grassroots organizing and pressure on the state and the medical profession. But as the 1990s unfolded, corporations and large foundations with a different conceptualization of proper citizenship, and of what constituted the problem of breast cancer, joined forces to promote the idea that the disease could be overcome by outpourings of individual, consumption-based, generosity.[23] Pink ribbons and 5K races thus started to replace petitions and protests as more legitimate vehicles through which to fight breast cancer, and the disease and responses to it came to be viewed as commodities, signifiers of identity and belonging that could be bought and sold. Left to the vagaries of the market, bodily well-being became increasingly subject to social and economic stratification, so that, for example, black-white disparities in breast cancer increased between 1975 and 2008, and indeed for other cancers affected by access to screening and treatment.[24] Thus, a body free of breast cancer became just one of many resources that were subject to dramatic "upward redistribution" under neoliberalism, and breast cancer itself yet another site at which inequality is widely tolerated and a concept of the public good gradually eliminated.[25]

Healthy Citizenship/Philanthropic Citizenship: The Emergence of the Thon

In order to understand how consumer-oriented, health-focused expressions of proper citizenship rose to prominence, it is also necessary to trace a related set of articulations that constitute the wide-ranging neoliberal project, namely, state-supported shifts in the approach of corporations to philanthropy and the rise of an industry devoted to fundraising. For it turns out that the present-day focus of the thon on health within a strictly domestic context, let alone on specific diseases like breast cancer, is quite far removed from its historical roots, which were entangled with the struggle to forge international cooperation in the post–World War II era and with issues of "third world" development.

During the 1950s, in response to high rates of poverty and malnutrition throughout the world, but especially in so-called developing countries, the Food and Agricultural Organization of the United Nations launched the

International Freedom from Hunger Campaign. As part of this operation, the American Freedom from Hunger Foundation (AFFHF) was established.[26] The AFFHF staged its first Walk for Development in 1968, and within a year 100 walks had raised more than $800,000 and involved more than half a million people in sixteen states. Between 1969 and 1970, 400 walks raised a further half million dollars and gained front-page attention in national media. The Walks for Development had three main purposes: to raise funds for development, to educate the public about poverty and malnutrition, and to develop youth leadership. Although health as measured by access to nourishment was a target of the fundraising, the language of health was largely absent from discourse surrounding the walk, and the health of the participants themselves was a nonissue.

According to former AFFHF officer Michael Seltzer, Walks for Development were different in other ways too. Operating under a donor choice format, the money raised often went to controversial causes such as National Welfare Rights and the America Indian Movement, and their public education frequently included radical critiques of structural inequality, racism, and colonialism. In addition, the walks were the means through which many youth became connected to the anti–Vietnam War movement. Seltzer claims that the professionalization and commercialization of fundraising events was the driving force in the gradual dissolution of Walks for Development. That is, these low-key gatherings run by volunteers working with small budgets could not compete with the splashy, costly, and professionally administered affairs that began to emerge in the 1980s—shifts that were the product of changes in both government and corporate approaches to the nonprofit sector.[27]

Although the US has long been characterized by a strong voluntary sector with close ties to prominent businesspeople, the existence of a fundraising industry, and the deployment of philanthropic initiatives as central components of corporate marketing strategy, are fairly recent developments. These shifts can be traced to the 1960s and 1970s, when federal funding for nonprofit organizations increased dramatically, leading to the rapid expansion of the voluntary sector.[28] During the late 1970s and early 1980s, however, publicly funded growth began to give way to increased commercial activity on the part of nonprofits, so that between 1977 and 1989, public-benefit nonprofit organizations experienced a 79 percent inflation-adjusted growth, over half of which was due to an upsurge in commercial activities.[29] The two most relevant reasons for these changes in the context of the present analysis were the Reagan administration's move to slash funding for social services, many of which were offered through voluntary sector partners, and its instruction to nonprofits to partner with the private sector, which was offered an incentive in the form of an increased limit on charitable deductions.[30]

In the context of an economic downturn marked by mergers and downsizing, the pressure to donate with the bottom line in mind intensified, and staff began to look for ways to "treat donations like investments" and thus to "expect some return from them."[31] It is this period that witnessed the emergence of strategies such as cause-related marketing, through which corporations sell products to consumers with the promise that a certain percentage of the sale price will go to a charitable cause, as well as other tools that had the effect of making businesses more conscious of the cost of giving and foundations more conscious of their marketability. By the 1990s, management guru Peter Drucker's argument that altruism cannot be the criterion by which corporate giving is evaluated had become a guiding assumption of contributions programs, as businesses discharged their social responsibilities by converting them into self-interest and hence business opportunities.[32]

Although the Reagan administration was the first to make corporate philanthropy an explicit part of a platform designed to undermine government health and welfare programs, all subsequent administrations have promoted philanthropy as a morally and economically viable means through which to respond to societal needs, in lieu of the state's role in mitigating the social effects of capitalism. In this context, Barack Obama's Office of Faith-Based and Neighborhood Partnerships, which allows government appropriations and tax benefits for church-based services, is only the most recent example of work undertaken since the Reagan era to replace general tax collections with voluntary revenue enhancers, and to devolve responsibility for functions previously administered by state agencies to individuals and nonprofit and for-profit organizations. The effect of this approach, to take just one example from the realm of health, is a piecemeal system deeply structured by social inequalities and oriented toward those causes that appeal to faith-based and other nonprofit providers. Although taxation and publicly funded and managed health care systems do not eliminate disparities, they attenuate them. Moreover, the governments that run them can be held accountable by the public, by the electorate, and by social movements. Public systems are not subject to the whims and fancies of individual donors or consumer-philanthropists who might at any time decide to put their dollars elsewhere.

Even with the immense injections of federal money into a range of industries and services in 2009 in response to the financial crisis, participation in voluntary giving—of time or money—continues to be touted as the preferable way to fund public services and, more important, for instilling civic responsibility and self-responsibility in the American people. Unlike the allegedly divisive and apathy-inducing technologies of nationalized health care or welfare, donning a brightly colored silicone bracelet or participating in a leisurely 5K stroll on a Sunday afternoon is thought to help rekindle America's "traditional" culture of personal generosity and constitutes a more harmonious, benevolent, active, and personally responsible citizenry. Thus, through corporate marketing and philanthropy programs with health themes (e.g., Bono's Product RED campaign, which raises funds for the fight against HIV/AIDS in Africa), and federal government policies to encourage voluntary initiatives in support of health research (e.g., the introduction of the breast cancer fundraising stamp in 1998), business strategy and political ideology have interacted in the production of techniques designed to encourage private giving.

From these developments, a new generation of philanthropic consultants trained in the principles of business administration has emerged. These consultants work for corporations and foundations and are also responsible for creating new tools and techniques of fundraising, such as overnight or late-night thons. Many of them populate the ranks of "special events" companies that partner with charitable organizations to manage their mass-participation activities. The nonprofit sector, in other words, has become more professionalized and more business-oriented. As the lines between the for-profit and nonprofit worlds are increasingly blurred, the competition for fundraising dollars intensifies. Sometimes such competition leads to the failure of low-key, small-budget events, and sometimes it leads to the proliferation of successful models, or at least models that are successful according to the measures of their creators.

To illustrate this point we can look to a series of transactions that have helped reconfigure the terrain of breast cancer special events in recent years. In May 2002, following criticism from activists upset with the high overhead cost and low returns of the Avon Breast Cancer 3-Day, a walk staged on behalf of the corporation by an events company named Pallotta Teamworks, Avon announced that it was abandoning its signature fundraising vehicle. Soon thereafter, the company revealed it would host its own series of thons— the Avon Walk for Breast Cancer—and Pallotta declared bankruptcy.

This sequence of events marked the end of Pallotta in name only, however. A few months later, the Susan G. Komen for the Cure Foundation began circulating advertisements for a three-day walk that looked remarkably similar to the publicity that Avon once used for its events; indeed, the logo was practically identical. The Komen Foundation, it turns out, had bought Pallotta's assets and hired former employees—who had obtained the rights to the 3-Day logo—to produce its new venture, which it would now run in addition to its Race for the Cure, a one-day, 5K run/walk. Then, in 2003, other former Pallotta employees took their trade to Canada, where they established the Weekend to End Breast Cancer. In 2006 their new company known as CauseForce, staged walks in six additional Canadian cities. That same year, CauseForce introduced the format to England, where it produced the Aviva Weekend to Breakthrough Breast Cancer in London and Birmingham.[33]

This series of transactions, from Avon's decision to leave Pallotta, but to maintain a walk, to Komen's decision to buy Pallotta's assets and establish a rival walk (when it already hosts another major series of events), to the movement of the format to new national markets, highlights the extent to which breast cancer thons have become highly valued commodities in themselves. Such events are now the subject of intense competition among a network of professional fundraisers who work across the corporate and nonprofit sectors. The main identification of these professionals is not with the particular cause that they are working to fund. Instead, they compete with one another for participants, and for the brand recognition that might enhance participation numbers in their particular thon. The amount of money any one thon might raise is of some concern, in part because of public skepticism about the overhead costs of these events, and in part because fundraising is their official purpose, but even the money generated becomes almost tangential in this model. Instead, the focus is on producing an experience for consumer-fundraisers that will keep them coming back, securing for the event its foothold in the marketplace for what are ultimately inefficient, low-return products, more effective at building name recognition for nonprofits and corporations than at raising funds.

The Avon Walk for Breast Cancer

In May 2004, I traveled to Boston to work as a volunteer for the Avon Walk for Breast Cancer (AWBC). Unable to meet the $1,800 minimum amount required to join the other walkers, and unsure that I wanted to ask friends to fund my research by contributing to an organization that I was to critically analyze, I thought a volunteer position would be the next most effective way to experience those aspects of the event that are inaccessible to the general public. My responsibilities lasted for only one afternoon, on the day before the walk, when I was assigned to work at the line for the registration desk and charged with verifying that participants had their paperwork in order.

It was here, in a large, windowless room on the campus of the University of Massachusetts, that I got my first, vivid, exposure to the microdynamics of power that give shape to events like the AWBC. Part of my job was to verify that entrants who had not yet met the minimum fundraising amount were now in possession of the dollars they owed before they reached the registration desk. If they were unable to pay the remaining money, I was to turn them away and inform them that they would need to come up with the correct sum within the next few hours—that is, before registration closed—or they would not be permitted to leave with the other walkers the following day. Nearly all participants I spoke with had met the target. Most of these women, like me, were white and middle-class in appearance. Although the age of participants ranged from sixteen to elderly, the event seemed to hold particular appeal for women in their late thirties and forties, many of whom had signed up for the walk with large groups of friends. The vast majority of walkers had a distinctly suburban aesthetic, with thick, long, shiny hair, slim, toned bodies, bronzed skin, and carefully applied makeup. Most were clothed in neat, brand-name athletic gear, and although many wore T-shirts or baseball caps that identified them as breast cancer survivors, I saw only one woman who was obviously sick (she was being pushed in her wheelchair by another participant). Of the 1,863 participants who came that day to register and pick up a large bag full of free goods, I estimated that approximately 3 percent were men (almost all of whom were white) and about 3 percent were women of color.

Although men made up only a tiny portion of the participants, a small group, dressed in luminous yellow T-shirts with "Men With Heart" emblazoned across the chest, stood out in what was otherwise a sea of pink and white, the official colors of the mainstream breast cancer movement. I soon noticed that these men were approaching the handful of women who the other volunteers and I had awkwardly and apologetically turned away. Listening to these exchanges, I learned that Men With Heart was a nonprofit organization composed of Boston businessmen who each year participate in the AWBC and the Komen 3-Day, as well as a range of smaller events. They were in the registration area to encourage eager participants to raise the extra funds they needed to walk. Members of Men With Heart would offer to write a check to get the women closer to the $1,800 minimum but, in the conversations I was witness to, not necessarily the full amount they required. One young woman, who was one of only a handful of African Americans among the potential participants, was a considerable way from her target, but her mother had recently undergone treatment for breast cancer and she desperately wanted to participate to show her support. After several exchanges with different men from the Men With Heart group, and after leaving the building at least twice to search for extra funds, she was finally presented with a check that enabled her to walk.

Clearly lacking the social networks or personal wealth of other participants, this woman had to depend upon these proper neoliberal subjects—entrepreneurial, economically self-sufficient, community-oriented—in order to join the other walkers. Put differently, her ability to practice proper neoliberal subjectivity—to make the physical sacrifices required to complete the thirty-nine-mile thon and to raise funds through personal interactions with private sponsors—relied on the generosity of others. Contrary to the idea proffered by politicians across the political spectrum that private giving, unlike state welfare, is a universal and inclusive practice free from divisive dynamics of race, gender, or class, this interaction reveals that such giving is in fact intimately and inescapably tied to these forces. As a young black woman of apparently modest means, she was always already situated through a discourse of welfare dependency that had been central to the ascendance of consumer philanthropy as the preferred mode of civic engagement in the 1980s and 1990s. The woman's receipt of the money reinvoked her dependence, but it did so without the mediation of the state and hence in a more personal way than it would have under a welfare regime. Simultaneously, the Avon walk provided a vehicle for the reproduction of the older white businessmen's privilege and the dynamic of obligation that was enabled by their gift.

In contrast to a collective, taxation-based model of economic redistribution, moreover, the consumer-oriented, individualist approach gave Men With Heart a *choice* in how they spent their money. They could decide who was deserving of their largesse and under what conditions. Ironically, within dominant discursive frameworks, this woman's need for financial assistance so that she could participate in the walk would be understood as legitimate in a way that it would not if she were seeking to, for example, feed her children. Such cultural validation stems in part from the ideological valence of active philanthropy and in part from those who are imagined as the recipients of the participants' largesse and sacrifice: in this instance, women with breast cancer who have been firmly situated in the national imaginary as courageous, innocent, and thoroughly deserving survivors.[34] Unlike the welfare queen—the quintessential antimother and, in the lead-up to reform, the primary symbol for the threat that a social state was said to pose to the nation's moral fabric—breast cancer survivors have come to represent the embodiment of white, middle-class, nationally sanctioned womanhood. They have been a spur to the outpouring of generosity that has signified and contributed to a shift away from the "nanny state" and toward a system in which the health and well-being of Americans is understood to be best left in private hands.

For the next two days, I joined my research assistant, Jennifer Scott, taking photographs, writing field notes, and talking with participants and other volunteers. The format for the walk was similar to other thons.[35] The event began and ended in Joe Moakley Park in the southern end of the city on a crisp and sunny spring morning. Participants began arriving at 5:00 am, although the walk was not due to begin until 7:00 am. They used this time to check in their overnight bags with volunteers (known as "crew members"), who piled the belongings into a fleet of large trucks that was waiting to drive them to the "Wellness Village," where the walkers would spend the night. They also helped themselves to bananas, yogurt, and granola bars that were laid out for breakfast, wrote personal messages on inflatable pink columns that were displayed at each walk, and chatted with other participants while stretching to the music that played from the main stage.

Following an inspirational opening ceremony that included addresses from Kathleen Walas, president of the Avon Foundation, Colleen Sullivan, an editor at *Health* magazine, a sponsor of the event, and Karen Cotton, a breast cancer survivor, walkers were sent on their way. Toilets and pits stops for snacks and drinks were set up at frequent intervals along the route, which took the walkers along Dorchester Bay, through the Inner Harbor, up to the North End, and into the city's suburbs. Participants had the choice of completing a full or half marathon that day. Both routes took them to the "Wellness Village" in Pine Banks Park, Malden, where they could enjoy showers, massages, yoga classes, hot meals, and live entertainment before going to bed in the tents that had been set up for them. There were long queues at the first aid stations and massage tables, where volunteers treated large blisters, swollen ankles, sore backs, sunburn, and other minor ailments, but the mood was generally festive.

By 4:00 pm the next afternoon, all the walkers were back in the park where they began their journey, having walked another 13.1 miles. Lined up in short rows, holding their joined hands high in the air, they marched toward the stage as music once again blared from the loudspeakers. The weather had turned cold, and the skies were gray, so the crowds of participants and their supporters were smaller than they were on the previous day, but the cheers for the volunteer crew who had been responsible for everything from security to food service were loud and enthusiastic. The closing ceremony was similar in content and format to the opening ceremony.

10.1. Participants write messages on a memorial column, Avon Walk for Breast Cancer, Boston, May 15, 2004.

10.2. Opening ceremony, Avon Walk for Breast Cancer, Boston, May 15, 2004.

10.3. Opening ceremony, Avon Walk for Breast Cancer, Boston May 15, 2004.

10.4. Closing ceremony, Avon Walk for Breast Cancer, Boston, May 16, 2004.

The most striking speech of the afternoon was given by Nelita Britos, who was introduced to the crowd as "an extraordinary woman who has been helped directly by your heroic efforts right here in the Boston area."[36] Through an interpreter, Britos explained that she "came to this country in search for the American Dream and for work to help my family that still lives in Uruguay;" but in 2002, she was diagnosed with breast cancer. She said: "The news was horrible. The first thing that I thought was not only that I may die, but that my son would be left here alone in a foreign country. I wasn't able to speak the language and I wasn't able to go out alone." At a moment when she was feeling particularly desperate, Britos received a call from an Avon patient navigator at Massachusetts General Hospital (MGH) in Chelsea offering to help. Britos admitted that at that point she told the woman, "I feel fine and I don't need anything" because she "already knew" she was "going to die." When the woman persisted, Britos agreed to go to the health center and "met these wonderful people with hearts," who helped her access medical and social services during her treatment and recovery. Britos concluded her speech by expressing her gratefulness for the program and her thanks to the employees at MGH. She continued:

> I would especially like to thank all of you because if it wasn't for all of you who are walking this weekend, and others who walked before, this program wouldn't have existed and I wouldn't have been able to get the care I needed. Without your dedication to fight this disease, I may not have been here today. But I am! Because of you! On behalf of my son and my family, I would like to thank you all from the bottom of my heart. Thank you!

As the crowd began a long and loud round of applause, Karen Borkowsky, the program director for the AWBC, said: "So congratulate yourselves because you're not only helping yourselves but you're helping thousands of women like this."

On the one hand, Britos's appearance represented a rare acknowledgment of cultural difference at a breast cancer special event. I have observed five such events over the past decade, and even in cities with sizable, or majority, racialized populations (e.g., Tucson, Arizona; Washington, D.C.), the figures who appear on stage during the opening and closing ceremonies do not come close to reflecting the diversity of women and men affected by the disease. Nor does the discourse that circulates at these ceremonies disrupt the homogenized image of the survivor—youthful if not young, light skinned if not white, ultrafeminine, and immersed in heteronormative relationships—

in whose name breast cancer fundraisers take place. Britos's speech also drew attention to the barriers faced by non–English speakers, recent immigrants, single mothers, and the economically marginalized when faced with serious medical diagnoses, as well the importance of providing services for them. Moreover, in the context of widespread, state-sanctioned, anti-immigrant sentiment, and as a Spanish-speaking worker from Latin America, Britos was far removed from the ideal recipient of American largesse. In this sense, her visibility at the Avon walk might be read as representing a provocative challenge to such sentiments, or to the idea that immigrants are undeserving recipients of US health and social services.

On the other hand, Britos's appearance and the response of Borkowsky and the crowd to it served to legitimize a system in which one's access to and quality of health care are dependent, in part, on the personal whims of individuals and the marketing concerns of corporations. There was no room in this format for questions about the social inequalities that leave people like Britos dependent on privately funded, haphazard services. Moreover, like the interaction between Men With Heart and the walker who had not met the minimum fundraising amount, Britos's appearance as the lone woman of color and lone non–English speaker at either the opening or closing ceremonies was structured by asymmetrical relations of power. Britos was situated—somewhat patronizingly—as the grateful recipient, forever obligated to the altruistic participants, many of whom, like her, were survivors of breast cancer. Unlike Britos, however, the survivor-walkers—largely American-born, financially secure, and insured—were able to act as both givers and receivers. More important, their ability to participate in the walk was representative of their heightened self-responsibility. They had been struck by breast cancer too, but their dependence on others for their recovery was not made visible; indeed, they were able to demonstrate their responsibility for their own well-being as well as that of women like Britos. These survivors were the picture of health, so to speak, in the neoliberal era: self-reliant, disciplined, apparently disease-free, physically active, and civically conscious.

Discipline and Consumption in Commodity Activism

In requiring participants to take responsibility for their fitness and to demonstrate compassion for those who will be the recipients of their private fundraising efforts, the thon supplies an "ethical rationale" for privatization and the shift away from general taxation toward corporatized individual philanthropy.[37] That is, as the realm of the social has shrunk and as politics is increasingly pursued in and through the realm of consumption, health practices like the thon gain increasing appeal, with both its physical activity and philanthropic components providing purpose and meaning. The self-discipline that allows participants to complete the long walk is not just a means to an end—a healthy body and some money raised in the fight against breast cancer; rather, the health of the participants becomes a means of expressing core social values and a criterion for judging others. It is a central part of their identities—a means of expressing themselves—and integral to their (consumer) styles of life.

To this point, I have not dwelled on the consumer dimensions of the AWBC. Yet it is in the relations of exchange that structure this event that the status of health as a supervalue is most clearly complicated and mitigated. For the control and denial that are integral to contemporary definitions of physical activity and health are in permanent conflict with the pursuit of pleasure that drives, and is at once driven by, consumer capitalism. As Susan Bordo argues in her now classic text, *Unbearable Weight: Feminism, Western Culture and the Body*, the conflict between the "producer and consumer sides of the self"[38] in this socioeconomic context is irresolvable. Proper subjects must necessarily oscillate between the "performance principal" and the "letting go."[39] The immanence of consumption to the healthy practices that constitute the thon makes these events an especially fraught site of social relations. Some form of corporate sponsorship supports even the smallest, most low-key thons, and at the bigger affairs brands are attached to T-shirts, banners, promotional materials, and, in the case of events like the AWBC, the name of the fundraiser itself. Furthermore, consumers pay in exchange for the opportunity to participate and to receive an official T-shirt and a variety of "freebies," which, like other commodities, become vehicles for fashioning their identities and expressing their values. Beyond the specific exchanges that characterize a typical thon, the ubiquity of the fitness and lifestyle industries in shaping contemporary subjectivities ensures that participants in these events are always already immersed in a whole range of purchasing practices related to health. In this context, the thon, a site of consumption and self-discipline, of receiving and giving, represents a potent tool for managing—if not rectifying—the contradictions of a health-obsessed capitalist culture.

Its success in this process and hence as a model for instilling neoliberal values is further enabled by a set of social norms that place good intentions and charitable works beyond political or intellectual reproach. Proponents of philanthropic citizenship repeatedly claim that the giving of time or money is a universal and inclusive practice, external to the realm of politics, transcendent of economic concerns, and free of the socially divisive forces of race and gender. What I have sought to argue, however, is that such renderings rely on the erasure of power relations that undergird charitable works. Rather than assuming that tools such as the thon can do no harm, that the good intentions of a healthy citizenry are enough to justify the existence of events like the AWBC, it is necessary to confront the deeply problematic deployment of philanthropic practice as an ideal of citizenship. In order to do so, we will need to resist the idea that social problems are best responded to with private giving, but also, and perhaps more challengingly, the status of health as a supervalue.

NOTES

1. http://www.uncoverthecure.org/index.html.

2. http://www.walkthewalk.org/Home.

3. http://www.acrossthedivide.com/home.asp.

4. "2007 Special Events Study," May 1, 2007, *Charity Navigator*, http://www.charitynavigator.org/index.cfm?bay=studies.events (accessed March 22, 2009).

5. Robert Crawford, "Health as a Meaningful Social Practice," *Health: An Interdisciplinary Journal for the Social Study of Health, Illness, and Medicine* 10, no. 4 (2006): 410.

6. Crawford, 2006.

7. Michel Foucault, *The History of Sexuality, Volume 1: An Introduction* (New York: Random House, 1990 [1978]).

8. Crawford, 2006.

9. Eberhard Wenzel, "Environment, Development and Health: Ideological Metaphors of Post-traditional Societies?" *Health Education Research: Theory and Practice* 12, no. 4 (1997): 414.

10. Crawford, 2006, 402.

11. Crawford, 2006, 402.

12. Crawford, 2006, 407.

13. Crawford, 2006, 407–8.

14. Alan Petersen, "Risk, Governance and the New Public Health," in *Foucault, Health and Medicine*, ed. Alan Petersen and Robin Bunton (London: Routledge, 1997), 189–206.

15. Cheryl L. Cole and Amy Hribar, "Celebrity Feminism: *Nike Style* (Post-Fordism, Transcendence, and Consumer Power)," *Sociology of Sport Journal* 12, no. 4 (1995): 347–69; Jeremy Howell, "A Revolution in Motion: Advertising and the Politics of Nostalgia," *Sociology of Sport Journal* 8, no. 3 (1991): 258–71; Alan Ingham, "From Public Issue to Personal Trouble: Well-Being and the Fiscal Crisis of the State," *Sociology of Sport Journal* 2, no. 1 (1985): 43–55; Susan Jeffords, *Hard Bodies: Hollywood Masculinity in the Reagan Era* (New Brunswick, NJ: Rutgers University Press, 1994).

16. Cheryl L. Cole, "American Jordan: P.L.A.Y., Consensus, and Punishment," *Sociology of Sport Journal* 13, no. 4 (1996): 366–97; Cheryl L. Cole and Samantha King, "Representing Urban Possibilities: Racism, Realism, and Basketball," in *Sport and Postmodern Culture*, ed. Genevieve Rail (Albany, NY: SUNY Press, 1998), 49–86.

17. Cole and Hribar, 1995.

18. Howell, 1991; Ingham, 1985.

19. Crawford, 2006, 409.

20. Crawford, 2006, 409.

21. Robert Crawford, "Healthism and the Medicalization of Everyday Life," *International Journal of Health Services* 10, no. 3 (1980): 365–88.

22. Crawford, 2006, 410.

23. Samantha King, *Pink Ribbons, Inc: Breast Cancer and the Politics of Philanthropy* (Minneapolis: University of Minneapolis Press, 2006).

24. Pinkowish, 2009.

25. Lisa Duggan, *The Twilight of Equality? Neoliberalism, Cultural Politics, and the Attack on Democracy* (New York: Beacon Press, 2003), xi.

26. Michael Seltzer, conversation with author, 1999.

27. King, 2006; Seltzer, 1999.

28. Elaine V. Backman and Steven R. Smith, "Healthy Organizations, Unhealthy Communities?" *Nonprofit Management and Leadership* 10, no. 4 (2000): 355–73.

29. Lester Salamon, "The Rise of the Non-profit Sector," *Foreign Affairs* 73 (1994): 109–22.

30. Edward Skloot, "Enterprise and Commerce in Nonprofit Organizations," in *The Nonprofit Sector: A Research Handbook*, ed. Walter W. Powellm (New Haven: Yale University Press, 1987).

31. John Dienhart, "Charitable Investments: A Strategy for Improving the Business Environment," *Journal of Business Ethics* 7, no. 1 (1984): 64.

32. Peter Drucker, "The New Meaning of Corporate Social Responsibility," *California Management Review* 26, no. 2 (1984): 59.

33. King, 2006.

34. King, 2006.

35. Samantha King, "Doing Good by Running Well: Breast Cancer, the Race for the Cure, and New Technologies of Ethical Citizenship," in *Foucault, Cultural Studies, and Governmentality*, ed. Jack Bratich, Jeremy Packer, and Cameron McCarthy (Albany, NY: SUNY Press, 2003), 295–316.

36. I have been unable to verify the spelling of Britos's name and so I have spelled it as it sounds on my tape recording of the event.

37. Crawford, 2006, 411.

38. Susan Bordo, *Unbearable Weight: Feminism, Western Culture and the Body* (Berkeley: University of California Press, 2003), 201.

39. Bordo, 2003.

11

Eating for Change

JOSÉE JOHNSTON AND KATE CAIRNS

Food shoppers are now regularly invited to practice their politics through their purchases. Whether it is upgrading to a fair-trade brew at a coffee shop, choosing organic milk at the supermarket, or perusing local fare at farmers' markets, consumers are increasingly encouraged to approach the seemingly mundane task of grocery shopping as a political event.[1] While varied, invitations to become ethical food shoppers are often organized around a central message: namely, that consumer food politics is a win-win enterprise, serving up delicious goods that also deliver a social or environmental "good." A food journalism article celebrating the rewards of locally grown vegetables exemplifies this sentiment: "We all know that eating in-season, locally grown produce is best—it's beneficial for the environment, for our health, and for the flavor of the dishes we prepare."[2] According to this account, the pursuit of individual self-interest offers the promise of social change—a narrative that, incidentally, has close parallels to classical market theorizing of private vices producing public virtues.

In this chapter we explore some of the tensions obscured by the seamless "eat for change" narrative of consumer food politics. While our focus is on food, we suggest that the win-win mantra is not unique to the politics of the plate. Rather, this seamless narrative circulates across many contemporary sites of commodity activism as a means of reconciling critical sticking points in the fusion of consumption and politics. To be clear, this chapter is not an attempt to expose the "truth" about consumer food politics, or to suggest that consumers are deluding themselves by thinking that their actions matter. On the contrary, we are equally wary of critical counternarratives that categorize all acts of ethical consumption as mere "bourgeois piggery."[3] Rather, our goal is to provide an analytic counterweight to the seamless narrative of consumer agency and to generate a more nuanced picture of the historical, cultural, and political convergences that give shape to consumer food politics.

We explore three sets of tensions associated with "eating for change," examining particular histories, subjectivities, and forms of collective action that are imagined and enacted across sites of food politics. First, we argue that we must contextualize current forms of political eating within their rich histories, particularly in relation to the market as a means of social change. Second, we consider how the seamless narrative of consumer food politics obscures contradictions surrounding the individual consumer, exploring entangled issues of agency, affect, and access. Third, we examine the tensions inherent in an "ethical foodscape" that is centrally reliant on market mechanisms. A classic debate for social movements, like the labor movement, was how to influence the state without being co-opted into the state. Today, a locus of tension centers on the question of market dominance and the retreat of the state. Reflecting upon these shifting tensions provides new insights into the current neoliberal landscape, and the particular challenges and possibilities therein. Before proceeding with this analysis, we briefly explore the ubiquitous "win-win" consumer food politics narrative.

Eating for Change: You Can Have It All!

Popular food discourse suggests that today's consumer can have it all—delicious, healthy meals and the satisfaction of contributing to a better world. This dominant account of consumer food politics is rearticulated across a range of institutional sites, such as food journalism, food policy, and marketing campaigns, as well as the daily practices of individuals. The apparent harmony of the ethical and the gastronomical makes consumer food politics an appetizing choice for those who consider themselves to be socially progressive and environmentally conscious consumers. An editorial in *Bon Appétit* sums up this logic: "Since better for the world means better tasting, this is one delicious revolution."[4]

It is this tension-free portrayal of political eating that we refer to as the seamless narrative of "eating for change." Drawing upon the democratic ideals of collective food projects like community supported agriculture, the seamless narrative packages political pursuits into a consumerist frame that centers on individual rewards like taste, pleasure and convenience. Prominent food celebrities further legitimize this narrative with heartfelt testimonials about how increased political awareness has enhanced their own culinary endeavors. According to restaurateur Joe Bastianich, business partner of celebrity chef Mario Batali, "Having a sustainable business is the way of the future. . . . But our fundamental principle is a better product. We're doing what we're doing to elevate the dining experience."[5] Similarly, we read that chef Thomas Keller is raising lamb, informed by "the philosophy that raising animals naturally and humanely will result in better meat. Sold under the Pure Bred label, it is excellently tender and flavorful."[6] From supporting local farmers, to protecting sustainability and animal rights, the overarching narrative of "eating for change" unites an array of diverse practices around the ideal of individual interests producing public goods, based on the idea that you too can create change through progressive (and delicious) purchases.[7]

The "eat for change" narrative is not limited to foodies and food writers but is also articulated in corporate settings. Corporations like Kraft, Kellogg's, and General Mills have adapted the countercultural messages of food activists and deliberately appeal to consumers' ethical sensibilities.[8] Hellman's, a mayonnaise brand in Canada owned by industry giant Unilever, launched a "real food movement" that encourages eating locally ("Eat Real. Eat Local") and planting urban gardens, and gives grants to initiatives that support "real food."[9] While many consumers are skeptical of the idea that corporations can orchestrate meaningful change, others see corporations as equal players in struggles to reform the food system. One young woman interviewed for a research project on Whole Foods Market (WFM) characterized Whole Foods as "almost like a . . . healthy community center."[10]

While popular food discourse depicts a consonant partnership of politics and consumption, scholarly assessments have also been critiqued for moving too far toward uncritically celebrating consumer agency. As Juliet Schor writes, "The field has ended up with a certain depoliticization and difficulty examining consumption critically."[11] Still, critical voices do have a place in food studies, and academic literature on food consumption is frequently depicted as congregating in optimistic and pessimistic accounts of political eating. Those who identify potential in consumer-based expressions of agency celebrate politicized food consumers for their success in mobilizing broad appeal and helping individuals relate their daily practices to larger issues.[12] More skeptical voices criticize consumer approaches as neoliberal technologies that download civic responsibilities onto self-auditing individuals, leaving the state less accountable for the public good.[13] For example, Guthman argues that Michael Pollan's individualized focus on what to eat fetishizes market solutions and obscures the food system's structural causes and collective solutions.[14]

Although both optimistic and cautionary perspectives have raised important issues, we are frustrated by the limitations of this binary, as well as the overly celebratory tone that dominates the public sphere. Just as the seamless narrative of "eating for change" flattens significant tensions, the dichotomous assessment of either celebration or condemnation is similarly restrictive. By contrast, we argue that there is rich analytic space in between the hopeful and the pessimistic. Cautionary accounts can be useful guides to social movement actors to avoid mobilization pitfalls,[15] and be conscious of the limits of market means for social change,[16] while hopeful analyses are important for focusing attention on what change can, and must, occur (especially given the earth's finite resources).[17] In the analysis that follows, we attempt to illustrate some of the complexity that exists within consumer food politics by exploring tensions that reside at the level of histories, individuals, and collective action.

Historical Tensions:
Struggles to Access, Control, and Restrict Markets

History is not a major theme in many accounts of consumption, and consumers are often presented as excitingly novel agents in contemporary struggles. Examining consumer history provides an opportunity to appreciate how consumers have collectively struggled to make transformative change while working within, against, and occasionally outside the market. Our brief account, which focuses primarily on US consumer history, is intended to situate the "eat for change" narrative in a larger historical context and to highlight the dynamic relationship between consumers, transformative projects, states, and market forces.

An early cooperative phase of consumer activism is most commonly attributed to 19th-century England,[18] focused on worker cooperatives that combated monopolies over grain milling and struggled to make food more affordable and accessible.[19] Cooperative members conceptualized themselves as both producers and consumers, and the goal was a cooperative model of self-help, which could serve as an alternative to the capitalist logic of profit maximization.[20] Struggles over food were central to these early consumer mobilization efforts. As Matthew Hilton notes in his history of consumer movements in the UK, most prewar consumer movements were driven by "the politics of necessitous consumption," like bread, rather than specialized luxury goods.[21]

The 20th century saw the rise of a distinct phase of consumer activism focused more centrally around the consumer identities that accompanied Fordist mass consumption, particularly in a US context. We think of this as "mass-consumption" activism,[22] and its foundations lay in the decline of household self-sufficiency, the growth of the middle class, the rise of Fordism, and the objectionable outcomes of anarchic markets—as famously exemplified in the appalling conditions of Chicago meat yards described in Upton Sinclair's novel *The Jungle* (1906).

The Great Depression confirmed public sentiments about the dangers of untrammeled market forces and inspired consumer organizations—often working with trade unions, the labor movement, and women's groups—to make demands for protective legislation and political representation.[23] Emerging consumer identities were not separate from other political identities but emerged synergistically. Lizabeth Cohen has written extensively on US labor and consumer history; her scholarship renders explicit the intricate relationship between consumer politics and political identities centered around race, class, and gender. For example, Cohen connects an emerging mass consumer culture in the 1920s and 1930s to the consolidation of workers' class-based identities and political action.[24] Women's groups and urban black groups also articulated consumer politics as they organized boycotts, and lobbied for stricter control over the quality and price of food in the depressed economic conditions of the 1930s.[25] Although women's consumer activism in the 1930s was frequently animated by the high price of food, the scope and reach of this activism were ambitious and frequently mobilized women across class and racial divides; some groups organized boycotts to support labor struggles, others organized letter-writing campaigns to demand protective legislation, and still others mobilized impressive grassroots constituencies.[26] Cohen notes, "At a high point during the meat boycotts of 1935, women in cities throughout the country succeeded in effectively shutting down the retail butcher trade as well as implicating the wholesale meatpackers whose profiteering they held greatly responsible for recent price hikes."[27]

With post–World War II prosperity, the focus of consumer activism shifted from necessary commodities to mass consumer items, and enthusiasm for protective legislation and government intervention waned. Advocates for price controls on essential foods (namely, women, blacks, working-class, and progressives) were cast in the public eye as "weak, dependent, and feminine," while proponents of reduced government regulation framed their struggles as ones of independence, masculinity, and strength.[28] Cohen argues that in the postwar US, the "citizen consumer" (who thought of the collective good and prompted government to protect it) eventually lost ground to a "purchaser consumer," who contributed "more by exercising purchasing power than through asserting themselves politically."[29] In these years, the mandate of consumer organizations focused more specifically on product testing and information (e.g., *Consumer Reports* magazine) to help consumers select products and abandoned earlier militant commitments.[30] Put differently, postwar consumer activism increasingly sought to help consumers take advantage of markets, "rather than trying to undermine the market through co-operative action or political agitation and lobbying."[31]

The mass-consumption phase of consumer activism helped improve the functioning of markets and solidified a sense of consumer goods as a universal right—even though access to consumer goods remained heavily stratified by race, gender, and class divisions.[32] State involvement was critical, particularly since consumer politics were characterized by an interest in basic living standards that dovetailed with emerging welfare regimes.[33] Even though consumer benefits were never fully universalized, consumer protection in industrialized states became, in varying degrees at different historical points, "a state project," and consumers were recognized as political actors who required a government response.[34] While the political response was muted in the postwar years, states became more responsive to consumers' demands in the 1960s and 1970s. A new wave of consumer activism emerged, fueled by concerns over product safety (e.g., automobiles like the Corvair, food additives and colorants, pesticides like DDT), frequently funded by labor unions, and animated by personalities like Ralph Nader and Rachel Carson.[35] Amid these concerns, Western governments reacted with hundreds of instances of protective legislation and new bureaucracies designed to protect consumers' interests.[36]

Building on the environmental concerns that arose in the 1960s and 1970s, new forms of consumer activism emerged in the 1980s and onward that have been variously termed alternative consumption, political consumption, and ethical consumption. The environment remains a core concern, while new issues have been taken on, like social justice (e.g., fair-trade coffee, sweatshop-free clothing), animal welfare (e.g., grass-fed beef or cage-free eggs), and anticorporate messages (e.g., anti-Nike and anti-Starbucks activism). As environmental awareness expanded, mass consumption became understood by some as a potential threat to planetary survival,[37] and an "unease with abundance" emerged alongside critiques of consumer society.[38]

Green and alternative consumption became enshrined in popular food discourse in the late 20th and early 21st centuries, evident in the expansion of shopping locations like WFM,[39] Academy Award–winning films like *Food, Inc.*, and the broad market expansion of alternative consumption discourses (e.g., WalMart organics). As consumers increasingly looked to "make change" through their food choices, governments were less interested in intervening to protect consumers from the vagaries of the marketplace. With neoliberal ideologies taking hold in Western governments from the 1980s onward, consumer protection took on a different tone from previous historical eras. The state retreated from its regulatory responsibility to offer protection to all citizens,[40] and individual consumers were framed as best able to protect themselves and discipline market actors through their purchases. With globalization processes, consumer regulations were standardized across multiple states, often to a lowest common denominator. This involved a vision of consumer protection focused on individual choice, which meant a lessening of concern to ensure protection for all, including marginalized populations that experience very little choice in the marketplace.[41]

As the state retreated and environmental awareness grew, critiques of consumption became divided between a radical message seeking to challenge corporate capitalism and consumerism,[42] and a second, more ameliorative message encouraging individuals to seek change and protect themselves by consuming differently—buying hybrid cars and pesticide-free organic foods.[43] In accordance with a neoliberal political climate where market relationships are sacrosanct, the second ameliorative message has become dominant in the "eat for change" narrative, leading to a prioritization of individual consumer choice in food markets—especially compared with universal-access, state-responsibility themes of previous eras.

The historical development we have briefly charted speaks to the shifting political alliances of consumption and food politics. In 19th-century cooperative consumer activism, labor unions and working-class people were central actors demanding access to basic foodstuffs and seeking alternatives to exploitative capitalist relationships. In 20th-century mass-consumption activism, an important, albeit inconsistent, theme was universalizing access to consumer goods and lobbying governments to keep corporate actors accountable in a complex consumption landscape. In the alternative consumption phase dominating the early 21st century, the environment has been targeted as a collective concern, the benefits of mass consumer society have been questioned, and market freedom from state interference has reemerged as a prominent theme. The contemporary focus on individual consumer choice ideologically underpins the emergence of upscale food markets that best serve upper-middle-class consumers with the resources to "eat for change"—markets that are regulated by private standards and regulatory systems.[44] As Hilton cautions, with the contemporary focus on individual consumer choice,

> protection became unevenly distributed. Those who can afford to choose alternatives, can bear the costs of deceptive practices, and can simply live to spend another day have their own protection mechanisms. But for the poor and disadvantaged, access to such protection is less readily available and their participation in consumer society comes at a struggle and a cost.[45]

Individual Tensions: Navigating Guilt, Pleasure, and Responsibility

The tensions outlined in this section revolve around the question of how individuals participate in consumer-based food politics, which is a dominant and popular theme in the "eating for change" narrative. Even so, consumers' political agency is up for debate, and the transformative potential of consumer-focused strategies remains unclear.[46] Popular and scholarly accounts focus on consumers' abilities to influence commerce and construct meaningful lifestyles and identities.[47] Feminist scholars highlight opportunities for women to engage politically through social reproduction practices, especially given their historical marginalization from formal politics.[48] Further, business literature emphasizes how consumer demand fuels the growth of socially responsible corporations promoting social justice and environmental sustainability.[49] In these appraisals, the politicization of everyday activities, like food consumption, creates new spaces and practices through which to foster political subjectivities.

Countering optimistic visions, a growing literature points toward neoliberal processes that may underpin ethical consumption projects.[50] Guthman suggests that the contemporary obsession with food politics reflects an individualized neoliberal model where political agency is reduced to shopping decisions: "Food politics has become a progenitor of a neoliberal anti-politics that devolves regulatory responsibility to consumers via their dietary choices."[51] Through her case study of agrifood activism in California, Julie Guthman demonstrates how ideals of "consumer choice, localism, entrepreneurialism, and self-improvement"[52] have been adopted by food activists, leading to greater focus on private forms of regulation (e.g., "buy local") at the expense of collective movements for state intervention (e.g., organizing in solidarity with migrant farmworkers). In fact, Guthman argues that neoliberal rationalities have been so deeply incorporated into contemporary food movements that these supposedly political projects are now cultivating activist neoliberal subjects.[53] Similar arguments have emerged from research on alternative agrifood movements,[54] non–genetically modified organism activism,[55] and community garden initiatives.[56] These studies find that despite efforts to create social transformation, consumer-based initiatives may inadvertently promote a neoliberal food system in which market mechanisms reign supreme and individuals assume the burden of political responsibility, as they are invited into self-regulating practices centered on making morally sound consumption choices.[57]

Within these debates, many scholars work toward a dialectical approach that "recognizes that meaning and agency are present in consumption decisions, but takes seriously the structural conditions shaping consumer agency."[58] One way of probing this dialectic is by exploring how individuals negotiate their own relationship to consumer food movements. Our research with foodies (i.e., individuals with a passion for eating, cooking, and learning about food)[59] offers some insight on this question. In this study, we interviewed thirty American foodies regarding their personal food preferences, including eating habits, shopping practices, and thoughts on the political aspects of food consumption. The people we spoke to encountered numerous tensions in their efforts to be ethical consumers and engaged these tensions with varying degrees of reflexivity.[60] For instance, one participant described her efforts to achieve "a good balance of pragmatism, but like, accommodating ethics," while others rejected the invitation to become ethical consumers and maintained a commitment to taste as the paramount value. In the words of another participant, "I'd have to say that I'm not ethical. [laughs] You know, a chicken's a chicken [laughs]." Notwithstanding extreme responses like this one, most foodies we interviewed drew on the dominant "eat for change" narrative, which offers them identities as discerning consumers capable of making decisions that are both delicious and politically progressive. However, few presented ethics as fully compatible with their gourmet preferences. The study reveals a significant gray area between the imagined consumer "hero" and "victim," as individuals develop personal strategies with which to navigate a complex food system.

Many foodies described struggling to make ethical choices in the face of competing objectives, like cost. One participant explains that he tries to buy local and organic food whenever "given a reasonable choice," but that ethics does not usually trump other consumer considerations like convenience or expense. Less obvious were those conflicts arising between ethical objectives, such as competing commitments to local versus organic food. While individual struggles varied in content and political sophistication, the very acknowledgment of these tensions reveals an element of complexity often overlooked in dominant food discourse. Moreover, these stories show how heavy political burdens are borne at the individual level, often resulting in feelings of guilt and uncertainty. One woman admits that although ethics are not paramount in her shopping decisions, they continue to "live in me as a kind of guilty conscience." Another describes how she has expended considerable effort to reshape her family's diet based on environmental and animal welfare concerns. Referencing a *New York Times* feature on factory farms, she says, "And so in fact this week, it was harder, I cooked less meat in what I cooked for my family, as a result of that article." This participant's food practices are shaped by feelings of personal responsibility that she connects to broader political discussions. Studying how individuals negotiate the affective tensions surrounding consumer food politics can provide insight into how neoliberal processes are lived at the everyday level, opening up space for an analysis that bridges agency and structural critique.

Within this sample of thirty American foodies, individuals took up vastly different subjectivities that might be plotted along a continuum of self-satisfying consumer to politicized food activist. A gendered pattern emerged in the way that participants approached ethical issues, with women tending to emphasize forms of care and community building through socially responsible food practices, and men more often prioritizing the ongoing development of their own food knowledge, researching political debates, and blogging on ethical eating strategies.[61] Many articulated a personal decision to support products that uphold a particular ethical standard—whether that be choosing to shop at WFM or supporting a community supported agriculture (CSA) farm. Clearly individual consumer efforts are often admirable, but they highlight a critical tension surrounding the politics of ethical consumption: political eating is often framed as a personal choice, but does everyone have access to this practice, and the subsequent rewards of a clear conscience and heightened social status?

Critical scholars demonstrate how the notion of moral correctness through shopping reserves the position of the ethical consumer for those with privileged access to economic and cultural capital.[62] No matter how committed one is to environmental sustainability and social justice, the products associated with these ideals—such as organic and fair-trade foods—incur costs that are prohibitive for many consumers. Indeed, most of our foodie sample was upper-middle-class. Furthermore, scholars have found that such class-based issues intersect with racial exclusions, such that consumer food movements tend to be normatively coded as white and middle-class.[63] Slocum argues that it is not simply individual preference that leads to the predominance of white consumers in alternative food spaces but rather the product of "a culture of food that has been made white":

How this food is produced, packaged, promoted and sold—engages with a white middle class consumer base that tends to be interested in personal health and perhaps in environmental integrity. White, wealthier bodies tend to be the ones in Whole Foods, at co-ops (e.g. in Syracuse's Real Food

Co-op, the Wedge in Minneapolis), the people attending CFSC confer-ences, those making certain purchases at the St. Paul Farmers' Market and the leaders of community food nonprofits.[64]

An individualized model emphasizing informed consumer choice can-not adequately address these racialized and classed exclusions. On the contrary, one significant tension obscured by dominant accounts of "eat-ing for change" is the fact that seeing social change through an individ-ual lens can make us blind to, or overwhelmed by, systemic inequalities. In our research with foodies, "green" environmental issues were given much more attention than social justice issues, such as labor conditions, global inequalities, and hunger.[65] This suggests there are serious limita-tions to an individualized approach that focuses on personal food choice, rather than instigating collective discussions about the need for struc-tural reform to the food system.

"Movement" Tensions and the Ethical Foodscape

The popular press is replete with references to the food movement, as well as its more specific manifestations—the "slow food movement," the "organic movement," and the "local food movement." While many consumers partici-pate in dimensions of political food consumption—such as buying organic salad greens—it is not clear that all of these consumers necessarily participate in a social movement. Sociologists generally understand social movements as having elements like collective mobilization, shared collective identities, sustained and organized conflict, and dense social networks that facilitate challenges to authorities, elites, and/or dominant values.[66] Grocery shopping, in contrast, is generally a personal rather than a collective affair. Products are selected in an individualized manner, the process is relatively noncon-flictual, and interactions with ethical products are often episodic rather than sustained. During interviews, WFM consumers identified myriad problems with the industrial food system but appeared to see themselves as individu-als confronting a food system behemoth rather than part of an organized collectivity engaged in a conflictual process.[67] This is not to say that there is not a social movement dimension to ethical eating. Think here of activ-ists lobbying Starbucks to sell more fair-trade coffee, or collective action around organic standards. Yet, our point is that food-related collective action needs to be empirically investigated and problematized rather than taken for granted as it is in the "eat for change" narrative.

For this reason, we find it conceptually useful to avoid reifying the food movement and instead think about an "ethical foodscape" that hosts a range of actors, collective identities, and contentious politics. The term "foodscape" has been used to describe the spatial distribution of food across geographic settings,[68] but can be analytically sharpened by drawing from geographic and sociological literature on landscape.[69] The suffix "scape" is most famously associated with Arjun Appadurai, who used it to theorize global cultural flows that are fluid, irregular, and "deeply perspectival," rather than a vision of "fixed" relationships reducible to one objective reality.[70] Influenced by Appadurai's emphasis on the fluid movement of people, ideas, and capital in the globalization period, we think of foodscapes as a social construction that captures and constitutes cultural ideals of how food relates to specific places, people, and political-economic systems. Just as a landscape painting has a mediated relationship to physical ontology, a foodscape may variously capture or obscure the ecological, political-economic, and social relations of food. Foodscapes are contested spaces where actors struggle to define the terrain of political action, including the extent of market involvement and private ownership of food. Goodman et al. have elaborated on the idea of an "ethical foodscape" to capture the range of actors involved in ethical eating (e.g., food corporations, social movement organizations, ethical food networks, individual consumers), as well as the way that "morality is a key and growing currency in the provisioning of food."[71] Seeing the ethical foodscape as an eco-social construct helps us resist the tendency to naturalize "ethical" food choices as morally superior and reminds us that social struggles to "moralize" food choices are inevitably tethered to material dimensions of food like land, seeds, and soil. Put differently, the "ethical foodscape" involves social constructions surrounding "ethical eating" (e.g., the idea of eating "green" as morally superior), but it is also connected to the material realities of food production (e.g., the fossil fuel consumed by eating conventional agriculture).

Working with the concept of an "ethical foodscape" leads us to examine a central quality of this terrain: the prominence of market-based mechanisms for social change. In contrast to earlier consumer activism, which critiqued capitalist relationships and demanded state action, a critical tenet of the ethical foodscape is the focus on social transformation through consumer choice in the marketplace. Market-based approaches can be roughly divided into small-scale market projects and agricultural initiatives that operate outside the industrialized food system (e.g., artisanal cheese, small-batch beer production, community supported agriculture programs), and large-scale corporate approaches that work within the dominant structures of industrial food production, distribution, and retailing (e.g., WalMart's organic offerings and programs for "heritage" agriculture).[72] While there is a notable "gray" zone between "alternative" and "mainstream" initiatives in the ethical foodscape (e.g., WFM often sources from small-scale operations), they share a well-rehearsed and popular logic: that incremental market change will produce positive transformation within the food system.

The dominance of market-based strategies is, in part, due to pragmatism. Working to shape consumption—toward heirloom tomatoes and artisanal cheese—is an easier sell than challenging unsustainable lifestyles or demanding institutional changes at a national or transnational scale. While regulatory bodies and government legislation often seem remotely related to everyday life, consumption is both familiar and intimate, accessible and pleasurable. For that reason, multiple movement actors have embraced the idea of "conservation through consumption."[73] Buy sustainable fish to prevent overfishing. Buy organic lettuce to save topsoil. Buy shade-grown coffee to protect tropical birds.

Despite these pragmatic underpinnings, the risks of focusing on market approaches within the ethical foodscape should not be understated. With respect to an "eating for change" narrative, three risks seem particularly salient. The first risk is that focusing on market mechanisms will produce a cornucopia of market options that has ambiguous, or even deleterious, consequences. Konefal argues that sustainable seafood initiatives have indeed generated "market diversity" (e.g., restaurant menus offer sustainable tilapia alongside overfished Chilean sea bass), but he raises questions about whether the market as a whole has moved toward greater sustainability.[74] Market research suggests that increased product diversity works to increase consumption,[75] which is a key problem underlying affluent Western lifestyles. This raises ideological questions about how market diversity—a cornucopia of food choice—works to perpetuate an anthropocentric notion of nature as eternally abundant, rendering it vulnerable to commodification and confusion in spaces like the Rain Forest Café.[76]

A second risk associated with market measures in the ethical foodscape is that social movements will find it difficult to distinguish their products from corporate initiatives with less progressive agendas. Research on the corporate-organic foodscape[77] demonstrates that the biggest and best-selling organic brands adopt key themes from food activism. Brand websites are imbued with the imagery of family farms, rural landscapes, and highly personalized narratives. These themes have become a key marketing feature of "Big Organic" food, even if they have little relationship to long-distance commodity chains and centralized corporate ownership structures. The corporate expansion and industrialization of organics has threatened the loss of public trust,[78] and firms have responded to resist these critiques. A marketing focus on dairy products from rural Vermont offers consumers a way to consume locality and responds to anxieties about placelessness that accompany globalized food production.

The inclusion of these themes in corporate-organics presents real challenges for food activism. While many food-related social movements employ market mechanisms, many share an interest in promoting food democracy— a fact that distinguishes them from corporations' legally institutionalized interest in profit maximization.[79] Food democracy represents a decentralized terrain of projects that seek to organize the food system at a scale where democratic needs are met, ownership is decentralized, sensitivity to resource depletion is heightened, and privileged core regions do not live off the carrying capacity of the periphery.[80] For activists in the ethical foodscape, it is not clear how to make food democracy projects an attractive option in a sea of corporate commodities, many of which seem to offer locally embedded, socially just foods that also comply with hegemonic consumer ideals (e.g., offer maximum choice, pleasure, and convenience). While food system activists must think strategically, to pose the question exclusively as a concern of market differentiation misses an essential point: that food democracy is not simply a product to be marketed but a normative vision for reorganizing the food system to provide access for the many, not just choice for the few.

A third risk related to the prominence of market-based solutions is the retreat of the state. When attention is devoted to the transformative potential of consumers and markets, states are framed as minor players, or even an antagonistic force preventing change.[81] Private solutions drown out public responsibilities from the collective imagination.[82] This point is difficult to prove empirically, but it is worth noting that in focus groups with environmentally motivated consumers, we found that the state was almost never mentioned as a locus for social change, and most consumers lacked basic information about the government agencies responsible for ensuring a safe, sustainable food system. Similarly, interviews with upper-middle-class consumers revealed that the state was almost never identified as a means to transform the food system—change was seen as primarily occurring through consumer demand in the marketplace.[83] These findings are striking, given that the state has significant resources to make structural change, regulate food system actors, redistribute resources, and mandate programs that provide access for people who cannot afford upscale market options.

As one example, we reference the Toronto-based community food security organization FoodShare.[84] FoodShare was born in part out of activist energies but is funded by both private donations and public resources. It has myriad programs, but its focus is providing a local market for regional food producers and delivering nutritious food to urbanites, particularly marginalized low-income and ethnocultural communities. Because of its funding base, FoodShare is able to do things outside of a pure market model—it can prioritize food access for marginalized communities but also offer appealing services for middle-class eaters, thereby creating a nonstigmatized way for accessing affordable (and frequently local/organic) food. Our intention is not to romanticize locally scaled organizations like FoodShare,[85] but to point out the potential synergy of state infrastructure and activist energy when it comes to providing healthy, sustainable food that is broadly accessible in the spirit of food democracy. This point was well recognized by earlier waves of consumer activists lobbying for universal access to goods and living standards, but it is often lost with a neoliberal focus on individual consumer choice and niche-market consumption.

Conclusions: Defending a Critical Vision of Consumer Food Politics

This chapter has identified a dominant message within contemporary food politics—the narrative of "eating for change"—and explored several tensions that operate beneath its smooth surface. Arguing that a historical perspective has much to offer studies of commodity activism, we have identified key shifts in the particular objectives, institutions, and sets of relations that have given shape to past consumer-based food movements. Our analysis highlights how a collectivist, state-oriented mode of food politics has been largely displaced by market-based approaches to ethical consumption centered on individual consumer choice. Building upon these insights, we have explored key debates regarding the kinds of subjectivities offered to, and adopted by, individuals in pursuit of ethical food consumption. After illuminating significant diversity and ambiguity in the ways that individuals negotiate their own food politics, we highlight structural issues of class-, gender-, and race-based exclusions that persist despite—and are furthered by—the narrative of "eating for change." Finally, we have offered the concept of the "ethical foodscape" as a means of conceptualizing the interplay of material and symbolic elements that shape the terrain of collective action around food, and highlighted what we see as significant risks associated with a primary focus on market-based mechanisms and individual consumer choice.

To conclude, we believe that binary accounts depicting consumer-based food movements as entirely hopeful or hopeless obscure possibilities for action that challenge a neoliberal model of consumer politics: namely, state-funded collective projects that may engage with the market but are not entirely driven by the ideologies of choice and individualism. While we fully appreciate how individuals can experience markets in creative and surprising ways,[86] we end with a vigorous defense of critical approaches to consumer culture that maintain analytic attention on the structural implications of consumer choice.[87] This attention is necessary to identify persistent forms of market exploitation, corporate power, environmental degradation, and ideological processes at work. At the same time, it is important to simultaneously appreciate the possibility and necessity of consumers working together to "moralize" markets and promote a food democracy where sustenance is sustainable, delicious, desirable, and equitable.

NOTES

1. Nick Clarke et al., "Globalizing the Consumer: Doing Politics in an Ethical Register," *Political Geography* 26, no. 3 (2007): 231–49; Mike Goodman, Damian Maye, and Lewis Holloway, "Ethical Foodscapes? Premises, Promises, and Possibilities," *Environment and Planning A* 42, no. 8 (2010): 1782–96; Julie Guthman, "Neoliberalism and the Making of Food Politics in California," *Geoforum* 39, no. 6 (2008): 1171–83; Josée Johnston, "The Citizen-Consumer Hybrid: Ideological Tensions and the Case of Whole Foods Market," *Theory and Society* 37, no. 3 (2008): 229–70; Josée Johnston, Andrew Biro, and Norah MacKendrick, "Lost in the Supermarket: The Corporate-Organic Foodscape and the Struggle for Food Democracy," *Antipode: A Radical Journal of Geography* 41, no. 3 (2009): 509–32.

2. *Bon Appétit*, February 2008, 105.

3. Josée Johnston, "Counterhegemony or Bourgeois Piggery? Food Politics and the Case of FoodShare," in *The Fight over Food: Producers, Consumers and Activists Challenge the Global Food System*, ed. Wynn Wright and Gerad Middendorf (University Park: Penn State University Press, 2008).

4. *Bon Appétit*, 2008, 4.

5. *Bon Appétit*, 2008, 39.

6. *New York Times*, March 12, 2008, F2.

7. This logic is not unique to food politics but shares intellectual roots with green capitalism. An exemplar "win-win" statement is found on the back of a recent book, *Green, American Style: Becoming Earth Friendly and Reaping the Benefits*: "Green is not about giving up. It's about gaining more money, time, opportunity, health, and well-being."

8. Johnston, Biro, and MacKendrick, 2009.

9. http://www.realfoodmovement.ca.

10. Johnson, Josée, and Michelle Szabo, "Reflexivity and the Whole Foods Market Consumer: The Lived Experience of Shopping for Change," *Agriculture and Human Values*,

28 (2011): 309–319. In this study, which involved in-depth interviews with twenty WFM consumers, about half of the sample was skeptical of the idea of corporate-engineered change in the food system, while the other half were generally positive about corporate responsibility.

11. Juliet Schor, "In Defense of Consumer Critique: Revisiting the Consumption Debates of the Twentieth Century," *Annals of the American Academy of Political and Social Science* 6, no. 11 (2007a): 17.

12. See Clive Barnett et al., "Consuming Ethics: Articulating the Subjects and Spaces of Ethical Consumption," *Antipode* 37, no. 1 (2005): 23–45; Clarke et al., 2007; Michele Micheletti, *Political Virtue and Shopping: Individuals, Consumerism, and Collective Action* (New York: Palgrave, 2003); Juliet Schor, "Consumer-Topia: Envisioning a New Culture of Consuming" (paper presented at the annual meeting of the American Sociological Association, New York, August 11, 2007b).

13. Julie Guthman, "Fast Food/Organic Food: Reflexive Tastes and the Making of 'Yuppie Chow,'" *Social and Cultural Geography* 4, no. 1 (2003): 45–58; Julie Guthman, "Bringing Good Food to Others: Investigating the Subjects of Alternative Food Practices," *Cultural Geographies* 15, no. 4 (2008): 431–47; Robin Jane Roff, "Shopping for Change? Neoliberalizing Activism and the Limits to Eating Non-GMO," *Agriculture and Human Values* 24, no. 4 (2007): 511–22; Michael Power, *The Audit Society: Rituals of Verification* (Oxford: Oxford University Press, 1997); Nikolas Rose, *Powers of Freedom: Reframing Political Thought* (Cambridge: Cambridge University Press, 1999).

14. Julie Guthman, "Why I Am Fed Up with Michael Pollan et al.," *Agriculture and Human Values* 24, no. 2 (2007): 261–64; Michael Pollan, *The Omnivore's Dilemma: A Natural History of Four Meals* (New York: Penguin, 2006).

15. For example, Amiee Shreck, "Resistance, Redistribution, and Power in the Fair Trade Banana Initiative," *Agriculture and Human Values* 22, no. 1 (2005): 17–29.

16. Jason Konefal, "The Marriage of Big Green and Big Food: A Case Study of Sustainable Seafood" (paper presented at the Association for the Study of Food and Society/Agriculture, Food, and Human Values Society conference, Bloomington, IN, June 3, 2005); Andrew Szasz, *Shopping Our Way to Safety* (Minneapolis: University of Minnesota Press, 2007).

17. Schor, 2007b; Juliet Schor, *Plenitude: The New Economics of True Wealth* (New York: Penguin, 2010).

18. Cooperatives did exist in the US in the 18th and 19th centuries but were less influential than their British counterparts. Interest in cooperatives in the US flourished in the 1930s but even then involved only 1.5 percent of retail sales nationally. See Lizabeth Cohen, *A Consumers' Republic: The Politics of Mass Consumption in Postwar America* (New York: Knopf, 2003), 25.

19. Yiannis Gabriel and Tim Lang, *The Unmanageable Consumer: Contemporary Consumption and Its Fragmentations*, 2nd ed. (London: Sage, 2006); Michael Schudson, "Citizens, Consumers, and the Good Society," *Annals of the American Academy of Political and Social Science* 6, no. 1 (2007): 17–29.

20. Gabriel and Lang, 2006, 157.

21. Matthew Hilton, *Consumerism in 20th Century Britain* (Cambridge: Cambridge University Press, 2003), 29.

22. Scholars have different, and more specific, ways of labeling various phases of consumer activism in the 20th century. For instance, Gabriel and Lang (2006, 160) refer to a specific "value for money" phase of consumer activism that emerged with Fordism, while Cohen (2003) identifies three specific surges of consumer activism in the 20th century—a first wave (early 1900s), a second wave (1930s and 1940s), and a third wave (1960s and 1970s).

23. Matthew Hilton, "Consumers and the State since the Second World War," *Annals of the American Academy of Political and Social Science* 611, no. 1 (2007): 66–81; Cohen, 2003, 28.

24. Lizabeth Cohen, *Making a New Deal: Industrial Workers in Chicago* (New York: Cambridge University Presss, 2008), 2.

25. Cohen, 2003, 31–53; Gary Cross, *An All-Consuming Century: Why Commercialism Won in Modern America* (New York: Columbia University Press, 2000), 123.

26. Cohen, 2003, 33–38, 51.

27. Cohen, 2003, 36.

28. Cohen, 2003, 134.

29. Cohen, 2003, 18–19; Cross, 2000, 135. As is clear in Cohen's historical account, the transition from "citizen consumer' to "purchaser consumer" was not seamless, linear, or simple. It is also important to acknowledge that other postwar social movements—apart from the consumer movement proper—involved elements of consumer mobilization and strong assertions of political identities. For example, the civil rights movement used consumer boycotts as a mobilization tactic, and the anti–Vietnam War movement involved boycotts of products associated with arms manufacturers (e.g., Saran Wrap was boycotted because of its ownership by Dow Chemicals, which also produced napalm).

30. Cross, 2000, 135; Cohen, 2003, 131.

31. Gabriel and Lang, 2006, 160.

32. Clearly, welfare regimes offered inconsistent protection that varied by race, class, and gender. The post–World War II GI Bill, for example, was an important policy instrument that benefited men over women, whites over African Americans, and was more advantageous for veterans with preexisting educational and financial resources. See Cohen, 2003, 137, 156, 166.

33. Hilton, 2007, 67; Cohen, 2003, 23.

34. Hilton, 2007, 68–69.

35. Cohen, 2003, 348–57.

36. Hilton, 2007; Cohen, 2003, 357. Although Hilton carefully documents the different consumer protection arrangements in Western Europe, the UK, and the US, he argues that what is most significant was "not that it was implemented in different ways throughout the world but that consumer protection existed at all" See Hilton, 2007, 75.

37. M. A. Hajer, *The Politics of Environmental Discourse: Ecological Modernization and the Policy Process* (Oxford: Oxford University Press, 1995), 10; Gill Seyfang, "Consuming Values and Contested Cultures: A Critical Analysis of the UK Strategy for Sustainable Consumption and Production," *Review of Social Economy* 62, no. 3 (2004): 323–38.

38. Hilton, 2003, 298; Kate Soper, "Rethinking the Good Life: Consumer as Citizen," *Capitalism, Nature, Socialism* 15, no. 3 (2007): 111–16.

39. Johnston, 2008.

40. In the neoliberal era the state does not abandon all regulation but, instead, actively regulates in ways that give more power to market actors (e.g., strengthening intellectual property rights). For this reason, Pechlaner and Otero suggest using the term "neoregulation" (rather than "deregulation") to describe the current food regime. See Gabriela Pechlaner and Gerardo Otero, "The Neoliberal Food Regime: Neoregulation and the New Division of Labor in North America," *Rural Sociology* 75, no. 2 (2010): 179–208.

41. Hilton, 2007, 78; Cross, 2000, 135.

42. Gabriel and Lang, 1995, 6; Seyfang 2004, 327.

43. Frances Cairncross, *Costing the Earth: The Challenge for Governments, the Opportunities for Business* (Boston: Harvard Business School Press, 1992); J. S. Dryzek, *The Politics of the Earth: Environmental Discourses* (Oxford: Oxford University Press, 2005, 189); Gabriel and Lang, 2006, 167.

44. Lawrence Busch and Carmen Bain, "New! Improved? The Transformation of the Global Agrifood System," *Rural Sociology* 69, no. 3 (2004): 321–46.

45. Hilton, 2007, 80.

46. Michele Micheletti, Andreas Folesdal, and Dietland Strolle, eds., *Politics, Products and Markets: Exploring Political Consumerism Past and Present* (New Brunswick, NJ: Transaction, 2004); Sharon Zukin and Jennifer Smith Maguire, "Consumers and Consumption," *Annual Review of Sociology* 30 (2004): 173–97; Soper, 2004; Don Slater, *Consumer Culture and Modernity* (Oxford: Polity Press, 1997); Margaret Scammell, "The Internet and Civic Engagement: The Age of the Citizen-Consumer," *Political Communication* 17, no. 4 (2000): 351–55.

47. For example, Pollan, 2006; Mark Bittman, *Food Matters: A Guide to Conscious Eating with More Than 75 Recipes* (Toronto: Simon and Schuster, 2008); John Fiske, *Reading the Popular* (London: Routledge, 1989); Nicholas Abercrombie, "Authority and Consumer Society," in *The Authority of the Consumer*, ed. Russell Keat, Nigel Whiteley, and Nicholas Abercrombie (New York: Routledge, 1994), 43–57; Schudson, 2007.

48. Johnston, 2008, 239; Cindi Katz, "Vagabond Capitalism and the Necessity of Social Reproduction," in *Implicating Empire: Globalization and Resistance in the 21st Century World Order*, ed. Stanley Aronowitz and Heather Gautney (New York: Basic Books, 2003), 255–70.

49. Cairncross, 1992; Marylyn Carrigan and Patrick De Pelsmacker, "Will Ethical Consumers Sustain Their Value in the Global Credit Crunch?" *International Marketing Review* 26, no. 6 (2009): 674–87; Peter Jones et al., "Corporate Social Responsibility: A Case Study of the UK's Leading Food Retailers," *British Food Journal* 107, no. 6 (2005): 423–35.

50. Allen et al., "Shifting Plates in the Agrifood Landscape: The Tectonics of Alternative Agrifood Initiatives in California," *Journal of Rural Studies* 19, no. 1 (2003): 61–75; Guthman, 2007; Guthman, 2008; Mary Beth Pudup, "It Takes a Garden: Cultivating Citizen-Subjects in Organized Garden Projects," *Geoforum* 39, no. 3 (2008): 1228–40; Roff, 2007.

51. Guthman, 2007, 264.

52. Guthman, 2008, 1171.

53. Guthman, 2008, 1172.

54. Allen et al., 2003.

55. Roff, 2007.

56. Pudup, 2008.

57. While we recognize the value of this critique, we must not overlook collectively organized struggles for global food justice that explicitly resist a neoliberal vision of globalized agriculture. Examples include rural collectives in postindependence India, mass violations of agricultural seed patents, the Zapatista struggles for food sovereignty in Chiapas, Mexico, the transnational peasant network Via Campesina, and many others.

58. Johnston, 2008, 234.

59. This book was coauthored by Josée Johnston and Shyon Baumann, while Kate Cairns worked as a research assistant. For more information on the data sources, see Josée Johnston and Shyon Baumann, *Democracy and Distinction in the Gourmet Foodscape* (New York: Routledge, 2010).

60. Johnston and Baumann, 2010.

61. Kate Cairns, Josée Johnston, and Shyon Baumann, "Caring about Food: Doing Gender in the Foodie Kitchen," *Gender and Society* 24, no. 5 (2010): 591–615.

62. Guthman, 2003; Johnston, 2008; Szasz, 2007.

63. Guthman, "Counterhegemony or Bourgeois Piggery?" 2008; Rachel Slocum, "Antiracist Practice and the Work of Community Food Organizations," *Antipode* 39, no. 2 (2006): 327–49.

64. Slocum, 2007, 526.

65. Johnston and Baumann, 2010, 231.

66. Sidney Tarrow, *Power in Movements: Social Movements and Contentious Politics* (New York: Cambridge University Press, 1998), 2; Kate Nash, *Contemporary Political Sociology: Globalization, Politics and Power* (Malden, MA: Blackwell, 2000), 145–50; James Goodwin and James M. Jasper, *The Social Movements Reader: Cases and Concepts*, 2nd ed. (Malden, MA: Wiley Blackwell, 2009), 4.

67. Josée Johnston and Michelle Szabo, "Reflexivity and the Whole Foods Market Consumer: The Lived Experience of Shopping for Change," *Agriculture and Human Values* (online only, July 2010).

68. Gisele Yasmeen, "'Plastic-Bag Housewives' and Postmodern Restaurants? Public and Private in Bangkok's Foodscape," *Urban Geography* 17, no. 6 (1996): 526–44; Anthony Winson, "Bringing Political Economy into the Debate on the Obesity Epidemic," *Agriculture and Human Values* 21, no. 4 (2004): 299–312.

69. For example, Don Mitchell, "The Lure of the Local: Landscape Studies at the End of a Troubled Century," *Progress in Human Geography* 25, no. 2 (2001): 269–81; Sharon Zukin, *Landscapes of Power: From Detroit to Disney World* (Berkeley: University of California Press, 1991).

70. Arjun Appadurai, *Modernity at Large: Cultural Dimensions of Globalization*, 7th ed. (Minneapolis: University of Minnesota Press, 2005), 32–33.

71. Goodman et al., 2010.

72. Dara J. Bloom, "Wal-Mart Goes Local: Defining Sustainability for US Agriculture" (paper presented at the Association for the Study of Food and Society; AFHVS = Agriculture, Food, and Human Values Society conference, Bloomington, IN, ASFS/June 3, 2010).

73. Johnston, 2008, 258.

74. Konefal, 2010.

75. Barbara E. Kahn and Brian Wansink, "The Influence of Assortment Structure on Perceived Variety and Consumption Quantities," *Journal of Consumer Research* 30, no. 4 (2004): 519–33; Barbara J. Rolls et al., "Variety in a Meal Enhances Food Intake in Man," *Physiology and Behavior* 26 (1981): 215–21.

76. Johnston, 2008, 258–61; John Beardsley, "Kiss Nature Goodbye: Marketing the Great Outdoors," *Harvard Design Magazine* 10 (2000): 1–6.

77. Johnston et al., 2009.

78. Laura B. DeLind, "Transforming Organic Agriculture into Industrial Organic Products: Reconsidering National Organic Standards," *Human Organization* 59, no. 2 (2000): 204.

79. Joel Bakan, *The Corporation: The Pathological Pursuit of Profit and Power* (New York: Penguin, 2004).

80. Brian Halweil, "The Rise of Food Democracy," *UN Chronicle* 42, no. 1 (2005): 71–73; Neva Hassanein, "Practicing Food Democracy: A Pragmatic Politics of Transformation," *Journal of Rural Studies* 19, no. 1 (2003): 77–86; Frances Moore Lappé and Anna Lappé, *Hope's Edge: The Next Diet for a Small Planet* (New York: Penguin, 2002).

81. For example, food activist folk hero and chicken farmer Joel Salatin (featured in the writing of Michael Pollan, as well as in the film *Food Inc.*) frequently espouses antistate rhetoric and argues vociferously for the power of the market to change the food system.

82. See Szasz, 2007; Norah MacKendrick, "Media Framing of Body Burdens: Precautionary Consumption and the Individualization of Risk," *Sociological Quarterly* 81, no. 1 (2010): 126–49.

83. Johnston and Szabo, 2010; Johnston et al., 2010.

84. Josée Johnston and Lauren Baker, "Eating Outside the Box: FoodShare's Good Food Box and the Challenge of Scale," *Agriculture and Human Values* 22, no. 4 (2005): 313–25; Johnston, 2008.

85. See Johnston and Baker, 2005.

86. Schudson, 2007, 241.

87. Schor, 2007a.

12

Changing the World
One Orgasm at a Time

Sex Positive Retail Activism

LYNN COMELLA

> When women talk about sex, it changes the culture. Our per-
> spectives have been hidden or misrepresented; any degree of
> change in that situation registers on a cultural level. Women
> have been fostered through feminism and our fervid conversa-
> tions about sex into activism.
>
> Carol Queen

In May 2001, Babeland, the women-run sex toy company, held
a rather unusual press conference at its retail store on the Lower East Side
of Manhattan. Provocatively dubbed a "Masturbation Summit," the event
brought members of the press together with an impressive group of feminist activists and educators who had been invited by the business's owners to
discuss the benefits of masturbation and the importance of sexual freedom.

In an effort to bring the topic of masturbation out into the open, a number of feminist sex toy businesses have joined together since 1996 in declar-
ing the month of May a nationwide celebration of masturbation. Conceived
by Good Vibrations in San Francisco, Masturbation May was created in
response to the firing of US surgeon general Dr. Joycelyn Elders by President
Bill Clinton in December 1994 after she suggested that information about
masturbation should be included in sex education courses. Although Masturbation May began as a way to speak out about masturbation and educate
the public about its benefits, it has since evolved into a highly successful public relations machine that helps promote women-run sex toy stores and the
business of masturbation as a matter of both sexual consciousness-raising
and commerce.

Babeland's Masturbation Summit kicked off a month of masturbation-
related events, including the release of the company's Masturbation Nation

Survey Results, masturbation education workshops at their stores in Seattle and New York City, and the Third National Masturbate-A-Thon. With the catchy slogan "Come for a Cause" the Masturbate-A-Thon is described as the most "fun philanthropy around." Similar to a walk-a-thon, the Masturbate-A-Thon is a fundraising event where participants ask their friends and coworkers to sponsor them for every minute they masturbate on a designated day in May, with proceeds going to various community-based organizations that promote women's health. The fundraiser serves several purposes: it is intended to raise "masturbation consciousness" and money for organizations like the Federation of Feminist Women's Health Centers and generate press and publicity for Babeland and other participating businesses.[1]

I begin this chapter with a reference to Babeland's Masturbation Summit because it provides a concrete illustration of how sex-positive retailers have used marketplace culture as a platform for advancing a feminist project of sexual liberation and education, one that combines second-wave feminism's emphasis on social transformation with what Rosalind Gill describes as a "postfeminist sensibility."[2] As many feminist scholars have noted, postfeminist culture draws on elements of feminism, including discourses of "choice," "empowerment," and "freedom," while simultaneously transforming these elements into a highly atomized, consumer-oriented politics of individualism, leaving feminism's emphasis on collective politics and social transformation in its wake.[3] The result is often an extremely contradictory, highly stylized, hypersexualized, and exceedingly commodified version of what Angela McRobbie views as a "faux feminism"[4]—a politically neutered version of popular feminism that simultaneously acknowledges feminism's gains while rejecting its seemingly "outmoded" and "strident" politics.

Ariel Levy's analysis of raunch culture is particularly illuminating in this respect. Raunch culture can best be described as a Girls Gone Wild style of sexual empowerment—a "tawdry, tarty, cartoonlike version of female sexuality"[5] that resembles a "fantasy world dreamed up by teenage boys."[6] According to Levy, raunch is an essentially commercialized brand of sexiness, which has "diluted the effect of both sex radicals *and* feminists, who've seen their movement's images popularized while their ideals are forgotten."[7] Despite her trenchant critique of raunch culture's "neo-sexism," Levy seems to indict all forms of commercialized female sexuality, suggesting they are intrinsically antifeminist and antiwoman—a claim I seek to challenge.

I suggest we would be conceding too much political ground if we handed over wholesale the messy, contested, and contradictory terrain of female sexuality and commercial culture to postfeminism. By positioning feminist sex toy stores as cultural sites where feminism *lives*—and has lived for more than three decades—I want to trouble the notion that feminism is always transformed into its postfeminist incarnations, and consequently evacuated of political import, when it comes into contact with sexualized forms of commercial culture within the context of neoliberalism.

This chapter details how sex positive feminist retailers in the US have used consumer culture as an instrument for sexual consciousness-raising and social change by imbuing sex toys and sex toy stores with new kinds of cultural and political possibilities. A number of critics argue that radical politics are at odds with or hostile to consumer-capitalism.[8] At the same time, others argue that the sex industry is the epitome of crass commercialism and gendered exploitation.[9] My research challenges these perspectives.[10] I argue that feminist sex toy stores have created a viable counter-public sphere for sex positive entrepreneurship and activism, one where the idea that the "personal is political" is deployed in the service of a progressive—and, ideally, socially transformative—sexual politics. As one staff sex educator at Babeland noted: "We don't just sell products. We sell information; we sell education; we sell our mission [which is] making the world a safer place for happy, healthy, sexual beings."[11] In other words, sex positive retailers promote a particular understanding of what it means to be a happy, healthy, and sexually empowered individual and offer individuals a consumer-oriented agenda for how this might be accomplished.

In this regard, the program of better living through orgasms promoted by sex positive retailers dovetails with a number of elements that characterize the broader neoliberal project, one marked by a shift from the state to the private sector, from the provision of social goods and services toward the cultivation of the self-sufficient, enterprising individual capable of governing him- or herself.[12] These elements include the following: the mandate that one's life—including one's sexual life—is an ongoing "enterprise of the self"; the role of experts in shaping and regulating individual choices; the managerialization of personal identity; and, importantly, the place of market culture in promoting strategies of personal empowerment.[13] Technologies of the self, as exemplified by makeover television, advice columns in women's magazines, and sex toy businesses that position themselves as sexual resource centers, figure prominently in neoliberal culture and, according to Foucault, "permit individuals to effect by their own means or the help of others a certain number of operations on their own bodies and souls, thoughts and conduct, and way of being, so as to transform themselves in order to attain a certain state of happiness, purity, wisdom, perfection or immortality."[14] The outcome of this operation—which may or may not be liberating—is ultimately an exercise in self-rule, illustrating the very idea of "governing at a distance" that is so central to neoliberalism.

However, not all exercises in self-rule are the same, nor do they produce a uniform set of effects. Sex positive retailers have made the care of the sexual self not only a cornerstone of their businesses but an ongoing social and political project, one that links technologies of personal empowerment to a broader, world-changing enterprise. The goal of these businesses, as I discuss in this chapter, is not only, or even primarily, about making sexual products available to consumers and turning a profit; rather, it is about creating new kinds of sexual spaces and communities where individuals of all genders and sexual orientations can engage with their sexual selves in a supportive and encouraging environment. As one of my interviewees stated, "I am in [the business] to help people have better orgasms and to have a better sex life, because I firmly believe that this makes everybody's quality of life better."[15] Indeed, the happy, fulfilled sexual self is not ancillary to neoliberalism but a central component of its operation.

In what follows, I briefly sketch the historical roots of sex positive feminist entrepreneurship, the mission of social change these businesses promote, and some of the challenges that have resulted from practicing feminist sexual politics through the marketplace. Despite the ambivalence that many retailers in my study express about the relationship between profitability and social change, money and the mission, I argue that the cultural terrain of neoliberalism is not inherently antifeminist, postfeminist, reactionary, or fixed. Instead, elements of neoliberalism, including the care of the self and the role of the marketplace in promoting technologies of empowerment, can be rearticulated and marshaled toward socially progressive ends that challenge, rather than uphold, the sexual status quo.

Tools of Liberation

Women's forays into the sexual marketplace as both entrepreneurs and consumers in the 1970s were the result of a number of intersecting currents: the sexual revolution, second-wave US feminism, the gay and lesbian movement, and professional sexology—all of which helped put the issue of women's sexual pleasure and satisfaction on the map. From the groundbreaking sex research of Alfred Kinsey and Masters and Johnson to Betty Dodson's Bodysex workshops and Lonnie Barbach's preorgasmic women's groups, the idea that "good sex" was something that could be learned and mastered took hold for many Americans. Emboldened by these cultural shifts, more and more women began turning to consumer culture to expand their sense of sexual freedom and autonomy, a move that invariably produced new discourses, new forms of knowledge, and new norms regarding female sexuality and the pursuit of pleasure.

Throughout the early 1970s, feminists were actively rewriting the patriarchal sexual script that had taught them that sex was an obligation, not something they were entitled to embrace and, importantly, enjoy. One of these women was Dell Williams. In 1974, at the age of fifty-two, Williams started Eve's Garden in New York City, the first business in the US devoted exclusively to women's sexual pleasure and health. A year later she placed her first classified advertisement in *Ms. Magazine*: "Liberating vibrators and other pleasurable things for women from feminist-owned Eve's Garden."

Eve's Garden was a direct outgrowth of second-wave US feminism and the politicization of female sexuality that was occurring in certain corners of the women's movement. In the early 1970s, Williams was an active participant in the women's movement percolating around her. "I was just passionate about our endeavor to change the world and bring about equal rights for women," she recalled in an interview. "I don't know whether younger women will understand the kind of passion and commitment we had for that, because we came from a time where women were conscious of the fact that [we] just didn't have all of the opportunities."[16]

Williams saw vibrators as "liberating appliances," and getting them into the hands of as many women as possible was a decidedly feminist act. "I never thought, 'this will be a great business and I'll make money.' That was never my intention," she told me. Rather, Williams was motivated by a desire to create a world where women could celebrate their sexuality and feel good about themselves. "My ultimate vision, and I had this vision when I started," Williams explained, "was that if women could really express their sexuality, get in touch with their energy, use it in their life and feel good, we can change the world. That was my bottom line."[17]

Several years after Williams founded Eve's Garden, sex therapist and author Joani Blank opened the Good Vibrations retail store in San Francisco. Blank was encouraged by the success of Eve's Garden, which had initially operated as a mail-order business. Blank wanted to create a different kind of sex toy store: a place where customers could touch, feel, and hold sex toys, and talk openly and without embarrassment about sex with a well-trained and knowledgeable staff. Her goal was to provide "especially but not exclusively" women access to a clean and well-lit sex toy store, one that defied the stereotype of adult businesses as inherently "seedy" and inhospitable places for women.

Much like Williams, Blank encouraged women to learn about their bodies, especially their clitorises. According to former Good Vibrations store manager Cathy Winks: "In creating Good Vibrations, [Blank] was responding to the need that was being expressed in the preorgasmic women's groups and the workshops that she led [and that was]: 'Well yeah, you say vibrators are so great and I would be happy to buy them but I just cannot find a place where I am comfortable doing it and I don't want to go into an adult store.'"[18] Anne Semans, a former Good Vibrations employee, made a similar point: "I think in the beginning Joani was really motivated by the very basic idea that was part of the whole feminist consciousness-raising of the seventies that wanted women to learn about clitoral orgasms. And certainly for ninety percent of us that went into the store, that's what was going on. We walked away with our little vibrators."[19]

By the early 1990s, Good Vibrations had developed a national reputation as a clearinghouse for sexual information and a leader in the alternative sex vending movement. The company's sex positive mission, one promulgated by Blank and her employees, permeated its stores and catalogs, and former staff members, such as Susie Bright—who went on to found *On Our Backs* magazine and write a number of best-selling sex books—became ambassadors for Good Vibrations' unique brand of sex positive retailing.

Sex positivity is a *discourse* about sex; it is a way of conceptualizing and talking about sexuality that draws on a particular constellation of sexual values and norms—or counternorms as the case may be (e.g., "anything goes" as long as it is between consenting adults). As a discourse and, one might argue, a *sexual ethic*, sex positivity seeks to intervene in a culture overwhelmingly shaped by sex negativity, which is the idea that sex is a dangerous, destructive, and negative force.[20] It includes the idea that the more encouragement and support people have around their sexuality, the better; that everyone deserves access to accurate information about sex; that people should not be embarrassed or ashamed for wanting more sexual pleasure and enjoyment in their lives. These ideas function as an ideological matrix that shapes the Good Vibrations model, informing virtually every aspect of the company, from marketing and advertising to product selection and customer service.[21]

Today, businesses based on the Good Vibrations model of retailing—an educationally oriented and quasi-therapeutic approach to selling sex toys— can be found in dozens of cities across the country and in other countries, too. Babeland, Early to Bed in Chicago, Self Serve in Albuquerque, and Sugar in Baltimore, among other businesses, have all adopted Good Vibrations' mission of making quality products and accurate sexual information available in a comfortable and supportive retail environment.

Cultural critic Michael Warner argues that sexual autonomy requires "more than freedom of choice, tolerance and the liberalization of sex laws. It requires access to pleasures and possibilities, since people commonly do not know their sexual desires until they find them."[22] Warner argues that although people do not go shopping for sexual identities, they nonetheless have a stake in a culture that enables sexual variance and freely circulates knowledge about it, because they have no other way of knowing what they might or might not want when it comes to sex without such access and information.

I argue that in a neoliberal culture, many Americans *do* in fact go shopping for sexual identities and information, and the range of practices that such knowledge enables. Within the context of feminist sex toy stores, for example, people can purchase sexual information and "technologies of empowerment" by attending in-house sex education workshops on topics as varied as masturbation, oral sex, or G-spot play, or they can buy any number of books or videos. They can also get this information for free just by talking to sales staff. Thus, Good Vibrations and its sister stores offer customers a range of pedagogical tools that can be used not only to increase sexual literacy but transform sexual subjectivities. As sociologist Meika Loe notes, the retail-based version of sexual empowerment promoted by feminist sex stores implies that people "might have to leave the home—and go shopping—to tap into the variety and significance of pleasure."[23]

"It Costs a Lot of Money to Change the World"

Sex positive feminist retailers do not think of themselves as "typical" retailers driven exclusively, or even primarily, by profit. Rather, they see their businesses as a way of providing consumers with a much-needed *service*—one of sexual education, empowerment, consciousness-raising, and, importantly, personal transformation. In the eyes of many store owners and employees, an emphasis on service trumps a focus on selling things and turning a profit, and thus sets them apart from more conventional adult businesses. A former Good Vibrations employee explained it this way: "I think [Good Vibrations'] mission is not about profits or about selling sex toys for the money in it. It is about selling sex toys as a vehicle to get accurate sex information out there and change people's attitudes about sex, which I think . . . has a really big impact on the way we do business. I think that is basically what makes us different from most of the other businesses out there."[24]

Negotiating the demands of market capitalism has been neither easy nor straightforward for many of the sex positive retailers in my study. In fact, ambivalence, if not outright antagonism, toward commercial culture shapes the narratives and experience of many of my interviewees. Perhaps no individual exudes greater antipathy toward traditional modes of consumer-capitalism than Good Vibrations founder, Joani Blank. Blank describes herself as an "anticapitalist" and prides herself on the fact that when she owned Good Vibrations (which she sold to her employees in 1992), she did not do "business as usual." When asked what she meant by this, she offered a one-sentence answer: "I didn't give a damn about profits.[25] Profits, she explained, were secondary to everything else that was important to her about running a successful business.

Blank brought to her business, and instilled in her employees, an alternative mind-set and a different set of values about what it meant to run a successful business. She cultivated a commercial universe where ideas about social good, right livelihood, and the dissemination of sex positive information superseded profit making. It was with a sense of great satisfaction that Blank recounted a story where someone once said: "Joani, you run your business like a social service." Without missing a beat, Blank replied, "Right. That is exactly it. Thank you. That is a compliment."[26] That Blank experienced this remark as a compliment rather than a condemnation of her business practices not only speaks to her understanding of herself as business person but also reflects the extent to which she muddied the taken-for-granted distinctions that typically characterize for-profit and not-for-profit enterprises—a blurring of values, practices, and ideologies that would for many years be a hallmark of Good Vibrations' retail operation and, later, shape the businesses that followed in Good Vibrations' footsteps.[27]

I saw ample evidence of this mind-set throughout the course of my research. Many people I spoke with were quick to dismiss the business-side of the business in favor of its sex positive mission. It was as though the business had two distinct parts—commerce and politics—that could be easily disarticulated from each other and understood on their own terms. This perspective was shared by store owners and sales staff alike. According to Claire Cavanah, cofounder of Babeland, "I didn't go into this business as a business person. I went into it as a feminist and a women's liberationist, with my own understanding of how sex fits into that." She continued: "The whole capitalist consumer thing has never been easy for me to deal with. I don't even shop. Not only did I not work in retail but I did not even go into retail stores."[28]

The act of keeping consumer-capitalism at bay while simultaneously reaping the monetary and social benefits it makes possible involves a complicated set of negotiations and deferrals. Sex positive retailers often find themselves swimming both with and against the cultural tide; they are at once hegemonic and counterhegemonic, mainstream and radical in their approach to both market capitalism and social transformation—a paradox that is not lost on them. Cavanah, for example, describes herself as an "uneasy, accidental capitalist" but also concedes that she is also very much part of the system that makes her so uncomfortable.

Rachel Venning of Babeland explains her discomfort with consumer capitalism this way: "Being a retailer in this culture is definitely like being a cultural player because [we live in] a consumer culture and it is so much of how people interact, and where they meet, and what they think about, and how they express themselves. I personally don't care for it. The whole shopping thing—buying and selling—is definitely not the highlight of anything; it is a kind of necessary evil or something."[29] Venning admits that she does not like thinking of herself as a businessperson but acknowledges that there is no adequate language to describe what she does for a living: "If I go around and say, 'I am a sex educator and I own Babeland,' I feel like there is something kind of false there. But I also feel that if I say, 'I am a businessperson,' that is not the whole picture either. Both are true."[30] Finding ways to bridge what is often thought of as dueling identities, that of "businesswoman" and "sex educator," or "retailer" versus "social activist," is an ongoing challenge and one that never seems adequately resolved for these entrepreneurs.

However, not everyone was conflicted about money or failed to appreciate the fact that generating a profit was an important part of running a successful business. I spoke with several people who invoked a much more pragmatic view of consumer-capitalism, one that took into account that money, especially in the context of American commercialism, was a form of power. "I have no problems whatsoever with the capitalist realities of our world," Jacq Jones told me. "I like money. I think money is good."[31] For Jones and a handful of other sex educators, it was understood that, as one person put it, "money can get you places": the more money you have, the more you can pay your employees; the more stores you can open; the better website you can design and build; and, ideally, the more people you can reach with your sex positive message. Brandie Taylor was one of the few people I interviewed who talked about the relationship between money and the mission in frank and unapologetic terms:

The mission is for everyone and there is no way we can spread our mission louder and clearer and wider than if we have more money in our belt. So we have to sell a lot of these toys and make a profit so we can spread the vision to everyone and promote positive sexuality to the whole world. . . .Underneath it all we are a business. Yes, we are a feminist business and I think we are a queer business, but we are a business. Period. And what is the common thing [that businesses share]? Businesses make profits. That's what they do. They sell things. So we have to come here and sell vibrators. That is our job.[32]

For Taylor, money not only greases the wheels of social change but keeps those wheels spinning. As a result, profit-making acquires a different kind of valence than if wealth accumulation was the only desired outcome. Thus, the project of social change advanced by sex positive retailers recuperates, and to some extent transforms, the capitalist underpinnings of these businesses, injecting them with new meaning and social value.

Cathy Winks described the moment when she realized just how important money was to advancing Good Vibrations' mission: "It wasn't really for me until about 1991 or 1992 when I suddenly realized that [Good Vibrations] had grossed a million dollars in revenues and it was like a light switch flipped and I was like, 'Oh for goodness sakes. We made a million dollars. We could easily make so much more.' Then my engines started revving up about how we could take this message out into the world and be successful."[33] Roma Estevez described a similar experience. During the nine years that she worked at Good Vibrations, her relationship to money began to shift once she saw how the company could make more money and "do bigger and better things in the world." The fact of the matter, she explained to me, is that "money can really get you places."[34] Winks echoed this idea. "This is America, money talks," she told me.[35]

The fact that money talks as loudly as it does implies that consumer-capitalism is a language that many people—at least in the US—understand. This is perhaps one way to explain the recent explosion of socially conscious businesses that strategically combine not-for-profit sensibilities with the logic of the marketplace. Not only does it make good fiscal sense to approach social reform as a business, but social entrepreneurs are tapping into a way of organizing the world that most people are familiar with. In other words, consumer-capitalism, and by extension a commercialized form of politics, brings with it a set of norms and a system of exchange that structures and mediates people's lives in absolutely fundamental ways. As Rachel Venning explained: "People know what to do with stores. They really understand that you go in and you get to look around. You can ask questions, you can buy or not buy, and you get to leave. If it was just a drop-in sex education center," she continued, "I think that would be a lot more intimidating for people to go to. If you could just stop by and ask people questions, if there were toys there and you got information but there wasn't a consumer purpose, I don't think people would come as much because it would feel strange."[36] Laura Weide, the former marketing manager at Babeland, expressed a similar idea: "Because [Babeland] is a commercial locale, I think it gives us a kind of legitimacy that if we were some small women's sexuality and pleasure activist organization and education center we [would not have]."[37]

Such comments are revealing and suggest that sex positive retailers invoke a range of signs, symbols, practices, and norms that constitute a familiar—and therefore perhaps more legitimate—part of the American cultural landscape. Despite many people's discomfort with a commercial world where "money talks" and where consumer capitalism is accepted as the norm, packaging sexual information and ideas about sexual liberation as though they were commodities might in fact be a highly effective means of providing sexual education and encouragement to people who might otherwise not have access to such things outside of the context of market culture.

Conclusion

For feminist sex toy businesses, changing the way society thinks and talks about sex requires not only entrepreneurial vision and missionary zeal but an ability to balance the books and pay the bills. As obvious as this statement may seem, it has been only relatively recently that these businesses have begun to bridge the ideological gap that long existed between money and the mission, feminism and capitalism, and profitability and social change, resulting in a new appreciation for the ways that profit both fuels and sustains them.

Getting to this place, however, has not been easy. Good Vibrations and its sister stores have been guided by an alternative set of commercial visions, values, and retail practices, ones that emphasized what these businesses *did* in the world—providing sexual education, promoting sex positivity, and increasing sexual literacy—as opposed to how much money they *made*. As a result, the demands of the marketplace frequently took a backseat to the goals of the mission, which reinforced the idea that profitability and social change were separate rather than interdependent spheres of activity and concern. And the fact that many people saw themselves as social workers and sex educators, rather than businesswomen and retail employees, seemed only to exacerbate this division, producing a business culture where "doing good" consistently trumped profit making as a means of evaluating commercial success.

In recent years, Good Vibrations and its sister stores have begun to close this long-standing divide and cultivate new forms of business expertise that can better support the goals of their sex positive missions while also turning a profit. As one staff member explained about Good Vibrations: "We have worked very hard in the last few years to try to develop more expertise in the business, and I think we are at a place now where we understand how to be profitable and I think that we haven't [understood that] in the past. And I guess we worked really hard to do that because there was a shift in wanting to do that."[38]

More important, perhaps, is that this shift needed to occur in order for feminist sex toy businesses to remain commercially viable in an increasingly crowded and competitive marketplace. Rather than seeing either consumer-capitalism or the sex industry as inherently antithetical to the broader goals of feminist transformation, sex positive retailers have found creative ways to meld feminist sexual politics with the realities of the neoliberal marketplace. While this has not always proved easy, the success of the Good Vibrations model suggests that consumer-capitalism, and the various technologies of empowerment it advances, can be organized in different ways and harnessed for multiple purposes—including socially progressive ones—that exceed an exclusive focus on wealth accumulation for a privileged few. Indeed, feminist sex toy companies demonstrate that consumer culture, and the resources, goods, and services it provides, can be put to use in the service of sex positive feminist intervention and, ideally, social transformation. In a world increasingly shaped by a postfeminist sensibility, where feminist values of freedom and empowerment have become individualized to the point of evacuating feminism of its collective politics, feminist sex toy stores are cultural sites where feminist goals of social transformation continue to live. In the end, these businesses challenge any simple bifurcation between sexual commerce and politics, profitability and social change, and feminism and postfeminism, demonstrating just how intertwined and mutually constitutive these domains can be within the context of neoliberalism.

1. Babeland has continued its "Come for a Cause" philanthropy by donating money to various not-for-profit and social change organizations. In 2009 the company donated more than $90,000 to over 300 organizations, which included Breast Cancer Action, Harvest Food Bank, and AIDS Alliance, among others. See http://www.babeland.com/about/come-for-a-cause-babeland-philanthropy/.

2. Rosalind Gill, *Gender and the Media* (Cambridge: Polity Press, 2007), 254–71.

3. In addition to Gill, see Angela McRobbie, *The Aftermath of Feminism: Gender, Culture, and Social Change* (London: Sage, 2009); Stephanie Genz and Benjamin A. Brabon, *Postfeminism: Cultural Texts and Theories* (Edinburgh: Edinburgh University Press, 2009); Yvonne Tasker and Diane Negra, eds., *Interrogating Post-feminism: Gender and the Politics of Popular Culture* (Durham, NC: Duke University Press, 2007); Ariel Levy, *Female Chauvinist Pigs: Women and the Rise of Raunch Culture* (New York: Free Press, 2005).

4. McRobbie, 2009, 1.

5. Levy, 2005, 5.

6. Levy, 2005, 17.

7. Levy, 2005, 196, emphasis in original.

8. For an example, see Alexandra Chasin, *Selling Out: The Gay and Lesbian Movement Goes to Market* (New York: St. Martin's, 2000).

9. See Robert Jensen, *Getting Off: Pornography and the End of Masculinity* (Cambridge, MA: South End Press, 2007); Gail Dines and Robert Jensen, "The Anti-feminist Politics behind the Pornography That 'Empowers' Women," www.opednews.com, January 24, 2008.

10. I have conducted more than seventy interviews with sex positive retailers, sales staff, marketers, sex toy manufacturers, and pornographers from across the country, and in 2001 I spent six months conducting participant-observation research at Babeland in New York City.

11. Jacq Jones, interview with author, April 12, 2002.

12. See David Harvey, *A Brief History of Neoliberalism* (Oxford: Oxford University Press, 2005); Lisa Duggan, *The Twilight of Equality? Neoliberalism, Cultural Politics and the Attack on Democracy* (Boston: Beacon Press, 2003).

13. For interesting discussions of these strategies, see Nikolas Rose, "Governing 'Advanced' Liberal Democracies," in *Foucault and Political Reason*, ed. Andrew Barry et al. (Chicago: University of Chicago Press, 1996), 37–64; Colin Gordon, "Government Rationality: An Introduction," in *The Foucault Effect: Studies in Governmentality with Two Lectures by and an Interview with Michel Foucault*, ed. Graham Burchell et al. (Chicago: University of Chicago Press, 1991), 1–52; Laurie Ouellette and James Hay, *Better Living through Reality TV* (Malden, MA: Blackwell, 2008).

14. Michel Foucault, "Technologies of the Self," in *Technologies of the Self*, ed. Luther H. Martin et al. (Amherst: University of Massachusetts Press, 1988), 18.

15. Chephany Navarro, interview with author, October 12, 2001.

16. Dell Williams, interview with author, November 20, 2001.

17. Williams, 2001.

18. Cathy Winks, telephone interview with author, June 27, 2002.

19. Anne Semans, telephone interview with author, June 25, 2002.

20. For a cogent discussion of sex negativity and its operations, see Gayle Rubin, "Thinking Sex: Notes for a Radical Theory of the Politics of Sexuality," in *The Lesbian and Gay Studies Reader*, ed. Henry Abelove et al. (New York: Routledge, 1993), 3–44.

21. Although the origins of sex positivity are difficult to trace, these principles can be found in a variety of cultural institutions and educational materials dating back to the late 1960s. They are present in printed materials published by the National Sex Forum, which was founded in San Francisco in 1968. Sex positivity also informed the counseling program at the University of California at San Francisco, where, prior to opening Good Vibrations, Joani Blank had worked with therapist Lonnie Barbach counseling preorgasmic women. Ideas about sex positivity also infuse a great deal of lesbian and queer sexual culture. Thus, while ideas about sex positivity did not originate with Good Vibrations and its sister stores, sex positive culture would not have proliferated, or proliferated in the ways it did, I argue, without businesses like Good Vibrations creating new kinds of distribution networks through which many forms of sex positive culture, including "how-to" guides, literary erotica, and pornography, found its way to consumers.

22. Michael Warner, *The Trouble with Normal: Sex, Politics, and the Ethics of Queer Life* (New York: Free Press, 1999), 7.

23. Meika Loe, "Feminism for Sale: Case Study of a Pro-sex Feminist Business," *Gender and Society* 13, no. 6 (1999): 712.

24. Ziadee Whiptail, telephone interview with author, March 29, 2002.

25. Joani Blank, interview with author, June 12, 2002.

26. Blank, 2002.

27. The kind of boundary blurring practiced by Blank and other sex positive retailers characterizes the concept of "social entrepreneurship." Social entrepreneurs creatively combine elements from the not-for-profit and for-profit realms in order to affect social change, mixing the idealism of a social worker with the fiscal aptitude of a seasoned CEO. Although no one I interviewed used this term to describe themselves, their business practices very much reflect this hybrid model of for-profit-business and social change.

28. Claire Cavanah, interview with author, August 30, 2001.

29. Rachel Venning, telephone interview with author, March 14, 2002.

30. Venning, 2002.

31. Jacq Jones, interview with author, April 12, 2002.

32. Brandie Taylor, interview with author, February 21, 2002.

33. Winks, telephone interview with author, June 27, 2002.

34. Roma Estevez, interview with author, November 11, 1999.

35. Winks, telephone interview with author, June 27, 2002.

36. Venning, telephone interview with author, March 14, 2002.

37. Laura Weide, interview with author, June 11, 2002.

38. Whiptail, telephone interview with author, March 29, 2002.

————————————————————————————————— 13 ——

Pay-for Culture

Television Activism in a Neoliberal Digital Age

———— JOHN MCMURRIA ————————————————————

As television has undergone significant industrial, technological, and cultural transformations with the expansion of cable/satellite delivery and its "convergence" through the Internet, so too have the strategies and orientations of television activism. At the height of television's classic network period in the 1970s when three broadcast networks drew nearly 90 percent of the viewing audience, advocacy groups representing communities of color, women, gays and lesbians, child advocates, religious conservatives, and other organizations campaigned to impact the prime-time network representations that held such symbolic power. Public interest provisions in federal broadcast policy gave advocacy groups legal leverage to mount national protests, challenge local broadcast license renewals, demand access to ownership and employment opportunities, and negotiate with the networks through their "standards and practices" divisions. But by the 1980s the social movements that had fueled much of this activism were marginalized as a neoliberal political movement advocated for free market mechanisms over redistributive programs and civil rights media advocacy organizations lost nonprofit foundation support.[1] Television policy changed too as deregulatory sentiments reduced broadcast public interest rules, insulated cable operators from public interests provisions, and facilitated the growth of media conglomerates with ownership ties across print, film, cable, broadcast, and Internet media. Broadcast networks no longer command such symbolic power as audiences have fragmented across proliferating cable/satellite networks, nor do they maintain such financial significance as they have become marginally performing assets held by larger media conglomerates—cable networks are now more profitable with dual income from advertising and subscription revenues.

Within this current period when television distribution is more dispersed, media ownership more integrated, and media policy more liberalized, this

254 |

essay considers how orientations to television activism have navigated this neoliberal environment. The essay begins with a consideration of two prominent orientations to television activism. The first targets media conglomeration as a threat to democracy and orients activism toward dismantling corporate ownership structures. The second looks to new forms of activism in fans of popular culture and how their grassroots communities can democratize television.[2] Each is concerned about the power of media conglomerates, but the first considers popular commercial television as a symptom of corporate media power and the latter a passionate avenue through which fans can challenge conglomerates to be more accountable to consumer interests. Though each orientation supports expanding democratic participation in a neoliberal media age, I consider how their invocations of neoliberal theories, particularly through adherence to the idea that individual direct payments for television programs constitutes a more democratic television culture, obfuscates the complexities of commercial television practices, and subordinates considerations for the historical conditions that have produced class, race, and gender privilege.

To further explore the issue of individual direct payment for television, the essay considers two case studies with particular attention to the cultural politics of activists supporting and opposing this neoliberal ideal of resource allocation. The first considers contestations over direct payment television in the postwar period, when a professional class of regulators, cultural critics, and educators promoted pay-TV to uplift a commercial broadcast network television culture they thought had sunken to a lowest common denominator. However, activists representing women's groups, veteran's associations, and labor unions perceived pay-TV as an unjust commodification of television that would stratify access to quality television based on viewers' ability to pay. Here structures of class privilege and hierarchical orientations to popular culture are integral to understanding activism and direct payment television. The second case study considers the more recent activism surrounding the issue of requiring cable systems to offer subscribers the option to purchase only the networks they want rather than having to purchase a package of networks. A bipartisan coalition of conservative religious organizations and progressive advocacy groups lobbied for so-called à la carte pricing as a more democratic form of television but did so with the assumption that this would promote "mainstream family values" despite the protests from civil rights and religious organizations. Unlike proponents of à la carte pricing who supported concepts of free market competition and consumer choice, historically marginalized communities opposing à la carte pricing framed access and participation in ways that recognized the socially constituted structures of media industries and broader sociohistorical axes of discrimination and exclusion.

The essay concludes with thoughts on how placing these formations of television activism in dialogue can help to expose the contradictory logics of neoliberal theories and identify productive spaces for activism within the complex practices of market formations, regulatory policies, and consumptive uses.

Anticorporate and Fan-Based Orientations to Television Activism

One prominent orientation to television activism targets "big media" for undermining the media's democratic function. In the wake of the political movement to deregulate media in the late 1970s, which facilitated the growth of large, diversified media conglomerates with ownership stakes across broadcast, cable, film, and print media, critics such as Ben Bagdikian, who published six editions of his widely read *Media Monopoly* from 1983 to 2000, focused media reform efforts on targeting corporate media power.[3] An extensively revised edition in 2004 identified similar trends despite the Internet's more prominent place in media culture.[4] More recently, media scholar Robert McChesney has been the most prominent and prolific advocate for focusing media activism on dismantling media conglomeration. McChesney situates his analysis within a long tradition of opposition to commercial "mass culture," and in particular, the broadcast reform movement in the early 1930s when mostly Protestant reformers organized and funded opposition to commercial radio.[5] McChesney argues that the profit-driven media conglomerates of today promote a "hypercommercialism" that deprives journalism of its critical independence and promotes an accessible entertainment culture that easily captures audiences' attention through "the tried-and-true mechanism" of "sex, vulgarity, and violence." This anticommercial and anticorporate media critique supports efforts to develop public-funded or nonprofit media alternatives and lobbies Congress and the Federal Communications Commission (FCC) to tighten regulations over these conglomerates, which otherwise stifle competition and limit the potential for smaller, more entrepreneurial media initiatives to develop.[6] In 2002 McChesney cofounded the media reform organization Free Press, which claims nearly half a million "activists and members" and has become a hub for anticorporate media activism through organizing conferences and coordinating lobbying campaigns.

Another emerging orientation to media activism focuses on how consumers actively engage with television in new media environments. Media scholar and popular culture fan Henry Jenkins argues that attacks on big media exaggerate corporate power, represent consumers as passive victims of corporate manipulation, and undervalue the pleasures of popular commercial culture. Rather, Jenkins considers how "grassroots fan communities" of popular commercial culture have utilized new interactive technologies to become more active participants in their media consumptive practices and increasingly successful in challenging commercial media producers to build stronger connections with them. Jenkins draws from the French Canadian philosopher Pierre Lévy's idea of "collective intelligence," which posits that the Internet has facilitated the formation of virtual communities that combine the expertise of each participant to form temporary and tactical "knowledge communities" around particular intellectual and emotional investments. This "knowledge culture" has emerged just as older forms of social community have dissipated, including those formed through physical proximity, family, or national belonging. Jenkins believes that media activism can learn from the ways in which first adapters of new technologies engage with popular culture and develop "new skills in collaboration and a new ethic of knowledge sharing that will allow us to deliberate together." These emerging participatory practices are more prevalent in the realm of commercial media, including through such franchises as Harry Potter, Star Wars, and *American Idol*, because the stakes for participation are lower than in politics, and more fun too. But Jenkins argues that these skills are increasingly applied to work, education, and politics. For example, during the political elections of 2004, activists used accessible graphics software to blend popular cultural images with representations of politicians to make political statements outside mainstream media coverage.[7]

Though these two predominant forms of television activism in the Internet age represent radically different orientations to popular culture—the anticorporate orientation signals commercial television's banality as proof of conglomerate power while the fan-oriented position derives its activist passions through it—both of these exemplify contradictory orientations to neoliberalism. To explore these contradictions it is useful to distinguish between the neoliberal theories invoked to promote deregulation and the complexities of market practices in deregulated television industries. Neoliberal theories emerged in the postwar period as a reaction to the advancement of a social welfare liberalism which invested the state with an important role in regulating market activity and redistributing resources to meet the basic needs of citizens. Neoclassical economists returned to classical liberalism's conception of the person as an autonomous individual who needed protection from state infringement and embraced "free markets" as better arbiters of human needs.[8] Neoliberal citizenship holds individuals personally responsible for their well-being and rewards those who can self-adjust to market permutations.[9] These free market ideologies informed media deregulations beginning in the late 1970s, facilitated by the idea that the new technologies of cable, satellite, and Internet delivery meant that most existing regulations were no longer necessary.[10] The result, according to pervasive liberal narratives of television progress, is as follows. While the broadcast network TV era was limited to just three national networks that each competed to reach a "mass audience," deregulations and new technologies facilitated the emergence of the "postnetwork" or "multichannel" era composed of numerous channels that "cater" to more distinct and individuated "niche audiences." While network programming pitched to "lowest-common-denominator" tastes, multichannel television caters to a broad spectrum of high- and low-quality programming to satisfy a range of tastes. The diversity goals of government-enforced public interest broadcast rules were finally realized as deregulation and the new technologies of cable and satellite proliferated programming that reflected registers of cultural, social, and economic difference. In this new age, viewers are less passive and more empowered to use new devices to watch what they want, as well as when and where to do so.[11]

To be sure, the volume of television has expanded, and new technologies have facilitated new ways to engage with television. But such narratives that represent this new environment as liberalized markets catering to diversified tastes subordinate cultural politics, obfuscate the complexities of cable television industry practices, and fail to account for the ways in which television culture promotes particular interests and behaviors or fails to engage others. Deregulations in cable television in the 1970s facilitated the development of monopoly cable franchises in most markets, enabled the business model of selling networks in bundles or tiers for monthly subscription fees, prompted cable operators to merge to form large multisystem operations, and allowed cable operators to own many of the cable networks they offered subscribers. Unregulated, subscription rates have ballooned, and cable operators have prioritized the networks they own through favorable marketing, channel positions, and pricing.[12] Forms of network and program "diversity" are constituted through these integrated operations, which can leverage risk so that new networks may run prolonged deficits while building audiences. Within increasingly transnational markets, programming networks themselves are less directed toward filling niche interests than toward commissioning programming that is thought translatable across the largest national television markets and often internationally coproduced.[13] Neoliberal narratives might perceive the Discovery Channel, for example, to have emerged to address the unmet needs of a niche of documentary or nonfiction programming enthusiasts. Its history suggests otherwise. A multisystem operator financed the educationally oriented network in the early 1980s to create goodwill during negotiations over federal cable legislation and grew to become a globally integrated operation. The network leverages high-cost blue-chip spectaculars such as *Blue Planet* to build global brand recognition and prestige to differentiate the network and facilitate carriage on cable systems, with low-cost reality programming filling out regular schedules.[14]

These industrial practices of multichannel television do not simply proliferate cultural difference through catering to viewer demands but constitute forms of inclusion and exclusion. Representations of ethnic and racial diversity on television are relegated to comedy and reality formats or placed on high-numbered channels in specialty "tiered" packages.[15] The case of the cable network Black Entertainment Television reveals how branding imperatives and profit motives first resisted airing hip-hop music videos, then overly relied on them to the exclusion of other forms of black representation.[16] The liberal feminist founders of the cable network and Internet portal Oxygen may "cater" to an intergenerational and multicultural audience of women, as Lisa Parks has shown, but when also designed to attract sponsors and distinguish its brand, the network exemplifies a form of gender commodification that constitutes viewers as market segments.[17] The rapid expansion of makeover reality programs is not just catering to unmet interests in "unscripted" programming but is equally invested in promoting the attainment of a particular lifestyle as a measure of social worth and rehearsing the entrepreneurial self-reformations required for success within neoliberal capitalism.[18] Neoliberal narratives that register progress by the effectiveness of commercial mechanisms in meeting existing viewer interests elide the complexities of these industrial production cultures.

Locating moments when anticonglomerate and fan-based activism evoke neoliberal narratives and theories can help to identify the ways in which they subordinate cultural politics, elide more complex industry practices, and/or promote conduct conducive to neoliberal capitalism. Anticorporate activism exemplified this in a 2010 Free Press campaign to stop cable, satellite, and phone companies from colluding to extend their lucrative monthly subscription TV business model to the Internet by allowing online access only for those who subscribe to their monthly service. In challenging this, Free Press contrasted this collusion with existing online TV initiatives that sounded as if they had realized the promise of a liberalized market. Free Press said this collusion threatened the "revolution in online video" that enabled "Americans to watch high-definition programs on the Internet from anywhere or on the family living room screen," including from services such as iTunes, Netflix, Hulu, Amazon VOD, YouTube, and other video-based start-ups. Though most of these services had ties to media conglomerates, Free Press said they represent "the benefits of competition and innovation in online TV." Central to this revolution was the opportunity for viewers to pay for networks or programs individually. Thus Free Press applauded Apple's iTunes, which sold video programs on an individual basis, but lamented reports that Apple may be developing a monthly subscription service. Consistent with a central focus on challenging "big media," Free Press evoked this more perfect commodity exchange process of existing online TV as a wedge to dismantle the corporate structures of cable television, a priority for Free Press and other anticorporate activists: "Online TV is this nation's best shot at breaking up the cable TV industry oligopolies and cartels."[19] In promoting online TV as a competitive environment that allowed viewers to watch anything anytime, Free Press sounded remarkably similar to Comcast's own promotional campaign for its "Fancast XFINITY" broadband service, which offered "customers more choice, more control, more speed, and more HD than ever before."[20] Here, anticorporate activism utilizes neoliberal theories of market competition, consumer choice, and the right to buy programs individually to critique the structures and business models of cable television.

While anticorporate television activism is less attentive to how users engage with online video than to using the promise of online video to promote regulating cable television, grassroots fan orientations conceptualize television activism through the actual uses of online video. This is a process that is not outside of the commodity processes of commercial media, but rather constituted through commodification itself. Following Lévy, Jenkins recognizes that fan communities have become important "engines" in the circulation and exchange of commodities as media industries increasingly accommodate these active consumers.[21] It is not surprising, then, to see Comcast branding its online TV service "Fancast XFINITY" to provide "fans instant access to an extensive video collection" so they can "tune-in, catch-up, and chat about their favorite programming," even as the cable company was colluding with other providers to find ways to restrict this content to cable television subscribers. For Jenkins, these fan practices within the commodity chains of commercial media are in a nascent stage but promise a fuller realization of democratic participation that entails a neoliberal ethical subjectivity of volunteerism, rather than government intervention, to solve social issues. For example, Jenkins offers *Global Frequency* as a "prototype" of what a more "mature, fully realized knowledge culture might look like" and an example of efforts to "democratize television." *Global Frequency* is a comic book series about a "multiracial, multinational organization of ordinary people who contribute their services on an ad hoc basis." These volunteers work in nonhierarchical ways to address problems through drawing on their localized knowledge. Because the government is an impediment to solving social problems in the world of *Global Frequency*, and in many cases the source of these problems, the series creator said the comic "is about us saving ourselves." When Warner Brothers created a television pilot for *Global Frequency* but canceled plans to run it as a TV series, fans circulated an illegal download of the pilot and, Jenkins suggests, applied these voluntary and ad hoc practices portrayed in the comic book to mount a grassroots campaign to pressure the company and the head writer and producer to continue with the series. Though the pilot never aired and plans for the series were canceled, this prompted the head producer to contemplate selling the DVD of the pilot directly to fans and prompted Jenkins to envision the potential to circumvent the institutional barriers of corporate media through selling television directly to fans on a subscription or pay-per-view basis.[22] Here television activism is constituted through the commodity process of direct viewer payments and articulated through the neoliberal values of volunteer rather than government actions.

Thus anticorporate and grassroots activist orientations represent forms of television activism that work through neoliberalism in contradictory ways. Anticorporate activism invokes neoliberal theory to petition the state to regulate the cable oligarchs, with the tacit assumption that Internet TV will not replicate the dull and standardized forms that have emanated from these corporate mavens. Grassroots fan activism emerges passionately within the commodity chains of commercial television to form voluntary associations to pressure corporate media to better respond to their passions, bypassing the state altogether. Uniting the two is the neoliberal idea that individual direct payment for television programs realizes a more democratic television culture. To further explore the social and cultural contexts that inform activist orientations to direct payment television, I consider the issue as it is manifested in contestations over the value of television in postwar America.

Taste Hierarchies and the Issue of Pay-TV in Postwar America

Currently almost 90 percent of US television viewers pay for their service through cable or satellite delivery, including many who pay for "premium" networks that have no commercials, and some who pay an additional fee for a single "on-demand" program. But these forms of pay-TV were not simply a technological evolution in television made possible by the emergence of cable and satellite technologies. Well before the modern cable and satellite television era emerged with the birth of HBO and other national cable networks in the mid-1970s, electronics manufacturers created devices in the 1950s to enable viewers to pay a fee to unscramble television programs transmitted through cable or over the air. The invention of these new technological devices was less significant than the *idea* that viewers should have to pay directly for something that was currently available free over the "public" airwaves for everyone with a television receiver. Economic stakeholders and activists converged in a series of public hearings on pay-TV convened by Congress and the FCC from 1955 through the mid-1970s.[23]

The hearings included activists supporting and opposing the idea of pay-TV. Proponents of pay-TV shared the cultural perspective that commercial broadcast television had catered to the low tastes of a "mass" audience with a barrage of sitcoms, soap operas, westerns, and variety and quiz shows. These proponents, including prominent educators, television critics, performing arts organizations, New Deal liberals associated with Americans for Democratic Action (ADA), and others who shared similar cultural tastes, argued that television viewers, if given the choice to pay for programs, would more likely choose more "sophisticated" programs such as televised Broadway plays, ballet, symphonic music, opera, and university lectures. In looking to pay-TV as a method to raise the cultural standards of television culture, these pay-TV advocates shared the cultural sensibilities of other educated professionals who felt their "minority" tastes were underrepresented on television. These cultural perceptions were widely expressed in television research and criticism in the 1950s that often contrasted the aesthetic value of television to the fine arts. In his widely read and cited survey of television research and criticism first published in 1956, Leo Bogart situates the social and cultural significance of television by counterposing television as a "popular art" to "elite art." He links aesthetic form to the social and economic position of audiences: "Whereas the elite audience tends to be heavily concentrated in an urban, well educated, upper-income milieu, the popular art audience is widely distributed and is characterized by considerable diversity of life styles, beliefs and tastes." Because of this, popular art "employs themes and symbols which are less complex than those of elite art" that "must be intelligible to a less sophisticated public" and "assume a less specialized universe of discourse and a lower level of interest." As contrasted to higher levels of rational and critical engagement in elite art, this "lower level of interest," especially evident in radio and television, entails emotional involvement and strong identification with characters and performers, which tends to "manipulate the audience's view of reality" through their "aura of glamour," "illusion of intimacy," "illusion of drama," and "illusion of two-way communication."[24] The prominent Stanford University professor Wilbur Schramm came to similar conclusions in his survey of a year later, finding that because "many people will identify strongly with the characters of popular art," they will "unquestionably contain more uncritical and suggestible persons than, say, the audiences of fine art."[25]

French sociologist Pierre Bourdieu's ideas are useful here for conceptualizing the relation between hierarchies of cultural taste and the maintenance of social and economic position. Culture deemed "high" involves extensive learning, which enables cultural readers to delineate fine distinctions that are often based on formal and stylistic characteristics and a purported distanciation from corporeal and immediate social needs. "Low" culture provides more immediate pathways to engagement based on everyday life experiences and "an affirmation of the continuity between art and life." Conversely, high cultural distinctions require the education and leisure time afforded by affluence, but these conditions are masked when these hierarchies are conveyed as universal measures for defining cultural worth. As perceived truths these cultural hierarchies legitimize economic and social differences as natural orders.[26] For Bogart and Schramm, the continuity of the popular arts and life through this strong identification and emotional involvement is an illusion of reality and thus a stealth manipulator that only the critical capacities and distanciated position of elite audiences can reveal. Both therefore advocate for more professional criticism in television to push the commercial broadcast industry to respond to professional class sensibilities.

Similarly, advocates for pay-TV embraced the possibility that direct payments would come from a more educated class interested in the elite arts. But in doing so, these advocates argued that pay-TV was a more efficient market mechanism for satisfying diverse consumer interests, often equating this supply-and-demand mechanism with a more democratic television culture. In advocating for pay-TV, the ADA put it this way: "A direct public payment for a product or service is a voluntary, selective ballot which not only measures the usefulness of that service but provides the economic incentive for invention, competition, and expansion."[27] This rhetoric of direct democracy not only displaces attention to this further commodification of television but also masks the class interests of this professional class wanting to exert more cultural influence on television.

Against these activist campaigns to support pay-TV to uplift television culture were groups and citizens expressing more populist defenses of commercial broadcasting. Women's groups, veteran's associations, and labor unions thought pay-TV would siphon programming away from free-to-air broadcasting and provide alternatives for only those who could afford them. The General Federation of Women's Clubs invoked the public status of the airwaves in pleading to Congress not to "sell our last free natural resource." The federation defended the value of morning talk shows and afternoon home improvement programs that white male opinion leaders often dismissed as trivial. Veteran groups, whose members subsisted on fixed incomes, and many strapped with hospital bills, described pay-TV as "one of the greatest giveaways of public property for private gain ever seen." In 1957, the AFL-CIO, the umbrella organization for most labor unions, warned Congress not to "break the pledge of the Federal Government, signed into law, that television would be free." By 1967, however, despite the broad opposition to pay-TV from most trade unions, the AFL-CIO reversed its position to support the powerful screen actors and writers guilds, which believed pay-TV would increase work for their members. Labor's changed position also reflected the need to adapt to Hollywood's transition from a centralized studio system model of production to a more flexible, decentralized model as Hollywood created a content ratings system to differentiate films for select audiences.[28]

Given these activist challenges to pay-TV and a powerful broadcast industry intent on warding off competition, the FCC did not authorize pay-TV until 1969 and restricted providers from selling certain motion pictures, sports, and "series type" programs to prevent the migration of staple broadcast programming to pay-TV. HBO challenged these "anti-siphoning" restrictions and won a Supreme Court case in 1977 which ruled that the FCC had infringed on cable providers' First Amendment rights. But the aesthetic quality of the programs pay-TV proponents hoped would flourish under this more direct payment method did not materialize, as existing popular commercial genres inspired most programming on cable networks, including HBO, ESPN, MTV, TBS, and USA. Rather, these professionals' evocations of consumer choice and free markets in pay-TV resonated with a cable television industry that lobbied for protection from the types of public service obligations that applied to over-the-air broadcasting. The first federal legislation for cable television in 1984 treated cable providers as private companies with strict First Amendment protections.[29] With limited regulations regarding rates and ownership ties, cable systems merged and profited to an extent that they now have much leverage in shaping the organization of media conglomerates.[30]

There are parallels in Free Press campaigns to challenge these cable "cartels" from inhibiting the potential of online television and the efforts of pay-TV advocates in the 1950s that suggest the uneasy contradictions of television activism and neoliberalism. Both looked down upon commercial television and promoted individual direct payment for programming, believing this represented a more efficient means for satisfying diverse consumer interests. Yet, in the case of postwar pay-TV, this facilitated rather than challenged the very deregulations that enabled cable television to hold such market power today. The case of pay-TV in the 1950s suggests that anticorporate critiques are not necessarily simply populist challenges to corporate power but reflections of situated perspectives on cultural value that themselves are invested in maintaining cultural authority that reproduces rather than challenges the material power relations of social position. This is evident in the more recent case of activism over the issue of à la carte pricing in cable television.

À la Carte Cable Pricing: Promoting "Mainstream Family Values" or "Media Sharecropping"?

In 2004 a coalition of public interest advocates joined forces to lobby for à la carte cable pricing, which would require cable operators to give subscribers the option to pay for only the networks they wanted to watch rather than require them to pay set fees for packaged networks.[31] The Parents Television Council (PTC) made "cable choice" a central component of its anti-indecency campaign. The PTC, founded in 1995 over concern that, according to its website, "gratuitous sex, foul language, and violence on TV (along with stories and dialogue that create disdain for authority figures, patriotism, and religion) are having a negative effect on children," mobilized its million-plus members to support a series of congressional bills introduced from 2004 to 2007 that called for à la carte pricing.[32] Though leery of government intervention, in advocating for government mandated à la carte pricing the PTC was in part advocating for a purer form of supply-and-demand mechanism than subscription packaging. Support for à la carte cable pricing from the progressive Consumers Union fit more easily into its pro-regulation ideologies and ongoing campaigns to break up the cable monopolies to create more competition and choice for consumers. But Consumers Union also expressed a shared cultural sentiment that cable television culture had grown increasingly distasteful as cable operations increased their monopoly power. According to Consumers Union's senior policy director Gene Kimmelman, à la carte would "help lower costs, increase incentives for quality fare, and give viewers the opportunity to not pay for channels they find objectionable or too expensive."[33] This echoed postwar pay-TV proponents' beliefs that individual viewer payments would elevate television culture against the monopoly broadcast networks that had catered to low tastes.

This integration of a neoliberal theoretical justification for direct viewer payment in television with the belief that this would likely reduce incentives for "indecent" programs and increase family-oriented options created an unusual consensus among the deregulatory-oriented Republican-appointed FCC commissioners and the more pro-regulation Democratic appointees. The cultural sensibilities that unified the FCC in support of à la carte cable pricing directly connected to the sensibilities of postwar pay-TV advocates when the FCC chairman Kevin Martin coauthored a commentary in the *Chicago Tribune* in 2007 with former FCC chairman Newton Minow, who assumed his chairmanship in 1961 with a speech describing television as a "vast wasteland." In his notorious speech to television broadcasters shortly after assuming the chairmanship, Minow defined the television problem as one of low "taste," professed his support for the "free enterprise system," and supported pay-TV as one potential solution to the problem.[34] Similarly, the 2007 commentary suggested that bundling family-friendly networks with programming that is either "inappropriate" or "uninteresting" fails to provide the proper market incentives that might otherwise reduce such programming.[35] These cultural sensibilities that favor mainstream family-oriented programming resonated with the supposedly objective microeconomic analysis of the FCC's Media Bureau. After initially accepting the findings of a report commissioned by the cable industry that found à la carte pricing would raise subscription rates and decrease program diversity, the bureau released its own study after prompting from Arizona senator John McCain, who supported à la carte pricing. The bureau report evoked the microeconomic language of "market efficiencies" and optimized aggregate "consumer value" to embrace the likelihood that à la carte would create more choices for "mainstream consumers" but less "niche programming that appeals to a small set of subscribers." The report concluded that "if a switch to *à la carte*

eliminated such [niche] programming, the result would not be a blow to program diversity, as the First Report suggests, but rather a restoration of programming to an efficient level, more consistent with consumer value."[36]

While this consensus among conservative and progressive advocacy organizations, the FCC, and other lawmakers supported free market competition
in the name of enhancing "mainstream consumer values," a coalition of cable
networks with programming of interest to people of color, women, and evangelical Christians strongly opposed à la carte pricing. The African American–oriented networks TV One and BET, the Latino youth-oriented *Si* TV,
the International Channel, Imaginasian TV, the women-oriented Oxygen
network, and the evangelical broadcasters Trinity Broadcasting Network and
the Christian Broadcasting Network all opposed à la carte.[37] These networks
argued that they would never have launched in an à la carte environment
because these less mainstream networks required time and broad exposure
to build an audience. Less beholden to the neoliberal supply-and-demand
theories of à la carte supporters, these networks spoke about the more complex practices of deregulated cable television markets, and in particular those
of bundling programming, which included how these practices helped cross-
promote new networks and even cross-subsidize new programming in the
processes of building viewership. Here viewing is not merely a practice to
best match existing interests with available programming but includes the
experience of surfing through a menu of networks and potentially discovering programs that initially might not have been of interest.

Although Beltway watchdogs discounted opposition from these networks
because many had ownership ties with cable operators, a broad coalition of
civil rights organizations also opposed à la carte pricing, including the League
of United Latin American Citizens, the National Hispanic Policy Institute, the
Hispanic Federation, the NAACP, the National Urban League, the National
Conference of Black Mayors, the National Coalition of Black Civil Participation, the National Congress of Black Women, the National Council of Wom-
en's Organizations, the Minority Media and Telecommunications Council,
and the National Asian Pacific American Legal Consortium. These organizations placed the issue within a history of people of color's marginalization on
television and demanded that cable regulations reverse this, rather than continue it through à la carte initiatives.[38] Following an FCC proposal for wholesale à la carte in 2007, which would allow cable operators to purchase single
channels from content providers rather than, say, all the networks owned by
Disney, a coalition representing people of color and women was joined by the
League of Rural Voters and the National Gay and Lesbian Chamber of Com-

merce to oppose this, calling it another attempt at "media sharecropping." The FCC chairman attempted to address these concerns by suggesting a policy that would require over-the-air broadcasters to lease time on their new digital broadcast channels to underrepresented groups. But Rainbow/PUSH Coalition founder Jesse Jackson described this digital leasing and à la carte cable pricing as an "antidiversity agenda." Other civil rights organizations agreed with the president of the National Coalition of Latino Clergy and Christian Leaders, who stated that "increasing minority-owned media outlets should be the FCC's top priority."[39] This was especially important given that, according to a 2006 study, women owned less than 5 percent of all television stations, African Americans only 1.3 percent, and Latinos just 1.1 percent.[40]

This attention to minority ownership has been a focus of civil rights television activism since 1973 when the US Court of Appeals for the District of Columbia required the FCC to consider race as a factor in broadcast licensing.[41] That year the National Black Media Coalition (NBMC), National Hispanic Media Coalition (NHMC), Native Americans for Fair Media, and Asian Americans for Fair Media were founded to hold the FCC responsible for setting and enforcing minority ownership and Equal Employment standards. Despite some success in increasing minority ownership in broadcasting, deregulatory currents in the 1980s saw the FCC, Congress, and the courts roll back these minority ownership rules.[42] But minority media ownership and equal employment opportunity have remained the principle focus of television activism for civil rights organizations. Since its founding in 1986 the Minority Media and Telecommunications Council (MMTC) has lobbied the FCC, Congress, and the courts to expand minority media ownership on behalf of the major civil rights organizations, including the NAACP and Rainbow/PUSH coalition, and minority media businesses and unions including the Communications Workers of America. In 2007, the MMTC successfully persuaded the FCC to adopt twelve actions to assist small media businesses, one of which directly addressed racial discrimination in the advertising industry by prohibiting advertisers from avoiding placing ads with black and Spanish-language radio and TV stations— a provision first sought by the NBMC in 1973. But under the relaxed media ownership rules more generally, the push for minority ownership has been difficult. In 2007 minorities owned only 8 percent of the nation's full-power commercial radio stations and just 3 percent of full-power commercial TV stations.[43]

Though the civil rights activists and the broad coalition of conservative and progressive public interest advocacy groups were all concerned about the power of media conglomeration that neoliberal deregulations had spawned, their opposing positions on the issue of à la carte cable pricing reveal more fundamentally different orientations to television activism in neoliberalism times. The direct supply-and-demand arguments made in support of à la carte cable pricing prioritize the individual consumer as a universal category of person whose interest can be better maximized through individual direct payments in the marketplace of television exchange. Yet these neoliberal justifications were contradicted by the coalitions' cultural support for more mainstream family programming, with little concern for the potential loss of networks oriented to marginalized communities. Civil rights groups made no such neoliberal justifications in prioritizing access to economic resources as a means to address the historical marginalization of groups of persons based on race, gender, class, sexuality, and religion, even if this meant supporting cable operators' profit model of bundling programming.

Conclusion

This essay considered how anticorporate, fan-initiated, and civil rights orientations to television activism have negotiated a neoliberal environment of dispersed television outlets, concentrated media ownership, and liberalized media policy. Placed in dialogue, these formations of television activism can help to expose the obfuscating logics of neoliberal theories and identify productive spaces for activism within the complex practices of market formations, regulatory policies, and consumptive uses. In the cases of postwar pay-TV, à la carte cable pricing, and recent online TV initiates, we saw how anticorporate activism promoted neoliberal justifications that equated individual direct payments for programs with a more democratic culture, obfuscating the class, gender, and race privilege of hierarchical value orientations to popular culture. Attention to fan activism, which forms through passionate engagements with commercial culture, can destabilize these hierarchical value orientations. Though fan activist orientations have found anticorporate critiques dismissive of fan consumptive practices, anticorporate activism has invoked populist sentiments that have galvanizing coalitions to lobby for regulatory changes, including historically marginalized groups that have joined this coalition to reduce barriers to ownership and employment opportunities. This focus on ownership and employment can inform the media literacy campaigns that Jenkins has promoted to close the "participation gap" so that those now left out can gain access to the knowledge communities that are forming through new technologies and popular culture. Attention to ownership and employment pushes these literacy efforts to think more broadly about the broader structural inequalities that have inhibited the success of such campaigns.[44]

This essay began by indicating that television activism had changed as television transformed from a network era with a few program networks to one of network abundance. The centralized symbolic target of network prime time has fragmented, and the broadcast public interest provisions used to leverage network era activism have given way to the more privatized policy climate for cable television. But the coalition of civil rights organizations and minority-owned media businesses that focus their campaigns on minority ownership and employment opportunities connects to the legacies of television activism of the 1970s and the broader social movement politics that placed television activism within the larger civil rights struggle that, as Nikhil Pal Singh has traced, continually linked the symbolic struggle for racial recognition with a material struggle over economic redistribution.[45] Maintaining this link is particularly critical in these neoliberal times. This is an activism that does not fit neatly into the liberal narrative that new technologies and deregulated markets have enabled television to progressively respond to diverse interests. It is an activism that calls for state actions to address market inequalities and one that requires public interest regulatory frameworks to leverage such activist campaigns. Support for this requires caution in asserting neoliberal theoretical justifications for activism inspired by early technology adapters or for anticorporate activism, which at times takes positions opposed to those of civil rights organizations and cable networks representing historically marginalized groups. Activists across these orientations certainly share this goal of challenging structures that marginalize citizens on the basis of class, gender, race, and other forums of exclusion—and it is likely that success in doing so will question hierarchical orientations to popular cultural pleasures, harness anticorporate populist sentiments, and reenergize a social movement politics that demands a closer integration of cultural and economic democracy.[46]

NOTES

Special thanks to Sarah Banet-Weiser, Roopali Mukherjee, and the anonymous reviewers at NYU Press for their insightful comments.

1. Kathryn C. Montgomery, *Target Prime Time: Advocacy Groups and the Struggle over Entertainment Television* (Oxford: Oxford University Press, 1989).

2. Dispersed distribution and ownership integration has made intellectual property another significant area of television activism.

3. Ben H. Bagdikian, *The Media Monopoly* (Boston: Beacon Press 1983). Sucessive editions were published in 1987, 1990, 1992, 1997, and 2000.

4. Ben H. Bagdikian, *The New Media Monopoly* (Boston: Beacon Press, 2004).

5. Robert W. McChesney, *Telecommunications, Mass Media, and Democracy: The Battle for the Control of U.S. Broadcasting, 1928–1935* (Oxford: Oxford University Press, 1993).

6. Robert W. McChesney, *Rich Media, Poor Democracy: Communications Politics in Dubious Times* (New York: New Press, 2000).

7. Henry Jenkins, *Convergence Culture: Where Old and New Media Collide* (New York: NYU Press, 2006).

8. David Harvey, *A Brief History of Neoliberalism* (Oxford: Oxford University Press, 2007).

9. Lisa Duggan, *The Twilight of Equality? Neoliberalism, Cultural Politics, and the Attack on Democracy* (Boston: Beacon Press, 2003).

10. Patricia Aufderheide, *Communications Policy and the Public Interest: The Telecommunications Act of 1996* (New York: Guilford Press, 1999).

11. Such narratives are found, to varying emphasis, in the following: Amanda D. Lotz, *The Television Will Be Revolutionized* (New York: NYU Press, 2007); Michael Curtin and Jane Shattuc, *The American Television Industry* (London: BFI Publishing, 2009); Megan Mullen, *Television in the Multichannel Age: A Brief History of Cable Television* (Oxford: Blackwell, 2008). For a critique of this narrative, see John Caldwell, "Convergence Television: Aggregating Form and Repurposing Content in the Culture of Conglomeration," in *Television after TV: Essays on a Medium in Transition*, ed. Lynn Spigel and Jan Olsson (Durham, NC: Duke University Press, 2004), 41–74.

12. David Waterman and Andrew A. Weiss, *Vertical Integration in Cable Television* (Washington, DC: AEI Press, 1997).

13. Timothy Havens, *Global Television Marketplace* (New York: Palgrave Macmillan, 2008); Barbara J. Selznick, *Global Television: Co-producing Culture* (Philadelphia: Temple University Press, 2008).

14. Cynthia Chris, "All Documentary, All the Time? Discovery Communications Inc. and Trends in Cable Television," *Television and New Media* 3, no. 1 (2002): 7–28.

15. Sarah Banet-Weiser, Cynthia Chris, and Anthony Freitas, eds., *Cable Visions: Television beyond Broadcasting* (New York: NYU Press, 2007).

16. Beretta E. Smith-Shomade, *Pimpin' Ain't Easy: Selling Black Entertainment Television* (New York: Routledge, 2008).

17. Lisa Parks, "Flexible Microcasting: Gender, Generation, and Television-Internet Convergence," in *Television after TV: Essays on a Medium in Transition*, ed. Lynn Spigel and Jan Olsson (Durham, NC: Duke University Press, 2004), 133–56.

18. Laurie Ouellette and James Hay, *Better Living through Reality TV: Television and Post-welfare Citizenship* (Oxford: Blackwell, 2008).

19. Marvin Ammori, *TV Competition Nowhere: How the Cable Television Is Colluding to Kill Online TV* (New York: Free Press, 2010).

20. Xfinity.com.

21. Jenkins, 2006, 27.

22. Jenkins, 2006, 250–52.

23. John McMurria, "A Taste of Class: Pay-TV and the Commodification of Television in Postwar America," in *Cable Visions: Television beyond Broadcasting*, ed. Sarah Banet-Weiser, Cynthia Chris, and Anthony Freitas (New York: NYU Press, 2007), 44–65.

24. Leo Bogart, *The Age of Television: A Study of Viewing Habits and the Impact of Television on American Life* (New York: Frederick Ungar, 1956), 21–38.

25. Wilbur Schramm, *Responsibility in Mass Communication* (New York: Harper, 1957), 298.

26. Pierre Bourdieu, *Distinction: A Social Critique of the Judgment of Taste* (Cambridge: Harvard University Press, 1984).

27. McMurria, 2007, 50.

28. McMurria, 2007.

29. Patrick R. Parsons and Robert M. Frieden, *The Cable and Satellite Television Industries* (Boston: Allyn and Bacon, 1998).

30. See Meg James, "Comcast to Buy Control of NBC Universal in $30-Billion Transaction," *Los Angeles Times*, December 4, 2009; Tim Arango and Bill Carter, "An Unsteady Future for Broadcast," *New York Times*, November 20, 2009.

31. This extends an earlier discussion of these issues in John McMurria, "À la Carte Culture," *Flow* 4, no. 3 (April 2006); John McMurria, "À la Carte Cable Pricing," in *Battleground: The Media*, vol. 1, ed. Robin Andersen and Jonathan Gray (Westport, CT: Praeger, 2008), 1–5.

32. See http://www.parentstv.org/PTC/aboutus/main.asp.

33. http://www.consumersunion.org/pub/core_telecom_and_utilities/000925.html.

34. Newton N. Minow, "The 'Vast Wasteland,'" in *Equal Time: The Private Broadcaster and the Public Interest*, ed. Lawrence Laurent (New York: Atheneum, 1964), 48–64.

35. Kevin Martin, Newton N. Minow, and Dan Lipinski, "For Kids' Sake, TV Must Go à la Carte," *Chicago Tribune*, July 20, 2007.

36. http://hraunfoss.fcc.gov/edocs_public/attachmatch/DOC-263740A1.pdf.

37. Piet Levy, "Evangelicals vs. Christian Cable: Under 'a la Carte' Plan, Viewers Could Bar Certain Channels," *Washington Post*, June 10, 2006, B9.

38. http://www.publicintegrity.org/telecom/report.aspx?aid=395; http://www.informationweek.com/news/management/showArticle.jhtml?articleID=203103274.

39. William Triplett, "Jackson Blasts FCC Agenda," *Daily Variety*, October 31, 2007, 16; William Triplett, "Orgs Blast FCC Plans," *Daily Variety*, November 19, 2007, 2.

40. http://www.stopbigmedia.com/files/out_of_the_picture.pdf.

41. Robert Horwitz, "On Media Concentration and the Diversity Question," *Information Society* 21 (2005): 181–204.

42. Marlyn Fife, "Promoting Racial Diversity in US Broadcasting: Federal Policies versus Social Realities," *Media Culture and Society* 9 (1987): 481–504.

43. www.mmtconline.org.

44. Jenkins, 2006, 23. See also Ellen Seiter, "Practicing at Home: Computers, Pianos, and Cultural Capital," in *Digital Youth, Innovation, and the Unexpected*, ed. Tara McPherson (Cambridge: MIT Press, 2008), 27–52.

45. Nikhil Pal Singh, *Black Is a Country: Race and the Unfinished Struggle for Democracy* (Cambridge: Harvard University Press, 2004).

46. For more on the integration of cultural and economic citizenship, see Toby Miller, *Cultural Citizenship: Cosmopolitanism, Consumerism, and Television in a Neoliberal Age* (Philadelphia: Temple University Press, 2008).

14

Feeling Good While Buying Goods

Promoting Commodity Activism to
Latina Consumers

MARI CASTAÑEDA

This chapter examines the ways in which commodity activism is marketed to Latina/o consumers, one of the fastest-growing and most diverse marketing segments worldwide.[1] Currently, nearly 45 million Latinos reside in the US, and by the year 2050, they will constitute more than 25 percent of the US population.[2] In Latin America and the Spanish-speaking Caribbean, the populations are expected to reach well over 600 million people by the middle of the century.[3] Although US Latinos are culturally and racially heterogeneous, with many people having family origins rooted in Mexico, Latin America, and the Caribbean and identifying as indigenous, Afro-Latino, Asian-Latino, or part of the Jewish Diaspora, the significant growth of this ethnic population across the Americas has spurred marketers on both sides of the border to develop more creative and assertive approaches to tap into this ascendant market.[4]

In recent years, commodity activism has become a very popular and prominent practice for reaching consumers while also promoting corporate social responsibility and brand awareness. After an era in which some multinational corporations have blatantly abused human rights, labor conditions, and product safety, the new approach aims to engender corporate loyalty and trust to an increasingly wary public. Commodity activism is thus becoming a two-for-one endeavor that promotes feel-good consumption through retail (store and online) fundraising for social and/or health campaigns that promote a public good, such as domestic violence prevention, AIDS research, peace in Darfur, reading literacy, or breast cancer awareness. In the increasingly social-networked environment, consumer culture is utilized "as an area for political action," as well as conscientious trade by private companies.[5]

However, since large numbers of consumers must purchase socially conscious commodities in order for long-term benefits to take effect, it is important to ask: How do corporations motivate consumers, for instance, Latina/os, to purchase their products, become loyal customers, and feel good about their brands? In addition, how are the practices of commodity activism simply part of the broader landscape of contemporary capitalist consumer culture? In an effort to address these questions, this chapter will first review the links between social marketing and commodity activism, since the former in many ways laid the groundwork for "feel good" consumption. It then will examine how and why Latina/o consumers are targeted as a desirable (transnational) market, demonstrating how the marketization of philanthropy is informed by the intersections of ethnicity, gender, and class. Finally, the chapter will address the implications and contradictions of Latino-oriented commodity activism, especially in an era in which they are both celebrated as consumers and demonized as citizens, by focusing on two corporate activist campaigns.

Laying the Groundwork for Commodity Activism through Social Marketing

Social marketing borrows from the best practices of social movements and commercial techniques in its effort to motivate individuals not only to act but also to commit to a broader social goal; whether encouraging seat belt safety, children's literacy, or recycling, it aims to "move beyond the message" and engage individuals to act for the cause. Social marketing is about inspiring community-wide behavioral or ideological shifts, as well as changes in popular behavior in order to motivate individual action and social change and in some cases to influence public policy.[6]

According to Hoye, advocacy campaigns are successful when they embody three key marketing elements: "a clearly defined problem, a solution, and a strategy for how supporters are going to help an organization or cause make that solution happen."[7] Since 2000, the US public health industry has been especially in favor of social marketing as a method for reaching communities with positive messages and shifting the public discourse about healthy living.[8] The industry's growing interest in social marketing is an attempt to bolster traditional health education by capitalizing on lucrative marketing techniques that emphasize "the needs, preferences, and lifestyles of the consumer audience."[9]

By collecting consumer data and applying commercial marketing practices in the development of public health campaigns, health educators can segment populations and create niche messages that better reach audiences in meaningful ways.[10] Such applications are increasingly viewed as more productive methods for "reaching the hard to reach" demographics while also producing positive results for perceived disenfranchised communities.[11] According to a health educator I interviewed, "If such marketing techniques worked for R. J. Reynolds and Budweiser, then why not use them to promote the local YMCA or the ways in which individuals can support environmental justice in their neighborhood?"

The assumptions in the link between social and commercial marketing are that behavioral changes can be marketed as products or commodities; targeted demographics can be imagined as consumers; and an exchange relationship between relevant advocacy and individuals is feasible. Ultimately, the neoliberal orientation to addressing social and health issues is alluring because it is viewed as a powerful intervention method that can successfully "persuade people of their personal responsibility and choice in the matter" at a moment when governments are reluctant to intervene in so-called negative societal trends.[12] Thus, there is a general belief that advocacy campaigns can also follow market logic in their messaging while also being culturally relevant and achieving desired results (i.e., consumer motivation and action).

The fact that minorities are often perceived as "hard-to-reach" consumers is one of the reasons social marketing has been applied more frequently to communities of color, especially in the areas of health. The emphasis on market segmentation and "customer insight" allows social marketers to gather copious data about specific minority communities in order to develop targeted campaigns that speak directly to desired clients.[13] Such data gathering is common practice within market segment research, and the wealth of information that is produced plays a key role "in helping corporate America improve its cultural competency, marketing strategies, and performance in a multiethnic marketplace."[14] For instance, Fisher noted that a survey of minority consumers revealed perceived key differences: Latinos are brand loyal, Asian Americans are price conscious, and African Americans are coupon friendly.[15] Although differences within each of the groups do not make them homogeneous, for the most part general trends are believed to exist that allow marketers to take note of "profitable evidence." For instance, in a thirty-day period, Latinos are 80 percent more likely than other groups to buy headache medicine; 40 percent of African Americans will likely purchase frozen vegetables; and Asian Americans, at 22 percent, have the highest percentage of nonmenthol cigarette purchases.[16] The production of specific information about the spending habits of minority consumers thus drives marketing campaigns and the quest for changes in consumption. With regard to social marketing, it is important to note that such data collection is more than just consumer research but also entails research on the cultural practices of ethnic populations that are then utilized to help sell (positive) behavioral, social, and consumer change.

Not surprisingly, generalized mainstream campaigns often fail to connect with communities of color, whereas social marketing is believed to provide the necessary methods for gathering information that will produce the most effective messages about AIDS screening, breast cancer awareness, domestic violence prevention, alcohol poisoning, and obesity prevention.[17] According to Neiger et al., social marketing is effective because it privileges "culturally innovative" messages as the goal to its marketing program rather than simply maximizing profit.[18] As a result, the class, residential, and cultural differences that influence health and social issues in communities of color are often prioritized differently by social marketers and taken into account rather than disregarded.

However, it is important to also note that while communities may be included in the development of campaigns, minority cultures are also being co-opted in the racial formation of social marketing strategies. This intersection of "identity and social structure" in social marketing is meant to include minorities in the marketplace of social good, but more often than not, it further racializes them and emphasizes the problems within communities without addressing the broader sociopolitical context that creates these conditions in the first place.[19] More troubling is the failure by health advocates to question the consumerist tactics of social marketing. By adopting a neoliberal framework for health advocacy, the broader questions as to why certain heath issues persist for communities of color, for instance, are left unanswered and unexamined, thus potentially reinforcing the status quo.

Additionally, the adoption of a discourse and practice that emphasizes consumer sovereignty alters the nature of social change where it is no longer produced in community but individually. Not surprisingly, this shift has broader implications, as Roff notes in her study of food politics:

> First, the neoliberalization of activism shifts the responsibility for social reforms from the state and manufacturers to individual consumers, bringing with it important social justice implications. Second, focusing on choice opens new spaces for profit without seriously threatening contemporary market structures. . . .Third, contemporary consumerist politics focus on eating right, not less and thereby provide few alternatives to the current trends towards convenience and processed foods.[20]

Similar limitations exist for health activism that emphasizes neoliberal models through social marketing campaigns. To make matters worse, funding retrenchment is decimating social and health services worldwide; therefore, health advocates are increasingly relying on and borrowing from market frameworks that seem to have a proven track record.

One response to the decline of funding is the development of public-private partnerships in which nonprofits and agencies partner with corporations in an effort to raise funds through social and cause marketing.[21] Such partnerships enable companies to promote their brand as a demonstration of corporate social responsibility while also developing philanthropic alliances with organizations that address health and/or social issues at the national and local levels, such as the American Cancer Society, the Make-a-Wish Foundation, Habitat for Humanity, and the American Lung Association.[22]

By combining social marketing, philanthropic fundraising, and consumerism, these partnerships allow consumers to participate in a "marketplace of meaning" by which their donations or consumption of commodities are marked as meaningful rather than wasteful. This is not surprising, as Conca, Princen, and Maniates note, since consumption is more than "rational decision making . . . but an individual's attempt to find meaning, status, and identity."[23] Corporations capable of linking consumption with cause marketing benefit as well; studies show that consumers will buy products from companies that demonstrate a social mission.[24]

One sector that is attracting companies interested in commodity activism is the global Latina/o market. In the US alone, the purchasing power of this consumer sector is expected to grow to $1 trillion by 2010.[25] It is also one of the youngest demographics and a population that has been consistently exposed to social marketing campaigns due to social and health concerns throughout the community. Given this background, the Latino market is poised to become one of the most important consumer sectors for commodity activism.

Marketing to the Latina/o Market

As mentioned earlier, there are 42.7 million Latinos in the US, and currently they constitute the largest ethnic majority group.[26] In many articles touting the size of the Latina/o market, writers often note that there are more Latinos in the US than there are Canadians in Canada, and thus their sheer numbers in the US can be tantamount to the population of another country.[27] In fact, 25 percent of all children born in the US (more than 1 million a year) are of

Latino heritage in an era when the overall birthrate in the US is declining.[28] Thus, it is no surprise that the immigration debate has highlighted Latinos, especially Mexicans, since the fertility ratio of Mexican-origin women, especially those who are foreign-born, is the highest among all Latino subgroups, and their birthrate patterns "account for the overall trends among all Latinos."[29] According to the US census, Mexicans constitute 66 percent (two-thirds) of the Latino population, whereas Puerto Ricans make up 9 percent, Cubans 3.4 percent, Salvadorans 3.4 percent, and Dominicans 2.8 percent.[30] Overall, Latinos' fertility rates are 71 percent higher than those of non-Latino whites; therefore, Latina mothers as a whole are an increasingly important niche within the global Latina/o marketplace despite differences between subgroups as well as the range of income and educational levels.[31] The quest to gain the confidence of Latina consumers is evident in the various marketing campaigns that companies have developed in recent years.

In 2008, Huggies developed a campaign called "Tren de Vida" (Life Train) in an effort to attract more Latina mothers to its brand. An executive noted that as a diaper maker, it was "trying to show Hispanic moms that Huggies is here for them. We provide products that make their life better and help them have a fun day so they can enjoy their kids."[32] A big component of the campaign were visits to popular Latino grocery stores, retail parking lots, and festivals where mothers would receive free diaper bags and baby blankets as well as have the opportunity to participate in its survey of parenting tips. The survey outcomes were compiled into a book titled *De Mama á Mama* (From Mom to Mom) and distributed for free to Latina moms on Mother's Day. Huggies credited the success of the "parking lot" campaign to face-to-face interactions and word of mouth because "members of the Hispanic community love this [kind of communication]."[33] Interestingly, the "innovative" marketing efforts by Huggies also came on the heels of the trade journal *Supermarket News* confirming that sales for corporate-brand disposable diapers were declining and environment-friendly cloth diapers were making a comeback. With 41 percent of Latino children and their families actually living below federal poverty standards, for Latina mothers, cloth diapers perhaps makes more economic sense, since disposable diapers are often a high-priced product.[34]

The news of declining milk consumption also provoked the California Milk Processor Board (CMBP) to expand its $2-million Spanish-language "Got Milk?" campaign, "Toma Leche!" (Drink Milk). It specifically promoted fluid milk and not powdered milk products, which are often consumed by low-income families.[35] In addition to television spots and print ads, the campaign included free salsa workouts and gallons of milk at various health fairs across the country.[36] This new development was an attempt to extend the campaign's broader theme, "Familia, Amor y Leche" (Family, Love and Milk), by linking it to social marketing efforts that nonprofit health professionals were implementing to attract Latino families, especially women and children, to healthier lifestyles. According to the CMPB press release:

> With more than 13 million Latinos living in California, health experts are becoming increasingly aware of the complications related to obesity and diabetes in this community. Statistics show that nearly three in four Mexican-Americans, the largest Hispanic group in the United States, are overweight or obese and about 2.5 million U.S. Hispanics have diabetes. To fight these alarming trends and to promote healthy living, [CMPB] will join other non-profit agencies in offering free health services and education to Latinos.[37]

It is important to remember that the expansion of the campaign also parallels the decline of milk consumption by Latinos; therefore, the CMPB's interest here is not purely philanthropic but largely an effort to prevent further losses to its Latina/o market.

In light of diminishing sales, other corporate consumer brands are also turning to social marketing and multiplatform techniques to expand their reach into Latina pocketbooks. Global companies like Disney and General Mills have created free direct-mail publications such as *Disney Familias* and *Qué Rica Vida* where advertising pages, advice columns, and recipes offer the modern yet Spanish-speaking Latina mom an array of ideas and tips for how to navigate life in the US. According to the publishers of *Kena*, another free publication targeting Latina households, the direct-mail magazine aims "to become a trusted friend to today's Hispanic women, offering guidance, support, and inspiration to help readers achieve balance across all areas of their lives."[38] In reality, corporate advertisers view "Latinos [as] a core consumer and considered key to the company's growth strategy" which is the primary reason the focus on Latinas is occurring. Consequently, for many of these magazines, it is important that they are viewed as information resources rather than simply multipage advertisements by Latina opinion leaders, since these individuals can make or break a company's connection to Latino communities. According to the founder of LatinWorks, one of the highest-grossing Latino-oriented ad agencies, Latinas in particular are often the linchpin to advertising and marketing campaigns; therefore, "segmenting and targeting is what makes a difference" when directing a message to a particular population.[39]

Yet the diversity of Latinos further complicates the development of audiovisual messages oriented toward social or commercial marketing. As noted previously, there is a wide array of cultural, religious, racial/ethnic, political, and national backgrounds across the Latino Diaspora, along with deep differences over citizenship, linguistic ability, and economic and assimilation/acculturation practices. According to Arlene Dávila, marketers have tried to work through this heterogeneity by applying what seem like "Foucaldian technologies and strategies of power" whereby differences are categorized, managed, and contained to "secure bases of commonalities and the perpetuation of 'authentic Hispanics.'"[40] Dávila further argues that when language, religious, and national trademarks are taken into account, it is done at the local and regional level rather than through nationwide advertising; thereby, "regions are associated with particular cultures, and particular cultures with their own traits."[41]

One issue that is becoming increasingly prevalent is the difference between Latinos who are foreign-born/immigrant and those who are not. Historically, the more connection Latinos had to Latin America "the more valuable they [were] as consumers," meaning they were viewed as more authentic Hispanics rather than "lost" to US culture.[42] In fact, "the Latino or Hispanic identity of the English-dominant or U.S.-born Latino is downplayed if not erased" within Spanish-language media because it is assumed that mainstream English-language media will somehow cater to their needs. This may help explain why Mother's Day has become the biggest card-buying holiday for the Spanish-speaking Latino market in the last ten years. Hallmark Cards and American Greetings, with their 450 variations of Spanish-language and bilingual Mother's Day cards, can attest to the holiday's popularity with Latina/os.[43] However, the immigration debate, with its battles over citizenship and racial profiling, has tempered the emphasis on difference between Latino subgroups. In turn, this has highlighted bilingual and family/community-oriented Latinas between the ages of eighteen and thirty-four as ideal consumers.[44] For companies like Avon and Verizon, which are aiming to improve "brand loyalty" through commodity activist campaigns, the focus on similarities rather than differences has facilitated their reach to Latinas, as the next section demonstrates.[45]

Avon Inc. and Verizon Wireless Really Care about Latinas

Avon is consistently rated as one of the top 100 companies for its support of female employees and one of the top 50 companies for Latina employment. Known as "The Company for Women," Avon has an annual revenue of $10 billion and a sales force of 5.4 million independent representatives in more than 100 countries.[46] For the past ten years, Avon has developed a reputation for extending its corporate responsibility ethos into a global program that includes commodity activism in the areas of breast cancer awareness and domestic violence prevention.

Although cause-related marketing has recently become a very popular method for fundraising and extending brand awareness, Avon has actually been involved in such practices since the early 1920s. According to Klepacki, Avon has a very long history of community involvement due to its development during the Progressive Era and an "earnest belief that in selling [the company's products], women were provided opportunities for personal fulfillment beyond the benefits of financial empowerment."[47] The effort to expand this belief system led to the creation of the Avon Foundation in 1955 with the goal to "improve the lives of women and their families."[48] Although the emphasis has largely been on women's education and job training, which of course benefits Avon, by 1990 the foundation extended its philanthropic work into an educational and awareness campaign called the Breast Cancer Crusade.

It was through this campaign that Avon's Pink Ribbon products were first developed, largely as a method for increasing awareness but, more important, as a venue for raising crusade funds through external sales. After the popularity of the $3 Pink Ribbon pin in the UK and US, Avon began offering other "pink products" such as "a pink rhinestone pendant on a silver tone chain for $7.50 and a heart-shaped locket with a key chain for $5 [in addition to] . . .celebrity-endorsed beauty items" like nail polish.[49]

As of 2005, Avon Products, Inc. has raised more than $65 million for the Avon Foundation's Breast Cancer Crusade and provided funding to hospitals, research institutes, health clinics, and nonprofit agencies worldwide. Most recently, Avon has developed a new campaign called "Speak Out against Domestic Violence," with spokeswomen Salma Hayek and Reese Witherspoon, two internationally recognized actresses who are increasingly speaking on behalf of women's issues. Finally, the global success of Avon's Pink Ribbon commodities has spurred other beauty companies such as L'Oreal and Revlon to develop similar products, and retailers such as Target have teamed up with these brands to provide ample shelf space for their cause-related commodities.

Despite the enormous positive reception of Avon's Breast Cancer Crusade, especially its Walk for Breast Cancer events, one of the downsides of Avon's commodity activism is that direct-sales representatives do not make any commissions on the pink items they sell. These items are specifically for fundraising, and as a result, Avon Ladies do not receive a percentage of the sales; instead, the proceeds are redirected to the Avon Foundation's breast cancer or domestic violence campaigns. According to one Latina Avon Lady, "I want to support these campaigns because they are very important and I feel proud that my clients are supportive too, but if they buy too much of these specific products, then my income goes down."[50] Actually, incomes can fall considerably, since representatives are required to pay a fifteen-dollar monthly sales fee in addition to a fifteen-dollar web access fee and two-dollar processing fee for every order placed. These fees do not include the transportation, phone, post mail, or delivery costs required for direct selling. One representative from the UK posted on a direct-selling website that despite the corporation's support of breast cancer research, "the only person who loses out on the deal is the Avon Lady—ME! Avon themselves are raking in the cash—the customer has a doorstep delivery but poor old Avon Lady has to spend untold hours filling in order forms—delivering and collecting—come rain or shine—always with a smile (through gritted teeth!)."[51]

Consequently, the expense of the breast cancer and domestic violence campaigns rests heavily (and unfairly) on the backs of already underpaid Avon Ladies. This is especially problematic for low-income sellers who rely on sales to supplement their income. Klepacki agrees that Avon's cause items "can cannibalize regular orders for the month [most notably Breast Cancer Month in October], since customers are not likely to buy both a Pink Ribbon lipstick and a traditional lipstick at the same time. But the reps feel it's worth it, given where the money goes."[52]

Several Latina Avon Ladies noted that the conflict between their need to make money and also support the company's philanthropic campaigns was difficult to resolve, especially when domestic violence and breast cancer for Latinas and low-income women are rising. Although addressing these serious social issues is critical, Avon's "charitable investing" largely occurs at the expense of its sales force.[53] More important, this neoliberal approach to philanthropy veils the disinvestment from the state to provide education and health resources in the first place, which was often unacknowledged by the Avon Ladies I interviewed.

In fact, the public policy realities that have made such campaigns necessary are often overlooked because of the deep trust Avon has generated through its breast awareness and domestic violence campaigns, as evident in an example presented by Klepacki. She discusses how a sales representative in Mexico wears Pink Ribbon pins and highlights pink products in the sales brochures in order to raise awareness about breast and uterine cancer.

Agustina Alvarez Diaz noted that her customers see the Avon Crusade as a noble cause, and selling as well as purchasing these products is a way of fighting the disease, especially in communities where there are limited resources for addressing women's health issues. Therefore, the income loss is worth the awareness that the campaigns engender.

Similarly, several Latina Avon sales representatives I interviewed in California and Massachusetts (two Chicanas, one Puerto Rican, one Dominican, and one Colombian) said the Pink Ribbon products were entry points through which they could discuss not only the Breast Cancer Crusade but, more important, their own health issues and possible resources. One of the Chicanas said:

> We start talking about the new beauty products, but it always leads to talking about [my client's] health. Some of my clients haven't been to the doctor in years, and many of them have health issues that should be examined by a health professional, but there's no one to talk to about what's wrong. My visit at least gets them thinking about how to take better care of themselves, and I really believe that my Avon products help with this process.[54]

Thus, sales representatives may be failing to gain commissions from products that support Avon's philanthropic campaigns, but the one-to-one connection of direct selling opens discussions and creates an awareness that otherwise may not happen.

Additionally, the Colombian sales rep from Massachusetts said she attended the Avon Latina Breast Cancer Survivorship Conference, and it was there that she witnessed how the proceeds she relinquished were being spent. She also noted that she was encouraged to organize a walk in her hometown in Colombia, since reaching clients south of the border (and on a global scale) is an important priority for Avon. To organize the walk she needed other fundraisers because she was told that the Avon Foundation only organized and funded such events in the US and Europe despite the fact that pink products are also sold in Latin America and the Caribbean. Yet she brushed away this tension by noting that "this issue is bigger than any of us." There seems to be a belief that at least something is being done, and that doing something is better than doing nothing, even if it is at the expense of sales representatives.

In the future, it would be best if Avon provided more resources and support for its sales force, especially those working in communities of color, since they seem to be carrying a heavier load for expanding the breast cancer and domestic violence product campaigns. In a recent advertisement, for instance, spokeswoman Salma Hayek asked readers to "please support [her] partnership with the Avon Foundation . . . by purchasing a Speak Out Against Domestic Violence product."[55] Yet this form of speaking out essentially commodifies the social issue at hand and reinforces the notion that shopping can solve problems, a contradiction that was rarely acknowledged by the Avon representatives I interviewed.

Samantha King notes that this contradictory exchange process in which consumers pay to participate in a social cause, such as the National Race for a Cure, "might be understood as a site for the production of both consumer-citizens and corporate citizens and as such exemplifies the ways in which citizenship advances through consumption at this particular moment in history."[56] The current financial crisis is further exacerbating the equation between citizenship and shopping, since many companies are advertising the notion that during tough economic times, it is more imperative than ever to feel good while buying goods. Unfortunately, as Johan Fischer argues, often the consumer-citizen alliance not only becomes a questionable public relations facade, but also allows US consumers to keep a comfortable distance from the real problems and fails to interrogate whether shopping is indeed a reasonable response to human suffering.[57] The lack of interrogation, however, is the result of an "emerging global consumer democracy," and it is this failure to investigate how consumption practices reinforce structures of power and access to resources that will make the promise of humanitarian efforts incomplete.[58]

On a positive note, funds from the Avon Foundation have created opportunities outside of the direct-selling environment to educate women about these two health and social issues. One case in particular is worth noting. In Marin County, California, a collaboration between nonprofit groups, educational institutions, and the Avon Foundation led to the development of a bilingual breast cancer awareness brochure that was oriented to "Latina students and young women who might not know about preventative health practices and cancer risk factors" at a time when the percentage of breast cancer exams for young women of color is low.[59]

The brochure, titled "Breast Cancer Tips for Latina Teens, Young Women and Families," was deemed successful because it spurred conversation between daughters and mothers over a topic that is rarely discussed yet increasingly important as more Latinas are diagnosed with breast and cervical cancer.[60] Given the religious conservatism of many Latino families, especially those of Mexican origin, which were the dominant group in Marin County, the bilingual brochure was useful for explaining the medical benefits of monthly breast self-examination and yearly Pap smears. Hurtado notes that many Latinas do not seek medical attention when it comes to parts of their bodies that are connected to sexuality because of conservative notions of femininity (i.e., the body is sacred and should not be touched except for procreation).[61] These notions have negatively affected not only Latinas' sense of sexuality but also the development of intimate knowledge about their bodies. The brochure was one small attempt to begin shifting how Latinas understand intimate health issues that affect them. Ultimately, Avon's increased emphasis on commodity activism deepens its connections to female consumers, and Latinas in particular are a critical niche within this broader demographic.

Another example of commodity activism oriented toward women, and Latinas in particular, is Verizon Wireless's HopeLine program, a domestic violence awareness and prevention campaign that encourages consumers to donate old used phones and accessories at local Verizon Wireless stores. These devices are then refurbished and given to HopeLine's nonprofit partners or sold to the public to raise funds for its cash grant program. Since its inception in 1995, HopeLine has donated $6.3 million in cash grants and received more than 5.6 million phones.

In addition to encouraging employees to support HopeLine through their activities at the local level, Verizon Wireless has also created new methods for expanding the campaign, such as "sponsoring the first ever TXT messaging poll as part of Liz Claiborne's and Marie Claire Magazine's 'It's Time to Talk Day' and HopeLine online phone auction to raise money for the National Coalition Against Domestic Violence."[62] The program also features toll and toll-free calls to the National Domestic Violence Hotline, which is available through the Verizon Wireless nationwide network by dialing #HOPE.

Through HopeLine and other media endeavors, Verizon Wireless, a company with $97.4 billion in revenue and a workforce of nearly 224,000 employees, has made a concerted effort to reach young Latina/o consumers.[63] Although domestic violence is a rampant social health issue in many communities, within Latino populations it is certainly a historical problem that has wreaked much havoc in families and communities. Publications such as *Latina* and *Hispanic* have consistently featured PSA-type advertisements about Verizon's HopeLine program in an effort to address domestic violence issues.

In one such advertisement *Hispanic* magazine, a Latina named Olga Mendez, who works at Verizon Wireless as a human resources manager and is a survivor of domestic violence, "helps Spanish-speaking women navigate the difficult road back to independence."[64] The ad's text also notes that since Olga survived and left an abusive relationship, she will be able to provide other Latinas with useful advice so they too can break the cycle, seek recovery, and "strike out in the world on their own."[65] The advertisement makes clear that Olga is not only training employees at her call center, "but she is also [helping] the company teach another important skill: life."[66] Thus, Verizon Wireless not only provides customers with the latest cell phone technology but also provides employees and customers with life skills.

While Verizon Wireless's program is noteworthy for its reach (currently, it has more than 200 partners across the US), the issue of domestic violence is not just a matter of having safe access to a phone or shelter in order to receive help. According to the National Latino Alliance for the Elimination of Domestic Violence, "Domestic violence in Latino populations must be understood within a legacy of multiple oppressions. . . .This social issue requires that research, policy, advocacy and services be approached with an understanding of the intersectionality of social forces that are at work in the occurrence of domestic violence in Latino families and communities."[67] Consequently, a multidimensional approach is needed for addressing the issue.

It is also important to understand that Verizon Wireless's interest in this issue extends beyond corporate social responsibility. As one of the largest wireless providers, its HopeLine program allows it to make the most of secondhand products by recycling and selling them for fundraising purposes. This gives the company a good name, which encourages consumers to support the company and its product, especially Latinos, who are not only the fastest-growing demographic but one of the consumer segments that uses wireless technologies, especially cell phones, more than any other minority group.[68]

According to market research, Latinos are "more engaged with their cell phones" than the average American, and 71 percent of Latinos as compared with 48 percent of other Americans utilized their phone consistently, especially to interact with online content.[69] This may in part be due to the lack of Internet or landline phone service in the home, and as a result, wireless multimedia phone service becomes a primary means of communication.[70] In addition, at-home telecommunication services are increasingly too expensive for calling internationally or require residence documentation for installation. As a result, consumer marketers are eager to reach Latino consumers via their mobile devices by developing Latino-centric campaigns.[71] According to Kim, such promotions are expected to quadruple this year not only by mobile providers but also by other consumer product makers that want to ride the Latino marketing wave.[72]

The positive reputation Verizon has developed through its HopeLine campaign was recently demonstrated at a local community meeting in Holyoke, Massachusetts, where the company was referred to as "a network that stands behind its people." The reference at this community event was not only in relation to the company's commercials, which show the Verizon guy backed by all the company's employees, but also the fact that HopeLine supports women's safety. If Verizon is committed, then maybe the community should be too.

Conclusion

The rise of commodity activism and cause-related marketing to motivate consumers to actively support a social, health, or political causes by purchasing products is increasingly ubiquitous. Take, for example, Kenneth Cole's latest media project, the book *Awearness: Inspiring Stories about How to Make a Difference*, a collection of essays by celebrities and politicians in which they discuss their social responsibility and commodity activism. Yet the fact that Kenneth Cole chose to spell the word "awareness" with the word "wear" highlighted in red reminds us that the book project is also part of a broader marketing campaign: to keep the clothing business front and center while still raising funds (especially through book sales) for the various social campaigns that are highlighted in the book. Consequently, consumers can feel good while buying these goods, whether they are books, clothing, makeup, or cell phone service, or buying into the hype of a cause-related campaign because a celebrity is hawking it.

Unlike charitable giving, where donors contribute to a public good but do not "directly consume the benefits," commodity activism is in fact centered on donors reaping the benefits of their economic contributions.[73] The consumerist orientation of commodity activism shifts the practice of donations from having use-value to exchange-value, thus transforming the donor from citizen to consumer in contradictory and complex ways. Although Canclini argues that such a transformation can be interpreted as a "democratizing project," it is nevertheless a shift that diminishes accountability from society as whole, and redefines charity as market logic.[74]

The bottom line, unfortunately, is the reality that this new era of social marketing in the name of commodity activism is not entirely altruistic, but this is beside the point. What is important here is that the consumer goods landscape is doubly competitive in the current economic downturn, but by linking products (and industrial brands) to broader social issues, transnational corporations can appear socially responsible and thus have the edge needed to stand out in a landscape of apparently innocuous commodities. We are thus witnessing the extreme ideology of shopping as a form of activism, although we are often unaware of how commodity fundraising dollars are spent. Yet as one Latina Verizon user expressed, "At least something is being done." Perhaps the power of consumption will lead to more cultural or political citizenship for marginalized groups. In a capitalist system, sadly, this may be the only way.

NOTES

I would like to thank the editors of this volume, Roopali Mukherjee and Sarah Banet-Weiser, as well as the anonymous reviewers for their insightful feedback during the revision process. I would also like to say "mil gracias" to Las Profes Online Writing Group for their unwavering support throughout the project.

1. This chapter will use "Latina/os" as the main term for people of Caribbean and Latin American descent, such as Salvadoran, Argentinean, Guatemalan, Cuban, Colombian, Dominican, Mexican, Puerto Rican, and even Brazilian and Spanish. Although it is important to consider the cultural heterogeneity as well as distinctive immigration histories, language uses, and socioeconomic differences of Latino subgroups, the purposes and page limitations of this chapter make it difficult to discuss each group separately. However, whenever possible, I will point out differences as it relates to the overall trajectory of this chapter.

2. US Bureau of the Census, *U.S. Hispanic Population: 2006* (Washington, DC: US Census Bureau, 2006).

3. US Bureau of the Census, "International Statistics: Table 1286, Population by Continent, 1980–2050," in *Statistical Abstract of the United States: 2009* (Washington, DC: US Census Bureau, 2009), 803–56.

4. Mari Castañeda Paredes, "The Reorganization of Spanish-Language Media Marketing in the United States," in *Continental Order? Integrating North America for Cybercapitalism*, ed. Vincent Mosco and Dan Schiller (Lanham, MD: Rowman and Littlefield, 2001), 120–35.

5. Matthias Zick Varul, "Consuming the Campesino," *Cultural Studies* 22, no. 5 (2008): 654–79.

6. Mike Rayner, "Social Marketing: How Might This Contribute to Tackling Obesity?" *Obesity Reviews* 8, no. 1 (2007): 195–99.

7. Sue Hoye, "Marketing Techniques Alone Won't Advance a Charity's Cause, Experts Say," *Chronicle of Philanthropy* 19, no. 19 (2007): 20.

8. Edward W. Maibach, Lorien C. Abroms, and Mark Marosits, "Communication and Marketing as Tools to Cultivate the Public's Health: A Proposed 'People and Places' Framework," *BMC Public Health* 7, no. 88 (2007): 1–15.

9. Brad L. Neiger, Rosemary Thackeray, Michael Barnes, and James McKenzie, "Position Social Marketing as a Planning for Health Education," *American Journal of Health Studies* 18, nos. 2/3 (2003): 78.

10. Jane Kolondinsky and Travis Reynolds, "Segmentation of Overweight Americans and Opportunities for Social Marketing," *International Journal of Behavior, Nutrition, and Physical Activity* 6, no. 1 (2009): 1–29.

11. Mary Ann Van Duyn, "Adapting Evidence-Based Strategies to Increase Physical Activity among African Americans, Hispanics, Hmong, and Native Hawaiians: A Social Marketing Approach," *Preventive Chronic Disease* 4, no. 4 (2007): 1–11.

12. Rayner, 2007, 196.

13. Julie Foxton, Val Thurtle, and Mavis Ames, "Selling Health: Social Marketing Approaches Are Increasingly Used in Health Promotion, but What Does It Involve and How Can Community Practitioners Use It?" *Community Practitioner* 82, no. 2 (2009): 32–34.

14. Geng Cui, "Marketing to Ethnic Minority Consumers: A Historical Journey (1932–1997)," *Journal of Macromarketing* 21, no. 1 (2001): 23–31.

15. C. Fisher, "Poll: Hispanics Stick to Brands," *Advertising Age*, February 15, 1993, 1.

16. Fisher, 1993.

17. Antronette K. Yancey et al. "Population-Based Interventions Engaging Communities of Color in Healthy Eating and Active Living: A Review," *Preventative Chronic Disease* 1, no. 1 (2004): 1–18.

18. Neiger et al., 2003, 16.

19. Michael Omi and Howard Winant, "Once More, with Feeling: Reflections on Racial Formation," *PMLA: Publications of the Modern Language Association of America* 123, no. 5 (2008): 1565–72.

20. Robin Jane Roff, "Shopping for Change? Neoliberalizing Activism and the Limits to Eating Non-GMO," *Agriculture and Human Values* 24, no. 4 (2007): 511.

21. Karen E. Lake, Thomas K. Reis, and Jeri Spann. "From Grant Making to Change Making: How the W. K. Kellogg Foundation's Impact Services Model Evolved to Enhance the Management and Social Effects of Large Initiatives," *Nonprofit and Voluntary Sector Quarterly 29, no. 1 (2000): 41–68.*

22. James E. Austin, "Strategic Collaboration between Nonprofits and Business," *Nonprofit and Voluntary Sector Quarterly* 29, no. 1 (2000): 69–97.

23. Ken Conca, Thomas Princen, and Michael F. Maniates, "Confronting Consumption," *Global Environmental Politics* 1, no. 3 (2001): 6.

24. Debra E. Blum, "After the Attacks: Consumers Choose Products Based on Corporate Philanthropy, Studies Find," *Chronicle of Philanthropy* 14, no. 4 (2001): 24–27; Brenden Kendall, Rebecca Gill, and George Cheney, "Consumer Activism and Corporate Social Responsibility: How Strong a Connection," in *The Debate over Corporate Social Responsibility*, ed. Steve May, George Cheney, and Juliet Roper (Oxford: Oxford University Press, 2007), 241–64; Remi Trudel and June Cotte, "Does It Pay to Be Good?" *MIT Sloan Management Review* 50, no. 2 (2009): 61.

25. Paul Harris, "Dispatches: Viva la Revolution!" *Observer*, November 4, 2007, 26.

26. US Bureau of the Census, 2006.

27. Research and Markets, *Hispanic Finances and Financial Services in the United States* (2009), Dublin, Ireland, http://www.researchandmarkets.com/reports/993138.

28. D'Vera Cohn and Tara Bahrampour, "Children under Five, Nearly Half Are Minorities," *Washington Post*, May 10, 2006, A1.

29. Dolores Acevedo-Garcia, Mah-J Soobader, and Lisa Berkman, "Low Birth Weight among U.S. Hispanic/Latino Subgroups: The Effect of Maternal Foreign-Born Status and Education," *Social Science and Medicine* 65, no. 12 (2007): 2503–16.

30. Elizabeth M. Grieco, *Race and Hispanic Origin of the Foreign-Born Population in the United States: 2007* (Washington DC: US Census Bureau, 2010).

31. Frederick A. Palumbo and Ira Teich, "Segmenting the U.S. Hispanic Market Based on Level of Acculturation," *Journal of Promotion Management* 21, no. 1 (2005): 151–73.

32. Julie Gallagher, "Changing Diapers," *Supermarket News*, November 24, 2008, 20.

33. Gallagher, 2008.

34. Sanford F. Schram, "Contextualizing Racial Disparities in American Welfare Reform: Toward a New Poverty Research," *Perspectives on Politics* 3, no. 2 (2005): 253–68.

35. Paul Grimaldi, "Latinos Are Drinking Less Milk, Studies Show," *Press-Enterprise*, February 9, 2006, 1.

36. M. Archer, "'Espanol' Illustrates Growing Strength of Hispanic Consumers," *New York Times*, April 9, 2007, 7B.

37. Hispanic PR Wire, "Drink and Dance Your Way to Health: TOMA LECHE Offers Free Salsa Workouts and MILK in National City Fair" (last modified March 7, 2005), http://www.hispanicprwire.com/news.php?l=in&id=13670.

38. "KENA to Launch in April," *PR Newswire*, April 18, 2007.

39. Laurel Wentz, "LatinWorks: The Ones to Watch," *Advertising Age*, January 19, 2009, 34.

40. Arlene Dávila, *Latinos, Inc.: The Marketing and Making of a People* (Berkeley: University of California Press, 2001), 75.

41. Dávila, 2001, 80.

42. Dávila, 2001, 79.

43. Krissah Williams, "To Latina Mothers, with Love: A Refrigerator from America," *Washington Post*, May 10, 2007, D1.

44. "LatinVision," 2010, LatinVision Latina Media Conference Blog, http://marketing-tolatinosentertainment.blogspot.com/.

45. J. Russell, "Target Demos: Moms, Youths," *Television Week*, September 12, 2005, 11–14.

46. "Avon Company Overview," http://www.avoncompany.com/index.html.

47. Laura Klepacki, *Avon: Building the World's Premier Company for Women* (Hoboken, NJ: Literary Productions, 2005), 19.

48. Klepacki, 2005, 218.

49. Klepacki, 2005, 221.

50. Sandra Rodríguez, interview with author, 2008.

51. "Can I Ring Your Ding Dong? Avon," http://www.dooyoo.co.uk/offline-shopping-misc/avon/331319/.

52. Klepacki, 2005, 221.

53. John McMurria "Desperate Citizens and Good Samaritans," *Television and New Media* 9, no. 4 (2008): 308.

54. Rodríguez, interview with author, 2008.

55. "Avon Foundation Advertisement: Speak Out against Domestic Violence," *Latina* 12, no. 7 (May 2008): 79.

56. Samantha King, *Pink Ribbons, Inc.: Breast Cancer and the Politics of Philanthropy* (Minneapolis: University of Minnesota Press, 2006), 39.

57. Johan Fischer, "Boycott or Buycott? Malay Middle-Class Consumption Post-9/11," *Ethnos: Journal of Anthropology* 72, no. 1 (2007): 29–50.

58. Varul, 2008.

59. The Latina Adolescent Outreach Project 2008.

60. Susan Schwartz, *Breast Cancer Tips for Latina Teens, Young Women and Families* (San Rafael, CA: Zero Breast Cancer, 2008).

61. Aida Hurtado, *Voicing Chicana Feminism: Young Women Speak Out on Sexuality and Identity* (New York: NYU Press, 2003).

62. "Verizon Wireless Advertisement," *Hispanic* 21, no. 10 (October 2008).

63. "Verizon Wireless Announces National Launch of Spanish-Language Short Film about Troubling Issues Faced by Latino Teens," *Business Wire*, May 6, 2005.

64. *Hispanic*, 2008.

65. National Latino Alliance for the Elimination of Domestic Violence, *Alianza Newsletter* 2, no. 1 (New York: National Latino Alliance for the Elimination of Domestic Violence, 2005).

66. Kim-Mai Cutler, "Wireless Carriers Woo Latinos," *Boston Globe*, July 4, 2009, D1; Rita Chang, "Mobile Marketers Target Receptive Hispanic Audience," *Advertising Age* 80, no. 3 (2009): 18; Paul M. Leonardi, "Problematizing 'New Media': Culturally Based Perceptions of Cell Phones, Computers, and the Internet among United States Latinos," *Critical Studies in Media Communication* 20, no. 2 (2003): 160–80.

67. National Latino Alliance for the Elimination of Domestic Violence (Alianza), *Domestic Violence Affects Families of All Racial, Ethnic, and Economic Backgrounds: It Is a Widespread and Destructive Problem in Latino Communities* (Alburquerque, NM, 2010), http://www.dvalianza.org/en/fact-sheets.html.

68. Chang, 2009; Cutler, 2006; Leonardi, 2003.

69. Ryan Kim, "Cell Phones Firms' Dream Demographic: Latinos," *Chronicle*, May 4, 2008, C1.

70. Karen Mossberger, Caroline Tolbert, and Michele Gilbert, "Race, Place, and Information Technology," *Urban Affairs Review* 41, no. 5 (2006): 583–620.

71. Matt Richtel and Ken Belson, "Cell Carriers Seek Growth by Catering to Hispanics," *New York Times*, May 30, 2006, C1.

72. Kim, 2008.

73. Lili Wang and Elizabeth Graddy, "Social Capital, Volunteering, and Charitable Giving," *VOLUNTAS: International Journal of Voluntary and Nonprofit Organizations* 19, no. 1 (2008): 23–42.

74. Nestor Garcia Canclini, *Hybrid Cultures: Strategies for Entering and Leaving Modernity* (Minneapolis: University of Minnesota Press, 1995), 12.

About the Contributors

SARAH BANET-WEISER is associate professor in the Annenberg School for Communication at the University of Southern California. She is the author of *The Most Beautiful Girl in the World: Beauty Pageants and National Identity* (University of California Press, 1999) and *Kids Rule! Nickelodeon and Consumer Citizenship* (Duke, 2007). She is the coeditor (with Cynthia Chris and Anthony Freitas) of *Cable Visions: Television beyond Broadcasting* (NYU Press, 2007) and has published articles and book chapters on gender, race, citizenship, and consumer culture. Her most recent project is a book on brand culture and political possibility, *Authentic™: The Politics of Ambivalence in a Brand Culture* (NYU Press, forthcoming 2012).

MELISSA BROUGH is a doctoral student at the Annenberg School for Communication at the University of Southern California. She received her B.A. in development studies and modern culture and media from Brown University. She subsequently worked in documentary film production and for FilmAid International, a nonprofit organization that uses film and video to promote health and strengthen communities. As program officer, she supported psychosocial and educational programs as well as participatory video projects for displaced communities in East Africa and elsewhere. She has volunteered with local and international community media projects, including the Chiapas Media Project in Mexico. Her current research interests include communication for social change, online video activism, community media development, and the visual culture of humanitarianism and international development.

KATE CAIRNS is a PhD candidate in the Department of Sociology and Equity Studies in Education at the Ontario Institute for Studies in Education (University of Toronto). Her primary areas of interest include feminist theory, cultural studies, sociology of education, and cultural geography. Cairns's doctoral research explores how rural youth envision futures in neoliberal times. Her work has appeared in *Gender and Education* and *The International Encyclopedia of Education*, and she has forthcoming articles in *Atlantis* and *Gender and Society*. Cairns has also contributed to major research projects exploring foodie culture (with Josée Johnston and Shyon Baumann) and specialized arts programs in public high schools (with Rubén Gaztambide-Fernández and the Urban Arts High Schools Project).

MARI CASTAÑEDA is associate professor of communication at the University of Massachusetts in Amherst. She is also currently director of the Five College Latin American, Caribbean and Latino Studies program. Most recently, she served as chair of the National Association for Chicana and Chicano Studies. Castañeda's fields of study include Spanish-language media and Latina/o cultural production, IT and communication policy, and political economy of media. Her most recent essays have appeared in *Latina/o Communication Studies, Technofuturos: Critical Interventions in Latina/o Studies*, and *Global Communications: Toward a Transcultural Political Economy*. She has also published her work in the academic journal *Television and New Media*.

LYNN COMELLA is assistant professor in the Women's Studies Department at the University of Nevada, Las Vegas. Her research and teaching interests include media and popular culture, sexuality studies, gender and feminist theory, and consumer culture and citizenship. Recent publications include a chapter in *Sex for Sale: Prostitution, Pornography, and the Sex Industry*, 2nd ed. (Routledge, 2009) and articles in *Contexts Magazine* (2008) and *Communication Review* (2008). She is currently completing a book-length manuscript on the history and retail culture of feminist sex toy stores in the US.

KEVIN FOX GOTHAM is professor of sociology and associate dean of academic affairs at Tulane University in New Orleans. His research focuses on the globalization of the real estate sector and the political economy of tourism. He is author of *Critical Perspectives on Urban Revitalization* (Elsevier, 2001); *Race, Real Estate and Uneven Development* (SUNY Press, 2002); and *Authentic New Orleans: Race, Culture, and Tourism in the Big Easy* (NYU Press, 2007).

ALISON HEARN is associate professor in the Faculty of Information and Media Studies at the University of Western Ontario, Canada. Her work combines cultural theory with critical political economy and focuses on the intersections of visual culture, consumer culture, reality television, new media, and self-production. She also writes on the history of the university as a cultural site. She has published in such journals as *Topia, Continuum, International Journal of Media and Culture Politics,* and *Bad Subjects* and in edited volumes including *The Celebrity Culture Reader; Reality TV: Remaking Television Culture* (2nd ed.); and *The Media and Social Theory.* She is coauthor of *Outside the Lines: Issues in Interdisciplinary Research* (McGill-Queens Univesity Press, 1997).

JOSÉE JOHNSTON is associate professor of sociology at the University of Toronto. She focuses her research on the sociological study of food, investigating aspects of culture, consumerism, politics, and the environment. Johnston coauthored (with Shyon Baumann) *Foodies: Democracy and Distinction in the Gourmet Foodscape* (Routledge, 2010). She has published articles in venues including *American Journal of Sociology; Theory and Society; Signs: Journal of Women in Culture and Society; Gender and Society;* and *Antipode: A Radical Journal of Geography.*

SAMANTHA KING is associate professor in the School of Kinesiology and Health Studies at Queen's University, Canada. Her research focuses on the sociocultural dimensions of health, sport, and the body and has appeared in journals such as *Social Text, Canadian Journal of Communication,* and *Sociology of Sport Journal* as well as a number of edited collections. King's book, *Pink Ribbons, Inc: Breast Cancer and the Politics of Philanthropy* (University of Minnesota Press, 2006), is the subject of a forthcoming documentary from the National Film Board of Canada. In addition to her scholarly work, King writes for mass-circulation newspapers and magazines on the politics of breast cancer.

JO LITTLER is senior lecturer in media and cultural studies at Middlesex University, UK. She is the author of *Radical Consumption: Shopping for Change in Contemporary Culture* (Open University Press, 2008), editor of *Mediactive 2: Celebrity* (Lawrence and Wishart, 2004) and coeditor, with Roshi Naidoo, of *The Politics of Heritage: The Legacies of "Race"* (Routledge, 2005) and, with Sam Binkley, of the special issue "Anti-consumerism and Cultural Studies: A Critical Encounter," in *Cultural Studies* (2008). She is on the editorial boards of *Soundings, Cultural Studies,* and the forthcoming Taylor and Francis journal, *Celebrity Studies.*

JOHN MCMURRIA is associate professor of communication at the University of California, San Diego. He is coauthor, with Toby Miller, Nitin Govil, Richard Maxwell, and Ting Wang, of *Global Hollywood 2* (British Film Institute, 2005). He is currently working on a critical cultural policy history of cable television in the US.

ISABEL MOLINA-GUZMÁN is associate professor at the University of Illinois, Champagne-Urbana. Throughout her educational and professional experience, Molina-Guzmán's work has centered on issues of social justice and the cultural politics of identity. Molina-Guzmán is author of *Dangerous Curves: Latina Bodies in the Media* (NYU Press, 2010), and her research has been published in numerous journals and edited collections. Currently she serves as director and chair of Latina/Latino studies and holds faculty appointments in Latina/Latino studies and media and cinema studies.

ROOPALI MUKHERJEE is associate professor of media studies at the City University of New York/Queens College. She writes on issues of race, politics, and US public culture and is author of *The Racial Order of Things: Cultural Imaginaries of the Post-Soul Era* (University of Minnesota Press, 2006). She is currently working on her next book focusing on material culture and black political subjectivities in "postracial" America.

LAURIE OUELLETTE is associate professor of communication studies at the University of Minnesota, Twin Cities. She is coauthor of *Better Living through Reality TV: Television and Post-Welfare Citizenship* (Blackwell, 2008), coeditor of *Reality TV: Remaking Television Culture* (NYU Press, 2004; 2nd ed., 2008), and author of *Viewers Like You? How Public TV Failed the People* (Columbia University Press, 2001).

MARITA STURKEN is professor and chair of the Department of Media, Culture, and Communication at New York University. Her work spans the fields of cultural studies, visual culture, American studies, and memory studies with an emphasis on cultural memory, national identity, consumer culture, art, and the cultural effects of technology. She is the author of *Tangled Memories: The Vietnam War, the AIDs Epidemic, and the Politics of Remembering* (University of California Press, 1997); *Tourists of History: Memory, Kitsch, and Consumerism from Oklahoma City to Ground Zero* (Duke University Press, 2007); and, with Lisa Cartwright, *Practices of Looking: An Introduction to Visual Culture* (2nd ed., Oxford University Press, 2009).

ALISON TROPE is clinical assistant professor in the Annenberg School for Communication at the University of Southern California. She is currently revising a manuscript that focuses on various sites that memorialize Hollywood and its history.

Index

ABC network, 57, 64–67. *See also* Better Community (ABC)
Activism: and agrifood, 226; alternative, 224–225; and class, 228–229, 233; collective, 234; consumer, 219–239; cooperative consumer, 222, 225, 233; corporate use of, 230–232; individual consumer, 225–226, 229, 230–231, 233–234; green, 30–35; mass consumer, 222–224; neoliberal, 226; and race/racism, 114–133, 209–10, 214–15, 228–229, 233; shifting modes of, 2, 225
Advertising, 19, 177, 178; the self, 28–29
AFL-CIO, 264
Africa, 180, 184, 185, 186; Darfur, 179; impact of neocolonialism upon, 121; Lord's Resistance Army, 185, 189n2; Uganda, 180–183, 185, 186, 187, 192n45; Western representations of, 121
African American(s) and commodity consumption, 117, 122, 124, 129n22; and citizenship, 117; and civil rights, 125–126; and corporate capitalism, 123; and male brotherhoods, 123; and pan-African solidarity, 124, 126; and political resistance, 120, 125; and racial politics, 120, 132n48; and social activism, 118, solidarities with the global South, 122–123
Americans for Democratic Action, 262–264
Amnesty International, 115
Anti-capitalism, 246–248
Anti-consumerism, 8; paradoxes of, 8
Appadurai, Arjun, 230
Army Corps of Engineers, 107
Arvidsson, Adam, 27, 69
Asian Americans for Fair Media, 268

Authenticity, 140–144, 147–150
Avon Products, Inc., 280–285; Avon Foundation, 281–284; Avon Ladies, 282; AvonWalk for Breast Cancer, 200, 207, 208–217

Babeland, 240–242, 247–248
Bagdikian, Ben, 256
Baumann, Zygmunt, 24, 25
Better Community (ABC), 58–59, 64
"Big Organic" food, 231
Black Entertainment Television, 259, 267
Blank, Joani, 244; and Good Vibrations, 244–246
Bling, 114, 116, 120, 124–125
Blood diamonds, 114–115; and hip-hop, 117–118; hip-hop music about, 116; Hollywood films about, 116; independent films about, 115–116; popular music about, 122; and Sierra Leone, 114, 115, 116. *See also* Conflict diamonds
Blue Planet, 259
Bogart, Leo, 262–263
Bon Appétit, 220
Bono, 180, 192n33, 207. See also Product RED
Bordo, Susan, 216
Bourdieu, Pierre, 263
Bourgeois piggery, 219
Brand: culture, 40, 42, 46, 47, 49, 52, 54, 69–70; manager, 19, 52
Branding, 19, 25, 27, 28–29; citizen, 63; green, 21; self, 28–29. *See also* Self
Breast cancer, 199, 200, 204, 281–282, 284, Pink Ribbon, 281–283
Bush, George W., 105, 119

Cable television: á la carte pricing, 265–269; First Amendment, 265; monopolies, 258–260

Capitalism: cultural, 52; death of, 4, 38n64; disaster, 15; and domination, 4; ethical, 61–62; and humanitarianism, 177–178; impact on modes of social activism, 13; neoliberal 2, 11; role of the state within, 14, 118

Cause: célebre, 30, 33, 34; -related marketing, 206

Celebrity: activism, 97–99, 111; as brand, 30–31, 34; as currency, 31; endorsements, 32; gossip 31, 32; Hollywood 31; as social critique, 105–108

Charities, 119, 181, 187; health, 199, 200

Child soldiers, 115–116, 127n6, 184; brutalization of, 121–123; night commuting, 174

Child workers, 120–121; brutalization of, 121–123

Christian Broadcasting Network, 267; Christian evangelism, 177

Citizen: brand, 62–63; civic, 6; civic action, links to, 5, 9 and community, 60–61, 67; compassionate, 60; -consumer, 5–6, 8, 11; virtuous, 200, 203. See also Consumer, citizenship

Civic: branding, 68–70; responsibilities of the media, 58

Clinton, Bill, 203

Cohen, Lizabeth, 117, 223

Cole, Kenneth, 287

Colonialism, 122, 177

Commodity, 14; feminism, 39, 46, 50; fetishism, 13, 46

Commodity activism: and affective or immaterial labor, 12–13, 30; backlash against, 87–89; and branding, 40; and celebrities, 30, 34; and citizenship, 2, 5–8, 117–118, 120, 124, 200, 204, 217–218; and civic virtue, 12; class implications of, 9, 12, 72; definition of, 2, 20; and democracy, differences from consumer activism, 11; and green consumption, 76, 86; historical antecedents, 6–8; and individual empowerment, 23–24, 44–46; limits of, 150;

moral frameworks of, 11; and neoliberal citizenship, 42; within neoliberalism, 11, 35, 42; and value, 12–14, 52, 71

Communication Workers of America, 268

Communitarianism, 59–61; training citizens for, 61

Community: gardens, 226; as corporate civic objective, 59

Community supported agriculture (CSA), 220, 228, 230

Conflict diamonds, global trade in, 114–115

Conservation through consumption, 231

Consumer: alternative, 234–235; activism/agency, 5–8, 219–239; boycotts, 42; citizenship, 11–12, 42, 44, 49, 52, 118, 120, 125, 223; as donor, 187; food politics, 219–239; generated-content, 40, 44, 47, 50, 54; movements, 6–7, 219–239; protection, 7, 224–225. See also Citizen-consumer; Consumption

Consumer culture, 117, 124; black, 117–124; and citizenship, 125–126, 130n26; histories of, 5–8; political action within, 6–8

Consumer Reports, 223

Consumerism: and activism, 276, 287; conscientious, 126. See also Consumption

Consumers' Republic, 5, 8, 117

Consumers Union, 266

Consumption, 200, 203, 216; activist, 5–8; alternative, 224–225, 234–235; and class, 228–229, 233; collective, 234; conspicuous, 5; cooperative 222, 225, 233; ethical, 9, 12, 42, 219–239; and gender politics, 6–7; green, 224, 229, 230; and immigrant politics, 6; individual, 225–226, 229, 230–231, 233–234; as liberating, 6; mass, 222–225; as patriotic, 5; vis-à-vis production, 12; and race/racial politics, 7, 117, 120, 228–229, 233

Cooper, Anderson, 162, 163, 167, 170, 171

Corporate organics, 230–232; and neoliberal capital, 10; and social responsibility, 9–10, 31, 33, 34, 61–67, 281, 286

Corporation, anti-, 224–225; and food, 221, 230–231

Crawford, Robert, 200–203

MTV, 154,159, 171
Music videos, relation to lyrics, 131n38

NAACP, 168
Nader, Ralph, 42, 224
Nanny state, 211
National Asia Pacific American Legal
    Consortium, 267
National Black Media Coalition, 268
National Coalition of Black Civil Participa-
    tion, 267
National Coalition of Latino Clergy and
    Christian Leaders, 268
National Conference of Black Mayors, 267
National Congress of Black Women, 267
National Council of Women's Organiza-
    tions, 267
National Gay and Lesbian Chamber of
    Commerce, 267–268
National Hispanic Media Coalition, 268
National Hispanic Policy Institute, 267
Native Americans for Fair Media, 268
Neoliberal capitalism, 42, 44, 45, 51, 52; cul-
    ture, 44, 43, 53; policies, 105
Neoliberalism: and the body, 28–29,
    201–204; and brand strategies, 42; and
    citizenship, 42, 257; and commodity
    activism, 24; contradictions of, 257;
    definitions of, 25–26; and democracy, 51,
    58; and democratic television culture,
    262–265; and discipline, 215–217; and
    entrepreneurialism, 53, 125–126, 261; and
    food, 220, 221, 224–225, 226, 228, 233,
    234; and governing at a distance, 243;
    and governing through freedom, 68;
    individualized ethos of, 8–11; ironies of,
    118, 126; and labor, 50, 77–78; market-
    driven ethos of, 26; and philanthropy,
    200; and post-feminism, 242; and
    promotional culture, 28; and race,
    117–118; and the self, 11, 25, 27, 243, 259;
    and self-rule, 242–243; technologies of
    empowerment 243, 246, 251; theories of,
    257; and welfare state, 118, 210–211
New media technologies, 174; and Web 2.0
    social networking, 176, 180, 181, 193n56

New momism, 167
New Orleans, 99, 103, 106–107; Ninth Ward
    of, 100–101, 103, 104–105
"NGO-ization," 118
Nielson, Trevor, 160, 161
Nonprofit: industrial complex, 118; organi-
    zations, 206, 207

Obama, Barack, 206
Oprah's Big Give, 57
Organic food, 227, 228, 230–232, 233
Oxygen network, 259, 267

Pallotta Teamworks, 207–208
Parents Television Council, 265
Participatory: culture, 47, 51; practices, 257;
    spectacle, 186
Philanthropy, 1–4, 61, 67, 176, 178, 180, 185;
    commodified, 180; consumer-oriented,
    196, 210; corporate, 34, 61, 204–208,
    215–16; gendered dimensions of,
    163–164; and hip-hop, 119; and Holly-
    wood celebrities, 154–171; privatized, 163;
    and rise of neoliberalism, 200, 204
Pickford, Mary, 158, 171
Pitt, Brad, 98, 100, 145, 162, 166; and celebrity
    activism, 98; and "Make It Right" cam-
    paign, 98, 100; and pink symbolism, 103
Political commodity consumerism, 125;
    food consumption and eating, 219–239;
    hip-hop, 123; subjectivity, 117–118, 120,
    122, 124–125, 129n19
Politics: black, 119–120, 124, 126, contra-
    dictions within, 120, 126; "end of," 118;
    outsider, 3
Pollan, Michael, 221
Pop culture, 176, 188; use of, 184, 191n21
Post: -feminism, 39, 45, 53, 241, 251–252;
    -Fordism, 24–25, 27, 32, 35; Fordist mass
    consumption, 222; -political, 3; -mod-
    ernism, 179, 188. See also
Privatization, 215
Product RED, 1, 40, 207; safety, 224–225.
    See also, Consumer, protection
Profitability, 248–249
Promotionalism, 23, 28, 34

Public service, reinvention of, 58
Public-private partnerships, 277
Purchaser consumer, 223
Putnam, Robert, 61–64

Rain Forest Café, 231
Rainbow/PUSH Coalition, 268
Reagan, Ronald, 206
Real food movement, 221
Refugee, 179, 191n26; forced displacement, 182; IDP camp, 182–183, 189n2
Reinvention of government, 64–65
Resistance, 1, 3, 4, 9; civic, 9; collective, 11; "commodity creep" within, 11; consumer, 5–8; cooptation of, 2; futility of, 2, 4; paradoxes of, 3; and popular culture, 12; tactical strategies for, 5
Robertson, Kellie, 29
Rose, Nikolas, 68–69

Sachs, Jeffrey, 154, 162, 169, 170, 171
Schor, Juliet, 221
Schramm, Wilbur, 263, 271n25
Self, 31, 32, 34, 35; and biography, 24–25; and the body, 27–28; and brand, 11, 23, 27–29, 32, 33, 35; and community, 24; construction of through consumption, 24–25, 29; as empty, 24; entrepreneurs of, 26; as enterprising, 11; -esteem, 39, 40, 45, 48, 50, 51, 53; interest, 11; as labor/work, 23, 26, 27, 29; as limitation of commodity activism, 24; narrative of, 25; within neoliberalism, 11, 23–27; promotional, 28; reflexive project of, 23, 25; working, 26
Sex positivity, 245, 253n21; and Good Vibrations, 245; and retail activism, 242, 251; and sex toy stores, 246, 250–251
Sinclair, Upton, 222
Singh, Nikhil Pal, 270
Slocum, Rachel, 228
Slow food movement, 229
Social entrepreneurship, 249–250, 253n27; marketing, 274–276; networks, 23, 29, 33, 35
Spanish-language market campaigns, 278–279

Spectacle, 97, 102, 104, 176, 179, 180; and disaster, 105; ethical, 186; limitations of, 104; marketing of, 105; and pop culture, 176; of suffering, 176
Spectacular consumption, 139, 147, 149
Spectacularization of disaster, 97
Starbucks, 40, 224, 229
State, and social responsibility, 61
Susan G. Komen Foundation for the Cure, 199, 207
Symbolic, colonization, 136–137, 140; rupture, 136–137, 140, 150

Television networks: and civic responsibility, 57; and communitarianism, 59; and corporate citizenship, 59; and democratic governance, 58, 64; and the do good turn, 57, 63–65
"Thons," 199, 207, 208–217
Time, 23, 35
Transmedia storytelling, 181, 192n37
Trinity Broadcasting Network, 267
TV One, 267

United Nations, 114; Children's Emergency Fund (UNICEF), 165; High Commission for Refugees (UNHCR), 157, 159, 160, 161, 162, 163, 166, 167, 170, 171
United States Supreme Court, 264

Verizon Wireless, 285–286
Vibrators, 244–245
Virno, Paolo, 26, 30
Virtuosity, 30
Visual culture, 176–189; film, 178, 180, 182, 187; photography, 177, 178; of suffering, 178; as visual economy, 177, 189, 188
Vogel, David, 10–11, 62
Walk for Development, 205
Walmart organics, 224, 231
Warner Brothers, 261
Web 2.0, 23, 33, 35, 44, 49, 51, 54
Welfare, 210
Welfare state, 4, 118; and privatized safety net, 120; and shadow state, 118; withering of, 5, 120, 130n24